# HISTORIC PHOTOS OF MINNESOTA

Text and Captions by Susan Marks

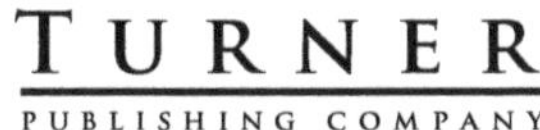

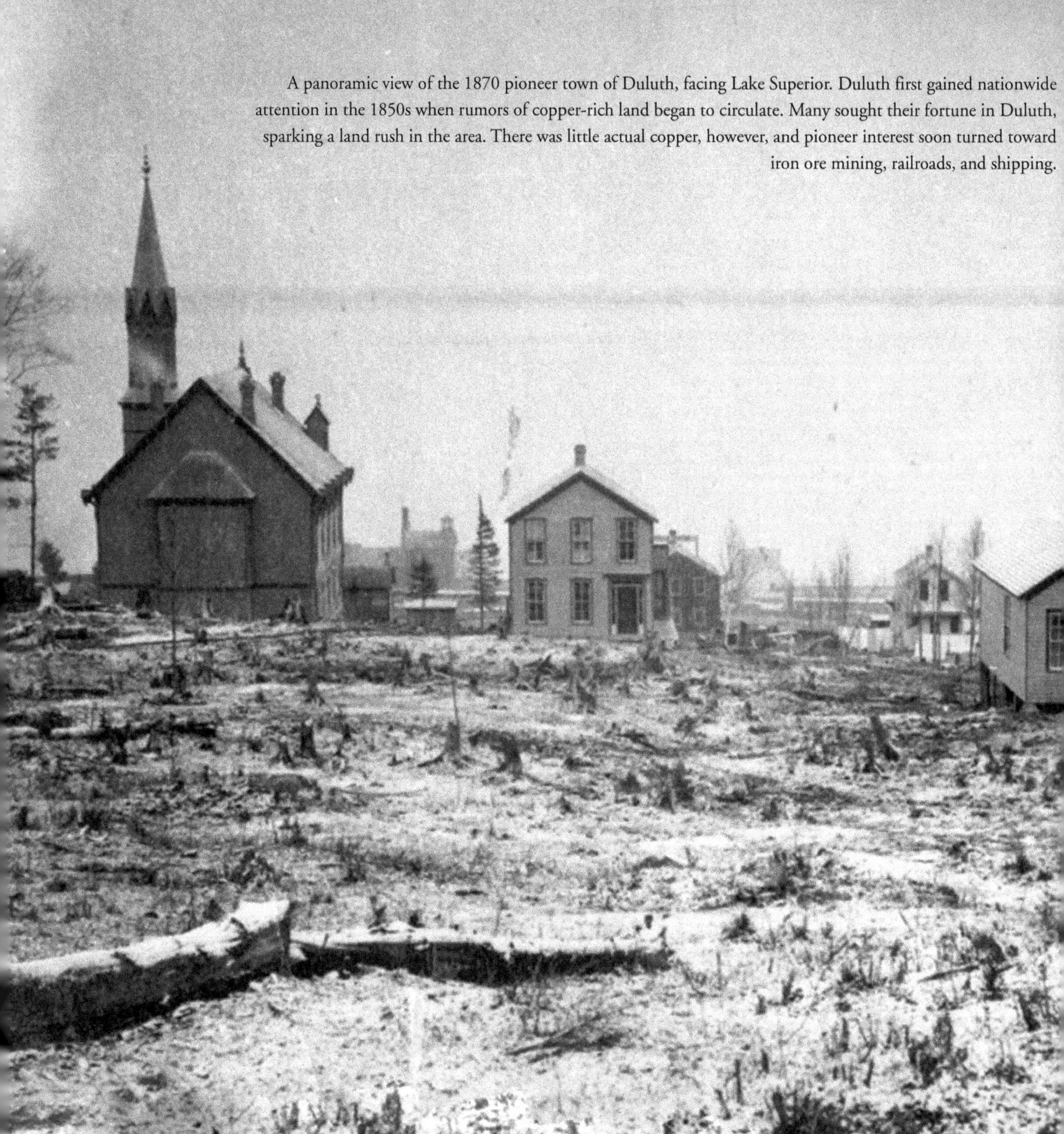

A panoramic view of the 1870 pioneer town of Duluth, facing Lake Superior. Duluth first gained nationwide attention in the 1850s when rumors of copper-rich land began to circulate. Many sought their fortune in Duluth, sparking a land rush in the area. There was little actual copper, however, and pioneer interest soon turned toward iron ore mining, railroads, and shipping.

# HISTORIC PHOTOS OF
# MINNESOTA

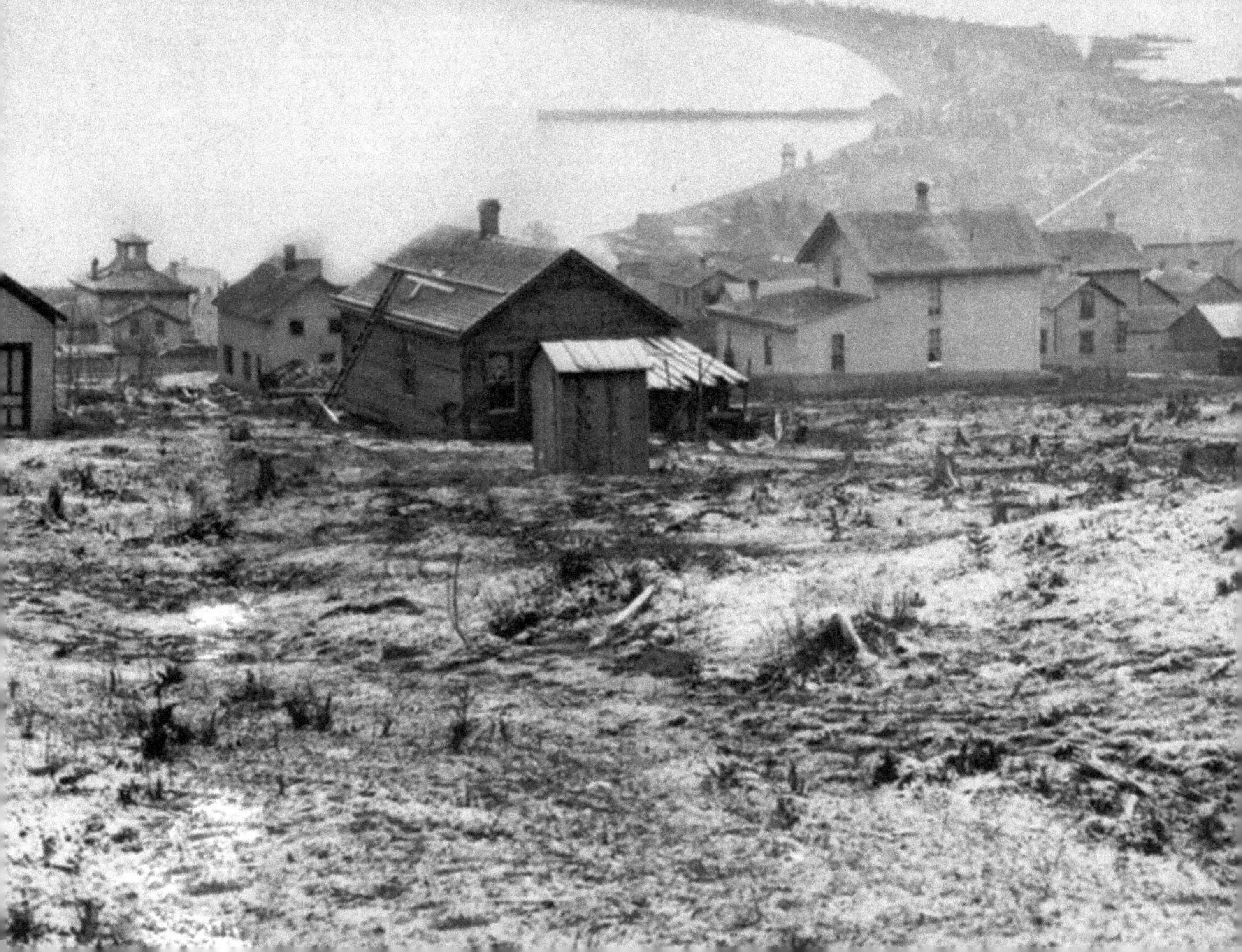

Turner Publishing Company
www.turnerpublishing.com

*Historic Photos of Minnesota*



Library of Congress Control Number: 2008910975

ISBN-13: 978-1-59652-523-8

Printed in the United States of America

ISBN 978-1-68442-079-7 (hc)

# Contents

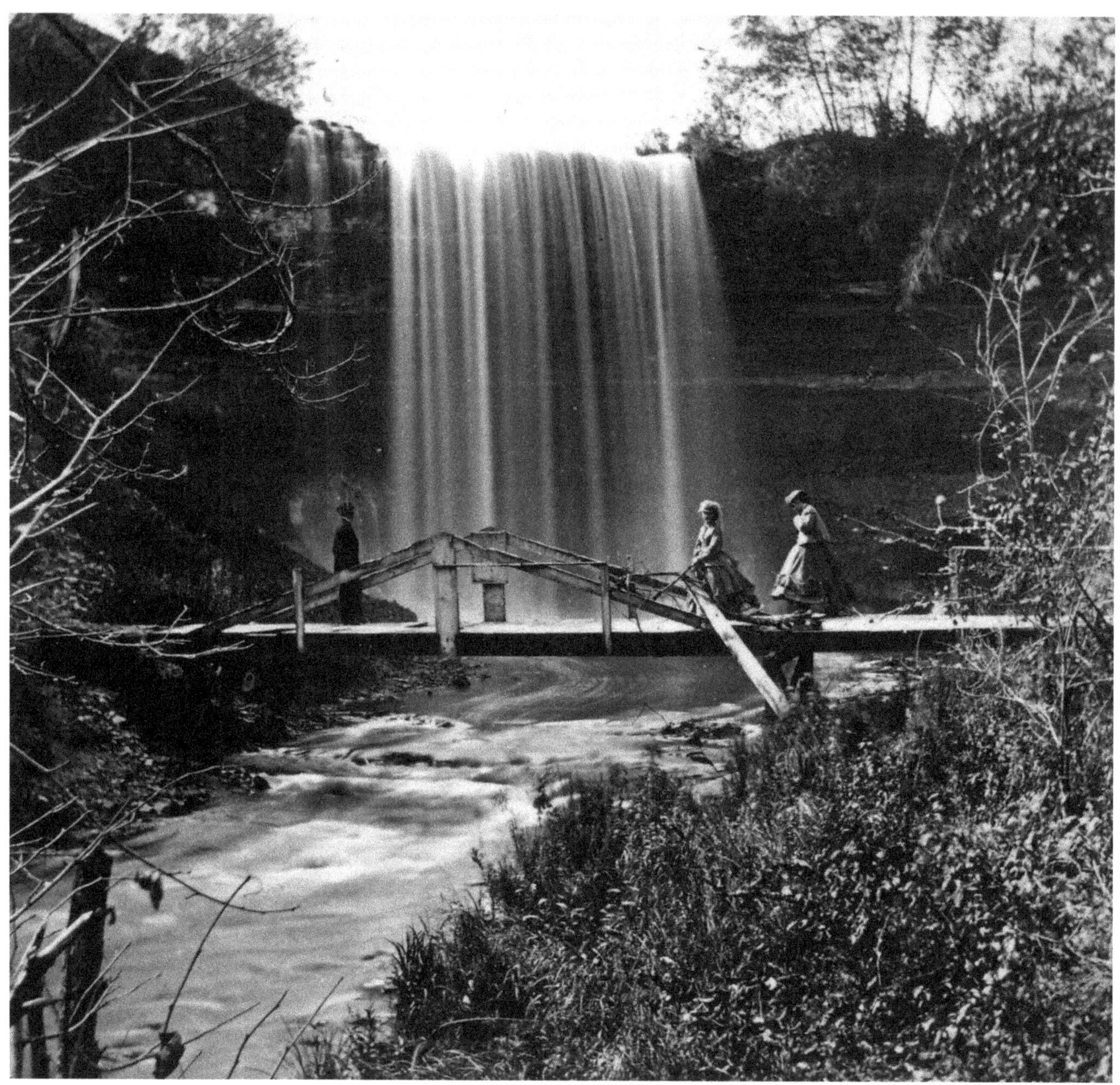

Visitors to Minnehaha Falls in Minneapolis, a popular tourist destination after the publication of the epic poem *The Song of Hiawatha* by Henry Wadsworth Longfellow in 1855. Longfellow never visited the falls, but he was inspired by the stories of Mary Eastman and Henry Rowe Schoolcraft about American Indian culture and the imagery of the falls.

# Acknowledgments

This volume, *Historic Photos of Minnesota,* is the result of the cooperation and efforts of many individuals, organizations, and corporations. It is with great thanks that we acknowledge the valuable contribution of the following for their generous support:

Library of Congress
Minnesota Historical Society

We would also like to thank the following individuals for valuable contributions and assistance in making this work possible:

Doug Bekke, Minnesota Military Museum
Jeff Forester
Carolyn Kneisl, Kandiyohi County Historical Society
Sarah LaVine, Stearns History Museum
Patricia Maus, Northeast Minnesota Historical Center
Bob Sandeen, Nicollet County Historical Society
David Stevens, the Mill City Museum, Minnesota Historical Society
Minnesota Historical Society's Library Staff

# Preface

Minnesota has thousands of historic photographs that reside in archives, both locally and nationally. This book began with the observation that, while those photographs are of great interest to many, they are not easily accessible. During a time when Minnesota is looking ahead and evaluating its future course, many people are asking, How do we treat the past? These decisions affect every aspect of the state—architecture, public spaces, commerce, infrastructure—and these, in turn, affect the way that people live their lives. This book seeks to provide easy access to a valuable, objective look into the history of Minnesota.

The power of photographs is that they are less subjective than words in their treatment of history. Although the photographer can make decisions regarding subject matter and how to capture and present it, photographs do not provide the breadth of interpretation that text does. For this reason, they offer an original, untainted perspective that allows the viewer to interpret and observe.

This project represents countless hours of review and research. The researchers and writer have reviewed thousands of photographs in numerous archives. We greatly appreciate the generous assistance of the individuals and organizations listed in the acknowledgments of this work, without whom this project could not have been completed.

The goal in publishing this work is to provide broader access to this set of extraordinary photographs that seek to inspire, provide perspective, and evoke insight that might assist people who are responsible for determining Minnesota's future. In addition, the book seeks to preserve the past with adequate respect and reverence.

With the exception of touching up imperfections that have accrued with the passage of time and cropping where necessary, no changes have been made. The focus and clarity of many images is limited by the technology and the ability of the photographer at the time they were taken.

The work is divided into eras. Beginning with some of the earliest known photographs of Minnesota, the first section records photographs through the end of the nineteenth century. The second section spans the first decade of the twentieth century. Section Three moves from 1910 through the 1920s. Section Four covers the Great Depression and World War II years, while the last section proceeds from the end of the war to recent times.

In each of these sections we have made an effort to capture various aspects of life through our selection of photographs. People, commerce, transportation, infrastructure, religious institutions, and educational institutions have been included to provide a broad perspective.

We encourage readers to reflect as they go traveling in Minnesota, strolling through its parks and the neighborhoods of its cities, and visiting its countryside and many lakes. It is the publisher's hope that in utilizing this work, longtime residents will learn something new and that new residents will gain a perspective on where Minnesota has been, so that each can contribute to its future.

—*Todd Bottorff, Publisher*

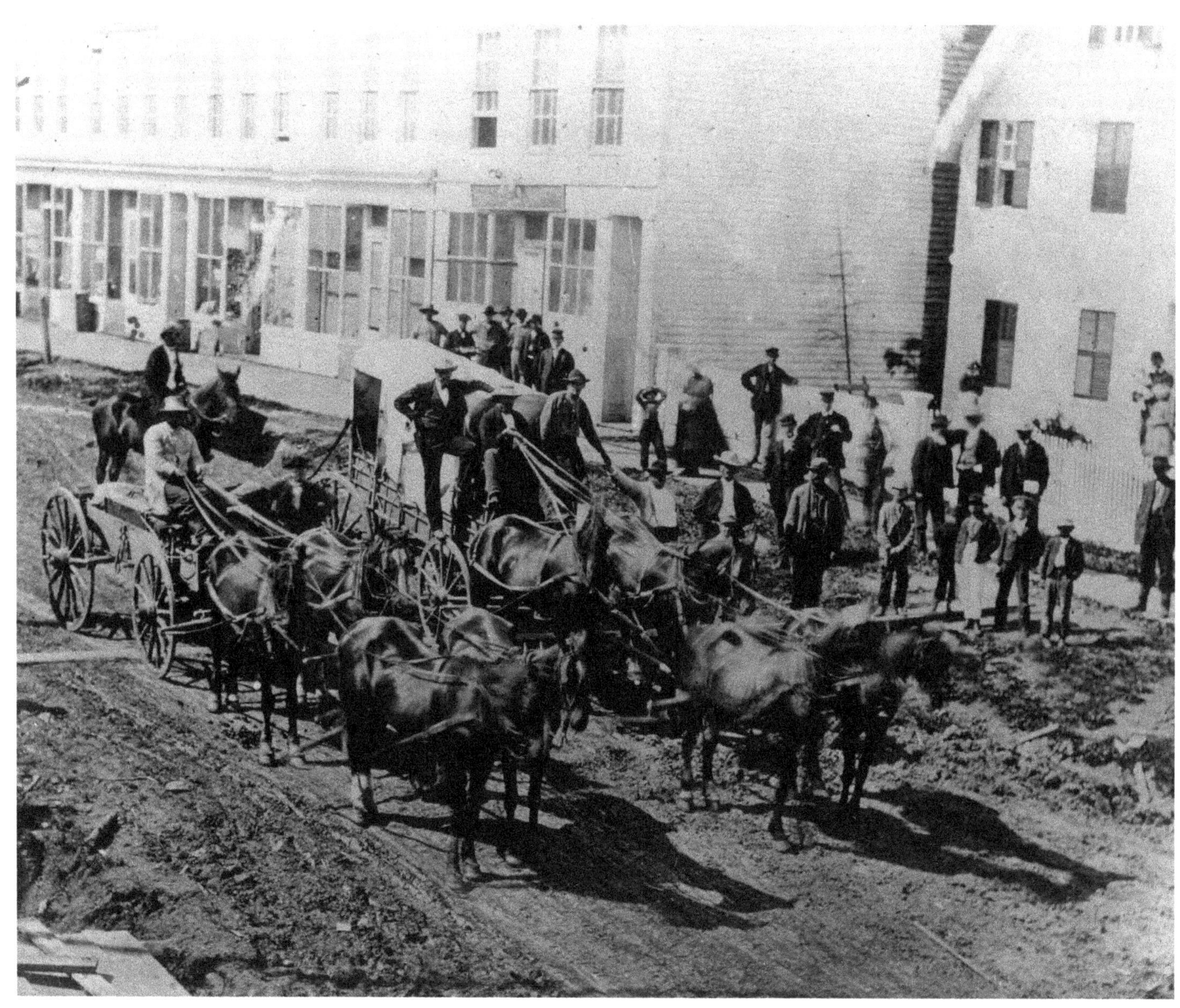

On August 1, 1870, the St. Paul and Lake Superior Stagecoaches ceremoniously quit service with the opening of the Lake Superior and Mississippi Railroad. On this day, the first train arrived in Duluth from St. Paul, a roughly 150-mile trip that took 16 hours.

# MINNESOTA ON THE MAP

# (1850–1899)

Long before Minnesota had a name, and long before cameras could capture the land's unspoiled, majestic beauty, Europeans took notice. Tales of thundering falls, towering pines, open prairies, fresh air, and rivers and lakes teeming with fish and wildlife proved irresistible.

Early explorers and fur traders were equally awed by the native Dakota and Ojibwe people, and their deep spiritual connection to this land. In 1682, the exaggerated travel accounts published by Father Louis Hennepin inspired widespread fascination with this mystical place just waiting to be explored and conquered.

Most of the area that we now know as Minnesota opened up for settlement when acquired from France via the 1803 Louisiana Purchase. Permanent white settlement ultimately appeared in the form of Fort Snelling at the confluence of the Mississippi and Minnesota rivers. Construction of the fort began in 1819 and was completed in 1825. Soon the "St." cities emerged—St. Paul, as Minnesota's capital city, and St. Anthony, at the Falls of St. Anthony. The worlds of the white settlers, fur traders, Dakotas, and Ojibwes often collided, but at times fell into harmonious rhythms.

Minnesota became a territory in 1849, and nine years later it became the 32nd state admitted to the Union. Around this same time, the west side of the Mississippi River opened up for settlement, and the city of Minneapolis was born on the other side of the Falls of St. Anthony. Minneapolis and St. Anthony eventually joined to become one city, Minneapolis.

The promise of rich farmland lured early pioneers to Minnesota. The vast forests of white pine had the same effect on lumbermen. Boomtowns and hamlets sprang up all over the state as the railroad industry increasingly became integral to Minnesota's way of life.

There was also darkness. The new state of Minnesota experienced a catastrophic blow with the U.S.-Dakota War of 1862. Relegated by treaty to small reservations along the Minnesota River, the Dakota Indians were near starvation and unable to persuade traders or the local federal agent to release stockpiled food. Desperation and tension grew as the Dakotas awaited overdue money promised by the United States government. When several young Dakota men launched a brutal attack on white settlers, a deadly war quickly erupted on Minnesota's prairies.

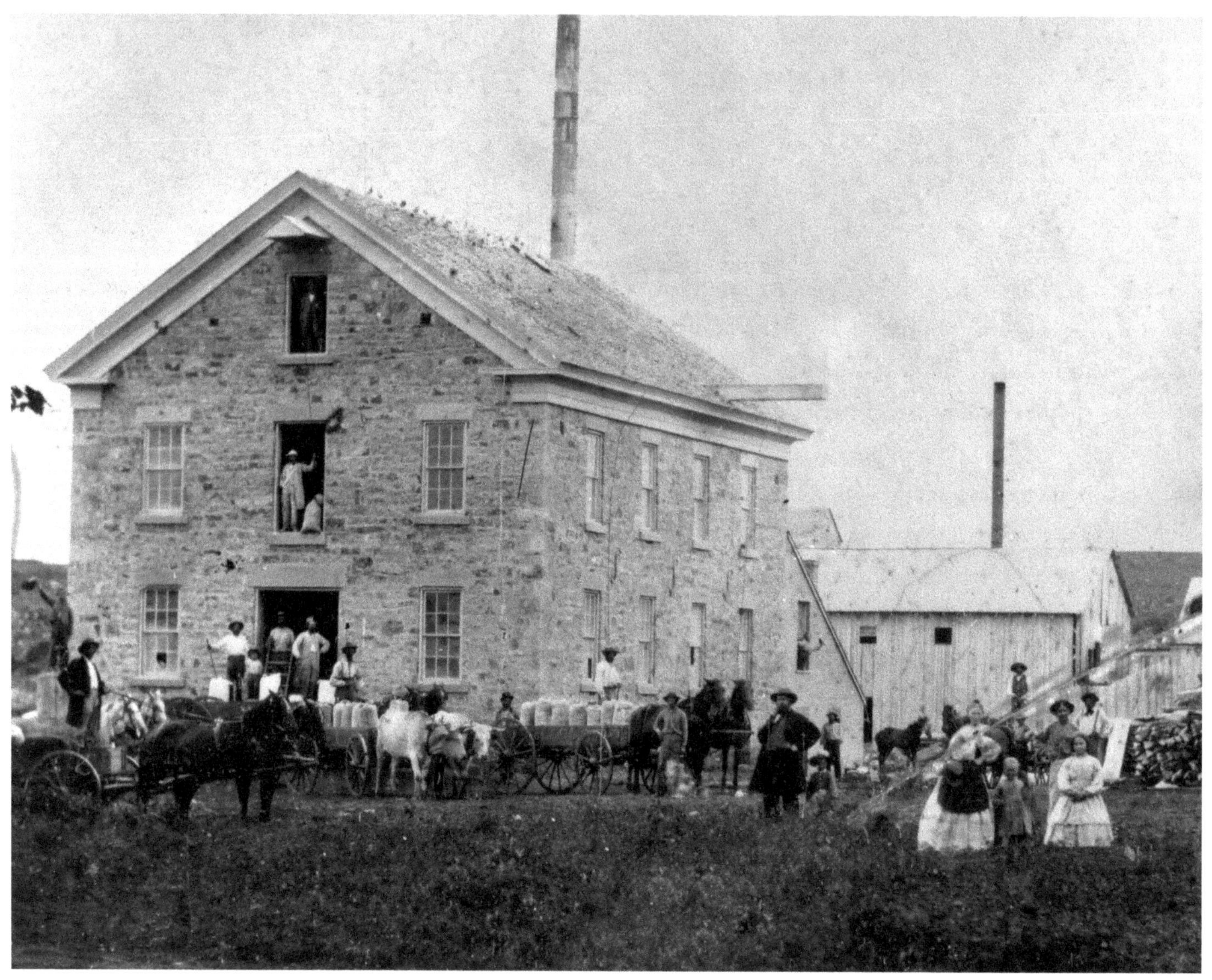

Early settlers pose in front of the Bierbauer Woolen Mill in Mankato sometime in the 1860s. The mill's owner, Wilhelm Bierbauer, fought in a battle against the Dakota Indians in nearby New Ulm during the U.S.-Dakota War of 1862. After the war, more than 300 Dakota men were tried for various offenses and sentenced to die. Upon review of the convictions, President Lincoln commuted the sentences of all but 38. Those 38 Dakotas were executed in a mass hanging in Mankato—the largest mass execution in U.S. history.

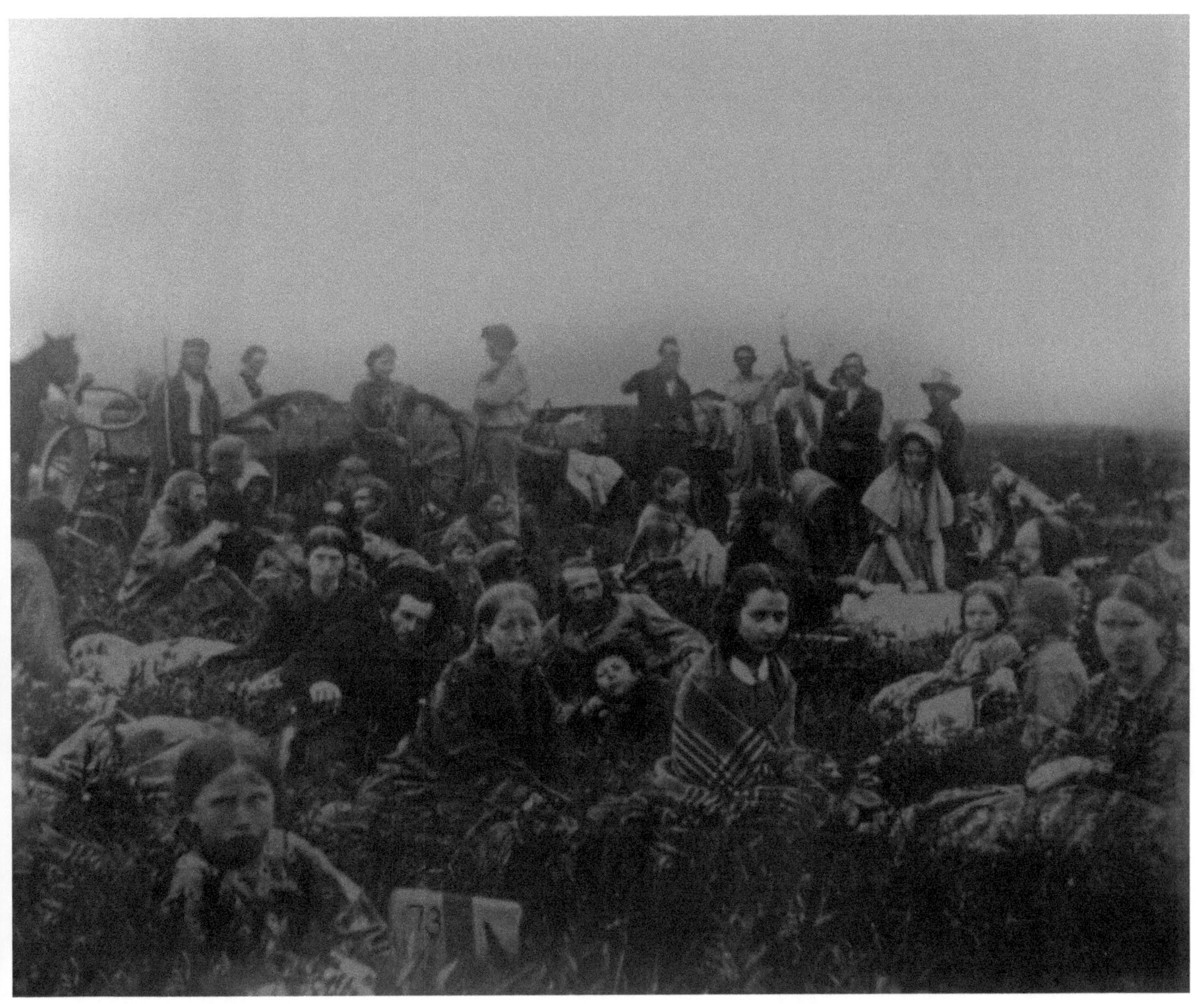

On August 21, 1862, white settlers sought refuge near the Upper Sioux Agency during the U.S.-Dakota War. Historians estimate that more than 500 settlers, including women and children, were killed during one of the most catastrophic episodes Minnesota has ever known. This photo, taken by refugee Adrian J. Ebell, is the only known photograph taken during the war.

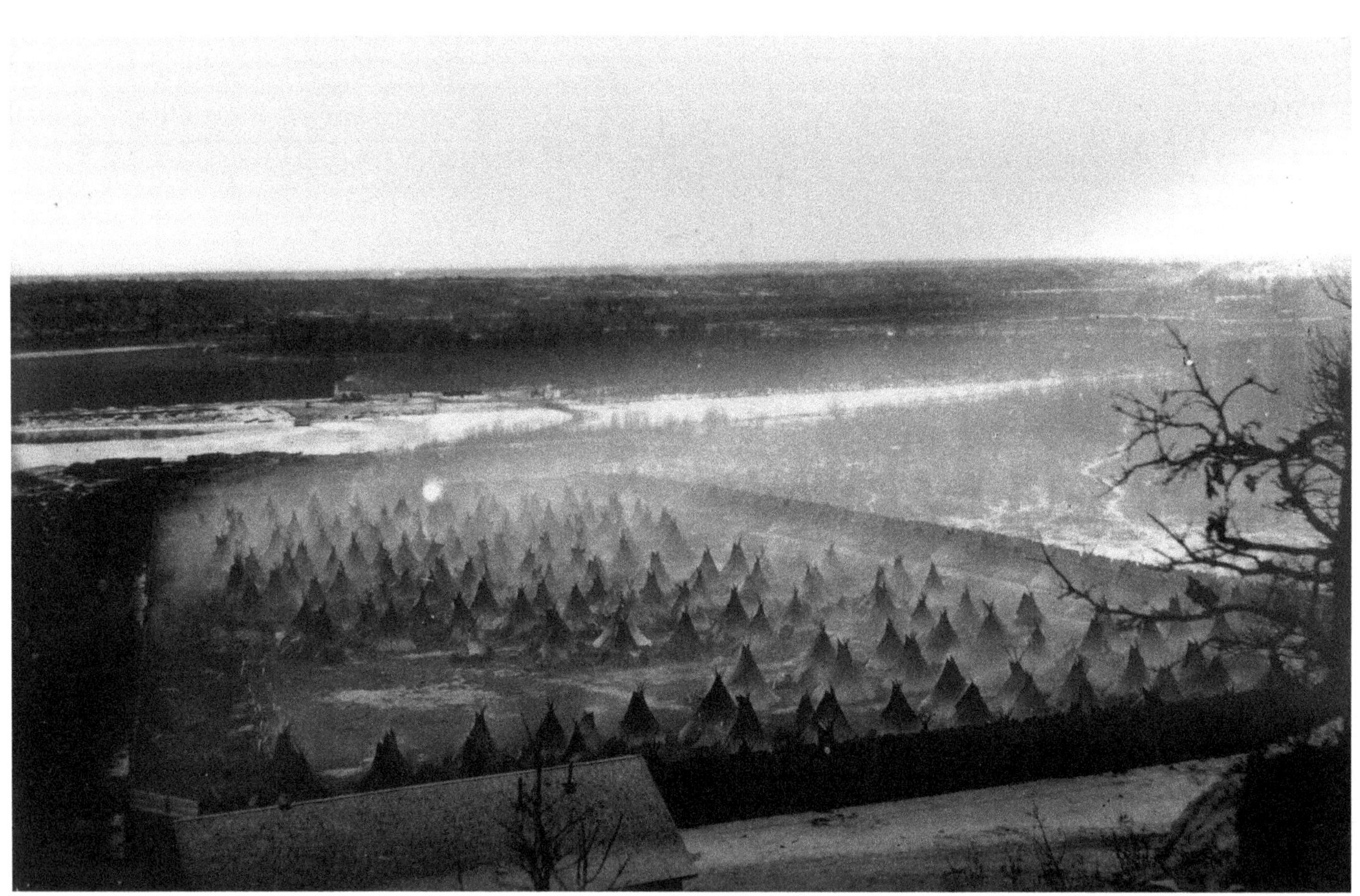

The camp where captured Dakotas were incarcerated on the Minnesota River flats below Fort Snelling, following the U.S.-Dakota War. About 1,600 other Dakotas—mostly nonparticipants in the war—were forced into this camp. Approximately 130 Dakota men, women, and children died due to food poisoning, starvation, disease, and exposure.

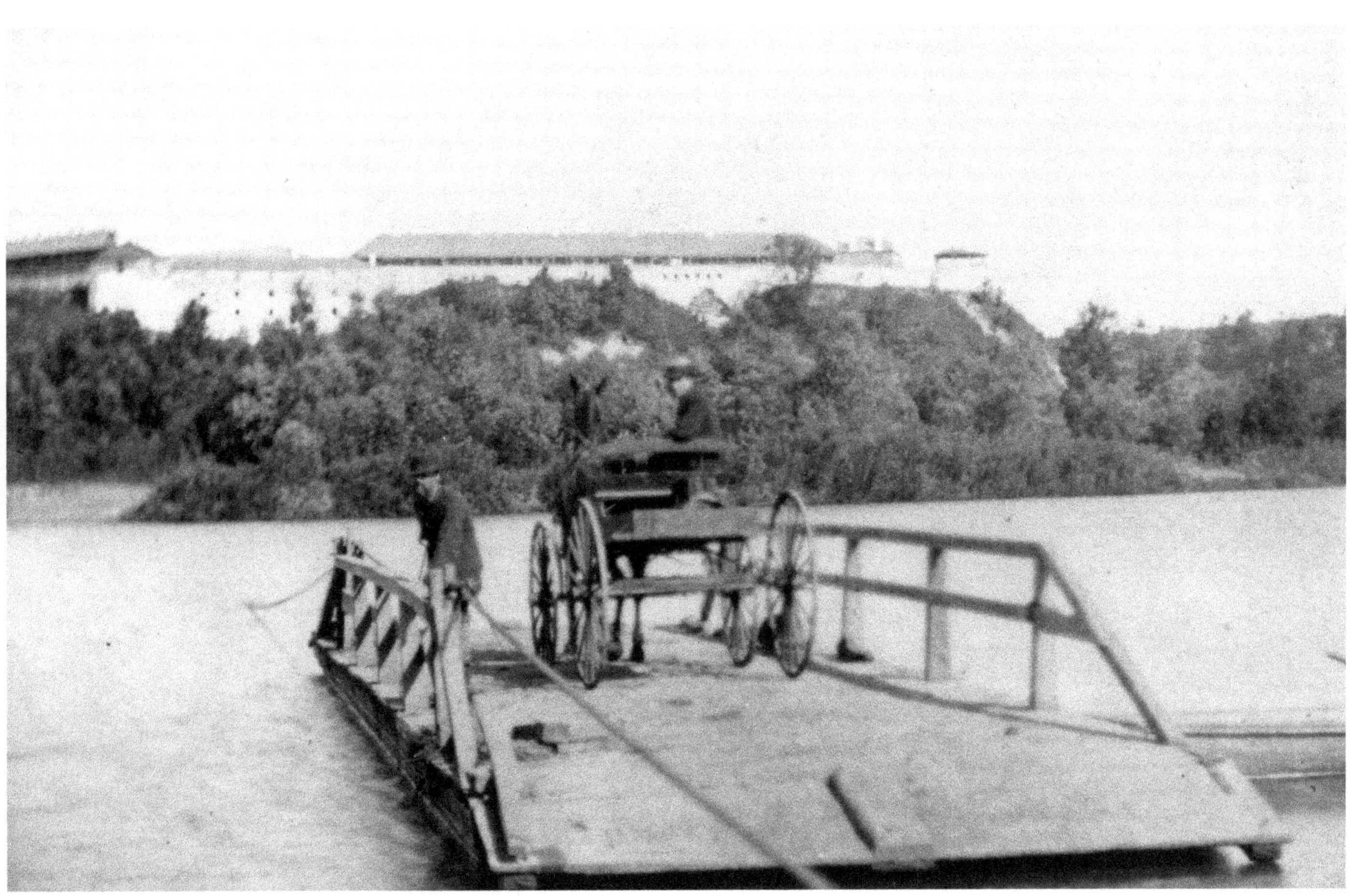

A ferryman pulls a cable across the Mississippi River to guide the ferry to Fort Snelling in 1861. The ferryboat was owned by Franklin Steele, the pioneering lumber mill owner and former shopkeeper of the fort, who was also the first legal settler in St. Anthony.

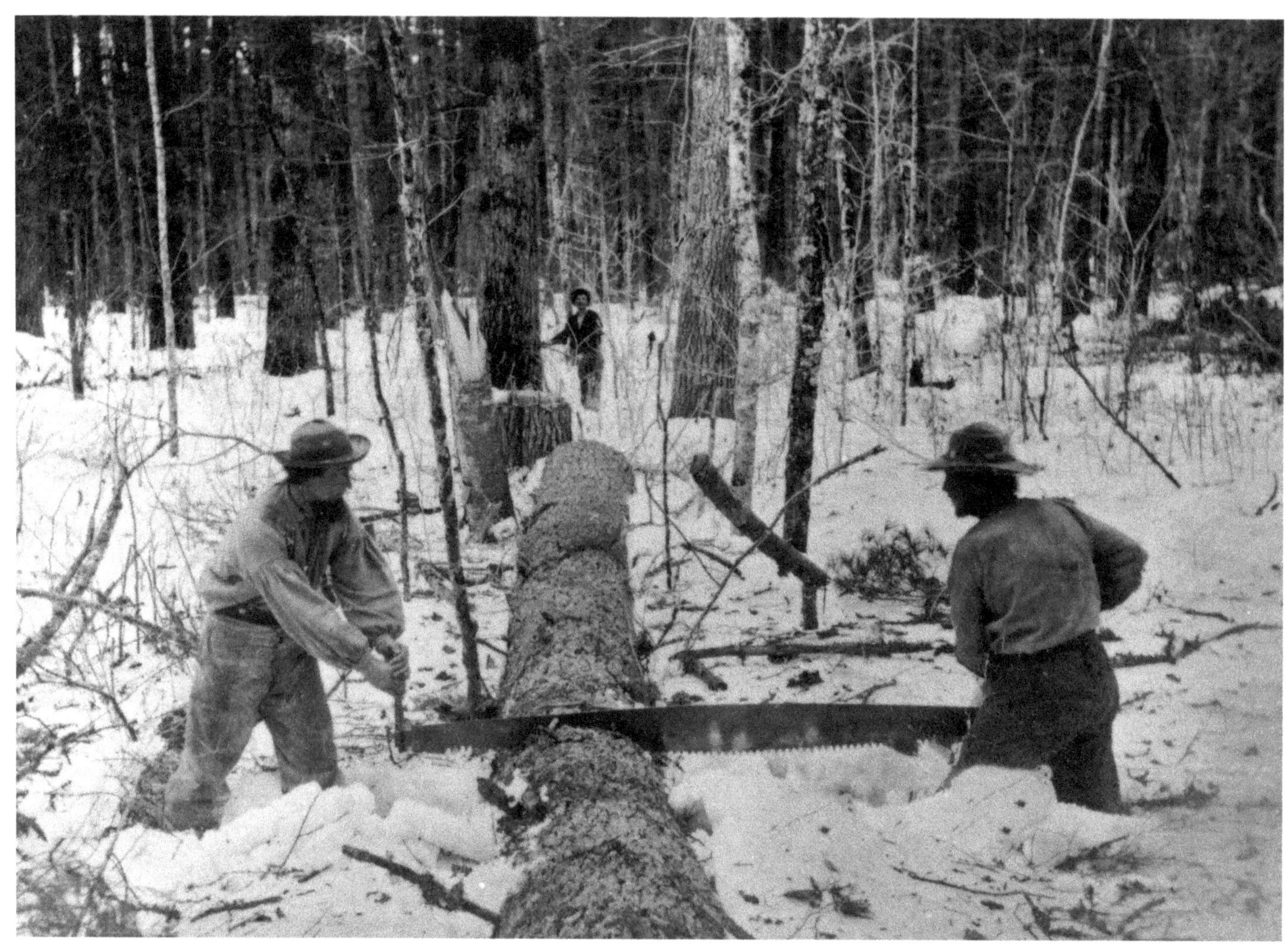

Lumberjacks sawing a white pine in one of Minnesota's many thriving pineries around 1865. Minnesota white pine was a lumberman's dream, because it was light, buoyant for the springtime river log drives, and easy to cut in the sawmills. At the same time, the pine was strong and durable.

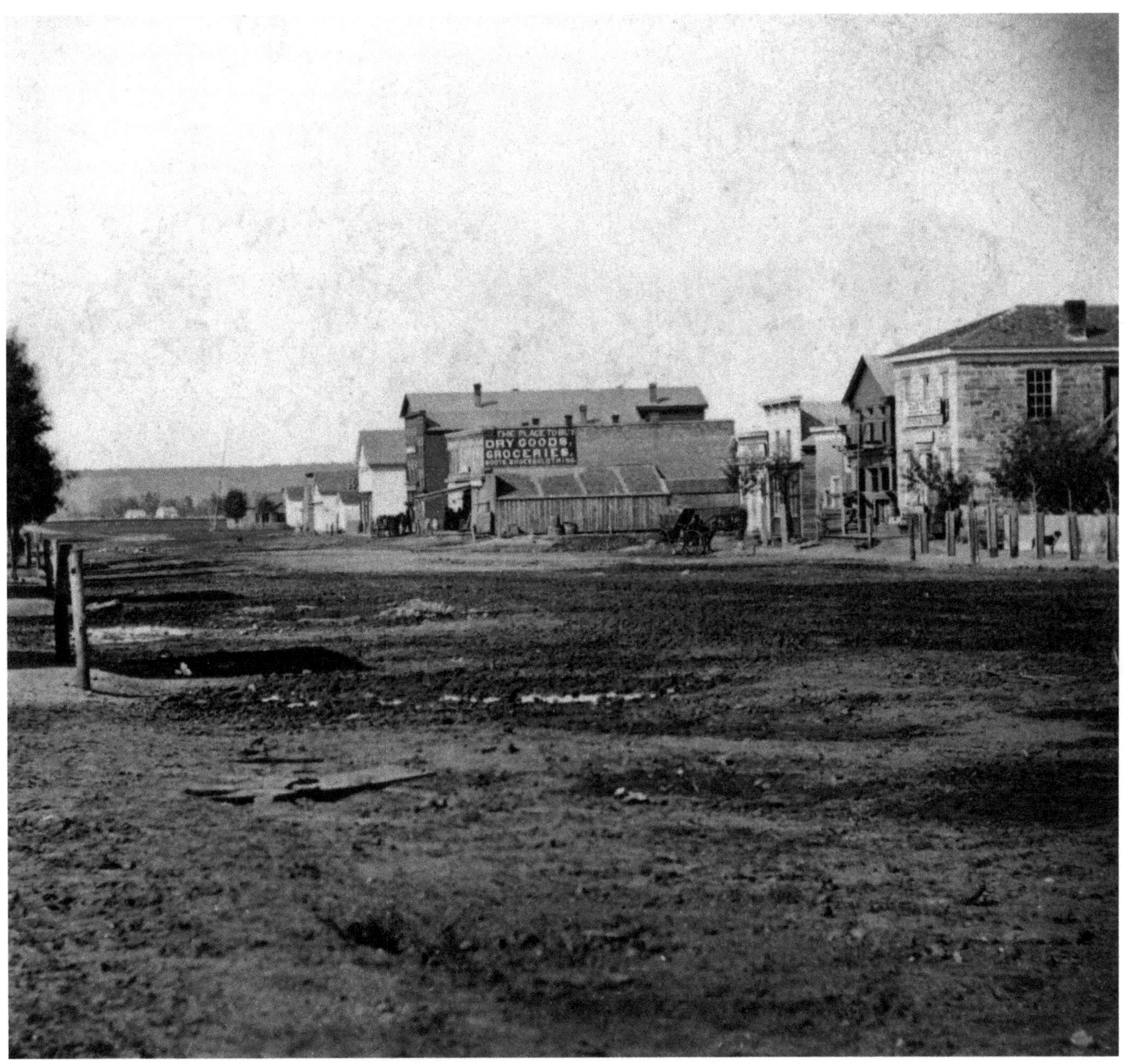


Minnesota Avenue in St. Peter as it looked in 1867. An attempt was made to move the territorial capital from St. Paul to St. Peter in 1857, but territorial council member Joseph J. Rolette famously took the legislative bill and hid with it in the St. Paul Hotel until the end of the legislative session, when it was too late for the bill to be signed.

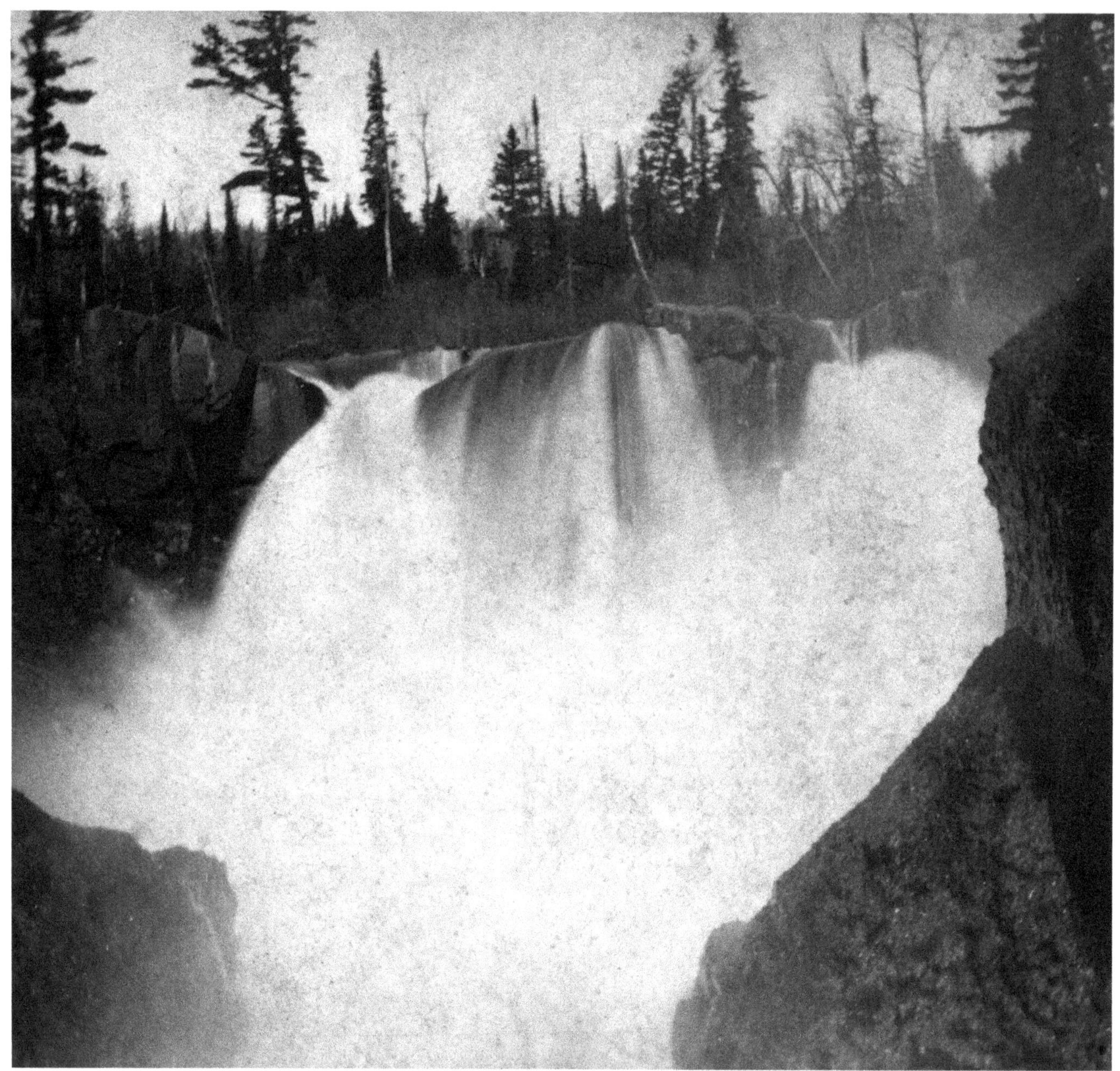

The Pigeon River Falls create part of the U.S.-Canada border between Minnesota and Ontario. The Pigeon River was an essential part of the route favored by fur traders from 1600 to the 1850s. This photo was taken in 1868, when the falls were reported to be 65 feet high and 100 feet wide.

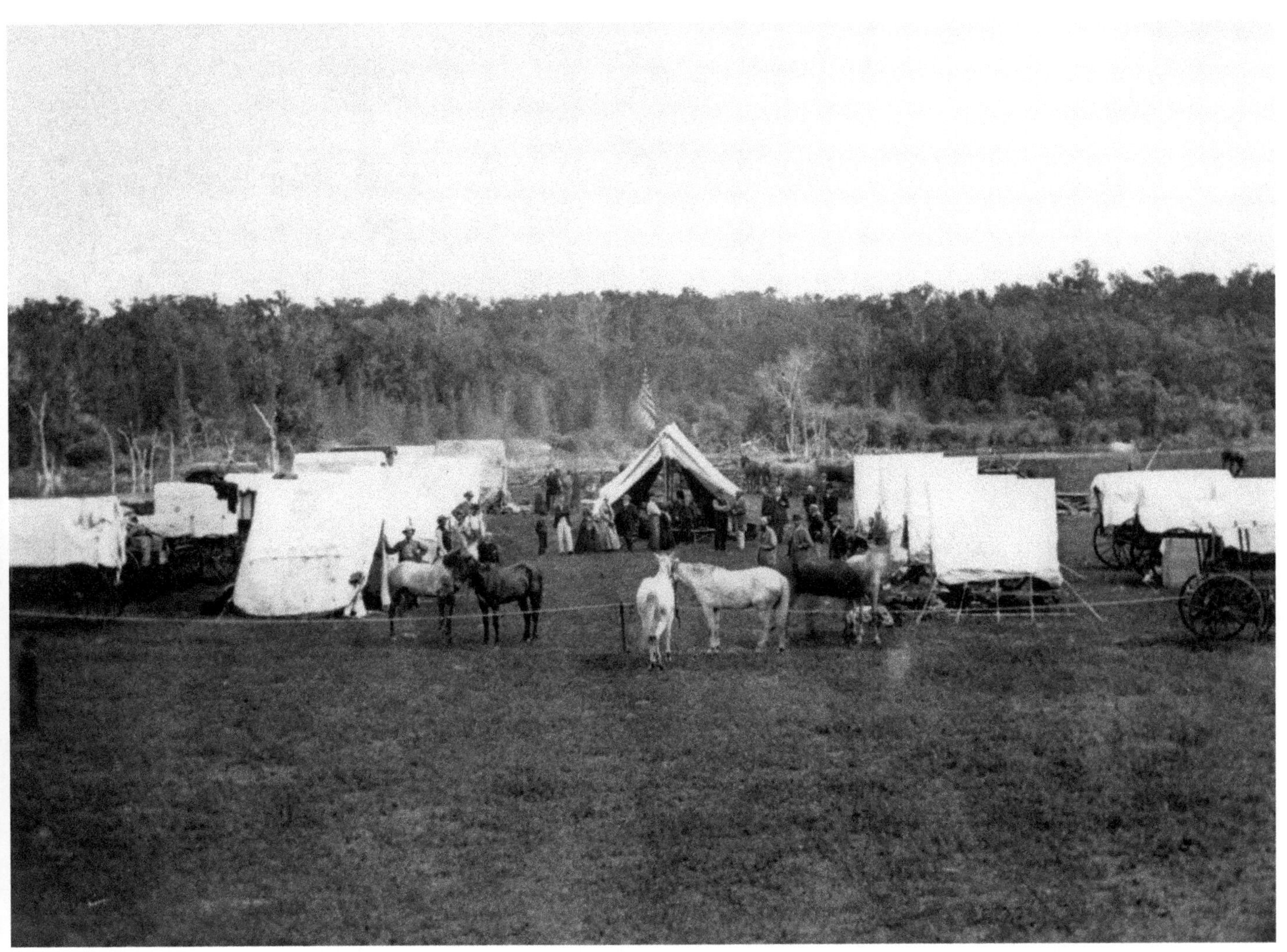

The expedition party for the Northern Pacific Railroad camping at Cold Spring, along an old fur trade trail, in the summer of 1869. Congress gave the Northern Pacific a colossal land grant to construct a railway from Lake Superior to Puget Sound.

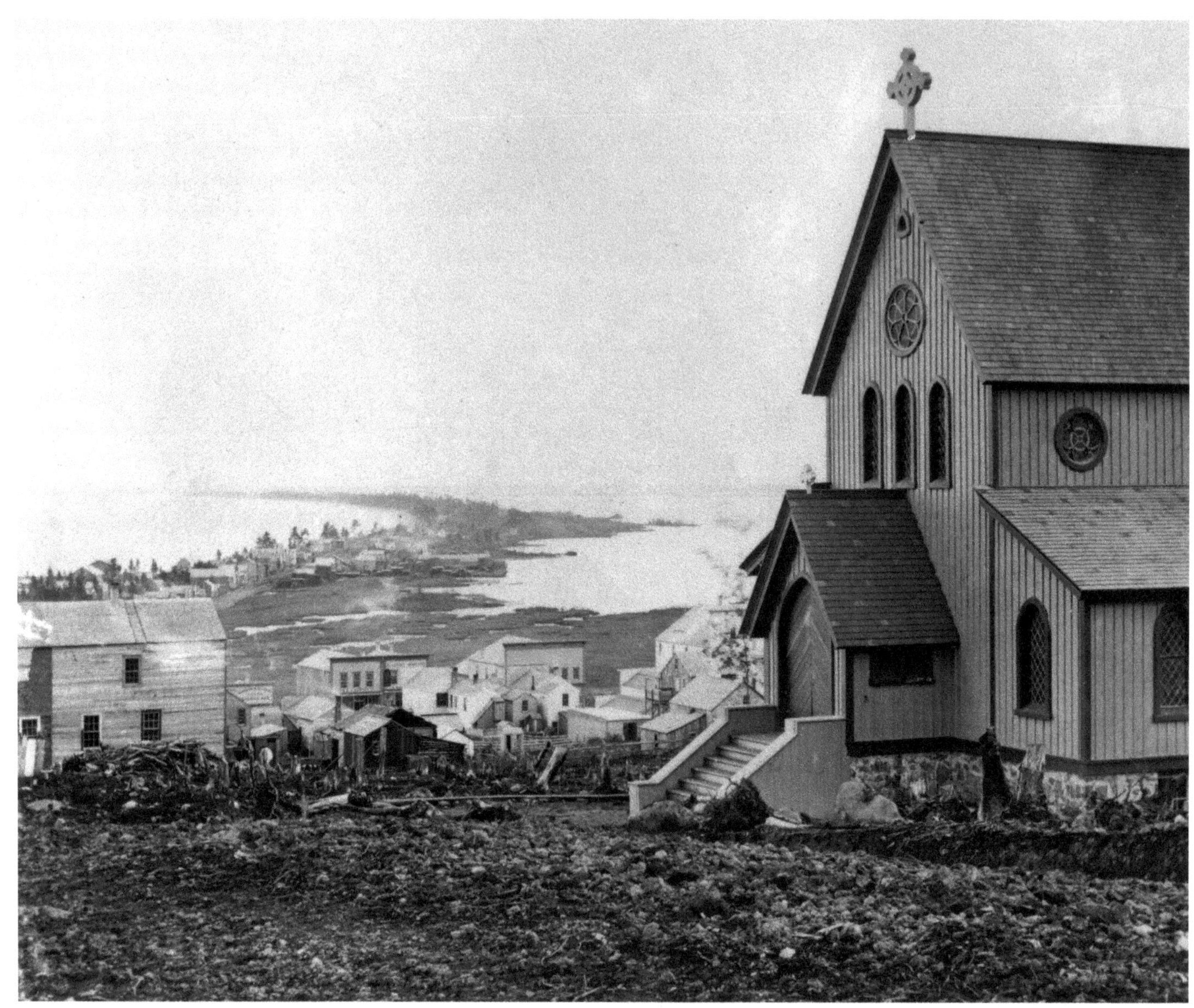

A view of St. Paul's Episcopal Church, Duluth's oldest church, as it looked in 1870. During its construction, the church was often referred to as "Jay Cooke's church," in honor of the town's Episcopalian financier. In October of 1870, Bishop Henry B. Whipple came to Duluth for a formal dedication, announcing the church's official name of St. Paul.

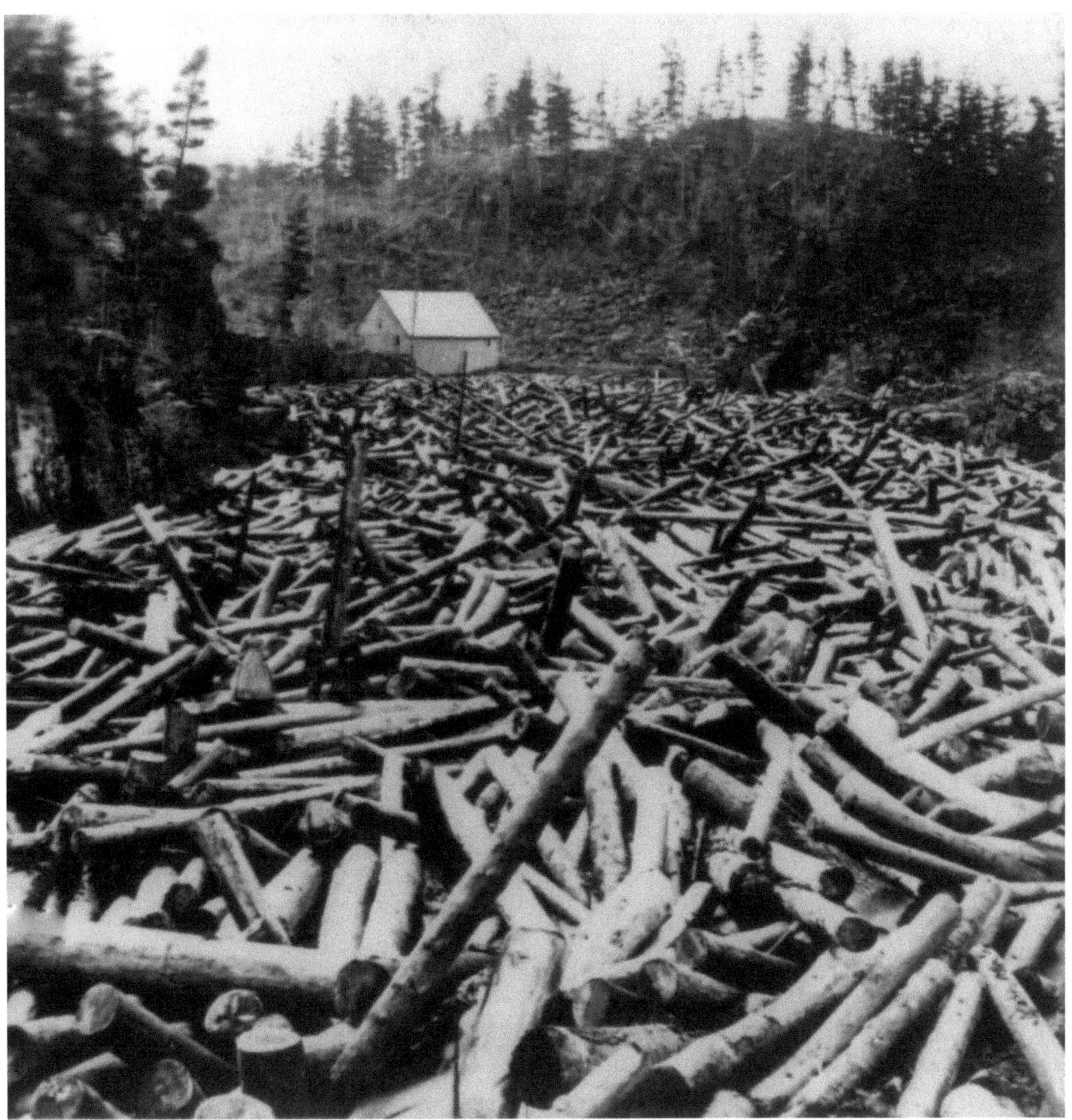

Logjams were an inevitable hazard on Minnesota rivers during the springtime drives. Before the expansion of the railroads in Northern Minnesota, lumbermen were almost completely dependent on river transportation. A team of lumberjacks called "river pigs" broke up jams and guided the logs to sawmills downstream.

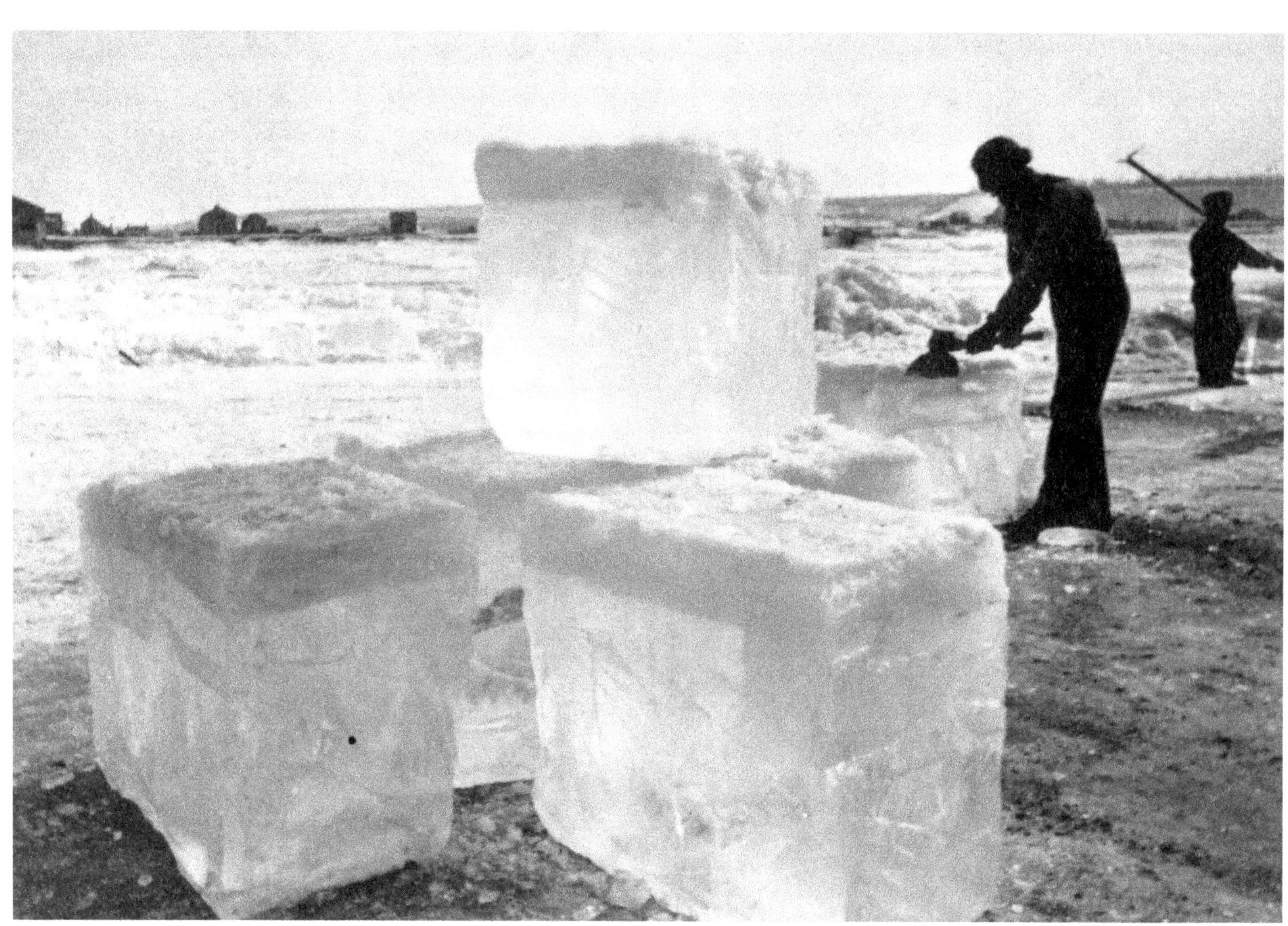

Across Minnesota, ice harvesting usually took place in January, when lakes and rivers were frozen at least 18 to 20 inches thick. Horse-drawn wagons or sleds hauled the ice to icehouses for storage. During the summer, ice was delivered, block by block, to homes and businesses for their iceboxes. Railroads, also a large ice clientele, used it to cool the boxcars when shipping produce, dairy, and meat.

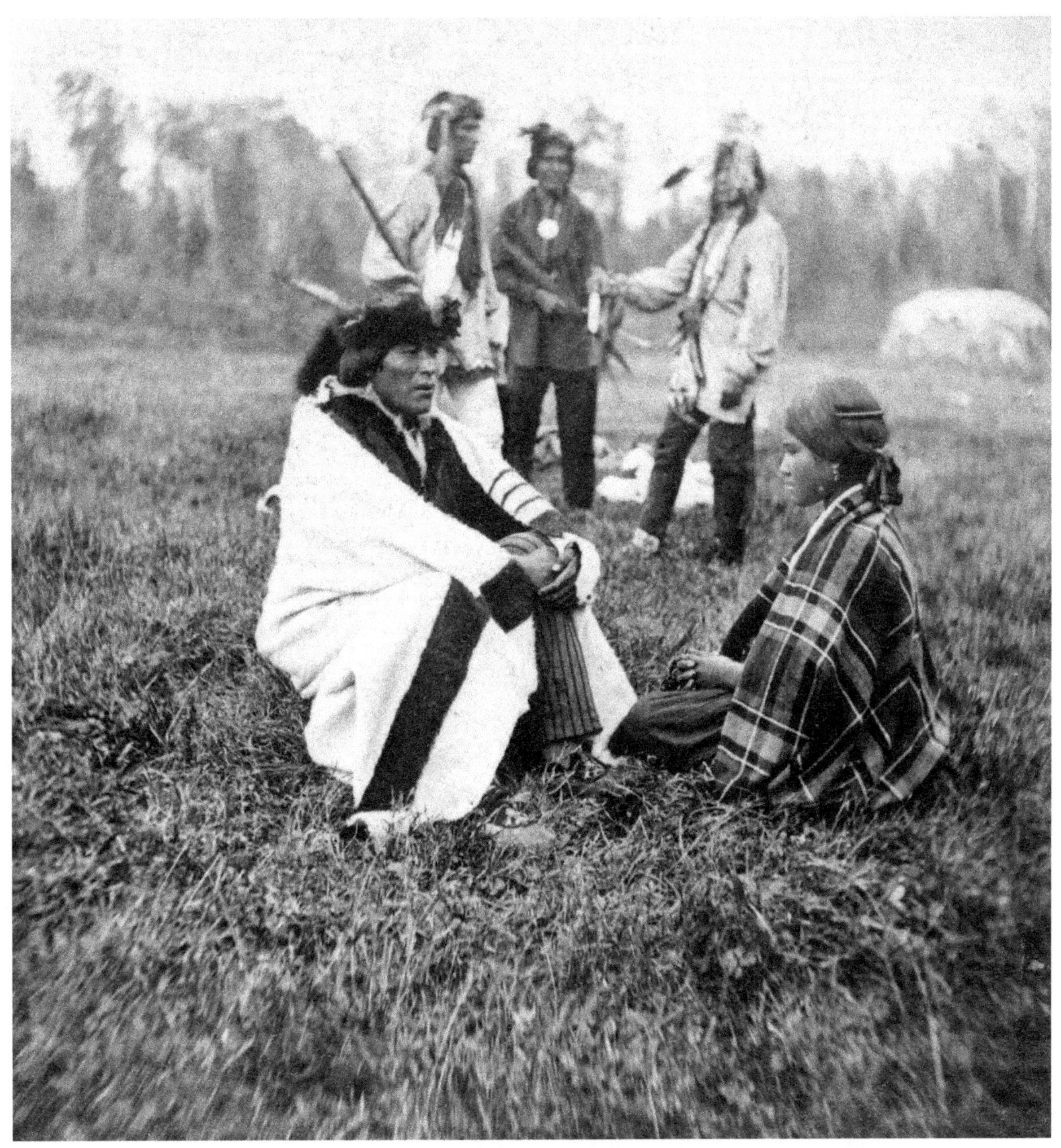

This image was recorded around 1870 and was originally titled "Chippewa Wedding," although it is likely that it was not a wedding at all, but a staged photograph of Ojibwe Indians that was sold as a stereoscopic image and postcard.

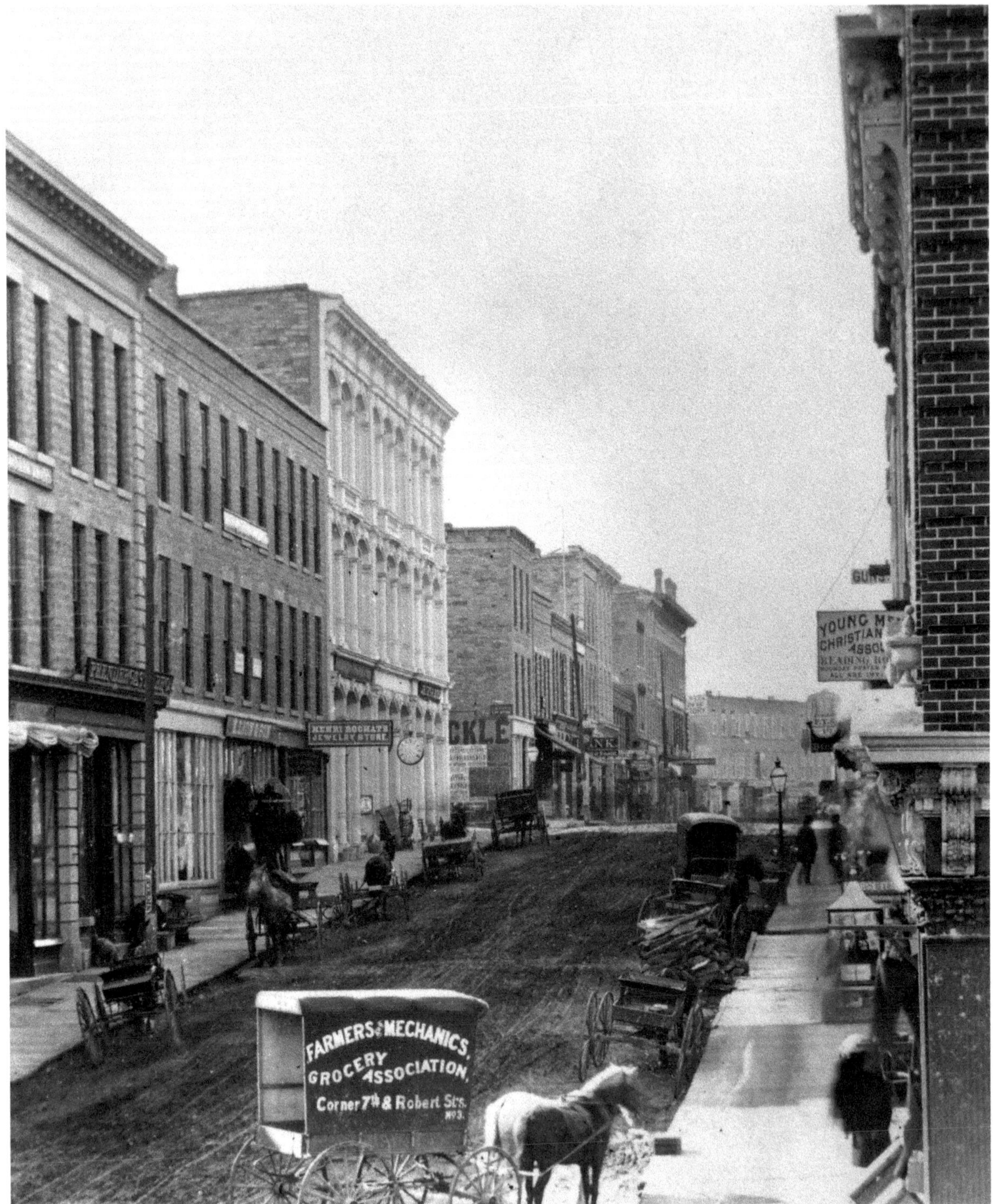


A view of Third Street in downtown St. Paul in 1873 with a horse-drawn wagon advertising the Farmers and Mechanics Grocery Association. The city evolved from a pioneer village in the late 1830s to a metropolitan area with strong agricultural roots. This thriving warehouse district connected nearby farms with the wide distribution network provided by railways and the Mississippi River.

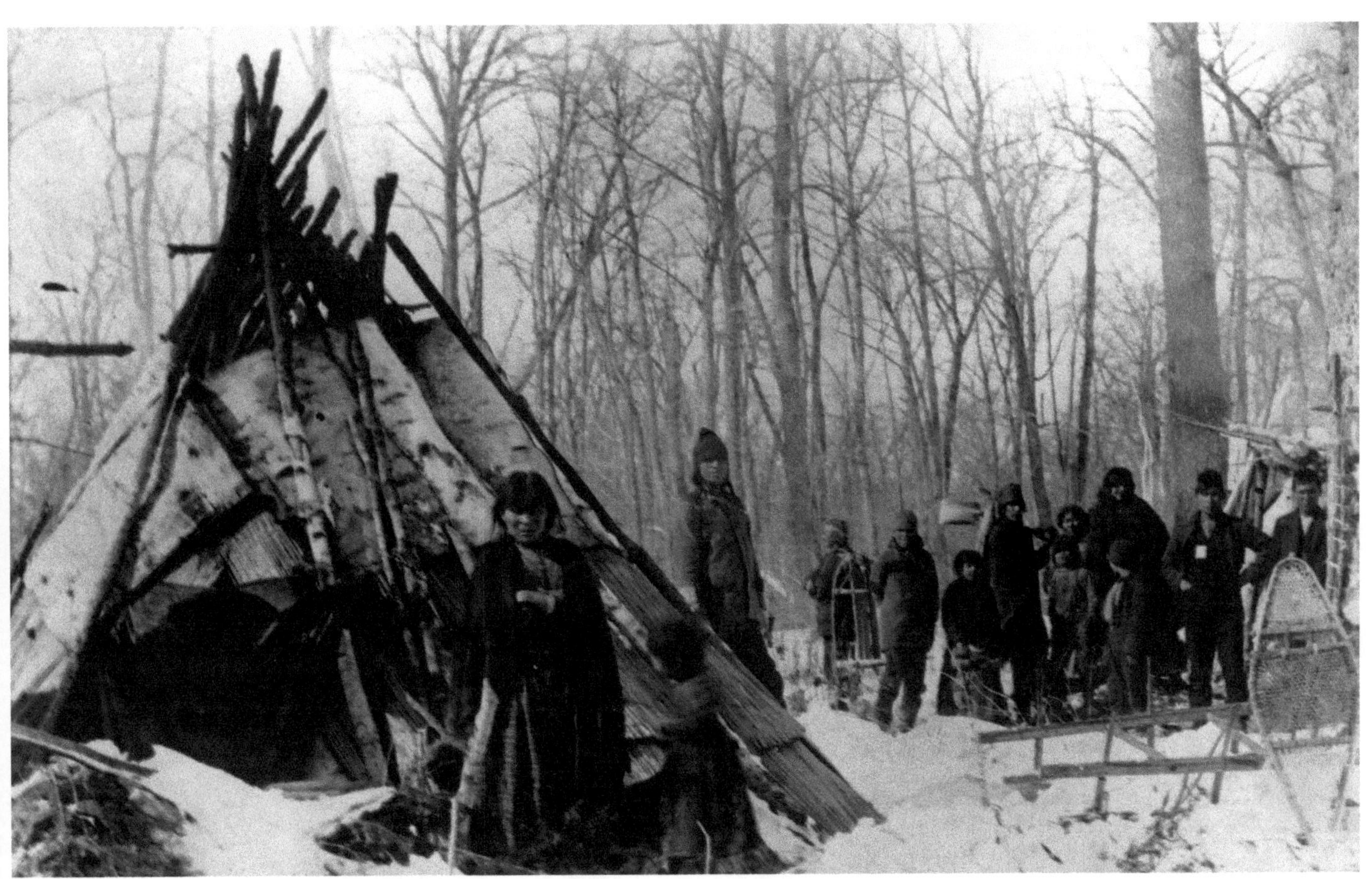

An Ojibwe winter camp in South Harbor Township around 1875. The township is located in the Mille Lacs Indian Reservation region, believed to have been one of the first areas in Minnesota settled by humans.

*Following Spread:* The Minnesota House hotel, shown here in 1876, was one of several hotels that catered to visitors in the St. Cloud area. Located in the center of the state, on the Red River Trail, the city was perfectly situated to accommodate the needs of travelers on their way from St. Paul back to North Dakota or Canada.

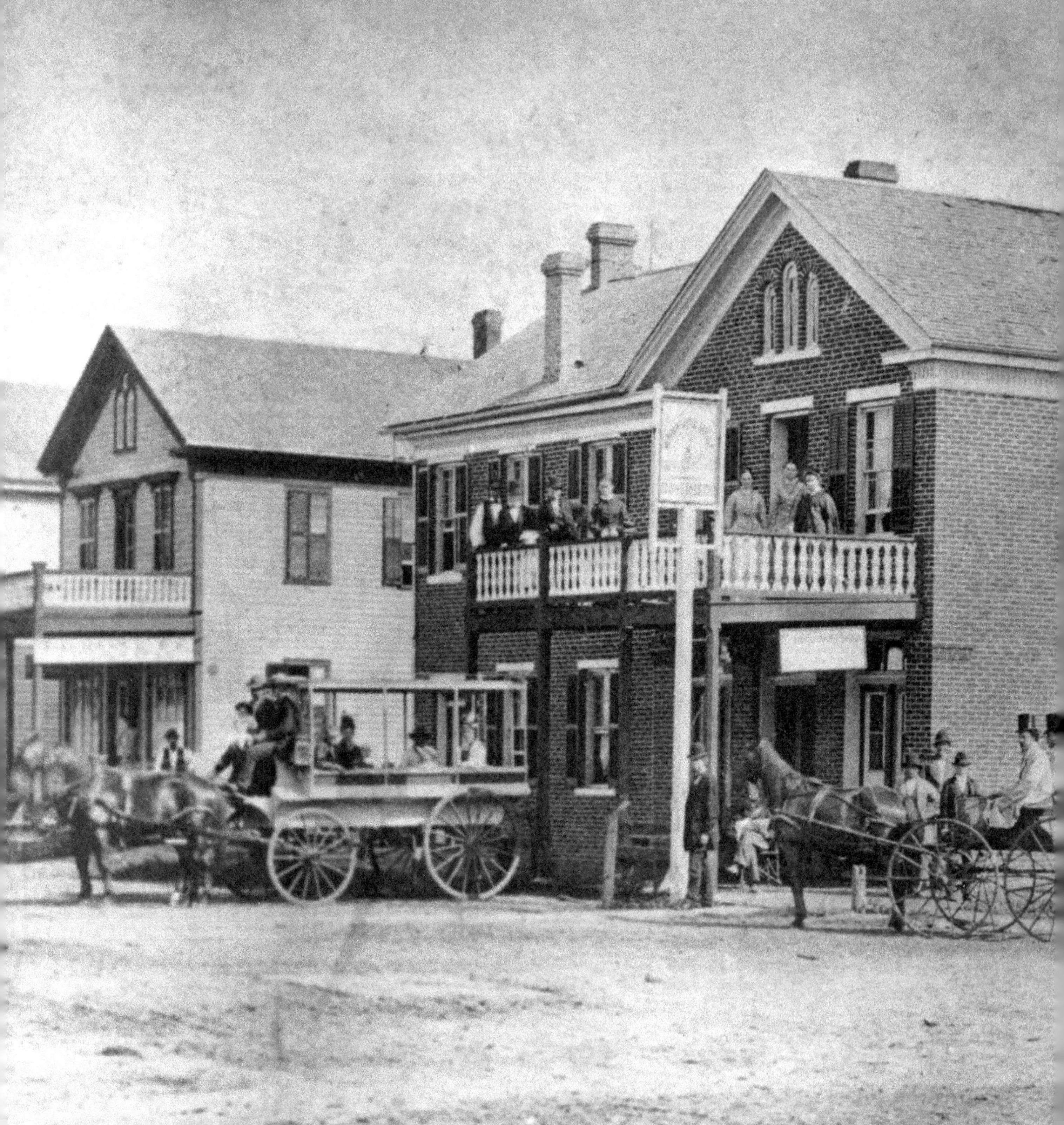

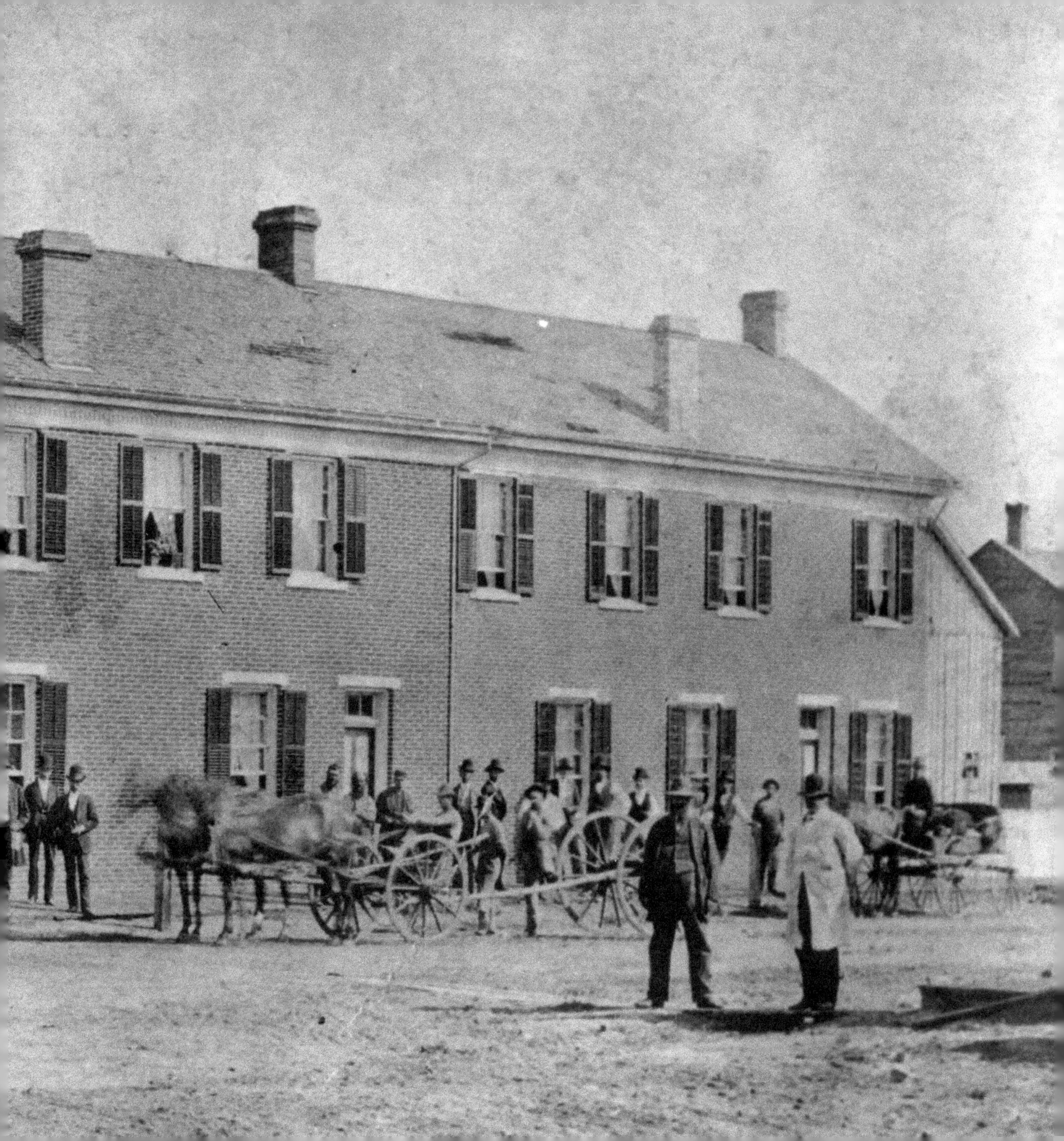

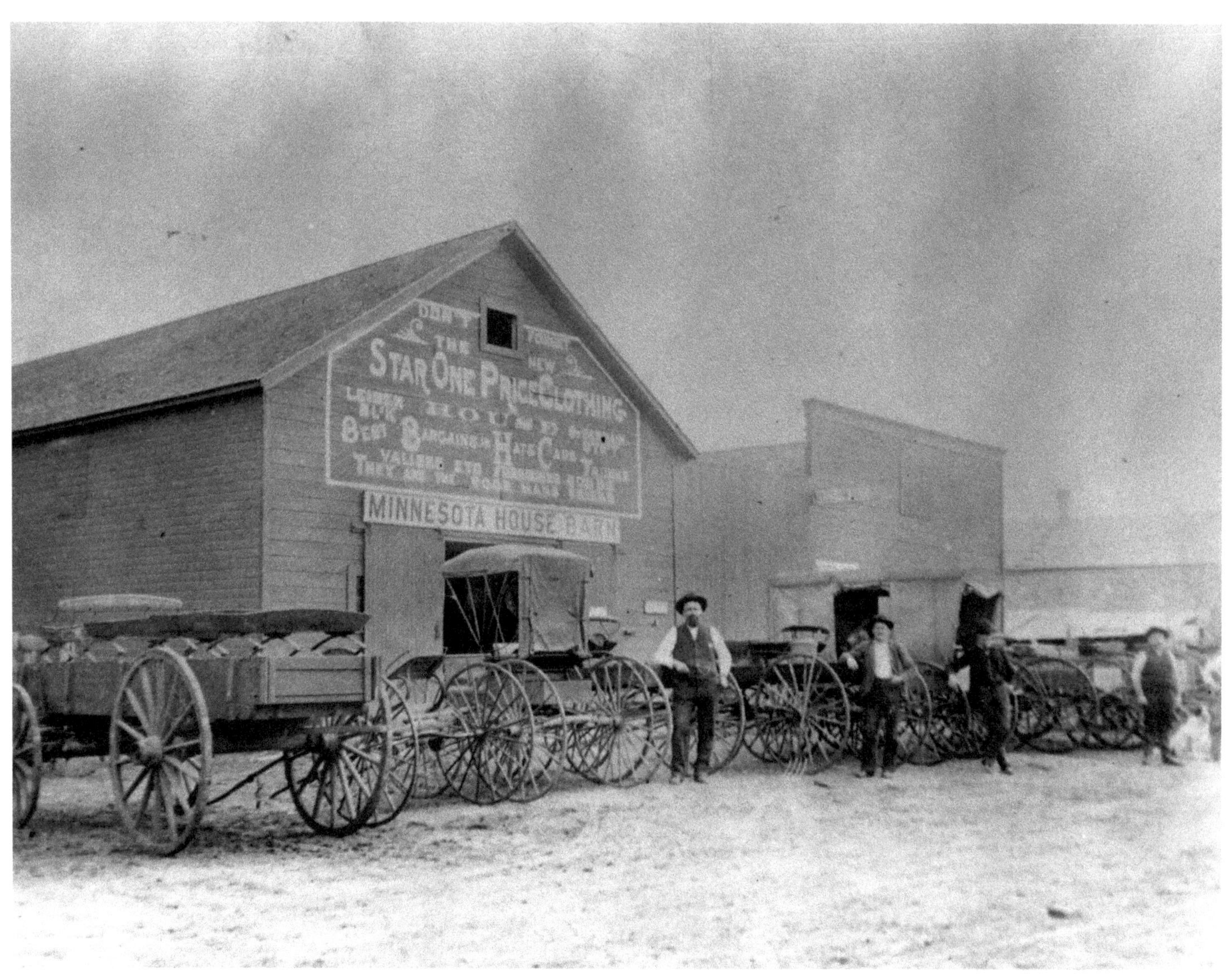


The Minnesota House barn rented wagons and stabled horses for overnight visitors. The barn and the Minnesota House hotel were located in the commercial hub of St. Cloud in 1876.

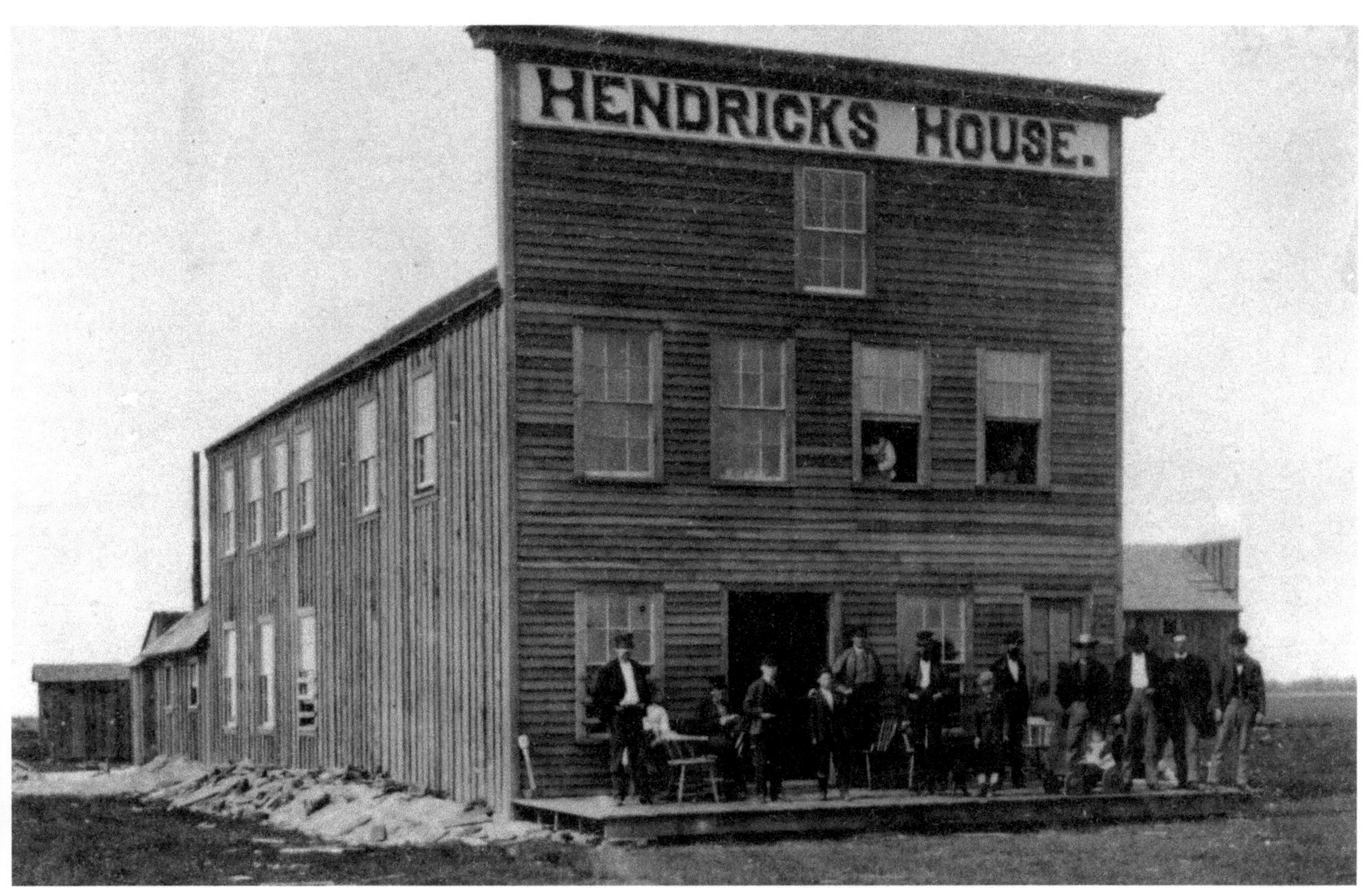


The Hendricks House hotel was located not in Hendricks, Minnesota, but on the North Pacific Railway line in Duluth, near Lake Street. Shown around 1876, the hotel is a perfect example of those that sprang up all over Minnesota to accommodate railroad passengers.

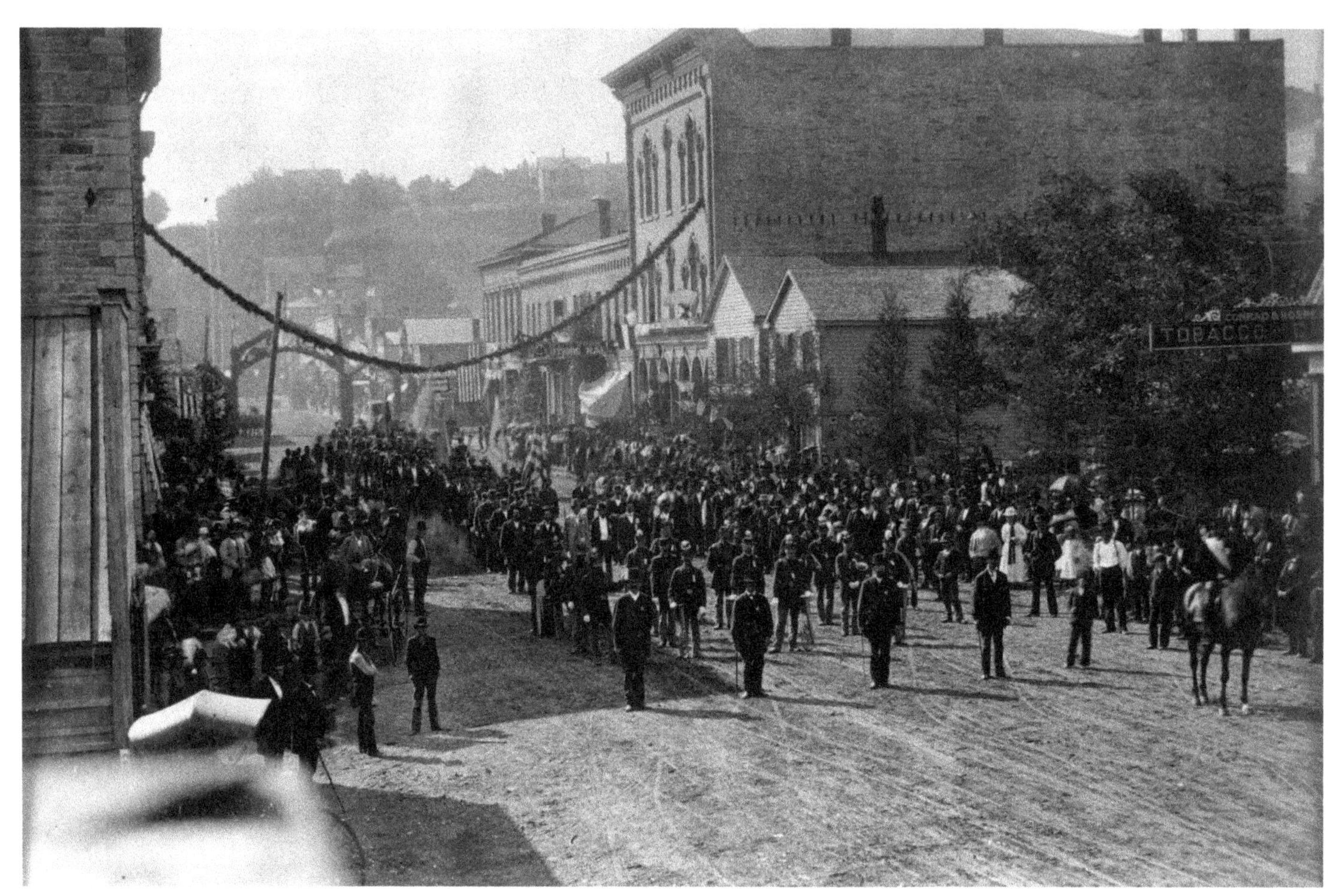


Stillwater celebrates the ninth annual Minnesota Saengerfest—a German music festival—in 1877. This event brought various German singing societies together for socializing, competition, and celebration of German culture.

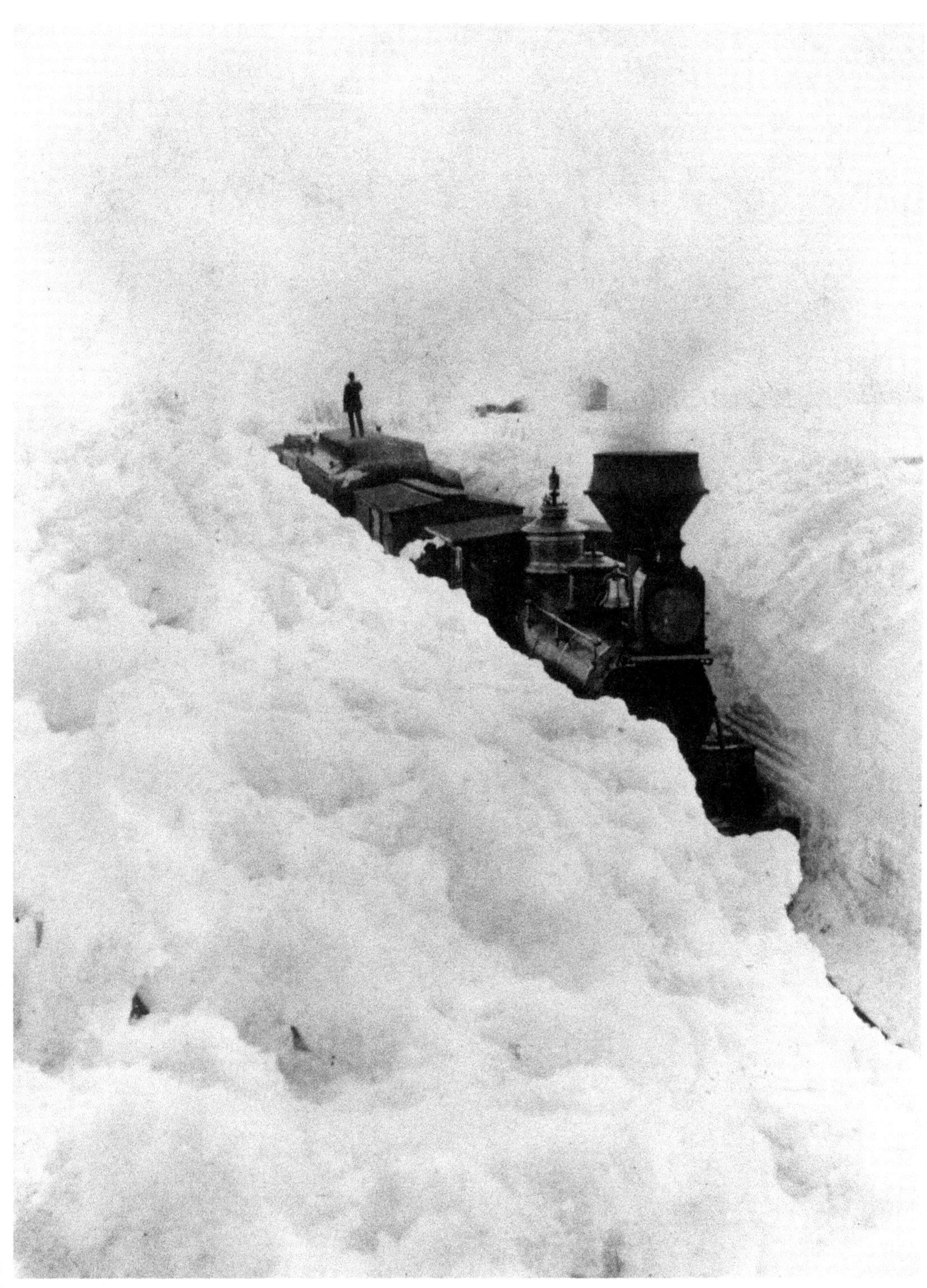

In late March of 1881, a blizzard hit Southern Minnesota, creating snowdrifts so high that trains could not pass. This image of a man standing on top of a snowbound train was massively reproduced for postcards and stereoscopes.

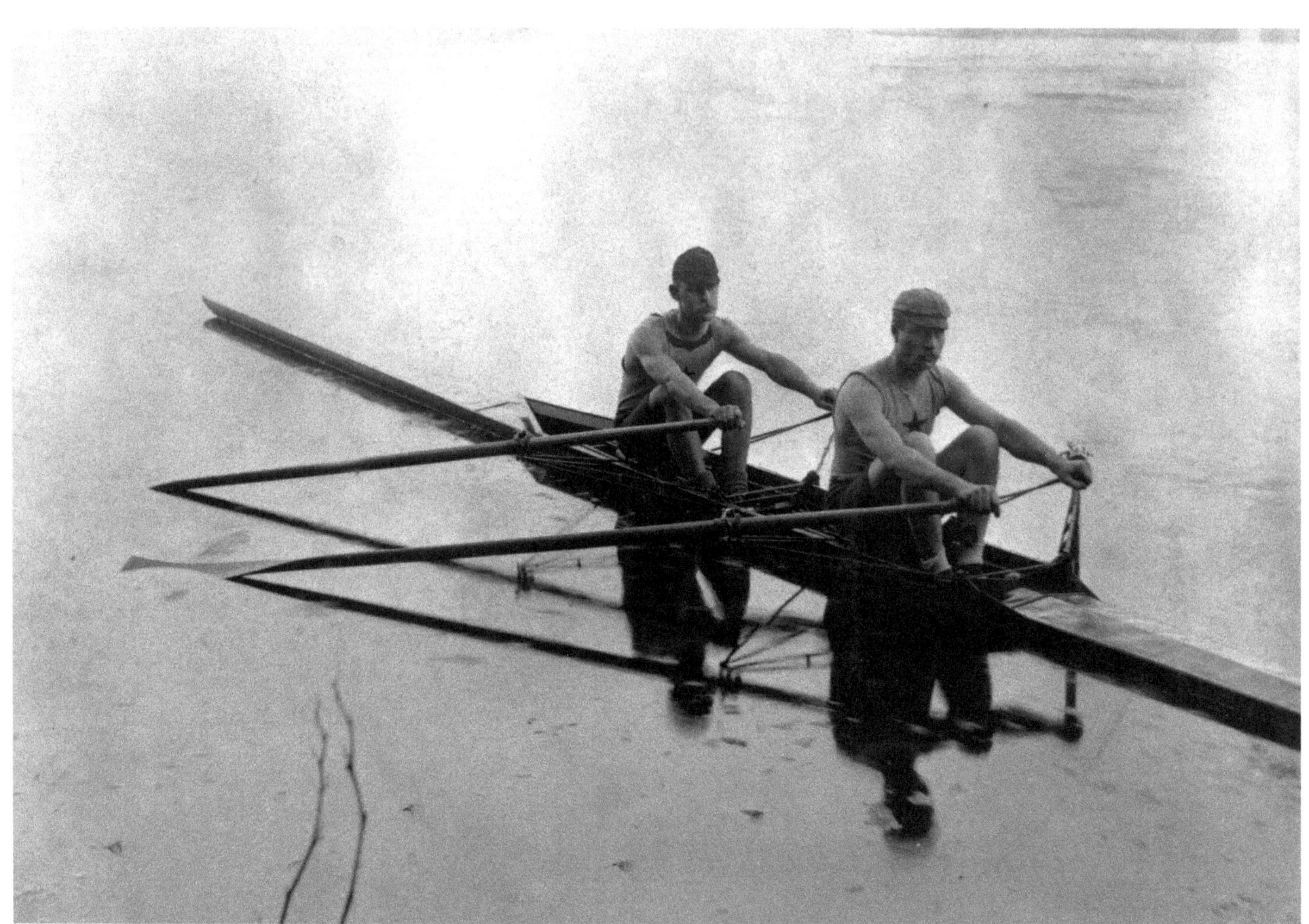

Two rowers from the Minnesota Boat Club in the 1880s. The club was established on Raspberry Island in St. Paul in the 1870s and is said to be the oldest athletic organization in the state. Members like these two had to adhere to strict rules, with punitive repercussions for breaking them. For example, refusing to obey captain's orders meant a fine of $2. Smoking in the dressing room brought a $1 fine.

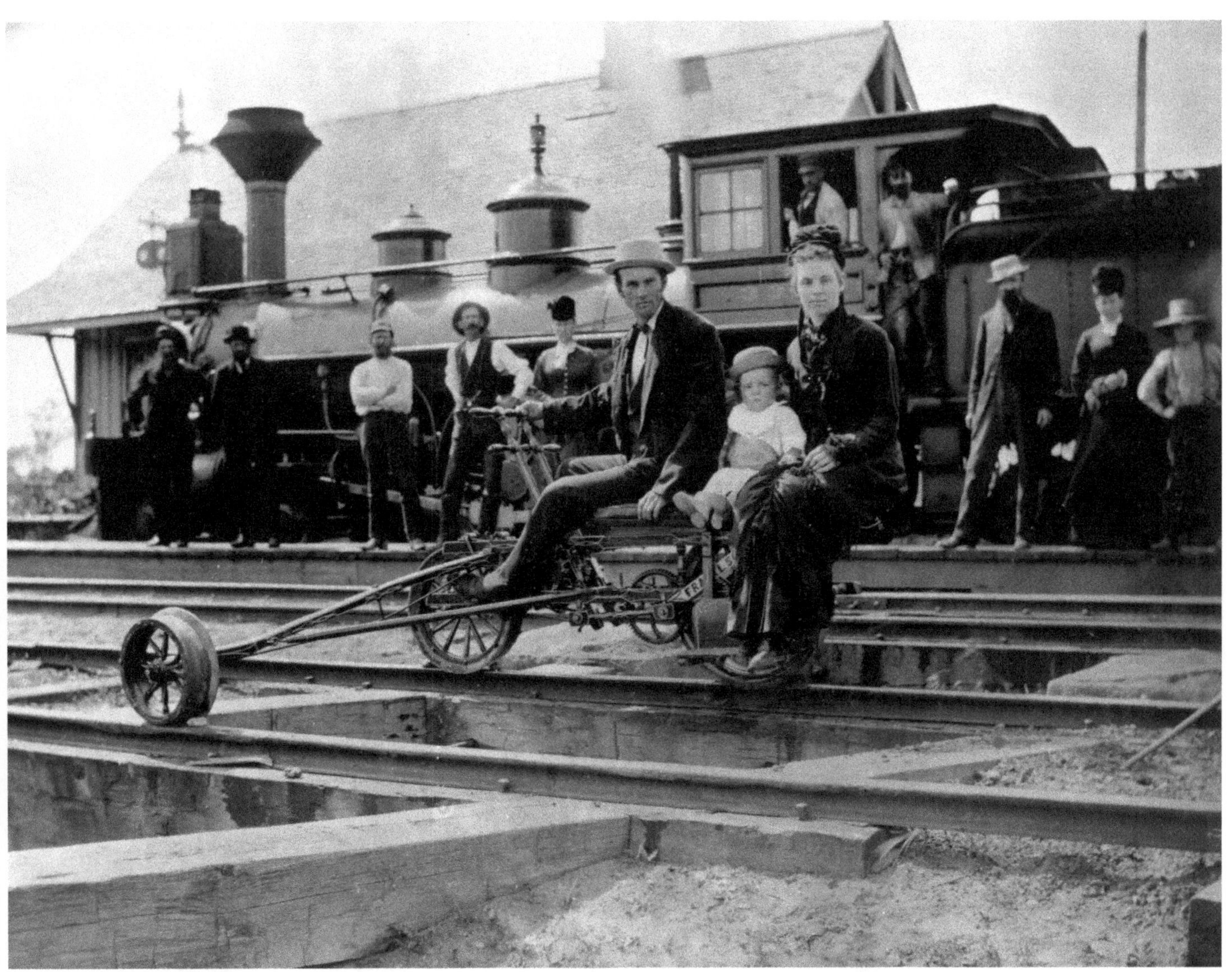

On July 13, 1881, a man, woman, and child pose on a velocipede handcar in a Minnesota rail yard. This novel, three-wheel railroad handcar was propelled by a combination of hand and foot power. The velocipede was likely used for track inspection, rather than the leisure riding this photo might suggest.

Construction pauses for a moment on the Minnesota Loan and Trust building, located at 313 Nicollet Avenue in downtown Minneapolis, in 1884. At the time, Minneapolis was flourishing financially, due to the seismic boom in flour and lumber milling and the growth of the railroads.

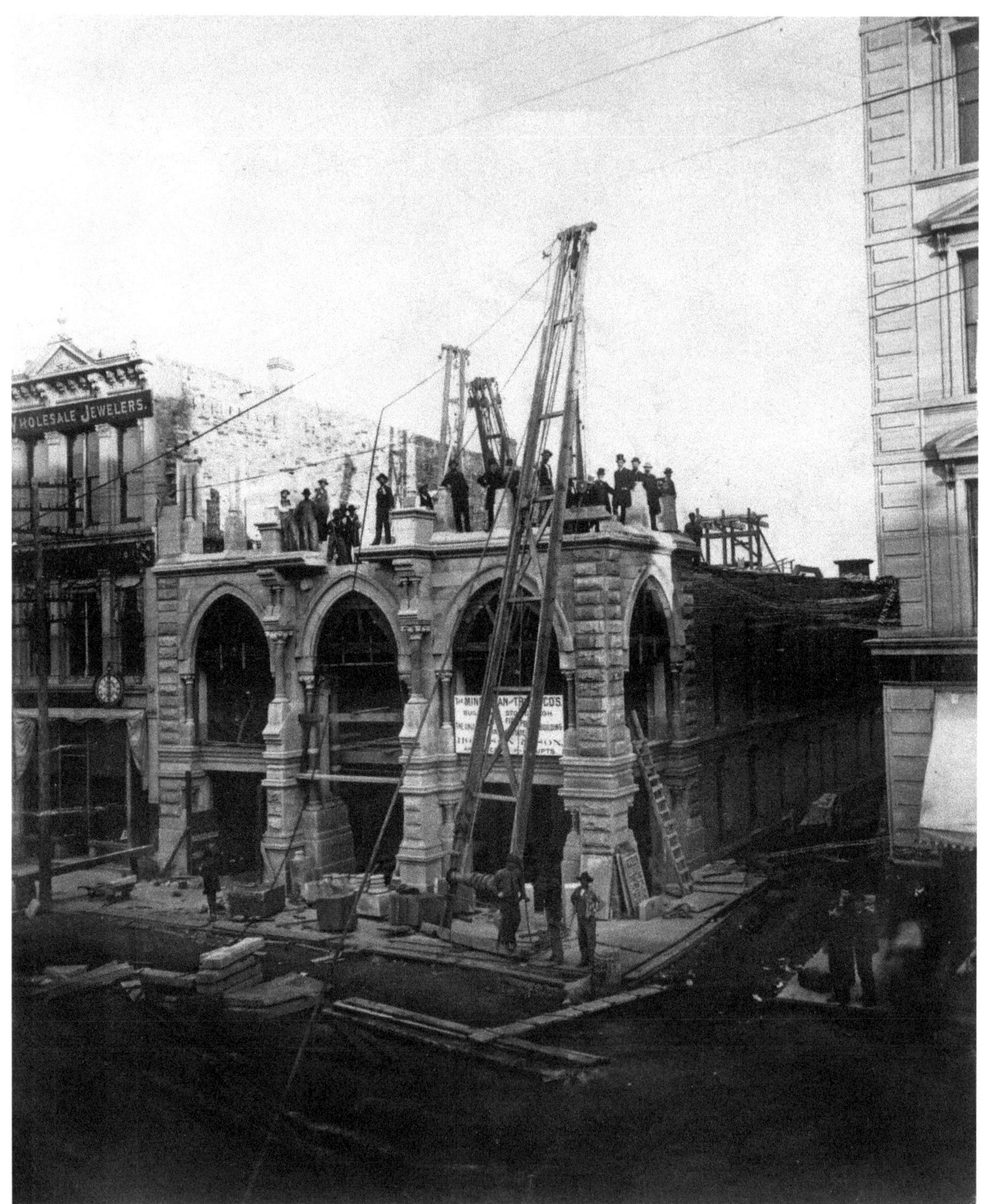

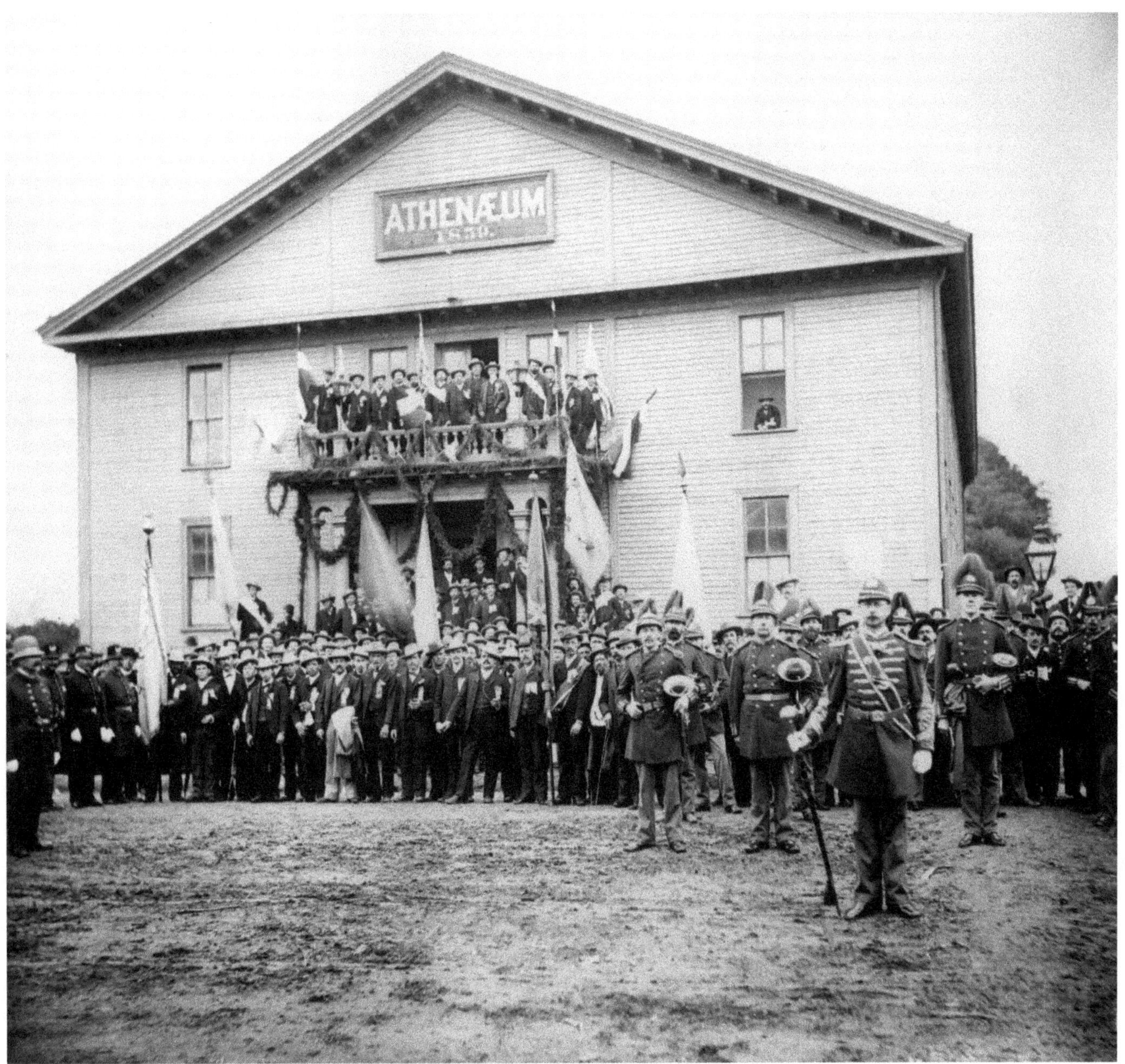


Pictured here around 1885, the Athenaeum in St. Paul, located at Exchange and Sherman streets, was built by the German Reading Society to serve as a meeting place for the German community in the St. Paul area.

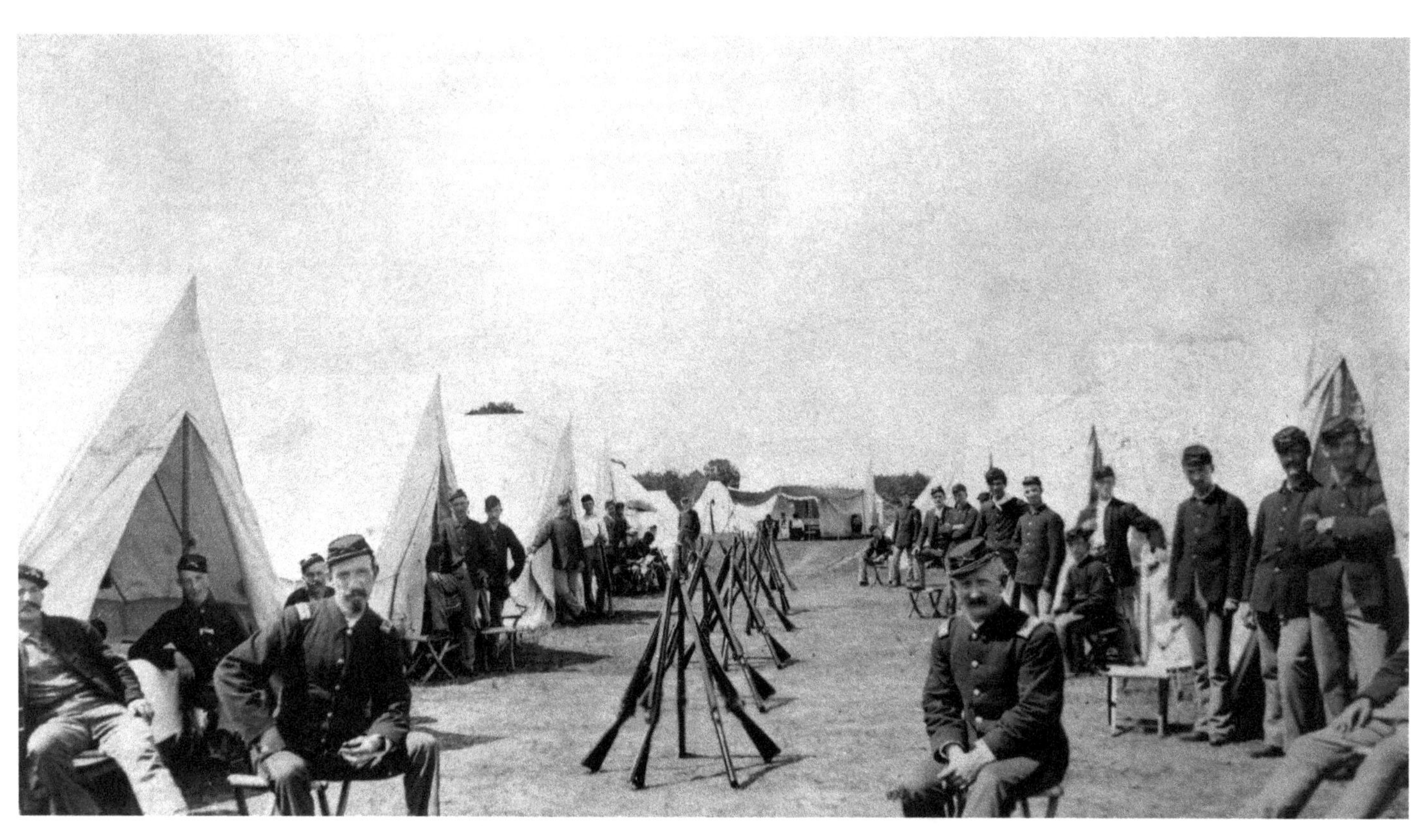

Members of the Minnesota National Guard's Company D pose outside their tents around 1885 at an encampment in either White Bear Lake or Fort Snelling. The tradition-rich military command of "stack arms" allowed weapons to be grounded in a uniform manner while keeping them clean and easily accessible.

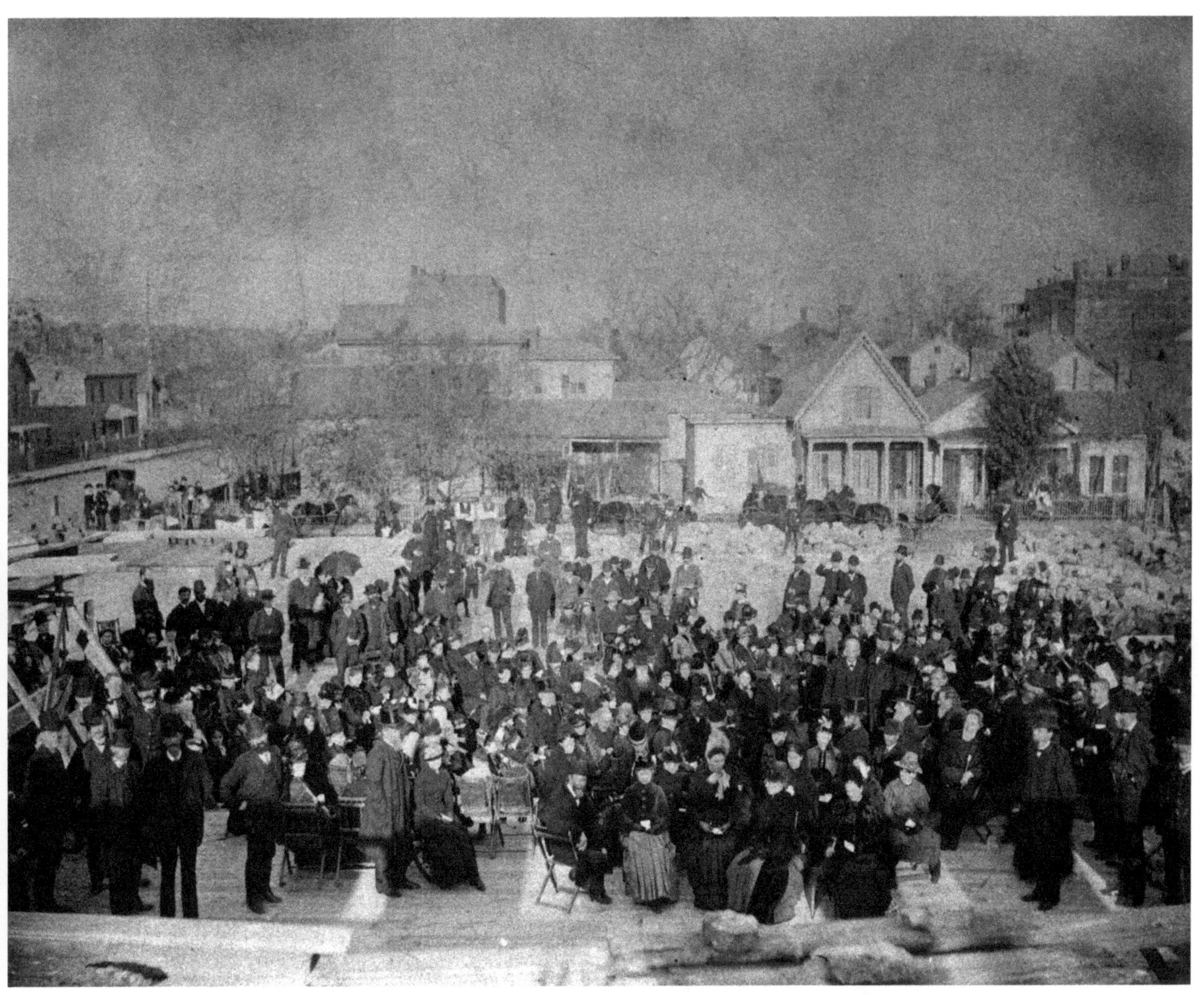

On October 12, 1886, a congregation gathers for the laying of the cornerstone of the Central Park Methodist Episcopal Church in downtown St. Paul.

A view of hunters camping at the St. Louis River around 1890. The picturesque St. Louis River is 179 miles long and the largest river to flow into Lake Superior.

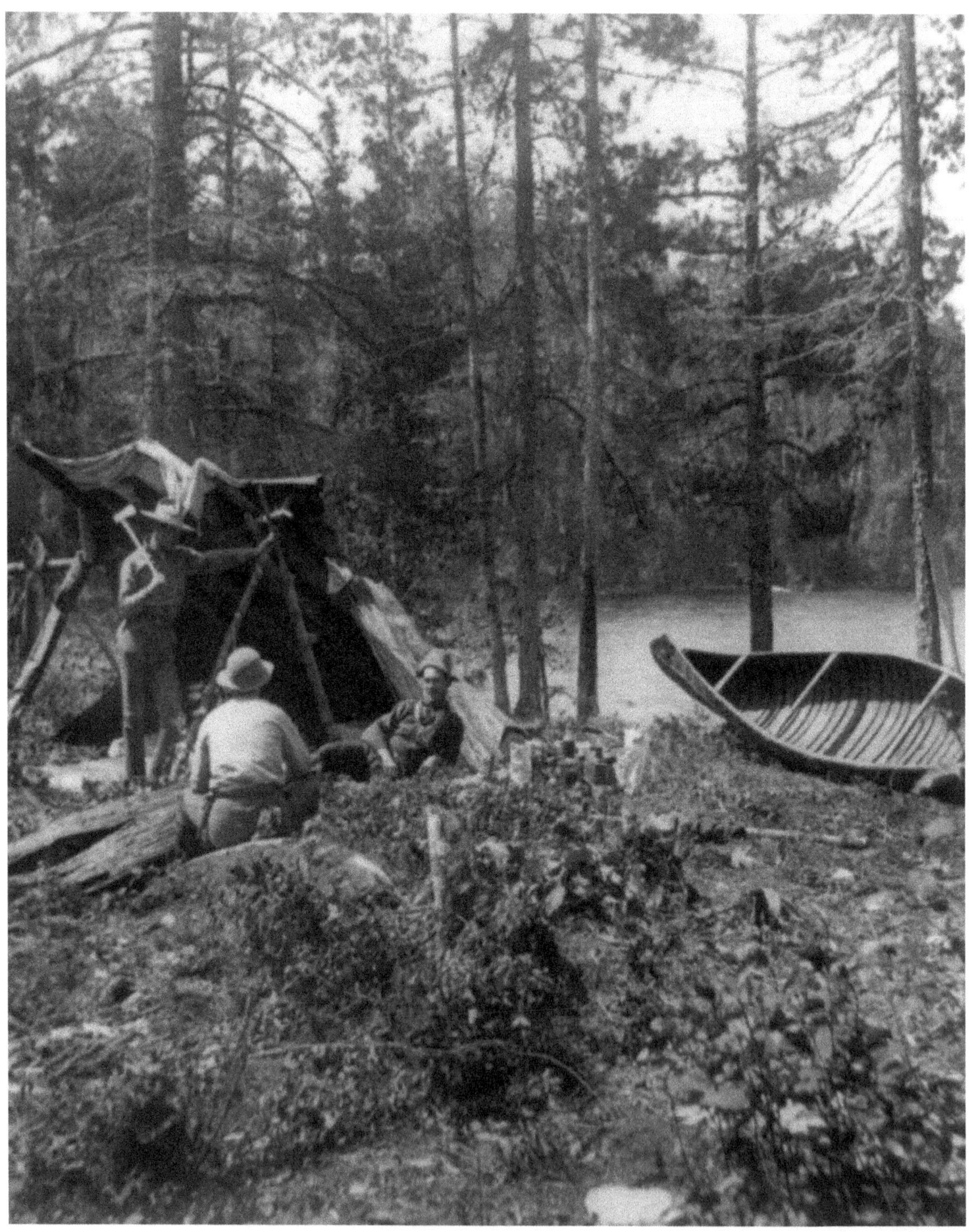

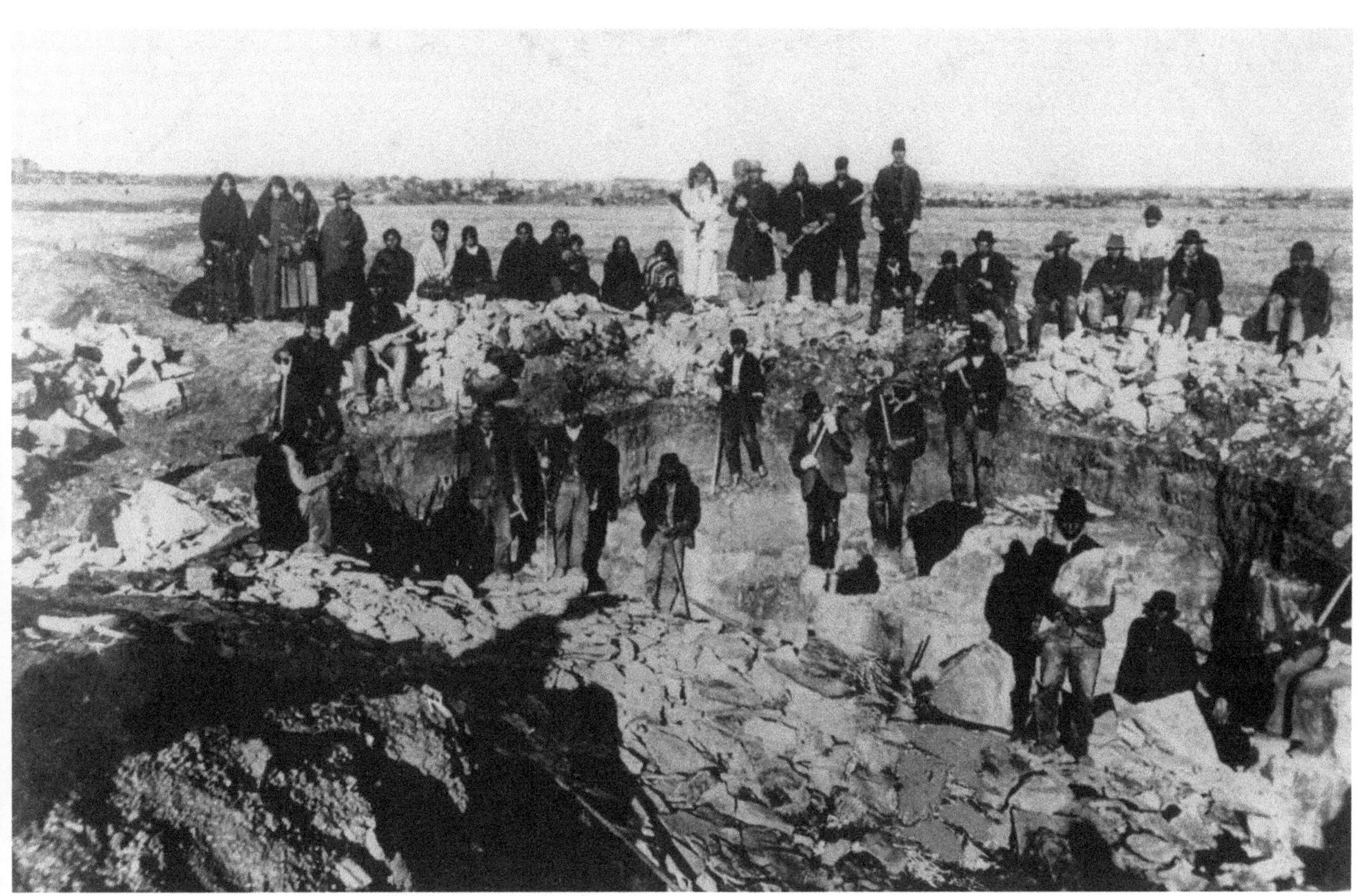

Dakota Indians pose for a postcard in Pipestone, located in the extreme southwest corner of Minnesota, in 1893. The Dakotas have a deep connection to the area, and a long history of mining the red quartzite used for making pipes. Pipestone National Monument, designated by the United States in 1937, is not a traditional monument but the quarry itself.

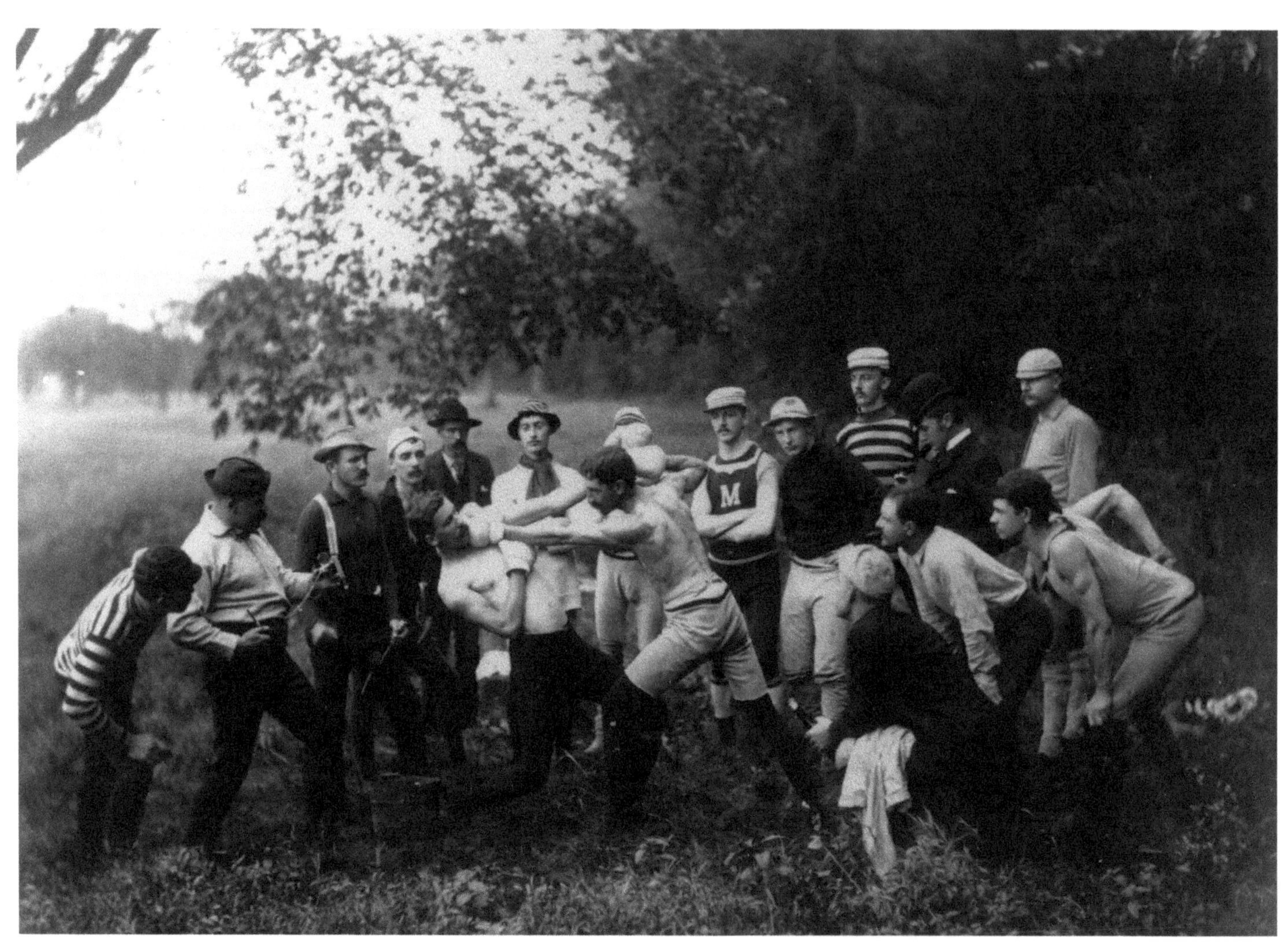


Members of the Minnesota Boat Club observe a boxing match, probably between two of their own, during an 1890s picnic excursion. The club's stated purpose was for the "mutual improvement of the physical bodily condition of its members."

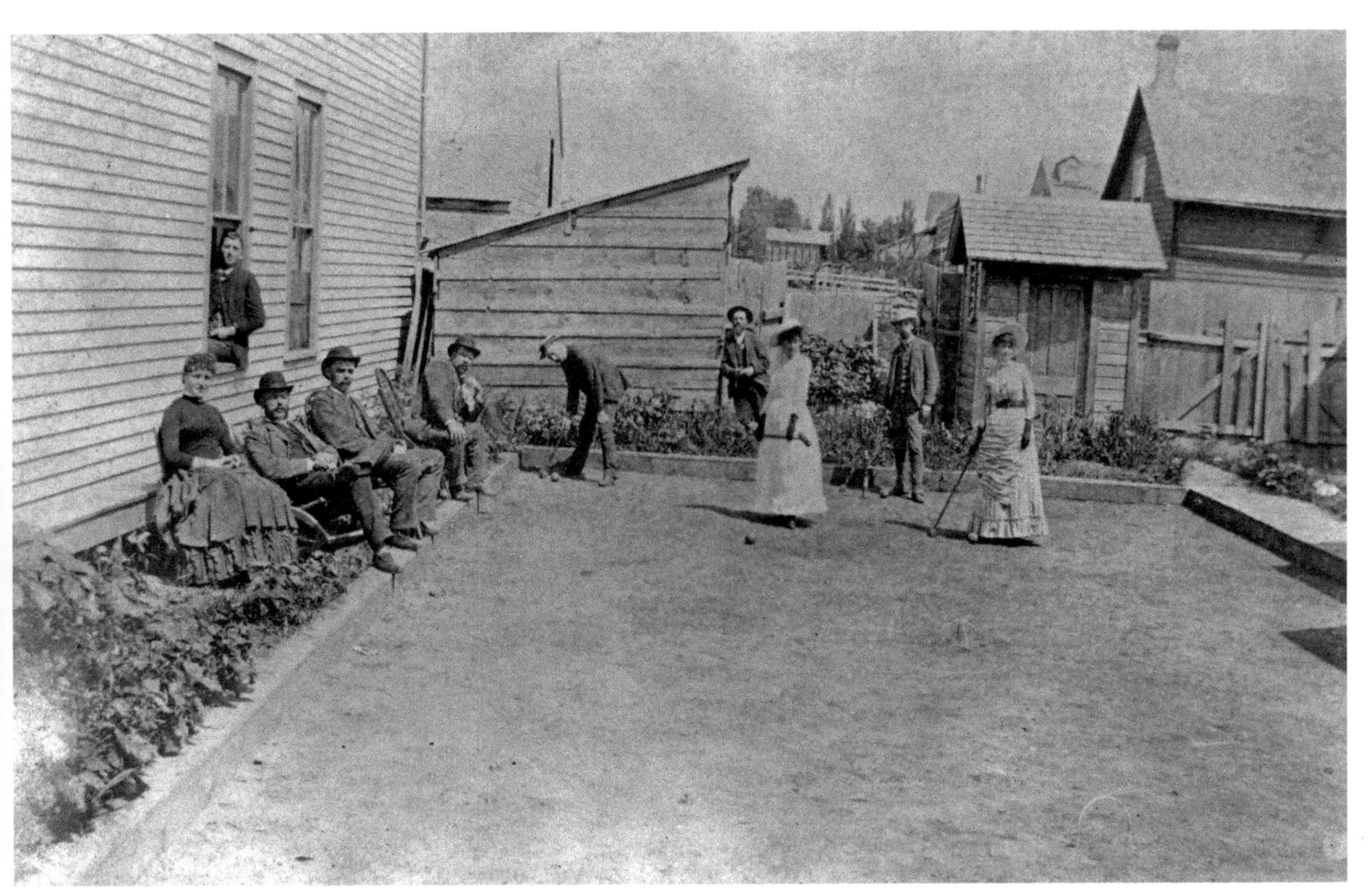

A group of men and women play croquet near the Hotel Merchant in Atwater, Minnesota, in the mid-1890s.

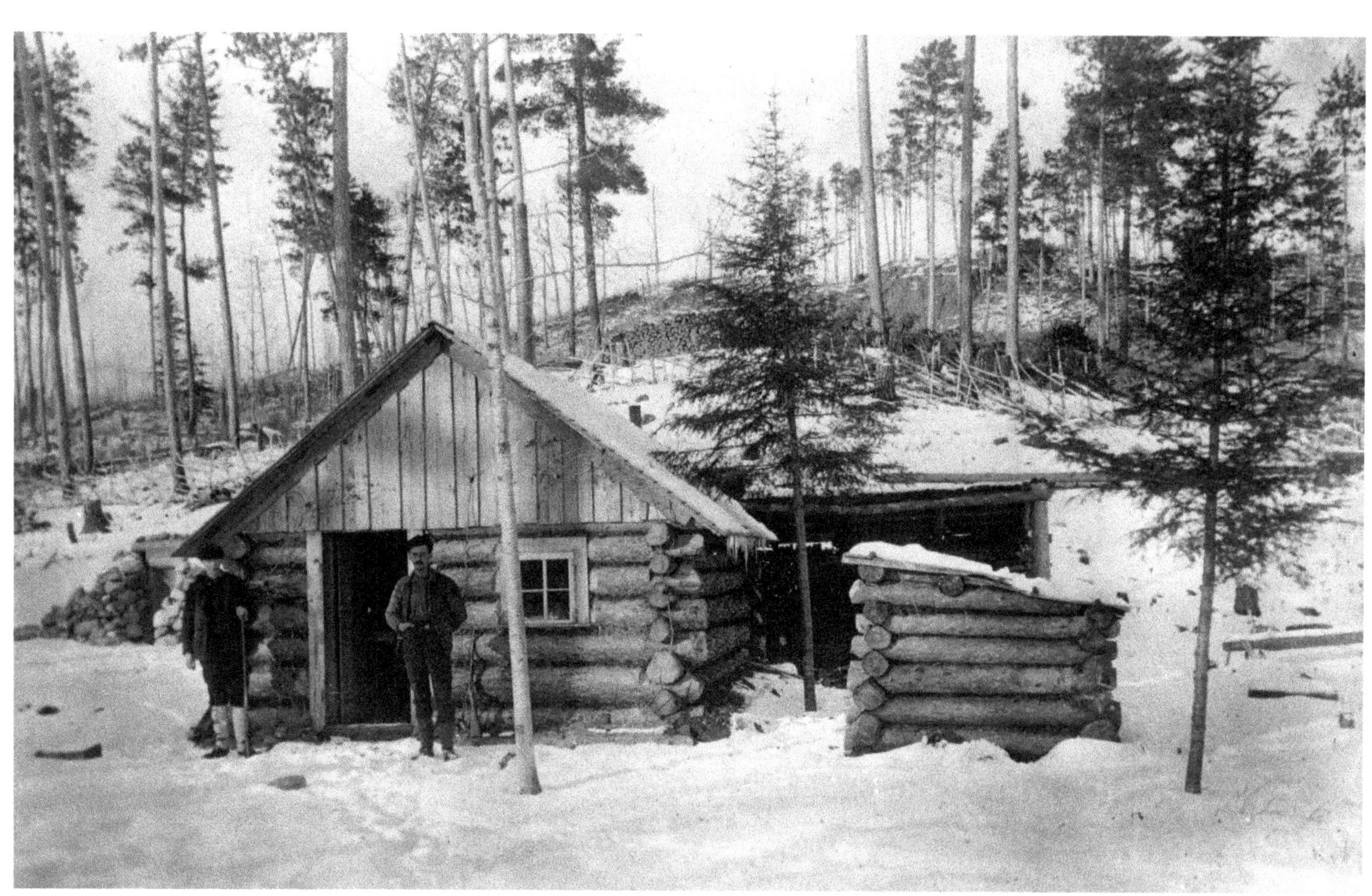

A claim shanty during Minnesota's second gold rush, in the mid-1890s. The discovery of gold in Northern Minnesota led to the Vermilion Lake gold rush of 1865-66. Very little gold was found, and prospectors abandoned the area by 1867. But gold was struck again in 1893, on Little American Island in Rainy Lake (along the United States–Canada border). The Little American Mine is the only productive gold mine ever to operate in Minnesota.

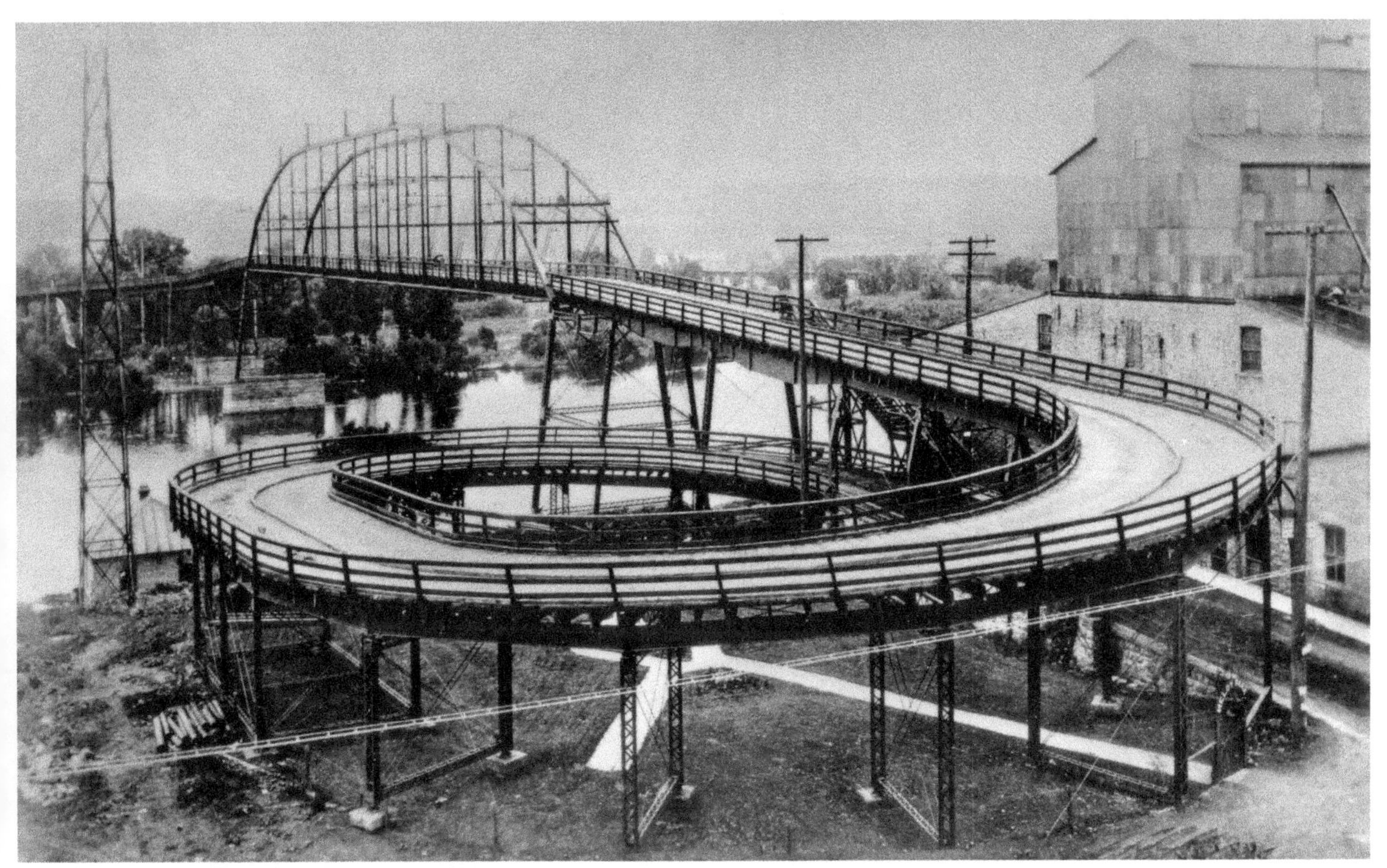

This wooden spiral bridge spanning the Mississippi River at Hastings opened in 1895 to great fanfare as reportedly the first of its kind. The spiral design, by Benjamin D. Cadwell of Hastings, was intended to minimize the impact of the bridge approach on the riverfront business district.

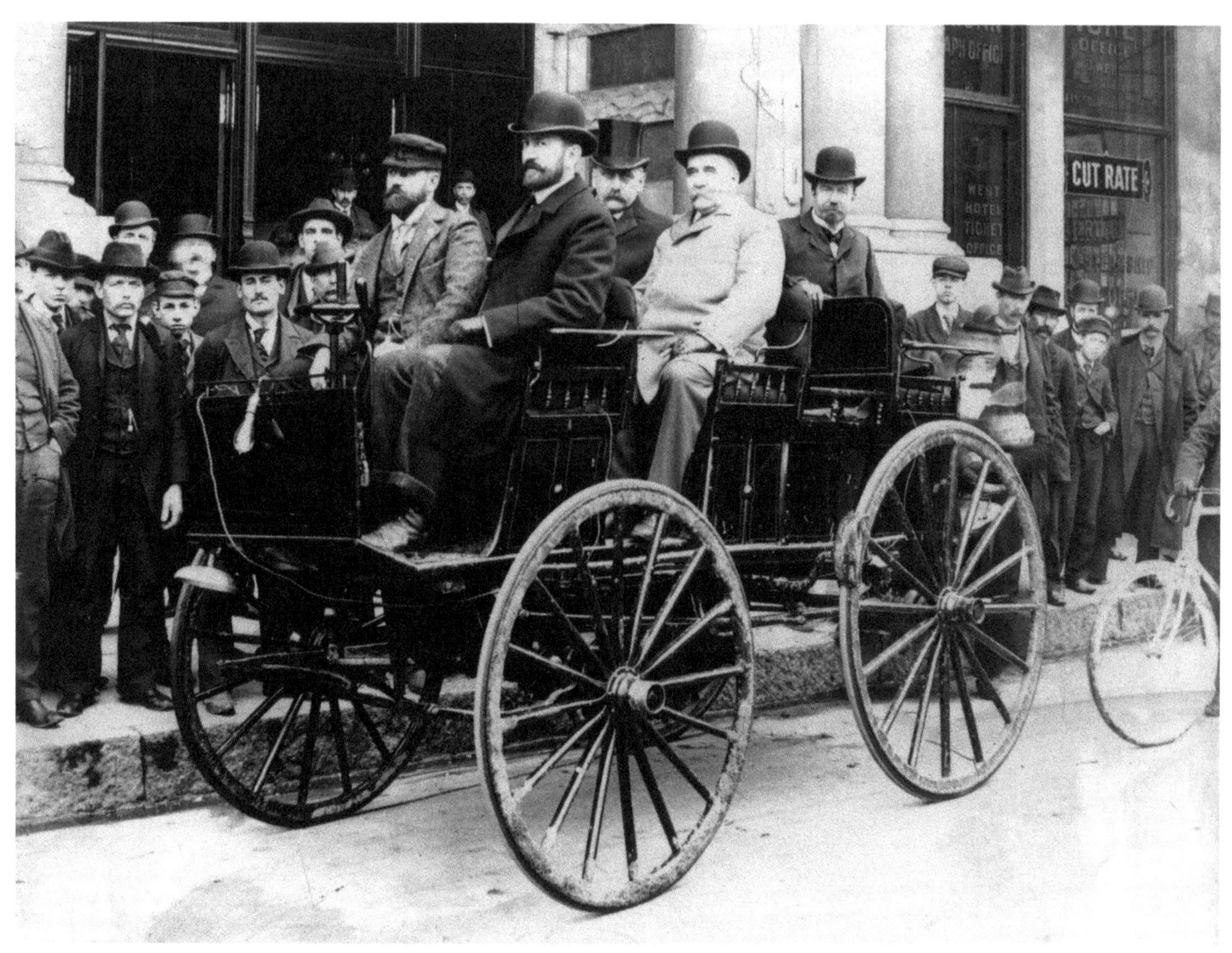


On April 14, 1896, a crowd gathers in front of the West Hotel in Minneapolis to get a look at one of the first electric automobiles in the city. This car was exhibited at the 1896 Bicycle Show held in the Exposition Building.

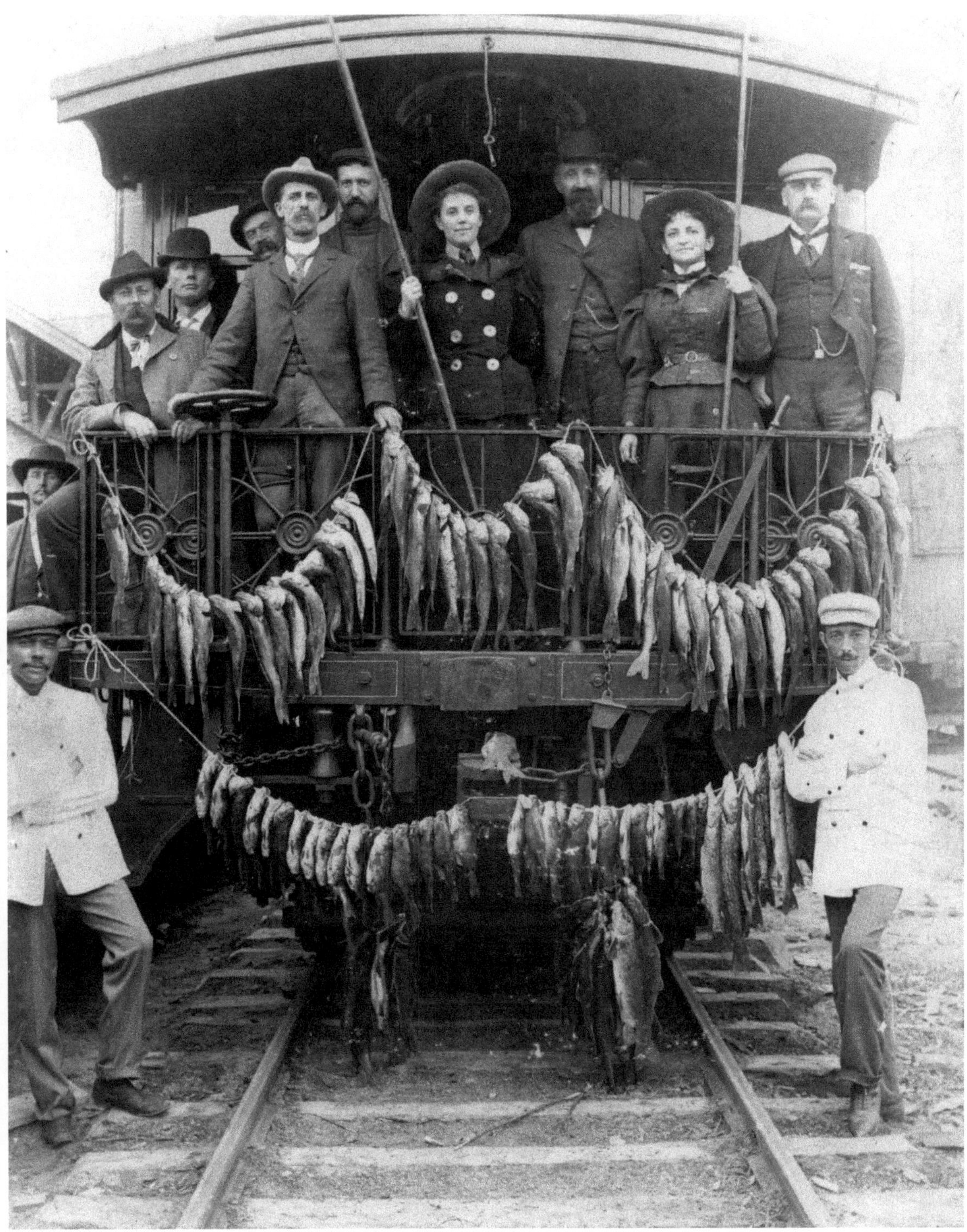

Men and women traveling back from an 1896 fishing expedition on Leech Lake display their catches after just one and a half hours of fishing. Leech Lake is located in Northern Minnesota and is renowned for its muskie, walleye, and northern pike.

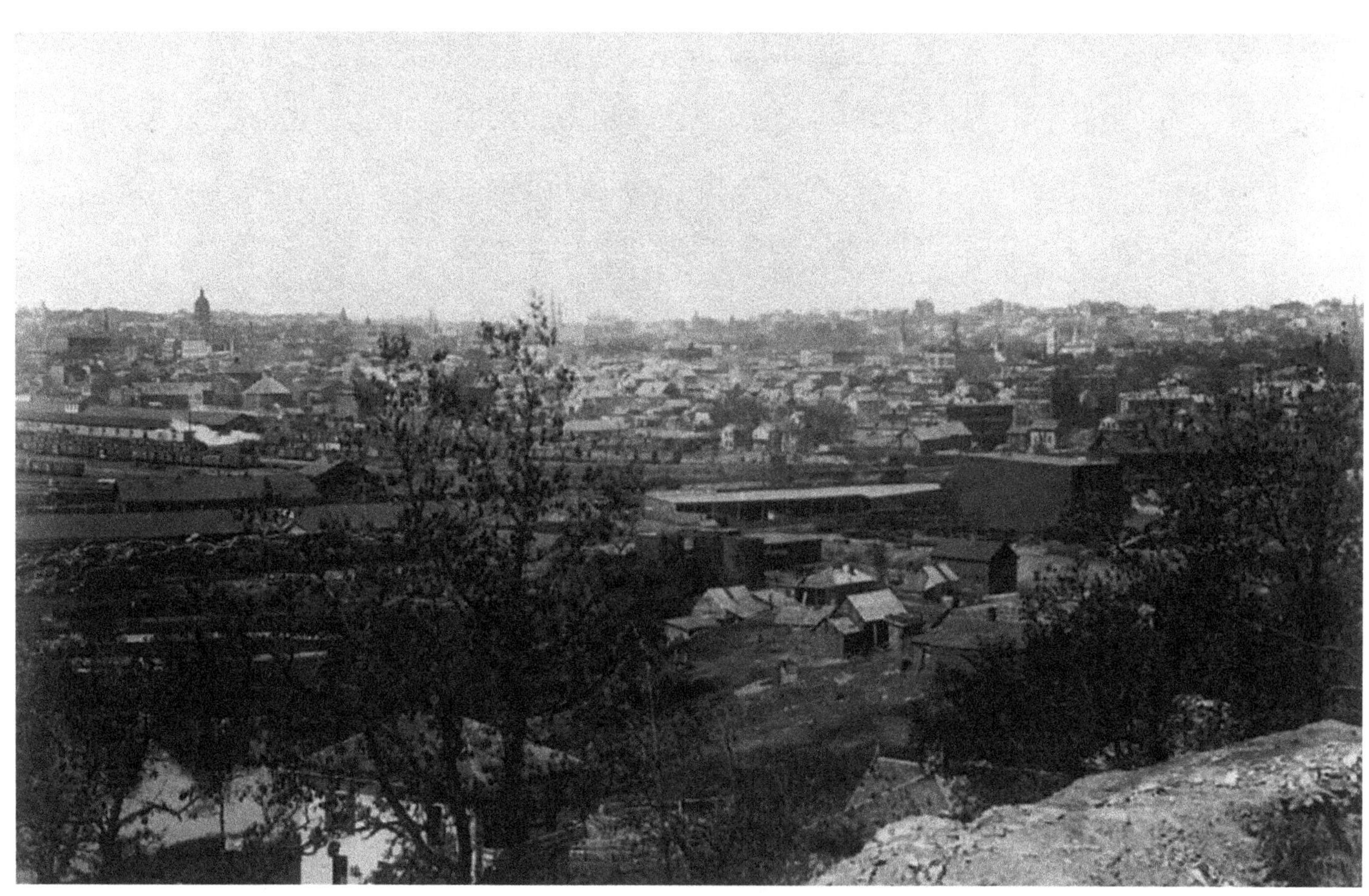

An 1896 view from Dayton's Bluff, a neighborhood located on the east side of the Mississippi in southeast St. Paul. The bluff is named for Lyman Dayton, a real estate investor and president of the Lake Superior and Mississippi Railroad. Dayton's Bluff was called "the most picturesque and beautiful district of the city" by the *St. Paul Pioneer Press* on January 1, 1887.

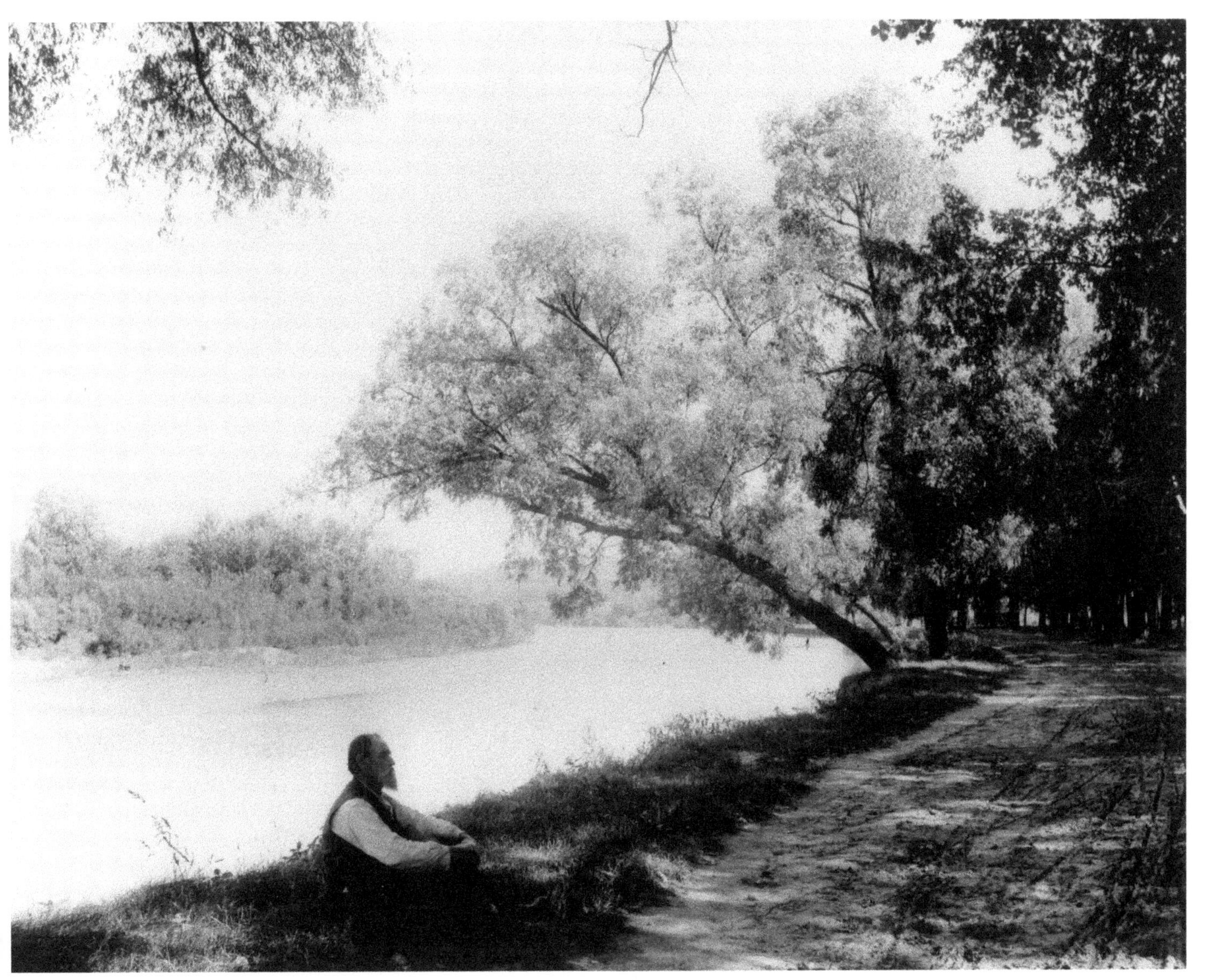

An unidentified man appears deep in thought on the shore of the Minnesota River in Mendota in 1897, near Fort Snelling.

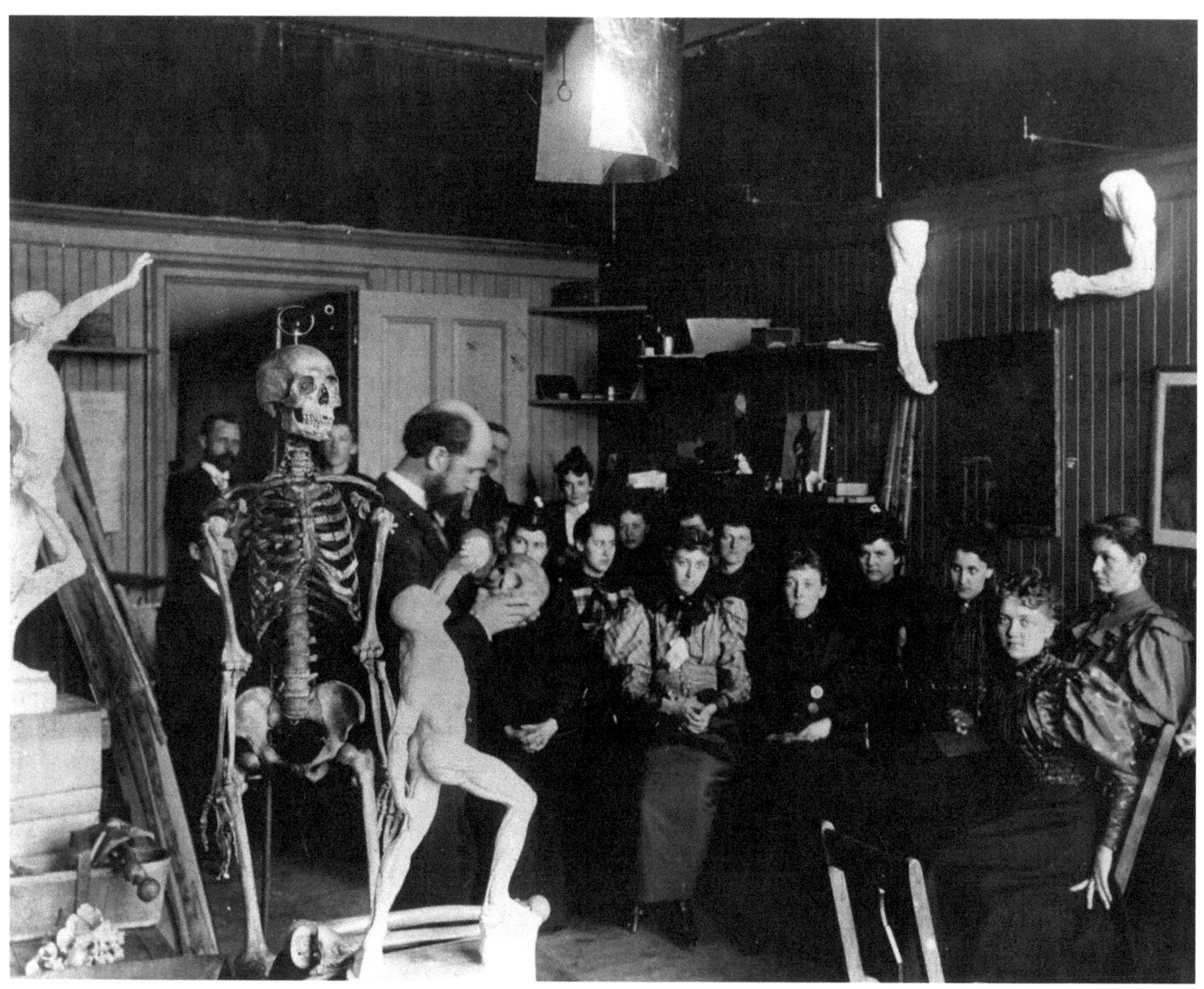

Art students at the University of Minnesota in the 1890s attend a lecture on the human body given by Dr. Richard Olding, a professor of physiology. When the university was founded, on February 25, 1851, women weren't allowed to enroll. Seven years later, enrollment was opened to women, but during the Civil War the university shut down. It reopened in 1869, with a class of 15 students.

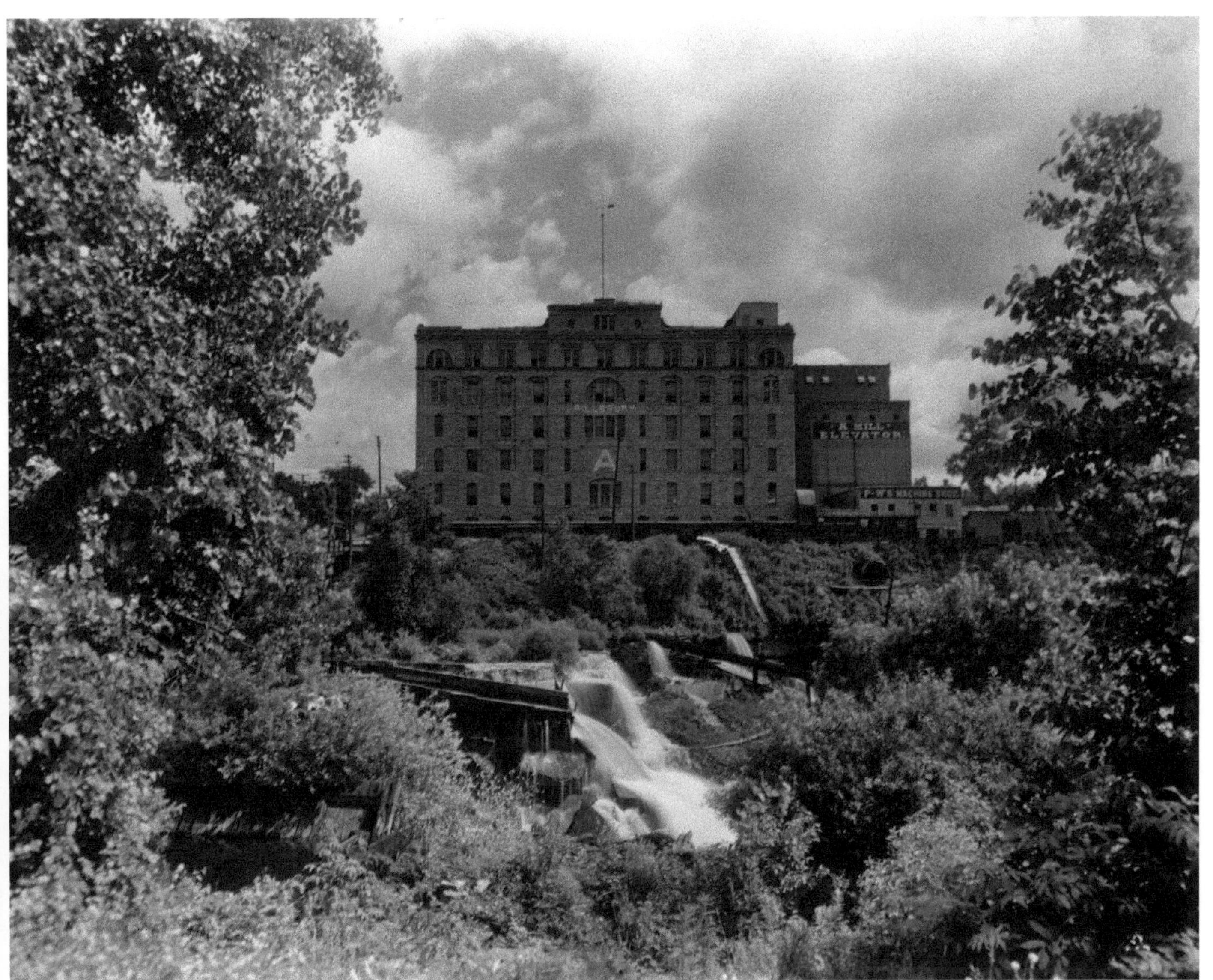


The limestone Pillsbury A flour mill, sluiceways, and tailraces in the milling district of Minneapolis around 1890. The "A" refers to the largest of several Pillsbury mills at the Falls of St. Anthony. This mill was the first in the area to use electrical lighting and had the capacity to produce 5,107 barrels of flour per day. On this exact location 33 years earlier, the Pillsbury family ran a hardware store.

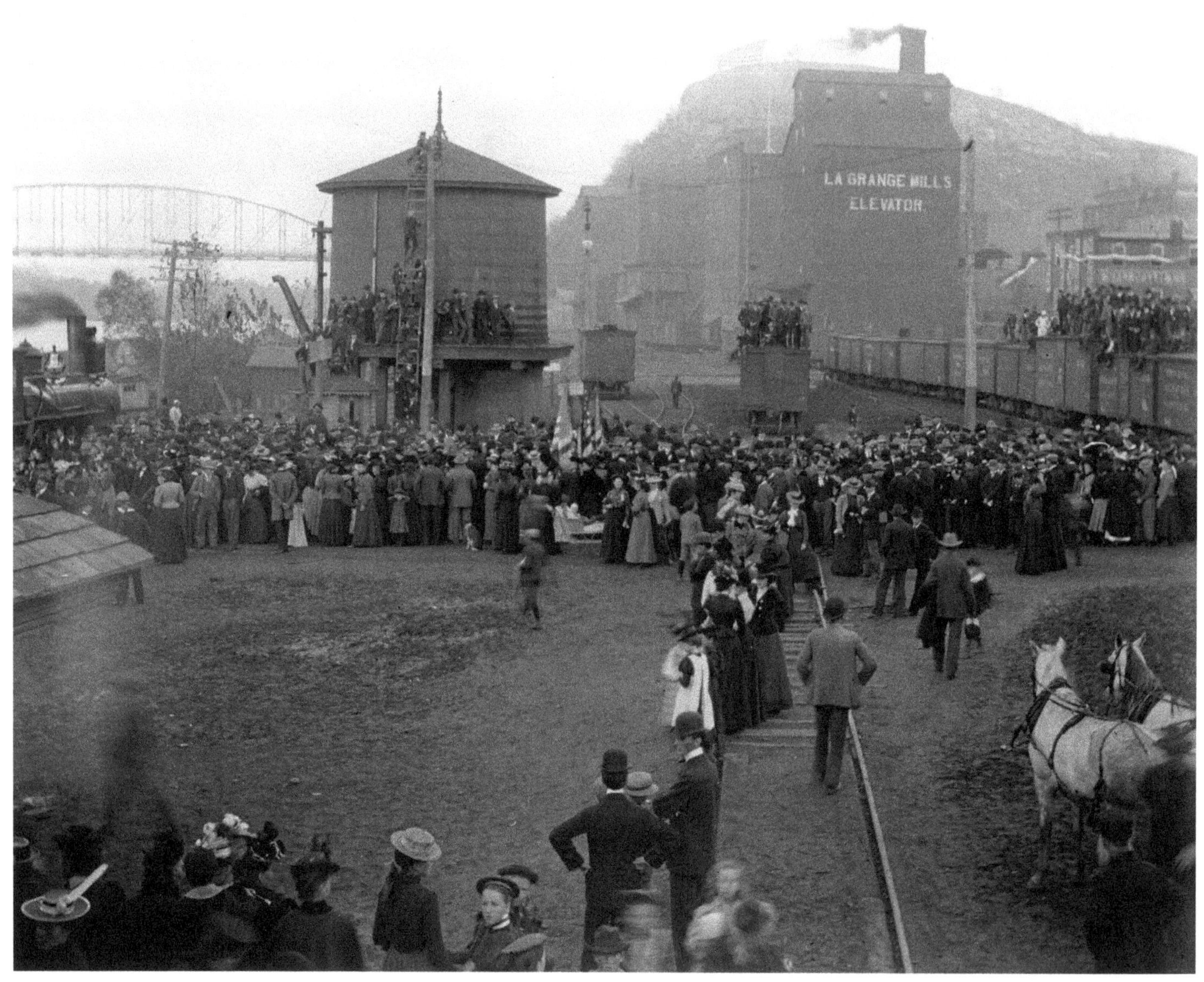


A crowd gathers at the railroad depot in Red Wing to show their support to the Thirteenth Minnesota Infantry as they depart in 1898 to serve in the Spanish-American War. The unit lost more than 40 men during the war, mostly due to disease.

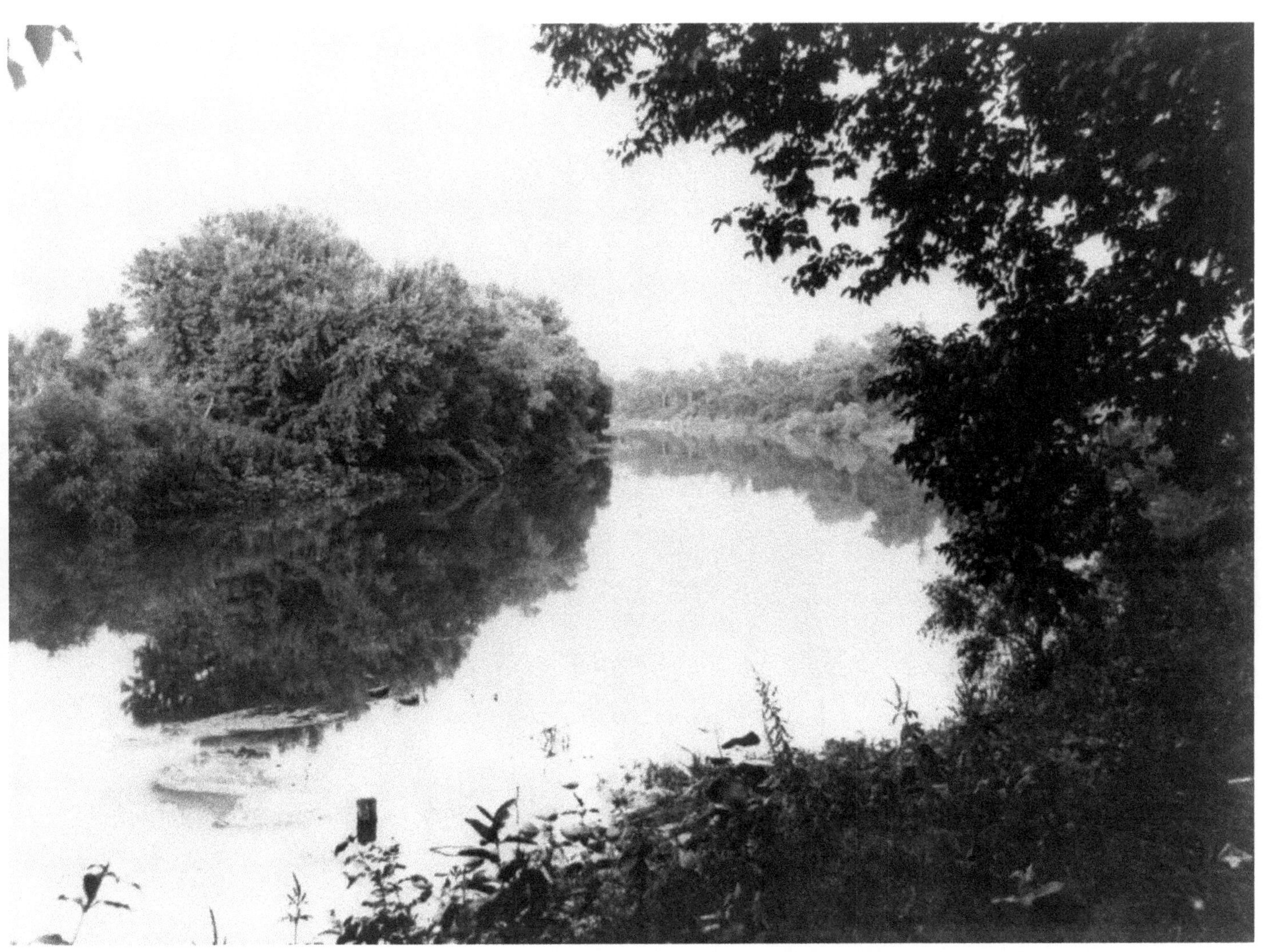

A view of the Minnesota River around 1898 in the city of New Ulm. German immigrants founded the city in Southern Minnesota, at the confluence of the Minnesota and Cottonwood rivers, in 1854.

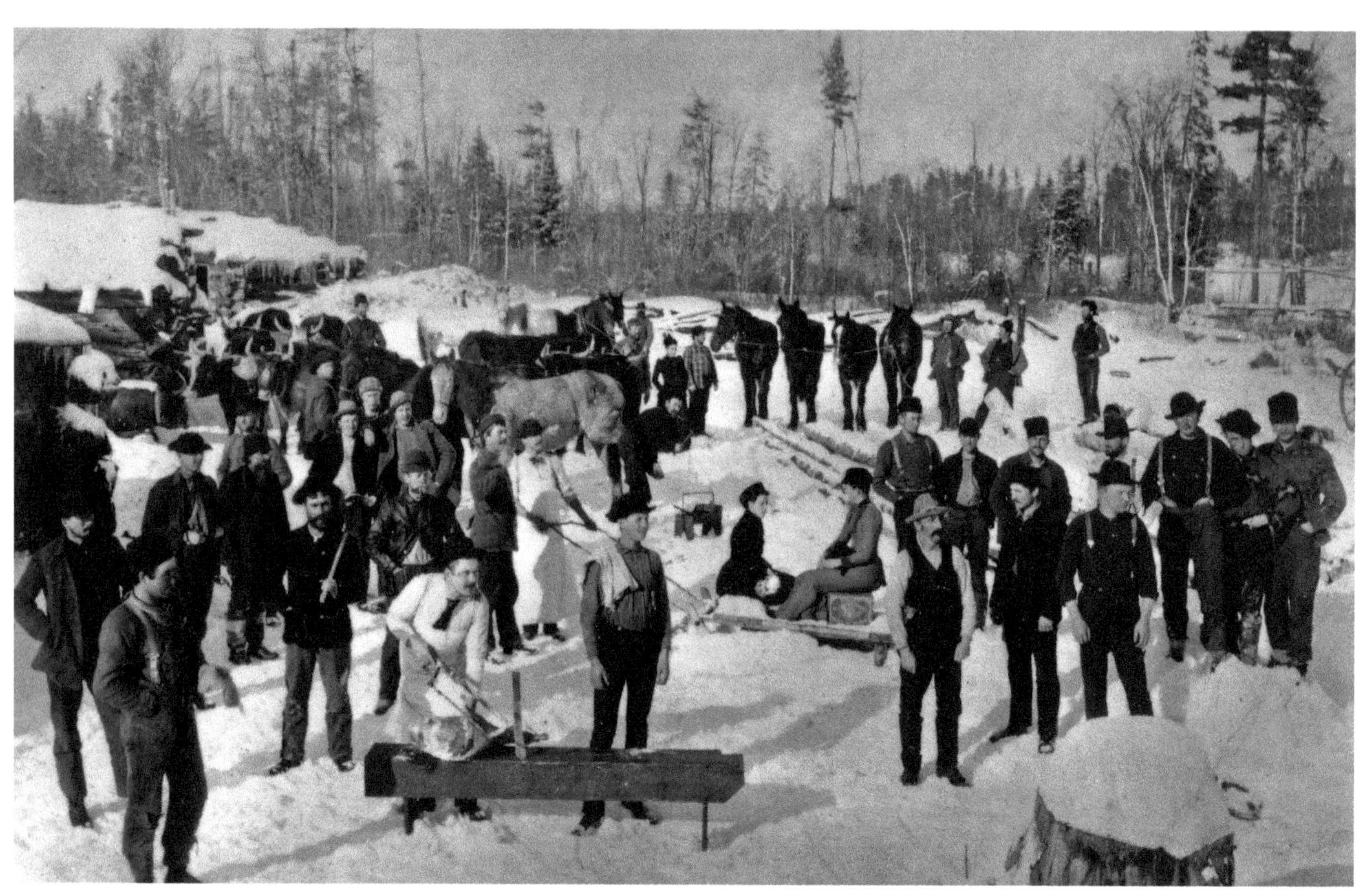

An uncommonly staged scene in a Northern Minnesota lumber camp around 1898. During the golden era of lumber in the state, lumberjacks were constantly on the move. More than 20,000 jacks and 10,000 draft horses worked in the pineries of Minnesota. Another rarity in this photo is the presence of women—who were not permitted in lumber camps.

# THE THREE FRONTIERS

## (1900–1909)

Minnesota experienced great prosperity and widespread transformation on several frontiers during the years just before and after the turn of the century. Railroads were ever expanding, stretching out across the Northern Plains, connecting small towns to the Twin Cities of St. Paul and Minneapolis. While rural Minnesota experienced great agricultural fluctuations throughout this era, the state's flour mills turned its bumper crops of wheat into gold.

The power of the Falls of St. Anthony on the Mississippi River was fully harnessed to Minneapolis, which became known as the "Flour Milling Capital of the World." Trains rushed Minnesota's flour to the eastern part of the country and to Duluth, where it was exported around the world. The city that developed around the falls grew rapidly and showed no signs of stopping. Minnesota's lumber industry also proved robust and reached its peak year of production in 1905. However, the future didn't look as promising for the industry, with the possibility looming that rampant deforestation could wipe out all of Minnesota's timber.

Another industry vital to the state was on the rise—iron ore. The discovery of iron ore on the Vermilion Iron Range in the Arrowhead region was soon followed by the discoveries of the Merritt brothers. Three of the brothers were the first to capitalize on iron ore deposits found in the area the Native Americans called Mesaba, meaning "mighty eagle" or "giant of the hills." In 1890, two more Merritt brothers and two nephews joined forces to drill the first successful mine in the region. The Duluth, Missabe and Northern Railway was built to carry the ore to ports in Duluth and Superior, Wisconsin.

New immigrants flocked to Minnesota's Iron Range to work in the open-pit mining operations, giving rise to about 100 new towns. By 1900, Minnesota led North America in iron ore mining.

For the tens of thousands of Minnesotans, this era was politics as usual. Local residents showed up in droves to hear presidential hopefuls speak from cabooses on their whistle-stop campaign tours through the state.

And increasingly during this era, Minnesotans got together for the annual Minnesota State Fair, held in late summer each year. What began as an agricultural showcase to help lure settlers to the state turned into a growing cultural and political event mixed with high style and a little entertainment.

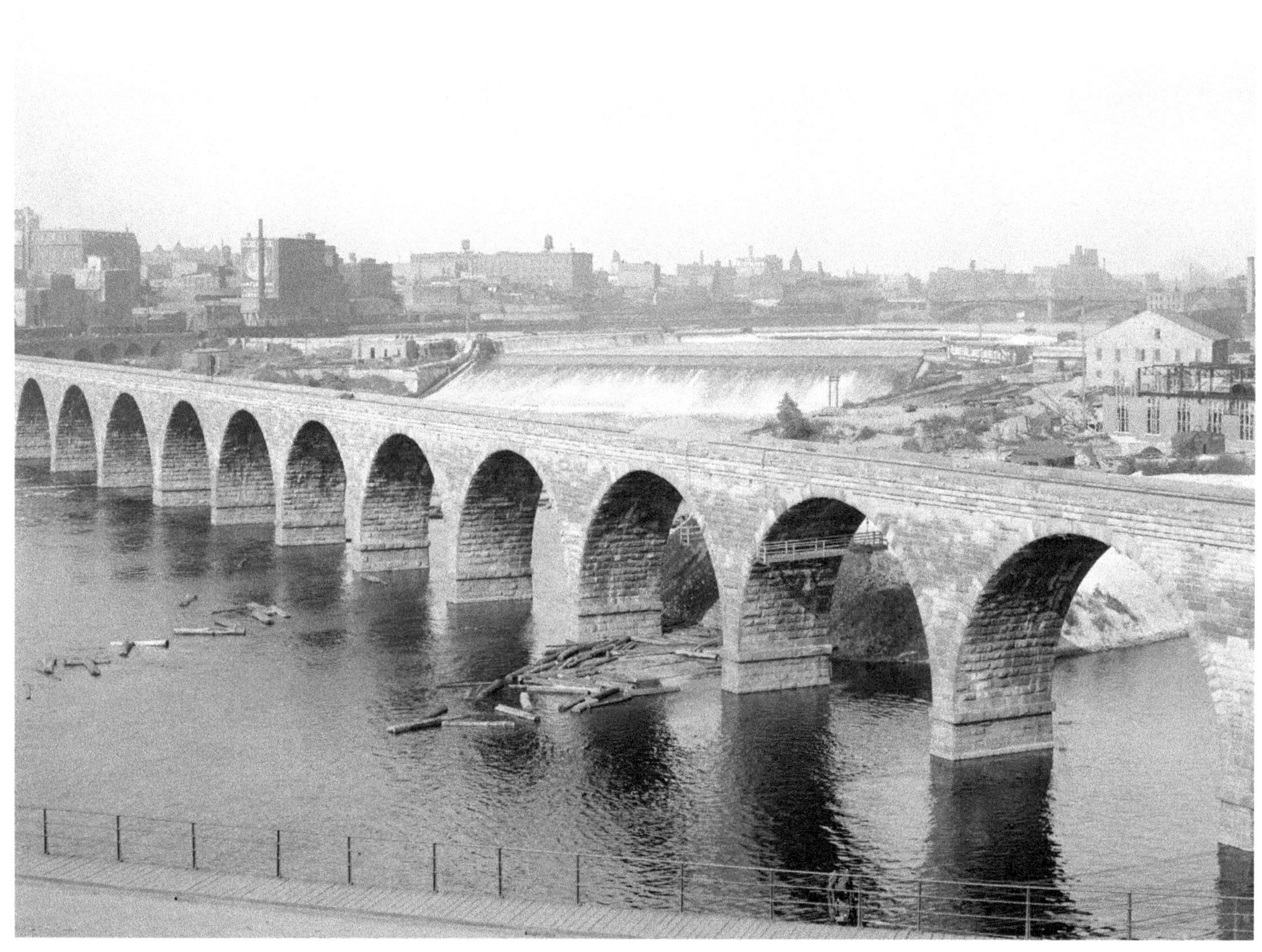

The Stone Arch Bridge, shown here at the turn of the century, spans the Mississippi River below the Falls of St. Anthony. Railroad tycoon James J. Hill built the bridge in 1883 to better connect his Great Northern Railway to the milling district of Minneapolis. The bridge eventually fell into long-term disuse but made a comeback in the 1990s as a newly refurbished bridge for pedestrians.

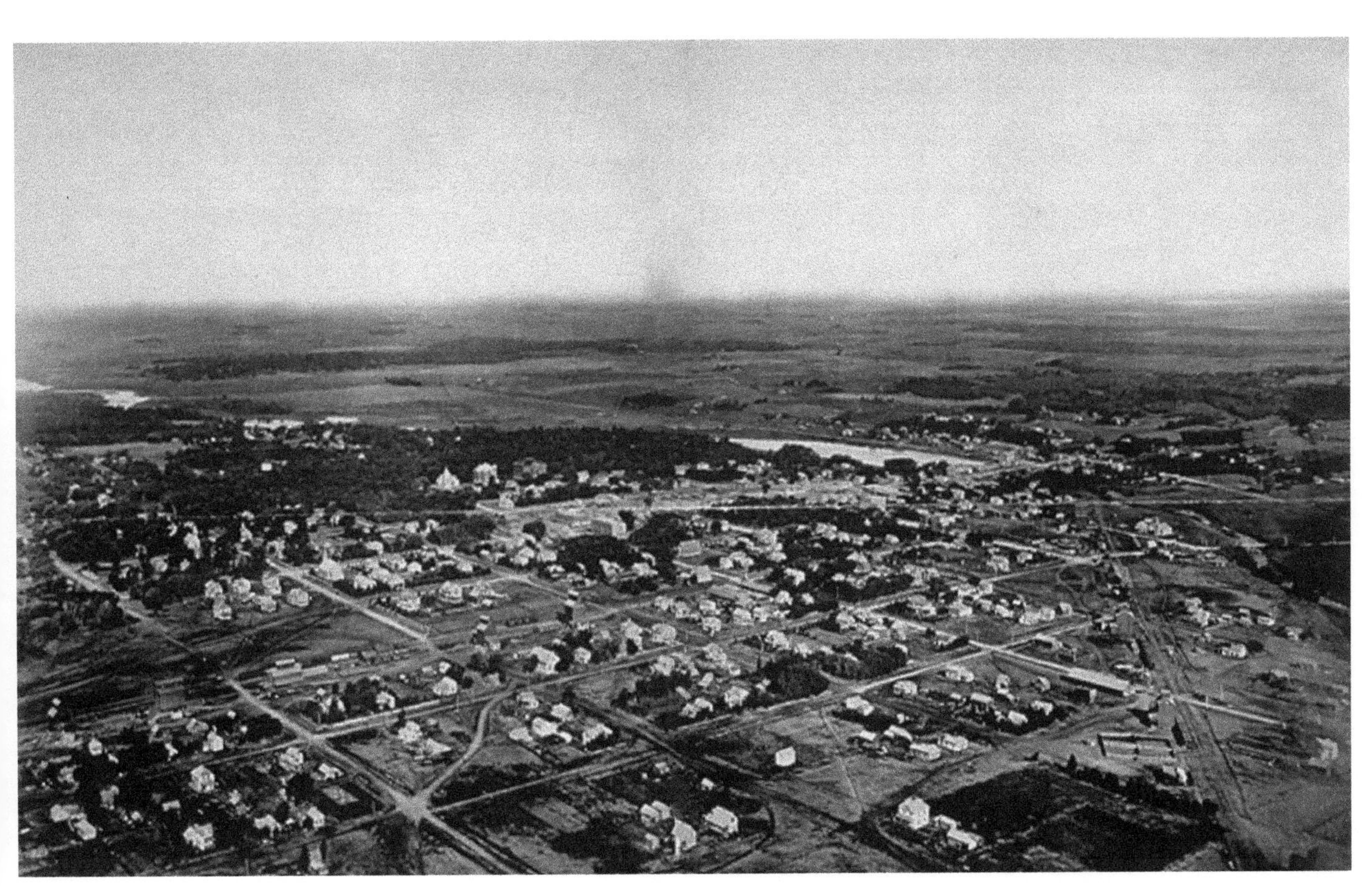

A 1901 aerial view of the farming town of Hutchinson, about 75 miles west of Minneapolis.

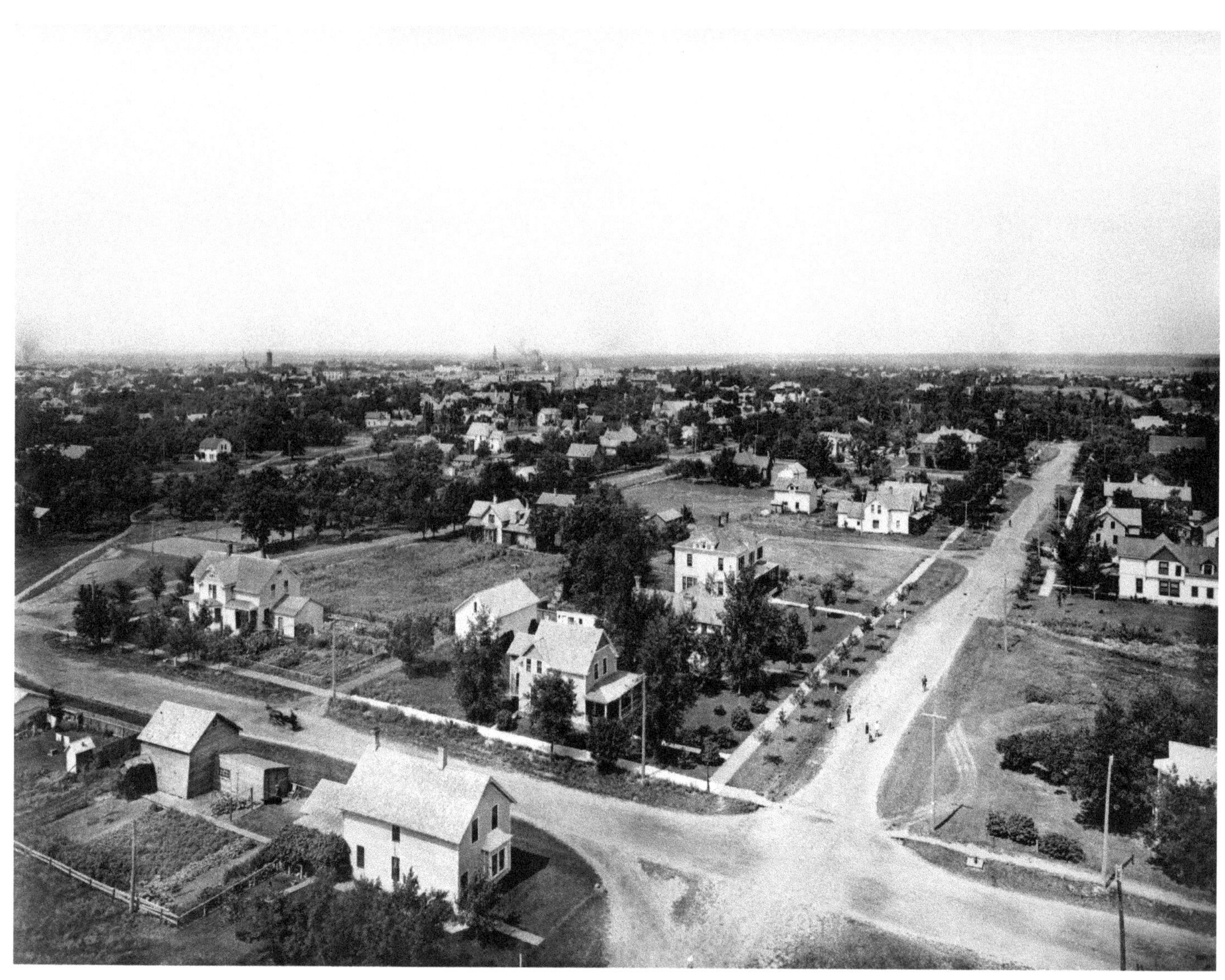

An aerial view of St. Cloud in 1902 at the corner of Second Avenue South and Seventh Avenue South. *Minneapolis Tribune* photographer George R. Lawrence scaled a newly erected, 100-foot "trestle-work tower" to get this shot of the city for the newspaper.

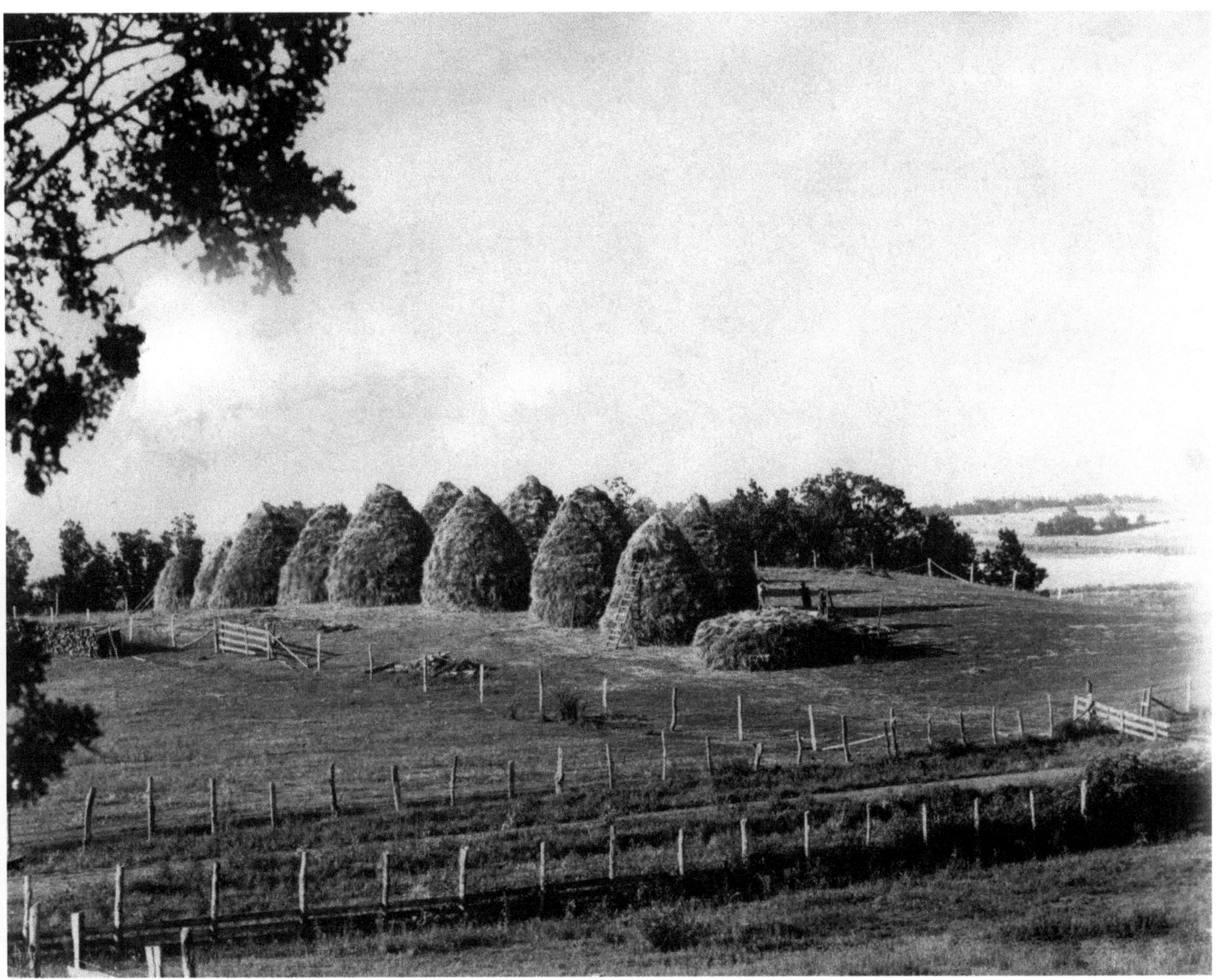

Wheat harvest on a Minnesota farm around 1905. The state's soil was ideal for growing wheat, and as wheat-milling methods became more refined in the milling district of Minneapolis, the demand around the world grew for Minnesota's "Number 1 Hard" spring wheat.

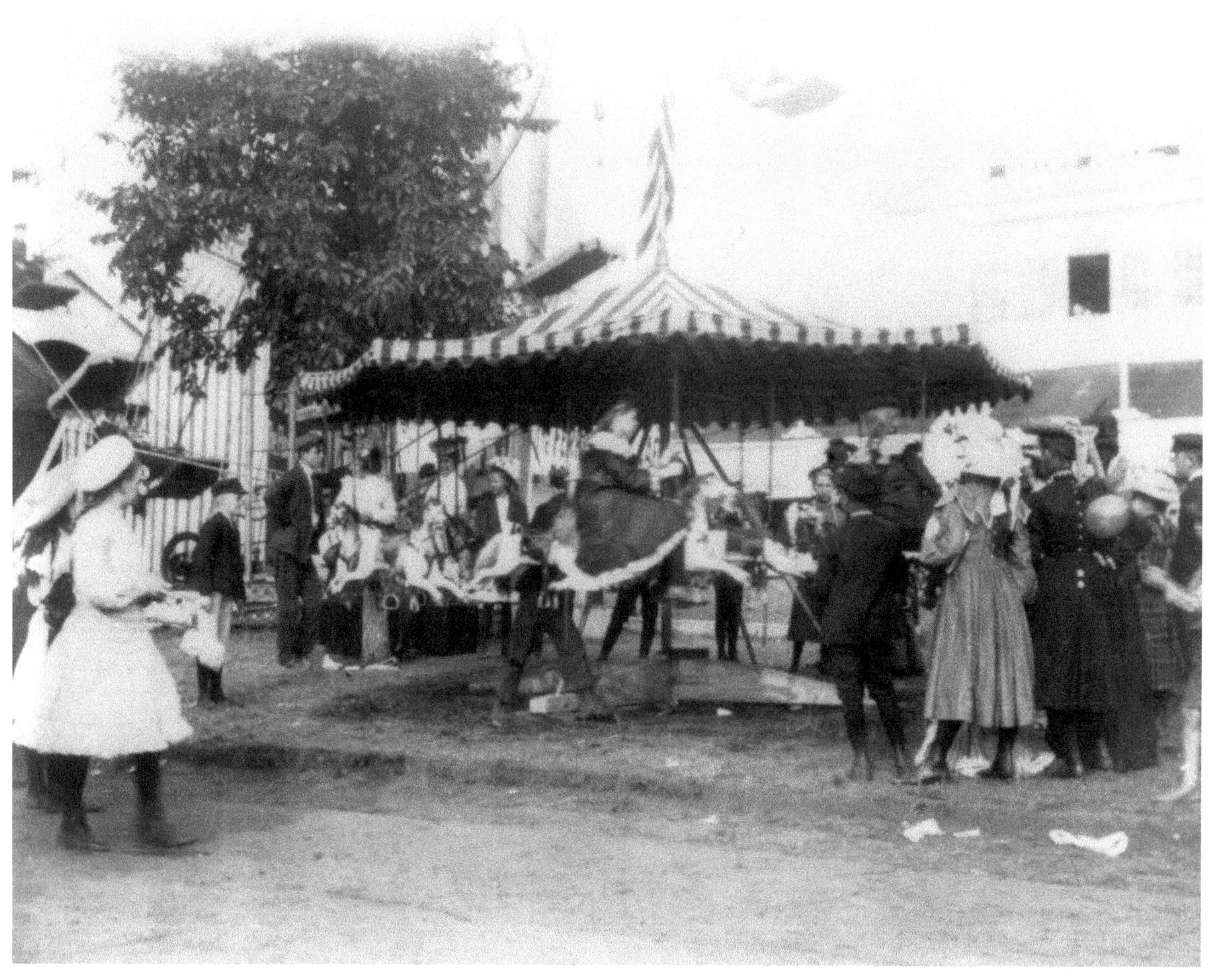

This hand-cranked, portable carousel was a big attraction at the Minnesota State Fair in 1903. The first Minnesota State Fair was held in 1859 to showcase the state's agriculture. The fair moved from various locations before it found a permanent home in 1885 on the site of the former Ramsey poor farm, midway between Minneapolis and St. Paul.

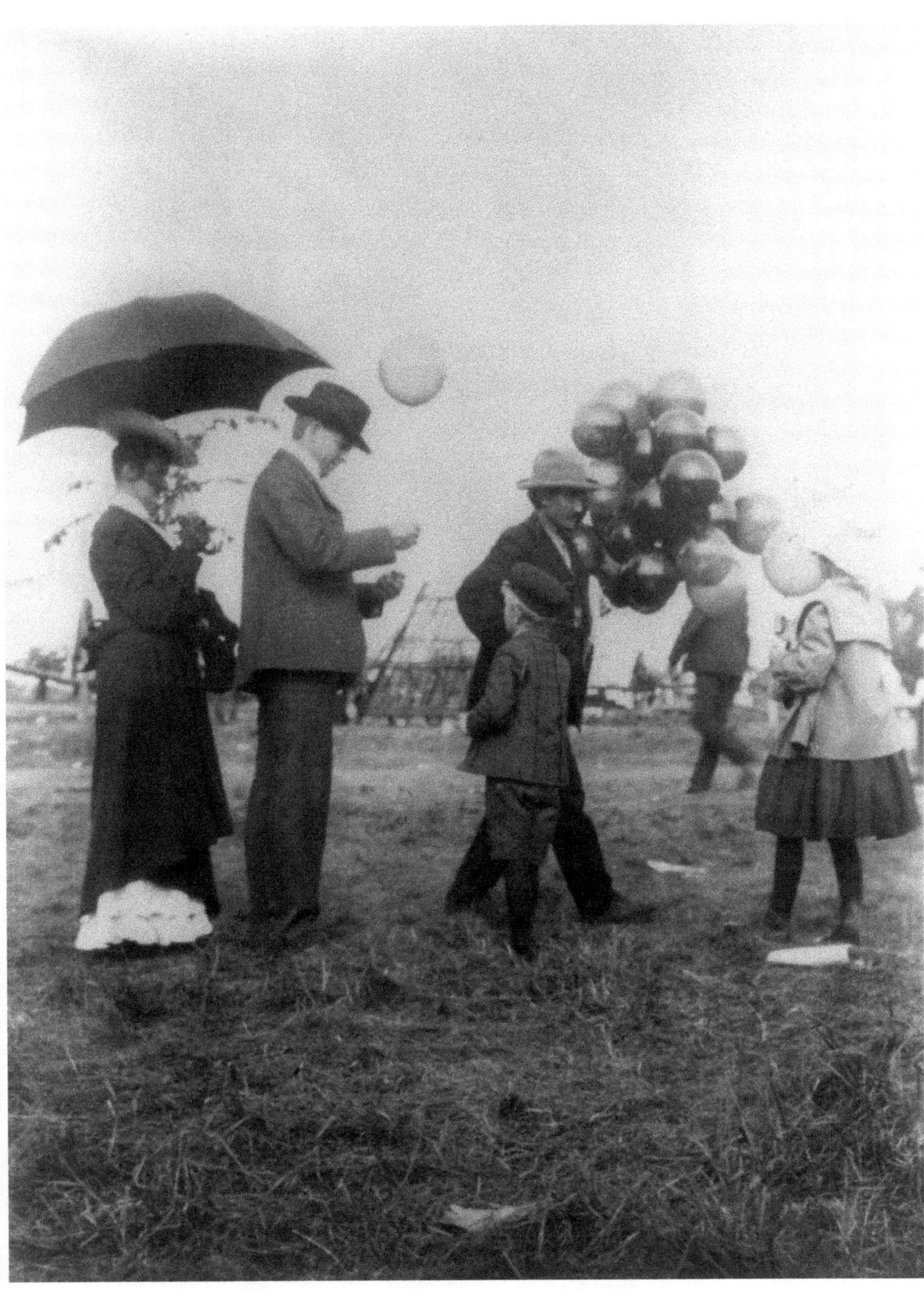

A vendor at the Minnesota State Fair in 1903 sells souvenir balloons for a penny to fairgoers.
The toy balloon as we know it was introduced in 1847 by J. G. Ingram of London.

Three elegantly dressed visitors at the Minnesota State Fair in 1903. Women fairgoers in full-length dresses, hats, and parasols, and men in suits, were a familiar sight around the turn of the century.

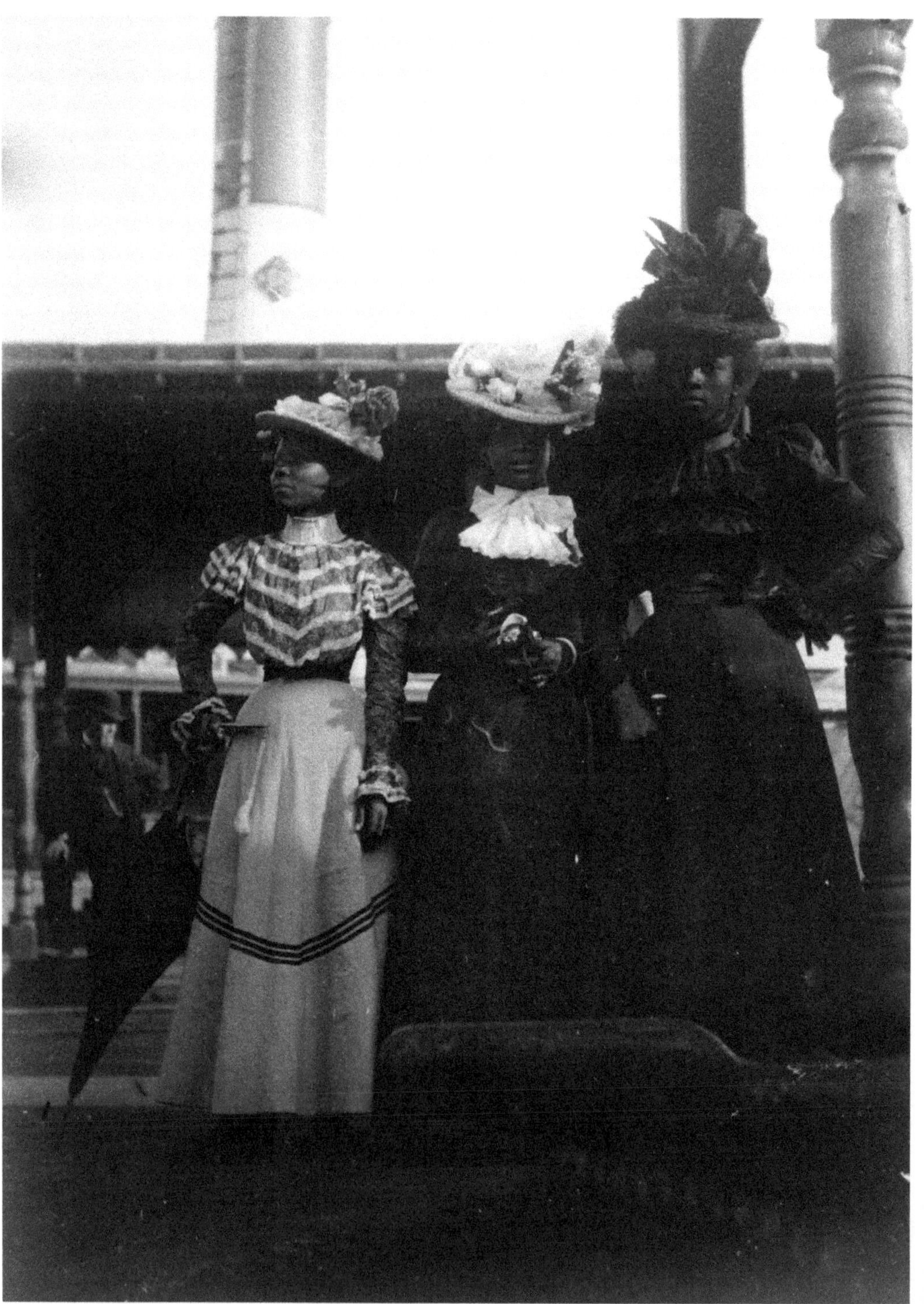

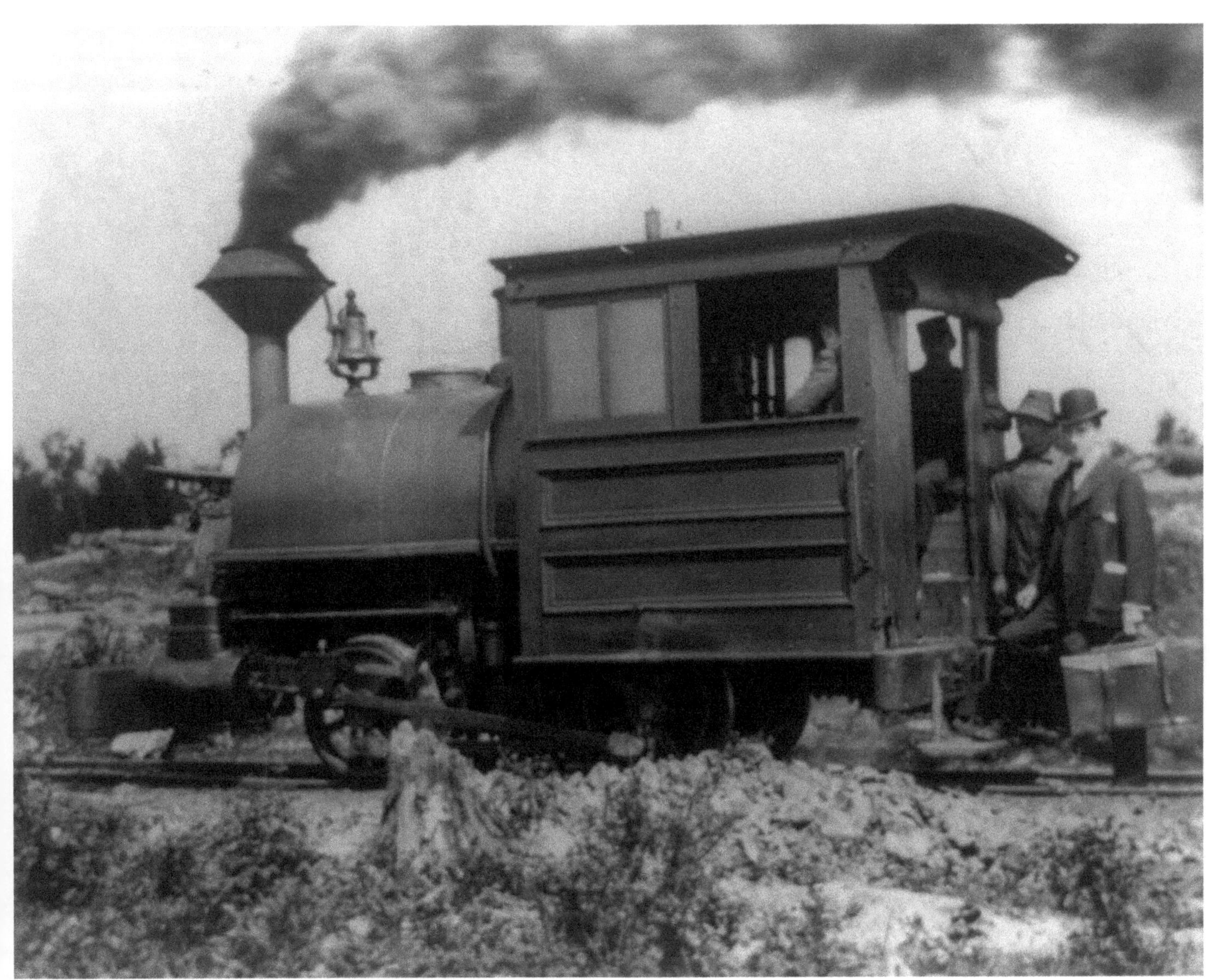

In 1903, men pose with an engine used to haul ore from the mines on the Mesabi Iron Range. Mesabi held a vast deposit of iron ore and was the largest of four major iron ranges in the region, collectively known as the Iron Range of Minnesota.

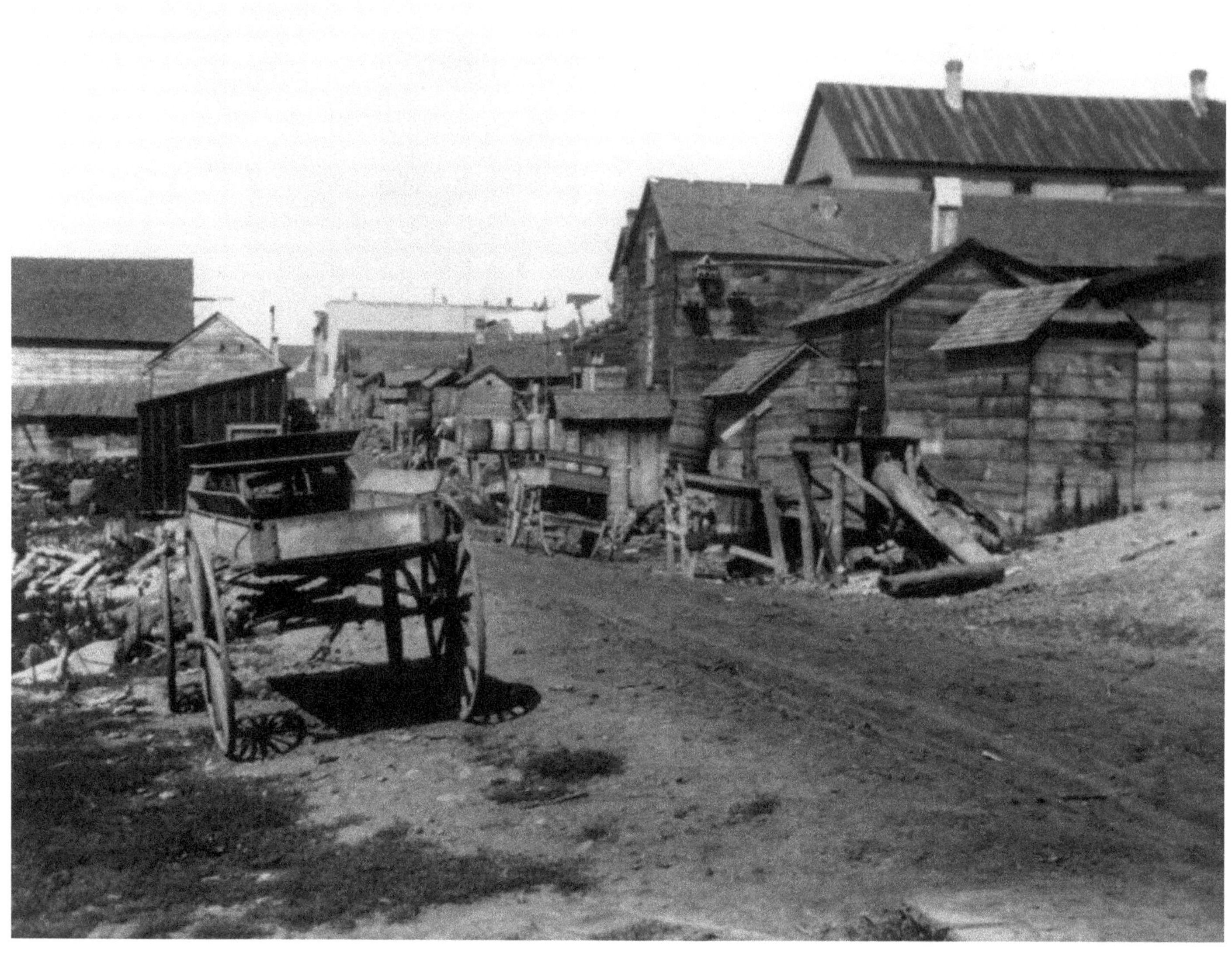

Wagons, office buildings, and miners' housing in 1903, near a mine on the Mesabi Iron Range.

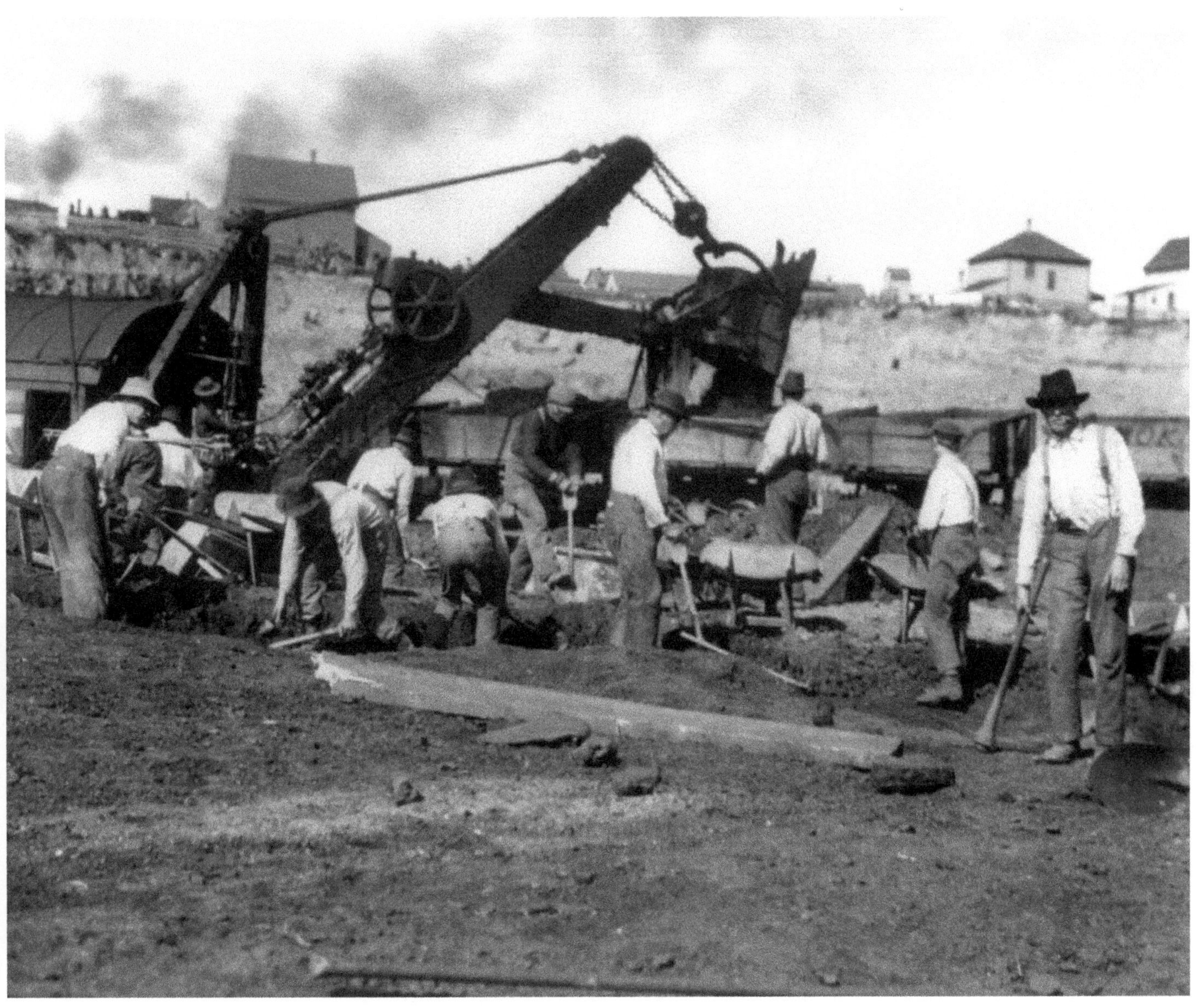

Miners dig iron ore in open pits on the Mesabi Range in 1903. The ore was carried by Duluth, Missabe and Northern trains to ore docks in Duluth or Superior, Wisconsin.

An unidentified miner on the Mesabi Range in 1903. The demand for men to work on the range coincided with massive emigration from Europe. Because mining required few English language skills and little in the way of prior experience, new immigrants easily found work on the range. By 1900, 70 percent of immigrants on the iron ranges came from Slovenia, Sweden, Croatia, and Finland.

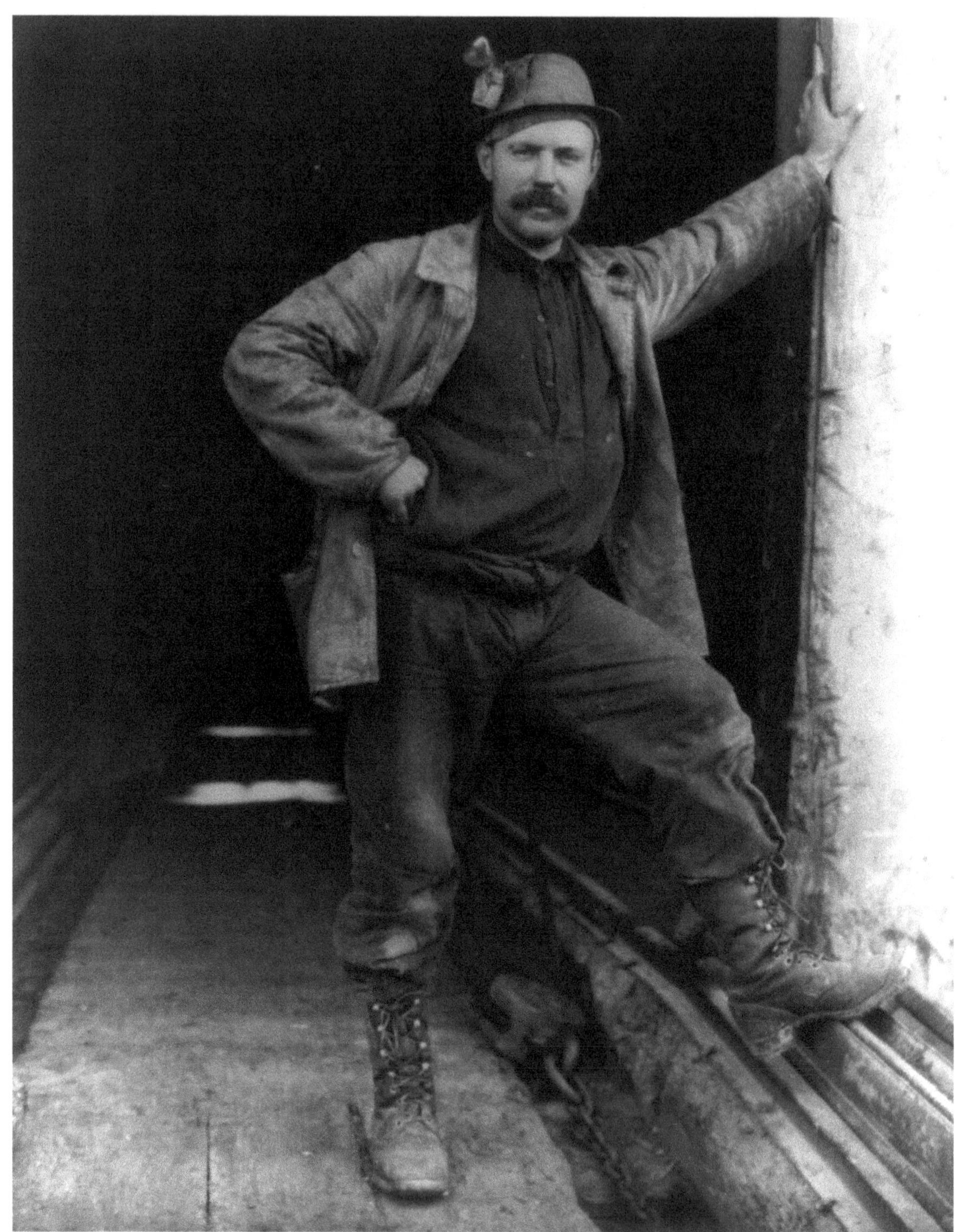

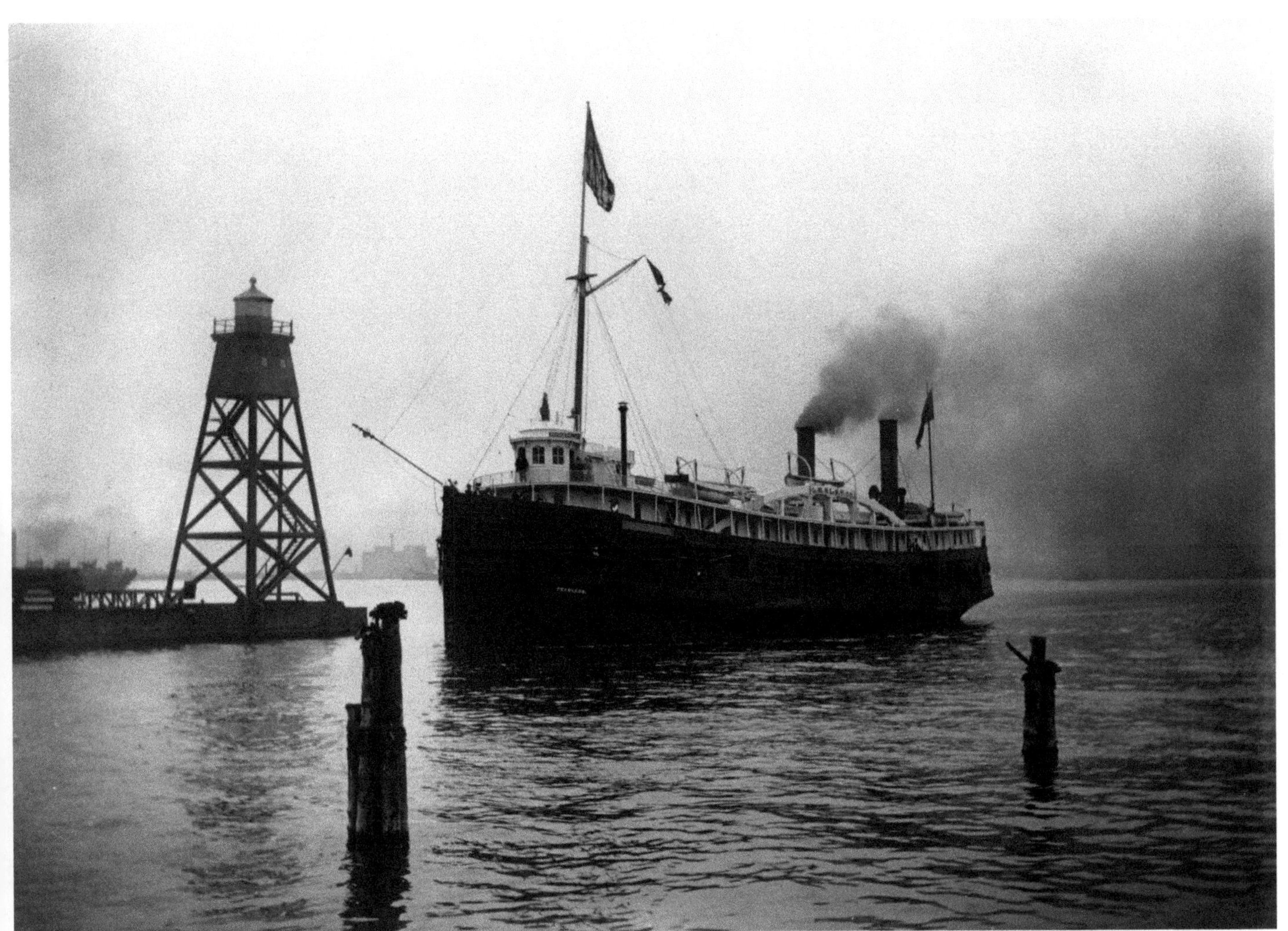

The steamer *Peerless* around the turn of the century, coming into Duluth Harbor. The ship was built for the Chicago and Duluth route in 1872 as an answer to the increasing traffic of passenger and package freight. On September 7, 1899, *Peerless* hit the barge *Stewart* in Duluth harbor. It took $8,000 to refurbish the 27-year-old *Peerless*.

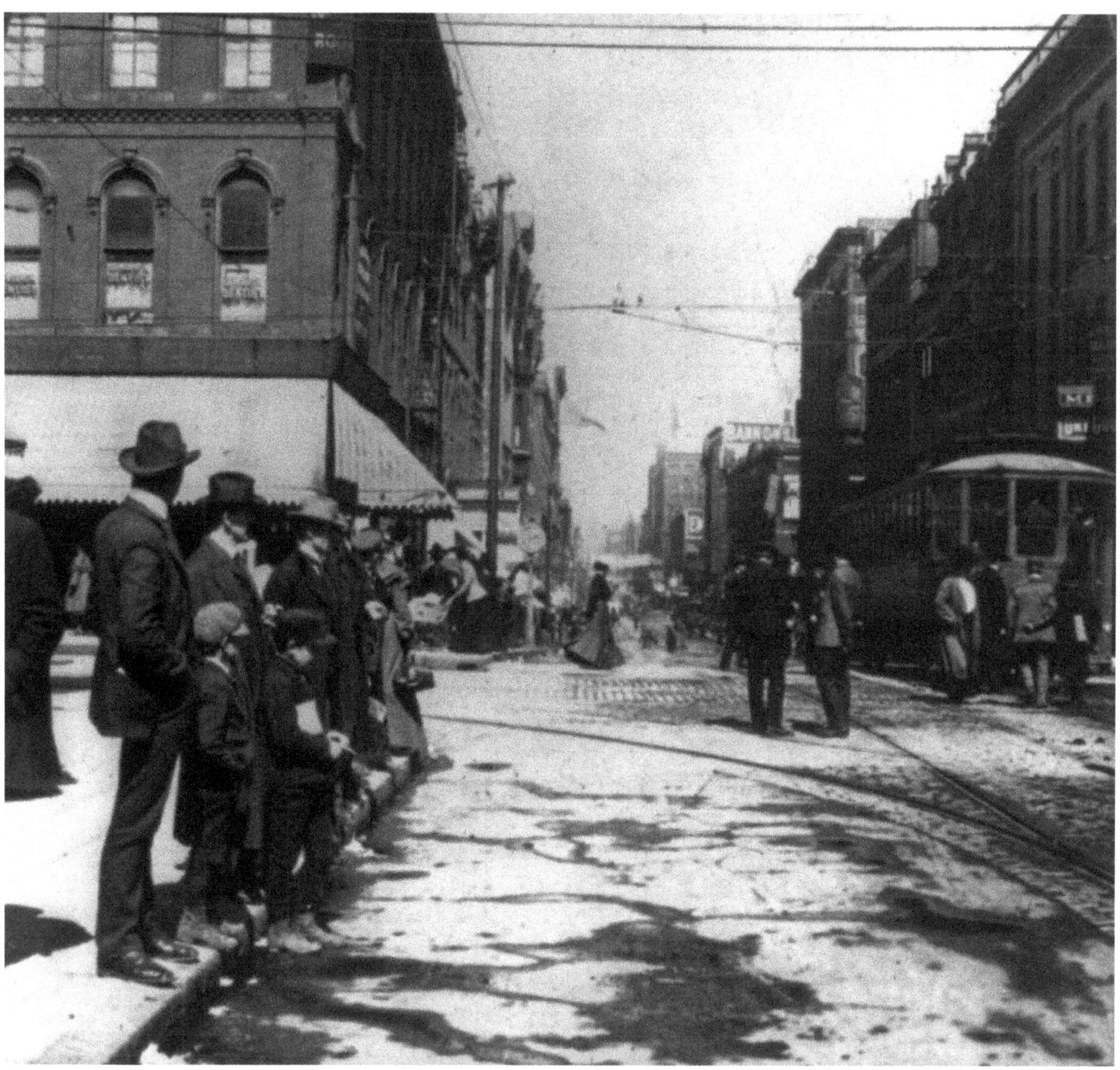

This view of Seventh Street shows a typical downtown St. Paul scene in 1905. The city's elaborate streetcar system connected St. Paul with Minneapolis and beyond. Increasingly, St. Paulites moved to "streetcar suburbs" on the outskirts of town, commuting to work each day.

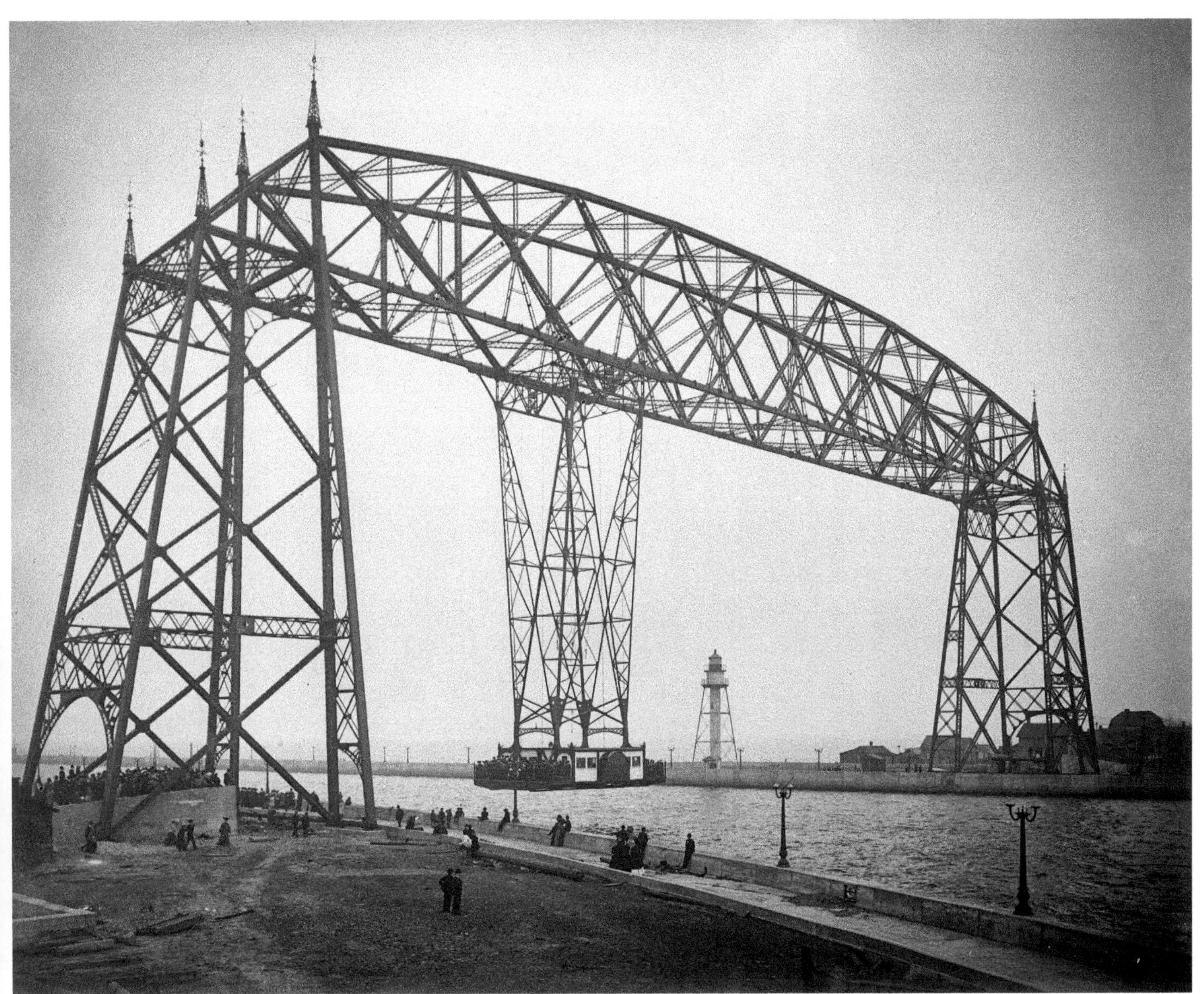

Originally built in 1905, the Aerial Bridge in Duluth was a popular tourist attraction. To accommodate both tall ships and land traffic, the bridge had a gondola that could carry 350 people, plus wagons, streetcars, or automobiles across the canal. The gondola was suspended below the main span and traveled on rails from one side of the bridge to the other. The trip across the canal took about a minute.

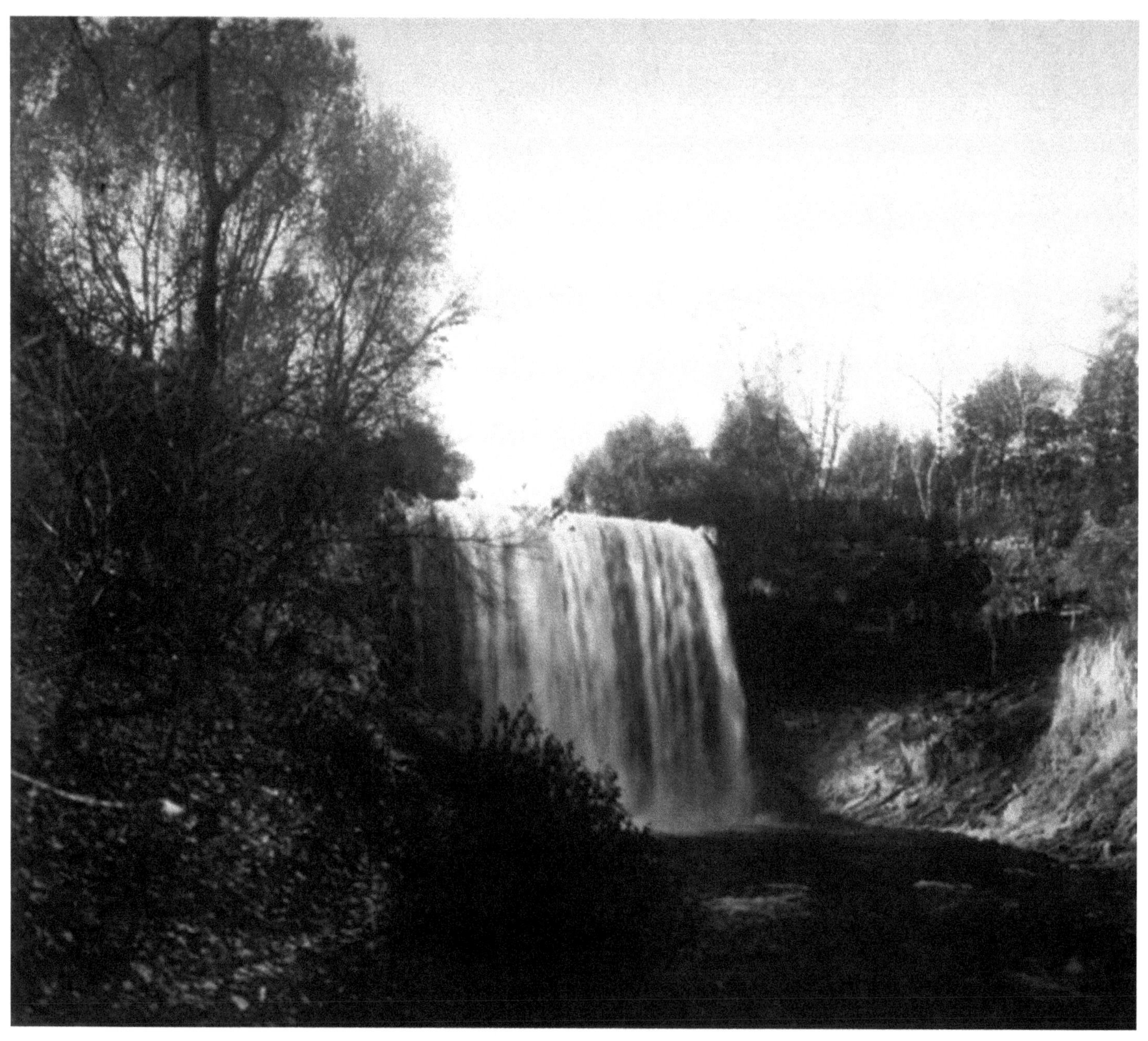

Minnehaha Falls in Minneapolis, pictured around 1906. The falls have long been an important spiritual site to the Dakota people. Minnehaha means "falling water" in Dakota—not "laughing water," as it is often translated. The "laughing water" translation comes from Mary Eastman's book *Dacotah,* published in 1849. The Dakota called Minnehaha Creek "Wakpa Cistinna," meaning "Little River."

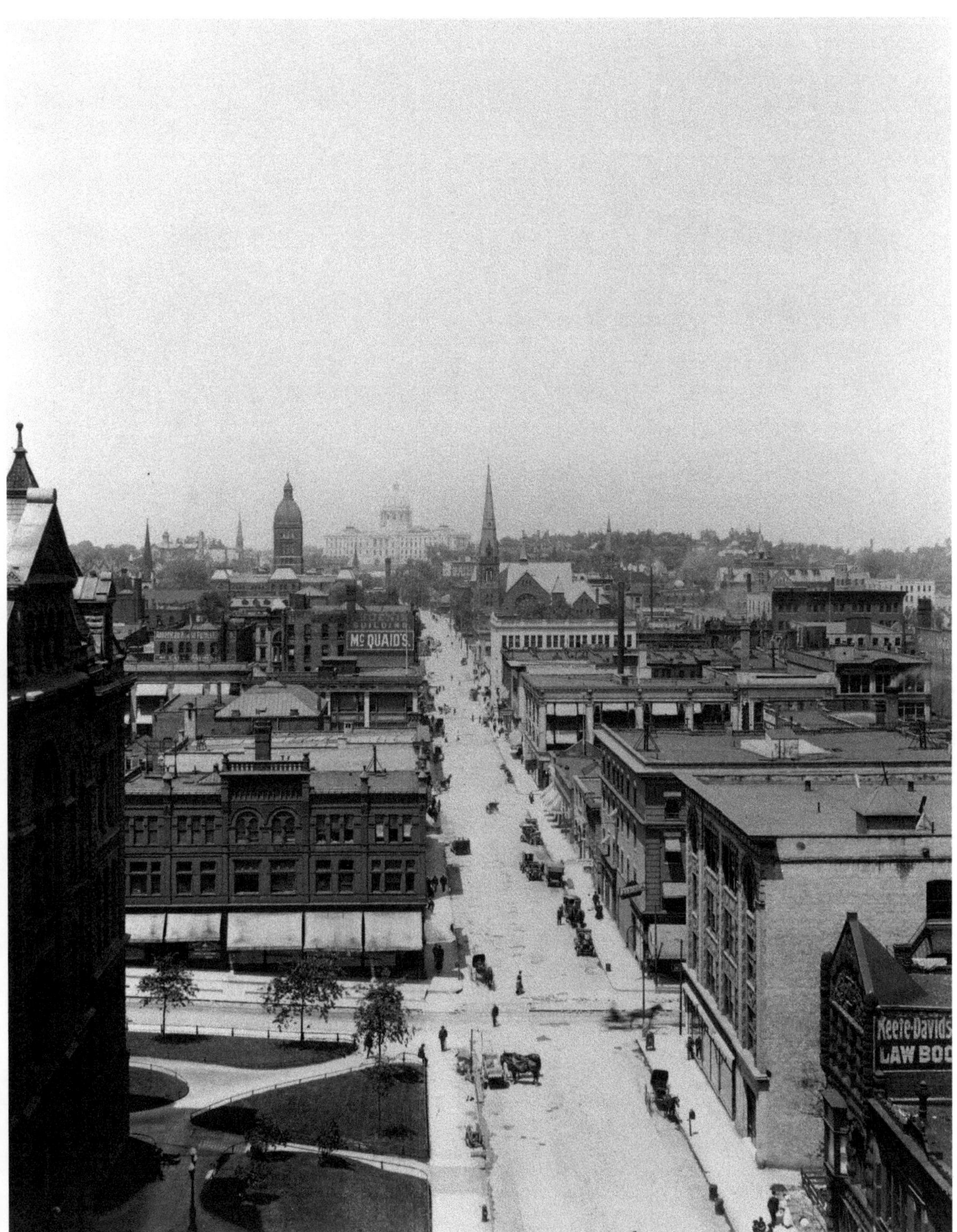


A bird's-eye view of downtown St. Paul on Cedar Street in 1908. While the city was outpaced by its rival Minneapolis in population and commerce, St. Paul was growing and expanding, especially its meatpacking industry and the production of beer, steel, leather goods, and butter.

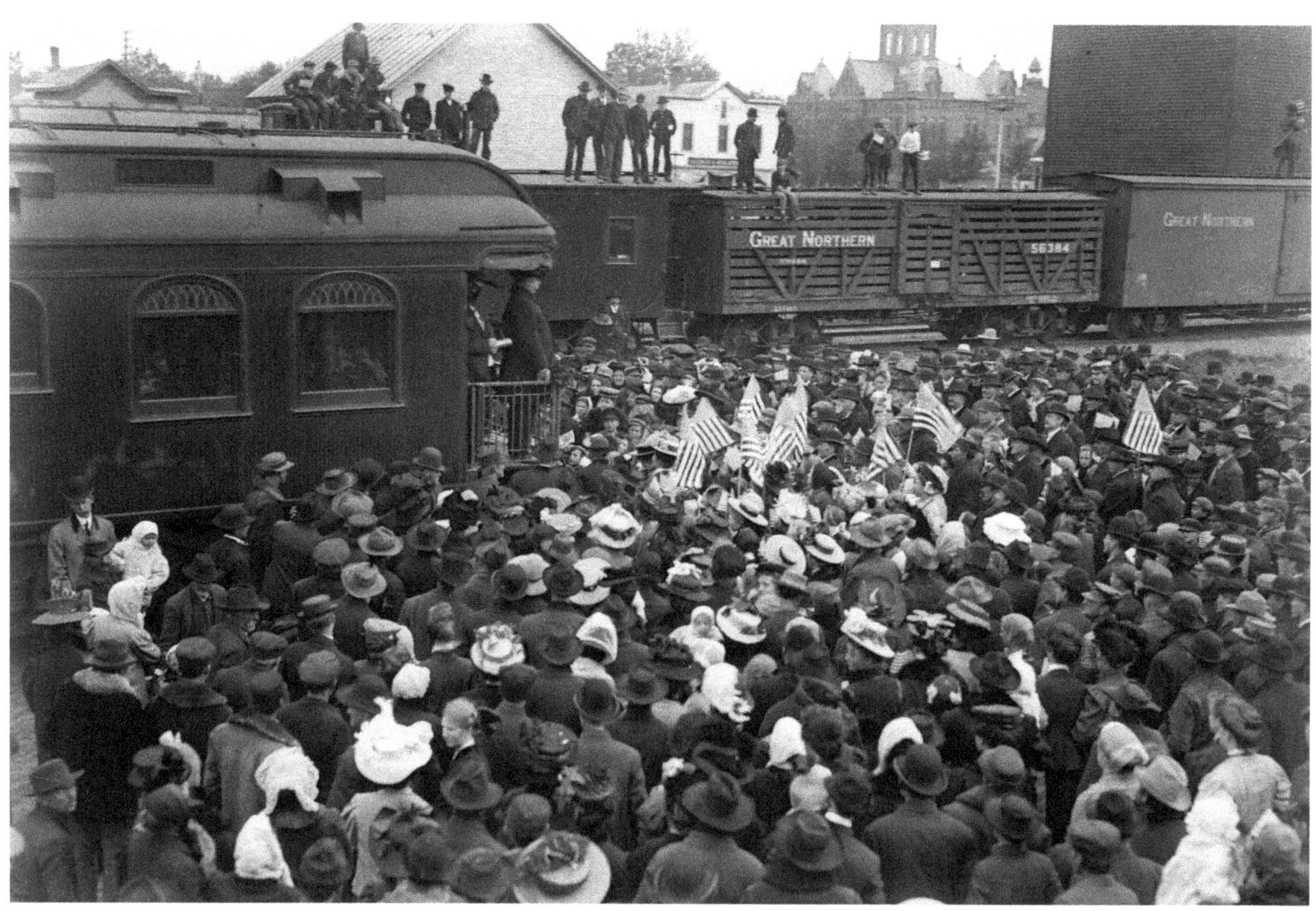


William Taft campaigned for president by train in 1908, stopping in Ada, shown here, after speaking in the Twin Cities, Southern Minnesota, and Iowa. During his campaign, Taft projected his voice to the crowds so often that he suffered from laryngitis. Members of his campaign team were quick to step in and do the talking for Taft.

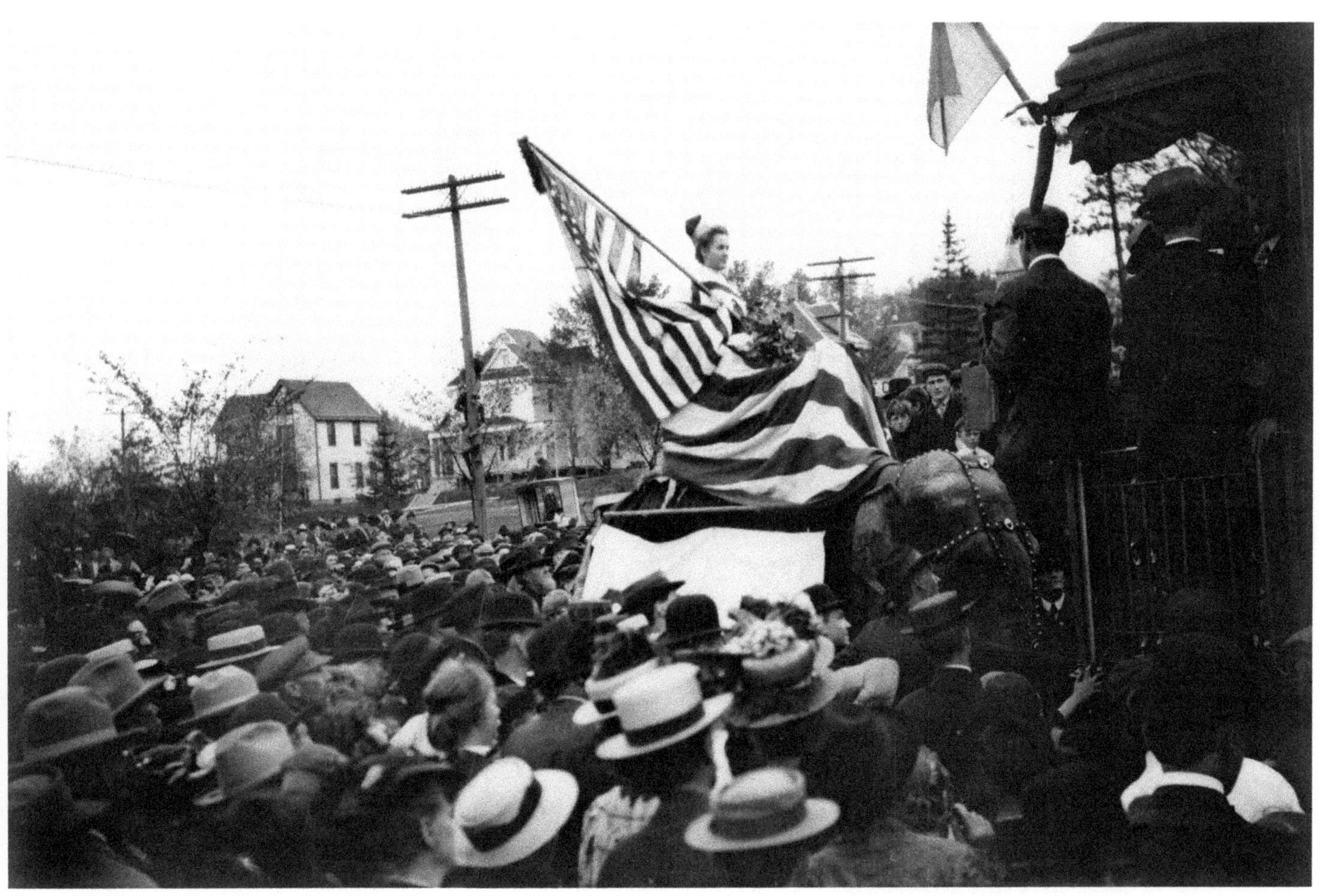

Eight thousand people showed up to hear William Taft's presidential campaign speech in Northfield in 1908. The Taft Club in Northfield borrowed an elephant from a street carnival to greet the train. Taft told the crowd that he was pleased to see such a great symbol of the Republican Party, and then he joked that he was too heavy to ride it himself (Taft weighed over 300 pounds).

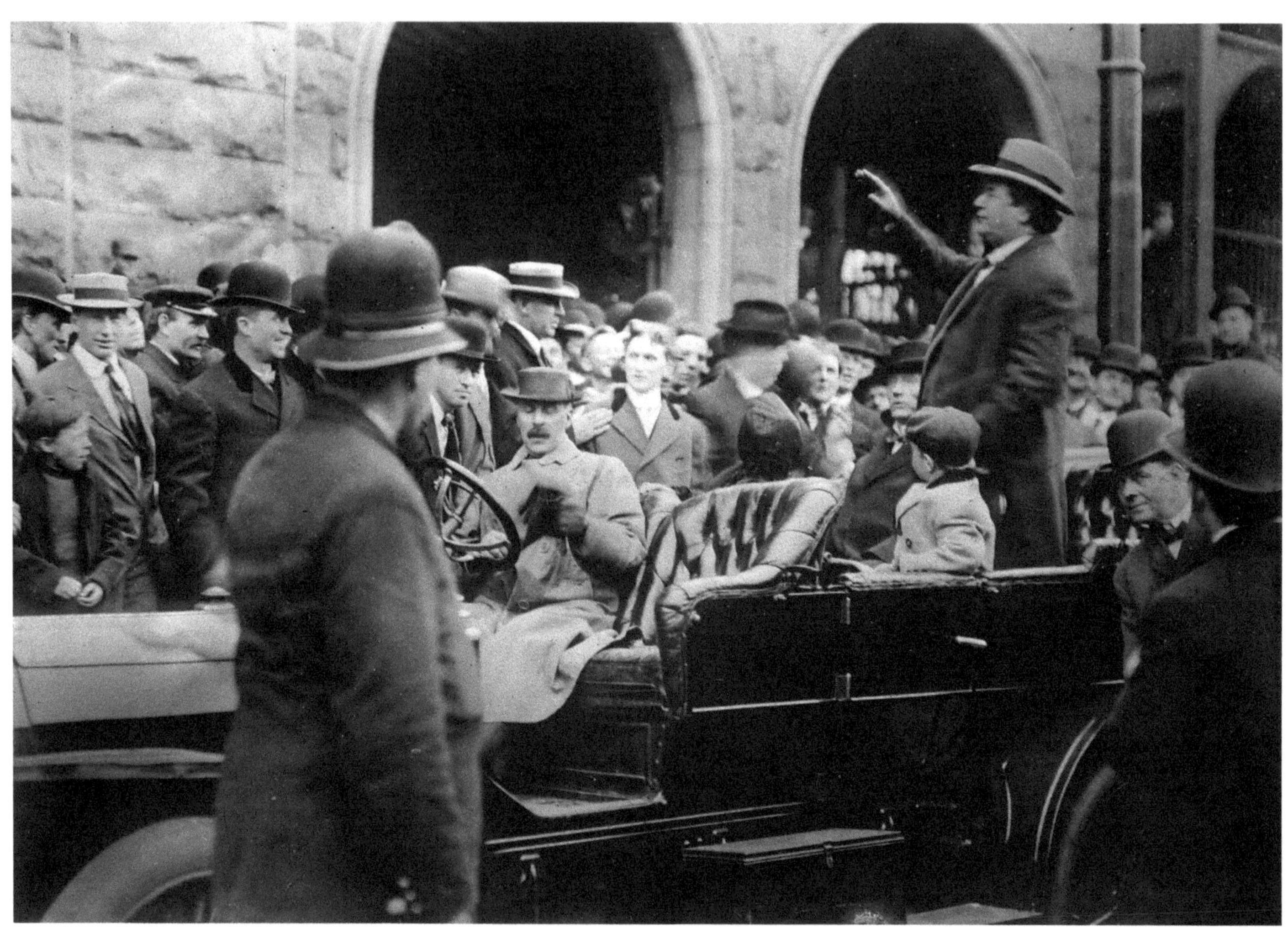

William Jennings Bryan, three-time Democratic Party nominee for president, visited Minnesota in 1908. Bryan was known as a great orator, but is pictured here, on a Sunday, refusing to speak. Bryan lost his presidential bid that year to William Taft.

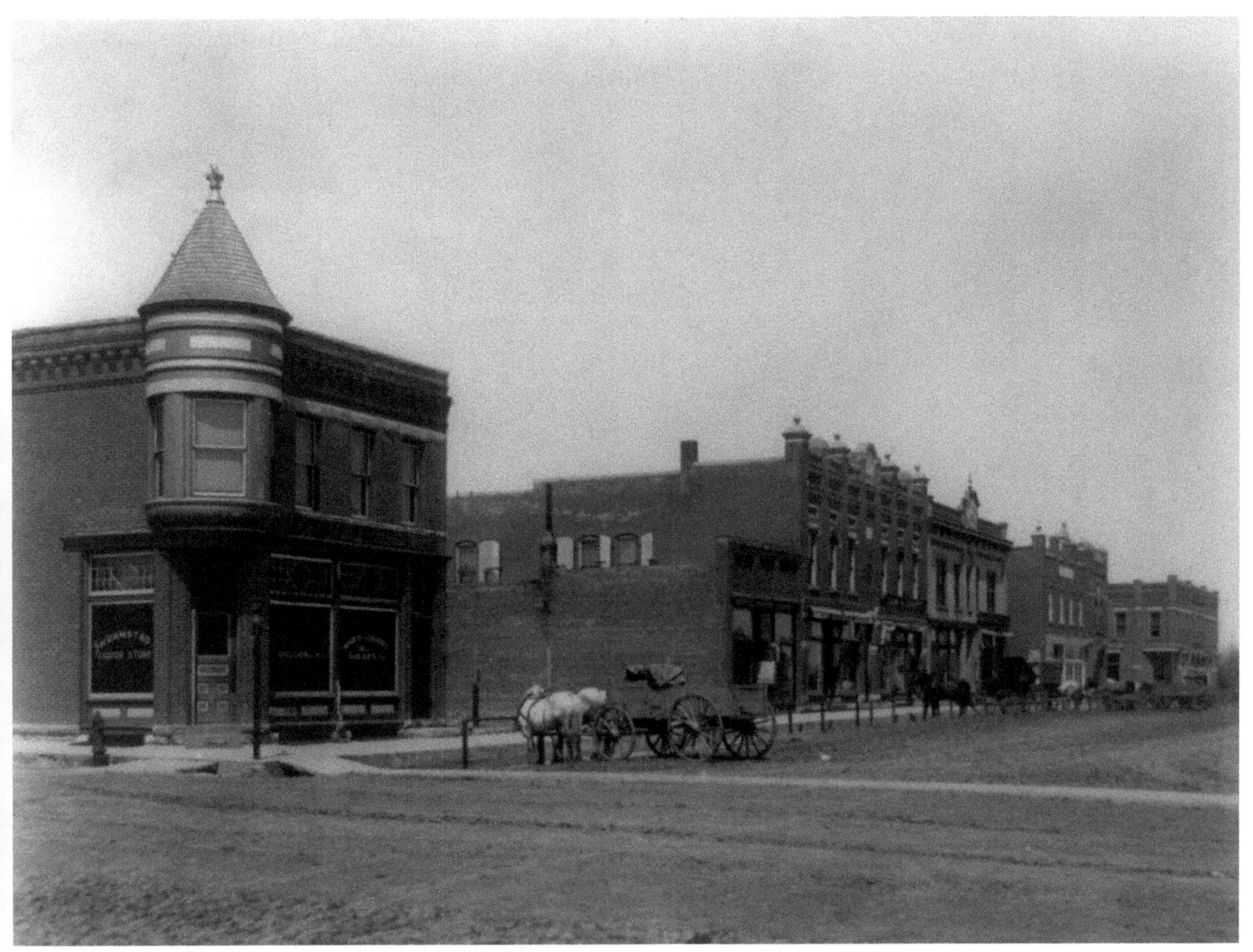

A view of downtown Goodhue, facing north, around the year 1908. Skramstad's liquor store and saloon is pictured on the corner at left.

A 1908 view of the Watab Dam in what is now Sartell, just north of St. Cloud, on the Mississippi River. It took two years to build this dam, and seven people lost their lives during the construction. The dam was used to power the Watab Pulp and Paper Company, visible across the river.

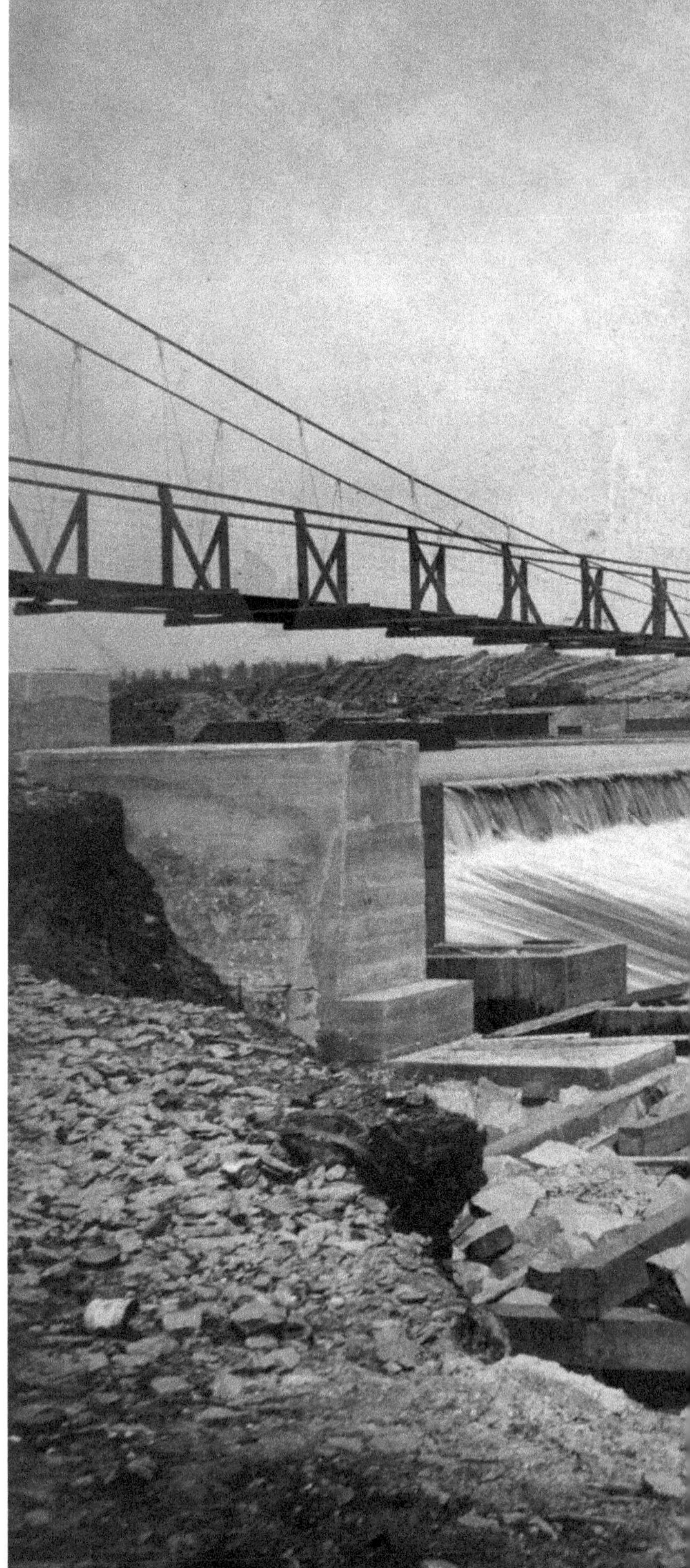

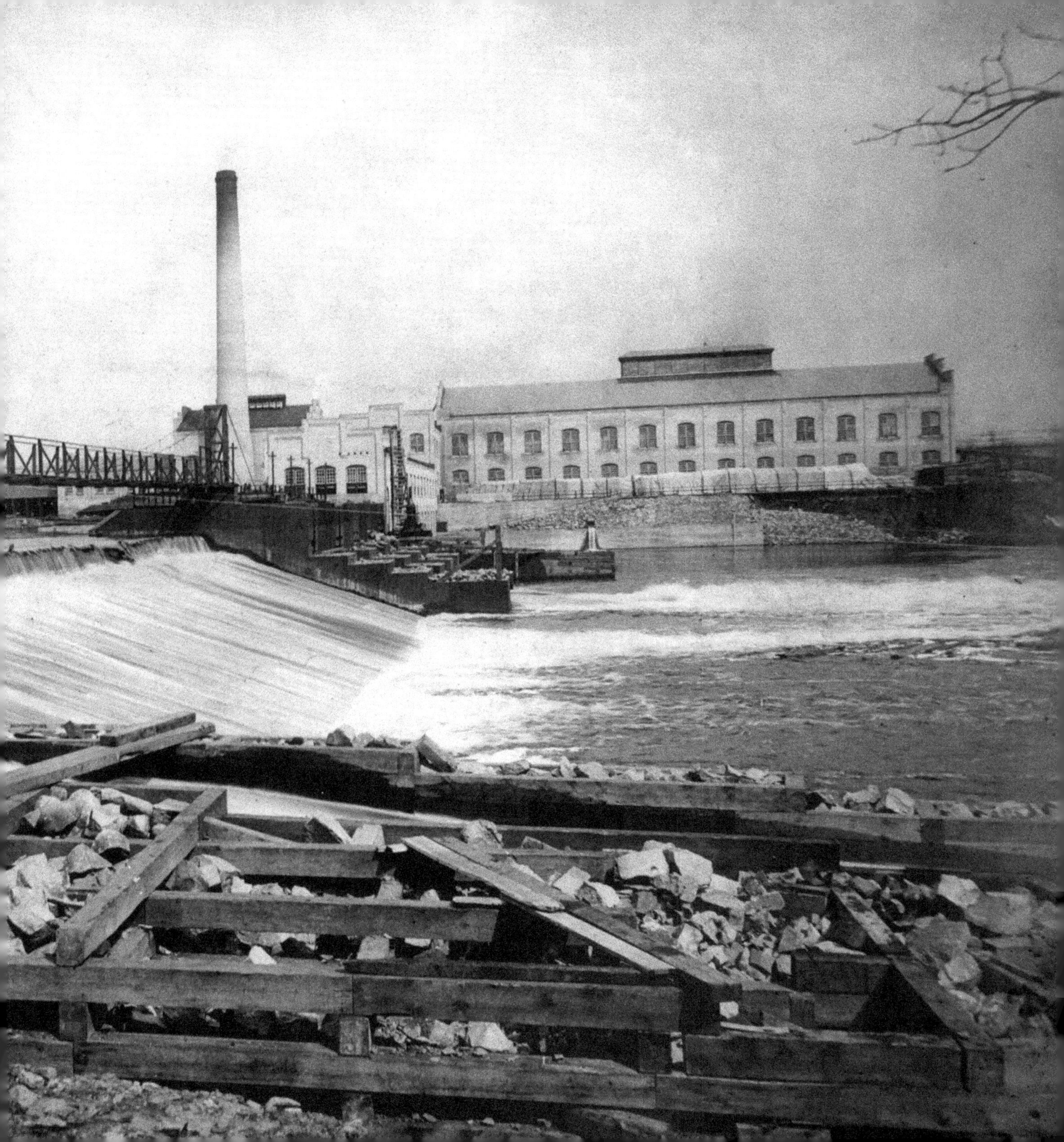

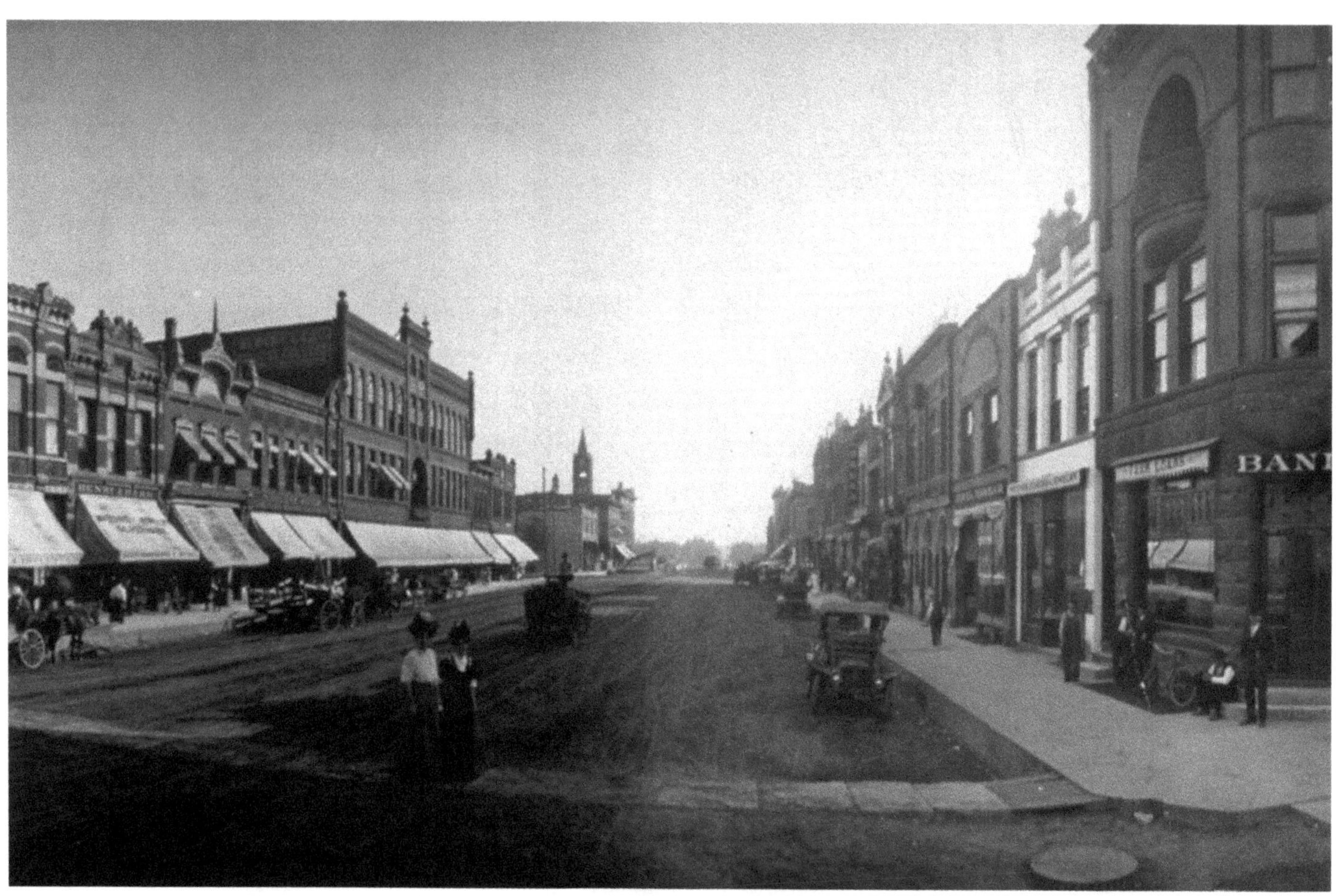

A view of downtown Albert Lea around 1908. The city is located in the southern region of the state and was an important trade center for Southeastern Minnesota and Northern Iowa. The downtown area was extensive, with grocery, hardware, and department stores, and bakeries, coffeehouses, barber shops, saloons, hotels, and restaurants.

# TRANSFORMATION

## (1910–1929)

During the early twentieth century, the population of Minnesota grew at an astounding rate, especially in the Twin Cities. In Minneapolis, Minnesota's largest city, the population ballooned from 203,000 in 1900 to 381,000 in the 1920s. In St. Paul, the second-largest city, it grew from 163,000 to 235,000. This population growth far outpaced infrastructure. In both Minneapolis and St. Paul, new city programs, planning, and public works were required to pave roads and sidewalks, expand the streetcar and telephone systems, electrify homes and businesses, and build better sewer systems.

Across the state, Minnesota's tight-knit communities, schools, churches, and businesses deepened their roots and carved out distinct identities. Still, young adults, including women, increasingly left their rural homes and headed for the Twin Cities. Many lived in settlement houses and found jobs on streetcar routes, creating new communities of young urban transplants. At the same time, more and more young people chose enrollment in universities and colleges located throughout the state, such as Hamline University and the University of Minnesota in the Twin Cities, Gustavus Adolphus College in St. Peter, and St. Olaf College in Northfield, just to name a few.

The United States entered World War I, the Great War, in 1917, with almost 200,000 Minnesotans serving. More than 15,000,000 people were killed in the war, roughly 1,500 of them from Minnesota. The state experienced additional devastation with the onset of the global influenza pandemic, which swept through the state in 1918 and continued for two years, claiming the lives of approximately 12,000 Minnesotans. Around the same time, the Cloquet–Moose Lake area was destroyed by forest fire, killing 453 people, and a tornado ripped through Fergus Falls, killing 59.

By the 1920s, the state's lumber industry was greatly diminished, and flour milling was starting to decline. However, Minnesota's economy was soaring in general, and famous Minnesota milling products such as Pillsbury's Best Flour, Gold Medal Flour, Bisquick, and Wheaties lined the shelves of grocery stores around the nation.

During the Jazz Age, changes at the national level—such as women gaining the right to vote, the growing popularity of the automobile, and the enactment of Prohibition—impacted and changed Minnesota. But as much as Minnesota changed, it also stayed the same; Minnesotans never ceased to enjoy the state's many lakes.

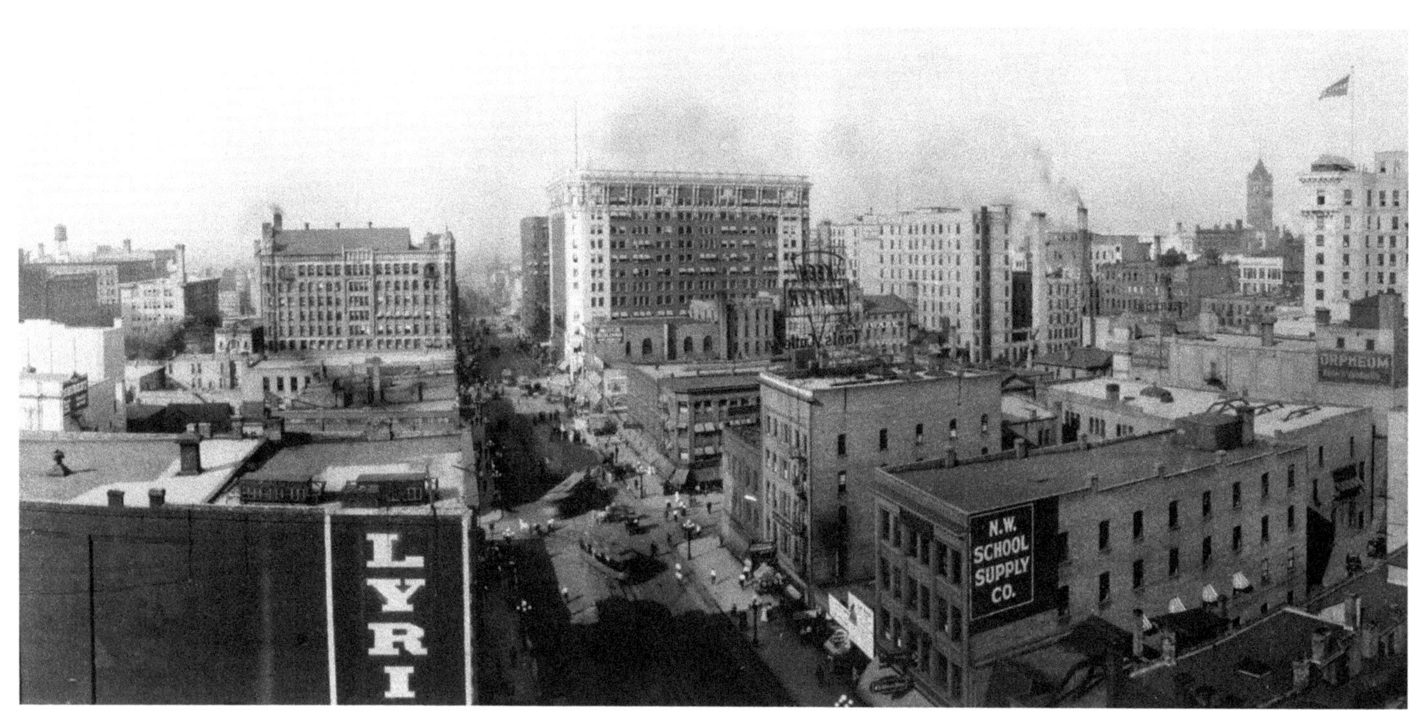


A panoramic view of downtown Minneapolis around 1911. The Lyric Theater is prominent, as is the major thoroughfare of Hennepin Avenue.

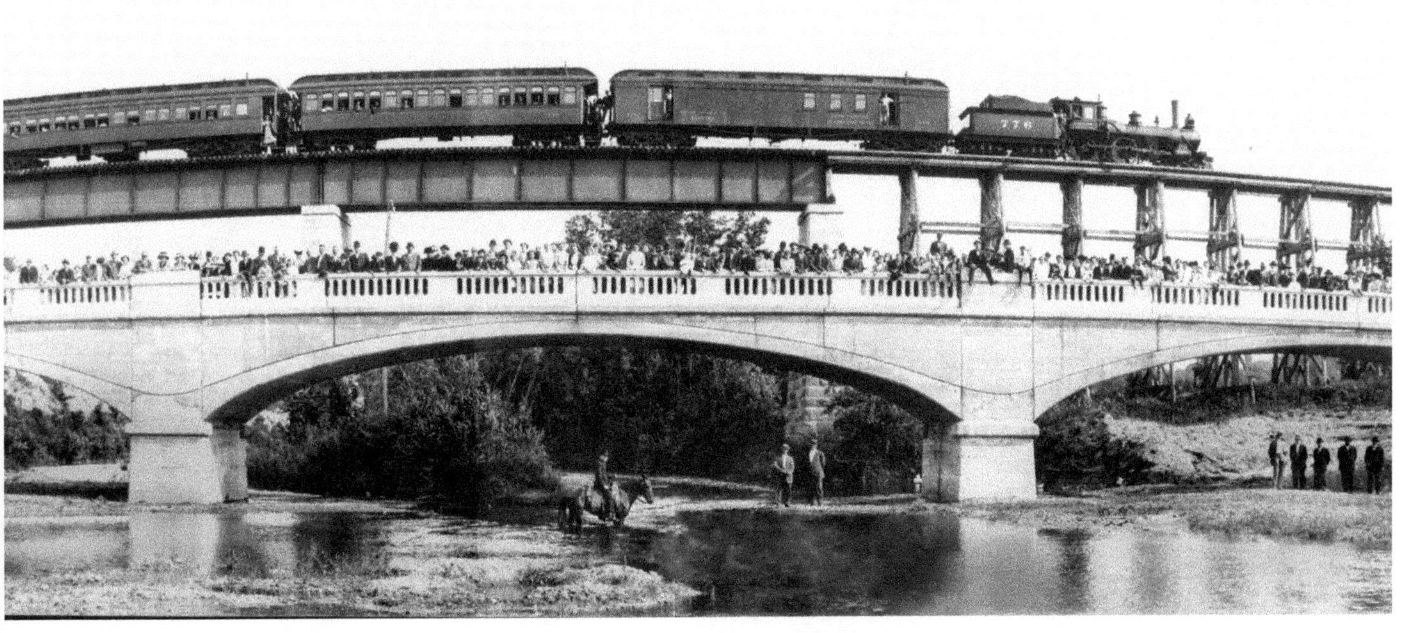

On August 2, 1911, the community of Red Jacket celebrated the opening of the Red Jacket Bridge. The new bridge was 276 feet long and 16 feet wide. A passenger train stopped for five minutes that afternoon to allow picnickers to pose for photos on the bridge below. Refreshments were provided for the cooperative train crew.

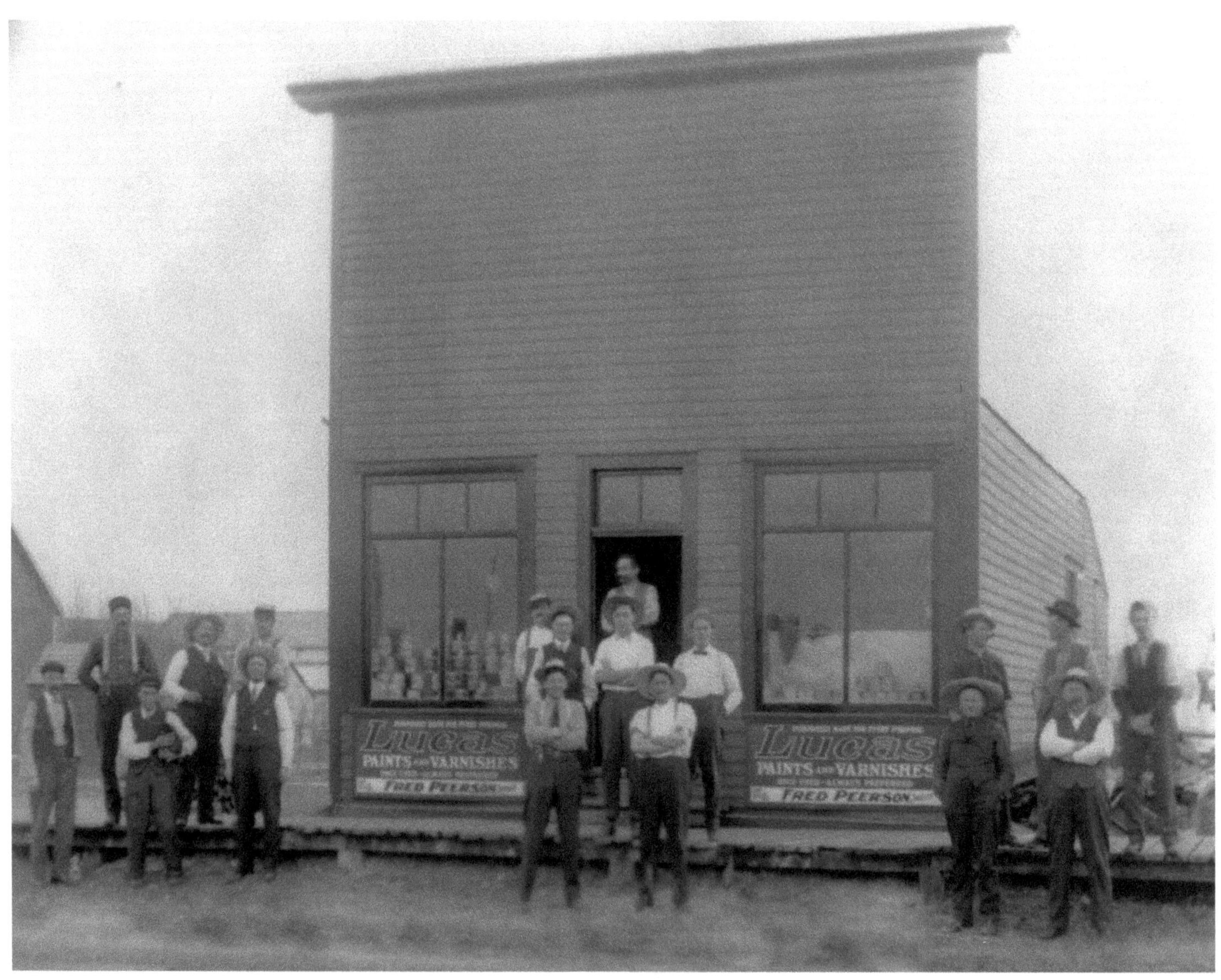


A group gathers in front of Fred Peerson's paint shop in Shelly on what appears to be an oddly balmy day in December 1913. The railroad was central to Shelly at this time, but automobiles were starting to make an appearance in the town, giving a hint of what the future had in store. Peerson was hired to paint auto speed-limit signs that same year.

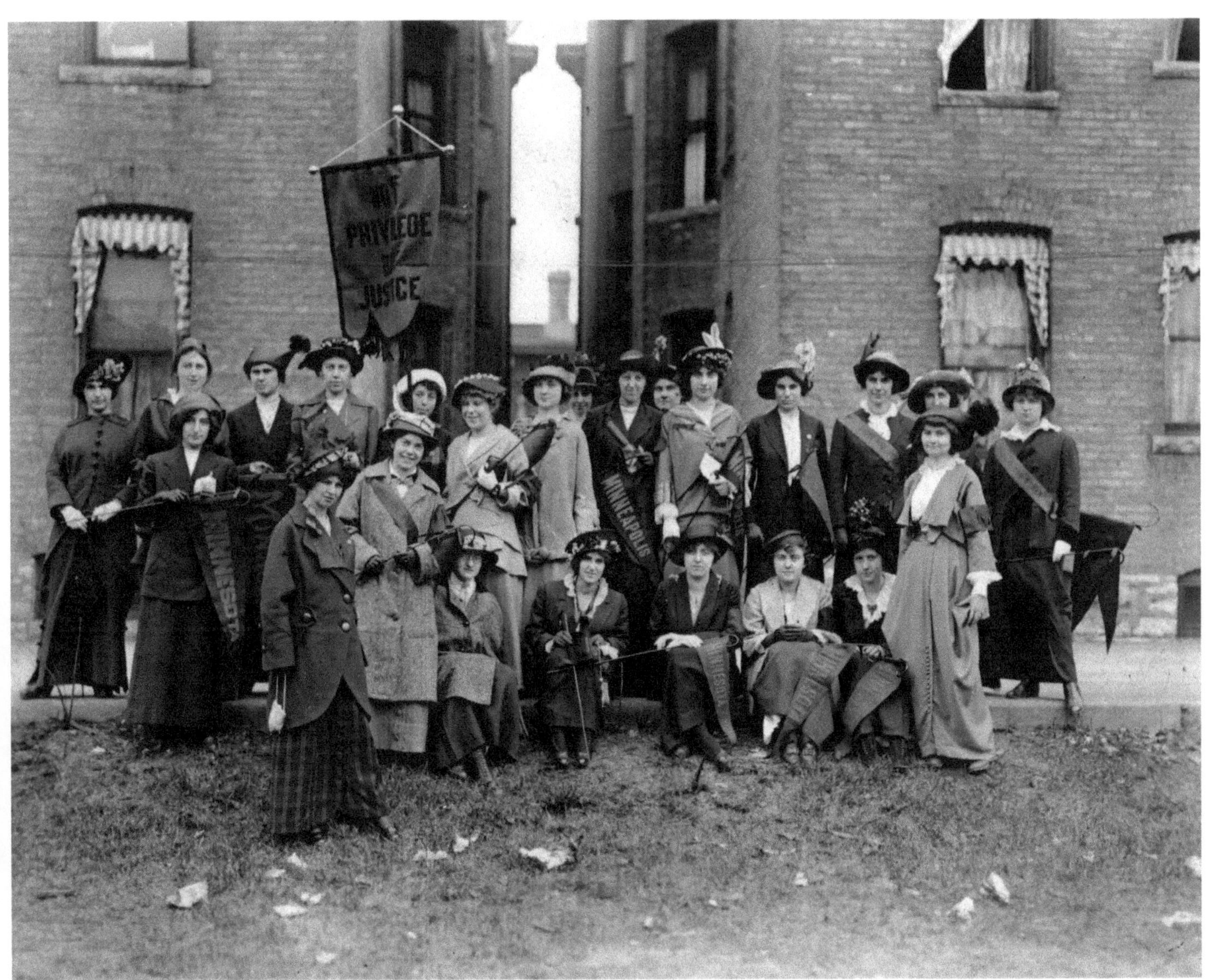


The University of Minnesota's Women's Suffrage Club, pictured in 1913, campaigned for the right to vote in United States elections. Suffragists participated in marches, rallies, speeches, and appeals to lawmakers. In 1920, women were granted the right to vote by the passage and ratification of the 19th Amendment to the United States Constitution.

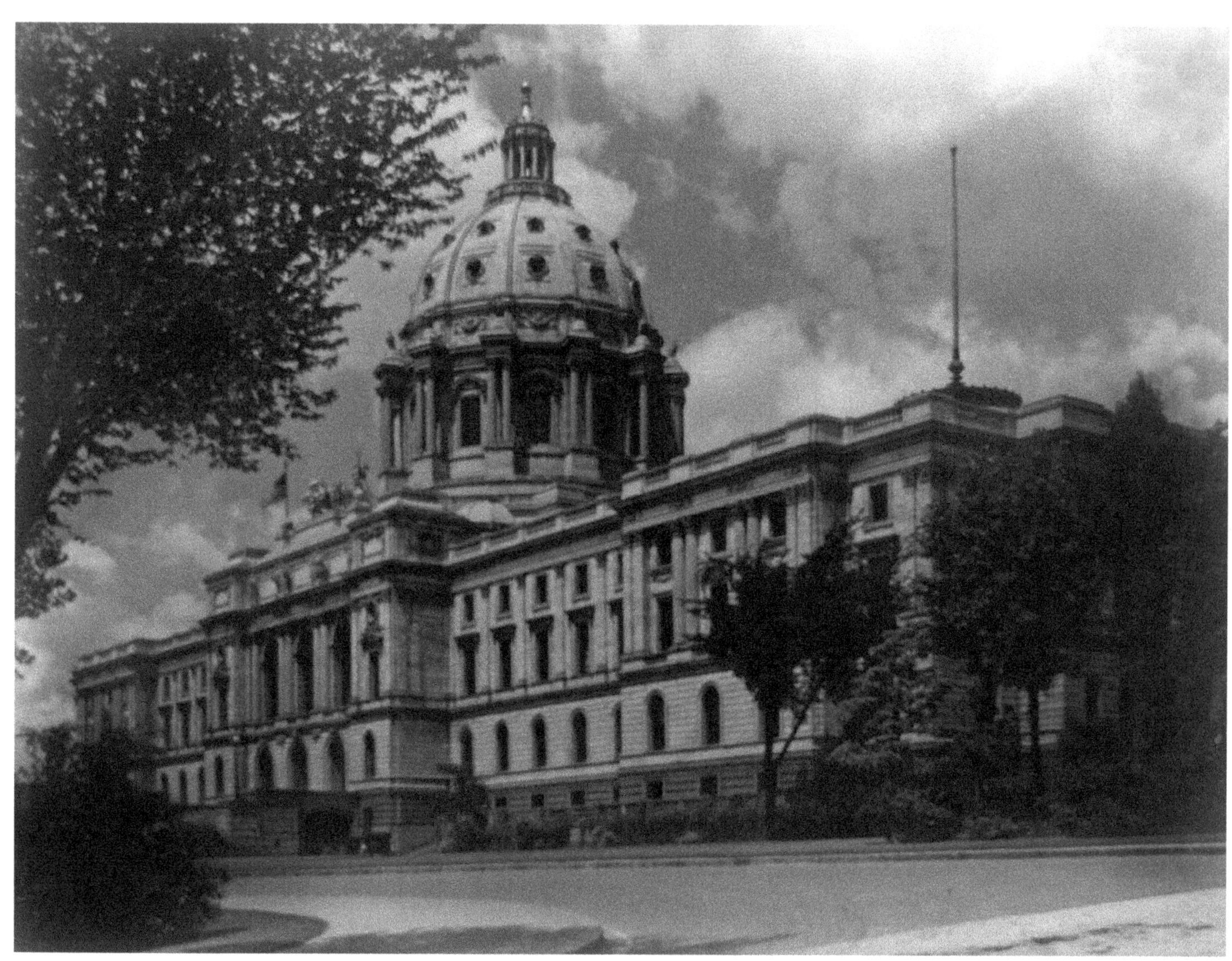

The Minnesota State Capitol in St. Paul, around 1915. The building was designed by pioneering architect Cass Gilbert. When the building opened its doors to the public, in 1905, it had state-of-the-art heating, electricity, and telephones. The planning and construction of the building took almost 12 years and cost about $4.5 million.

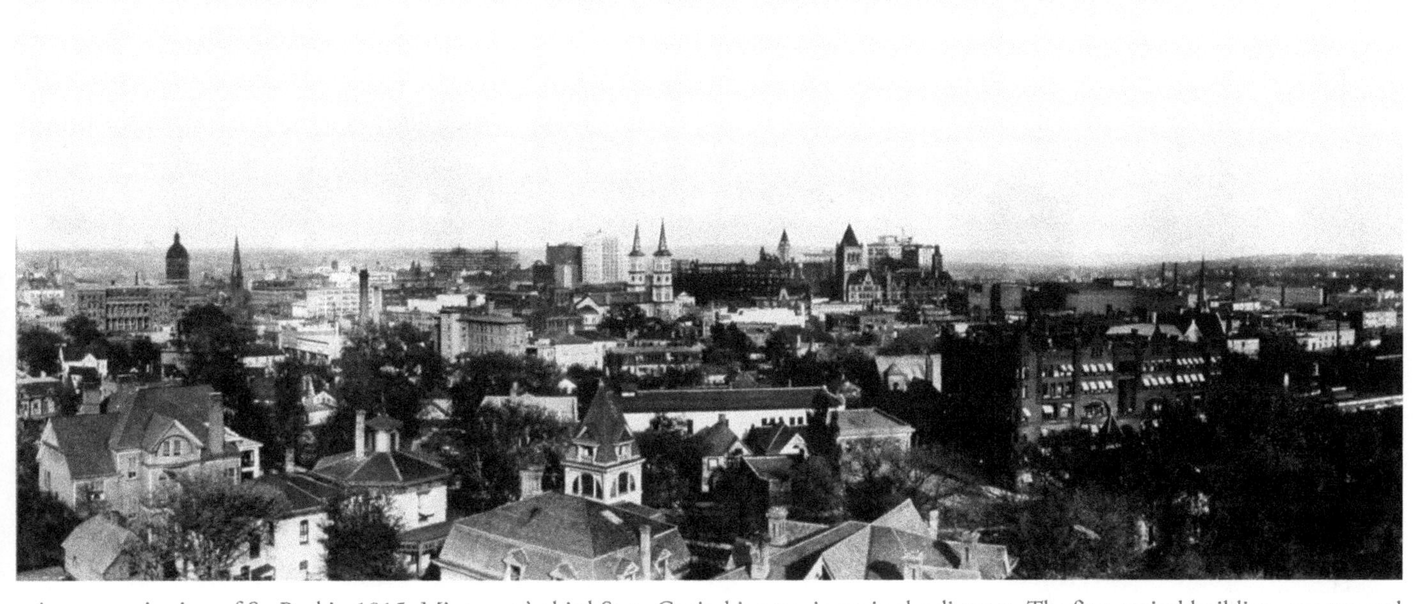

A panoramic view of St. Paul in 1915. Minnesota's third State Capitol is prominent in the distance. The first capitol building, constructed at Tenth and Cedar streets in 1853, was destroyed by fire in 1881. A second capitol, built on the same site, was deemed too small and poorly constructed. For this third capitol, legislators chose Wabasha Hill above downtown St. Paul.

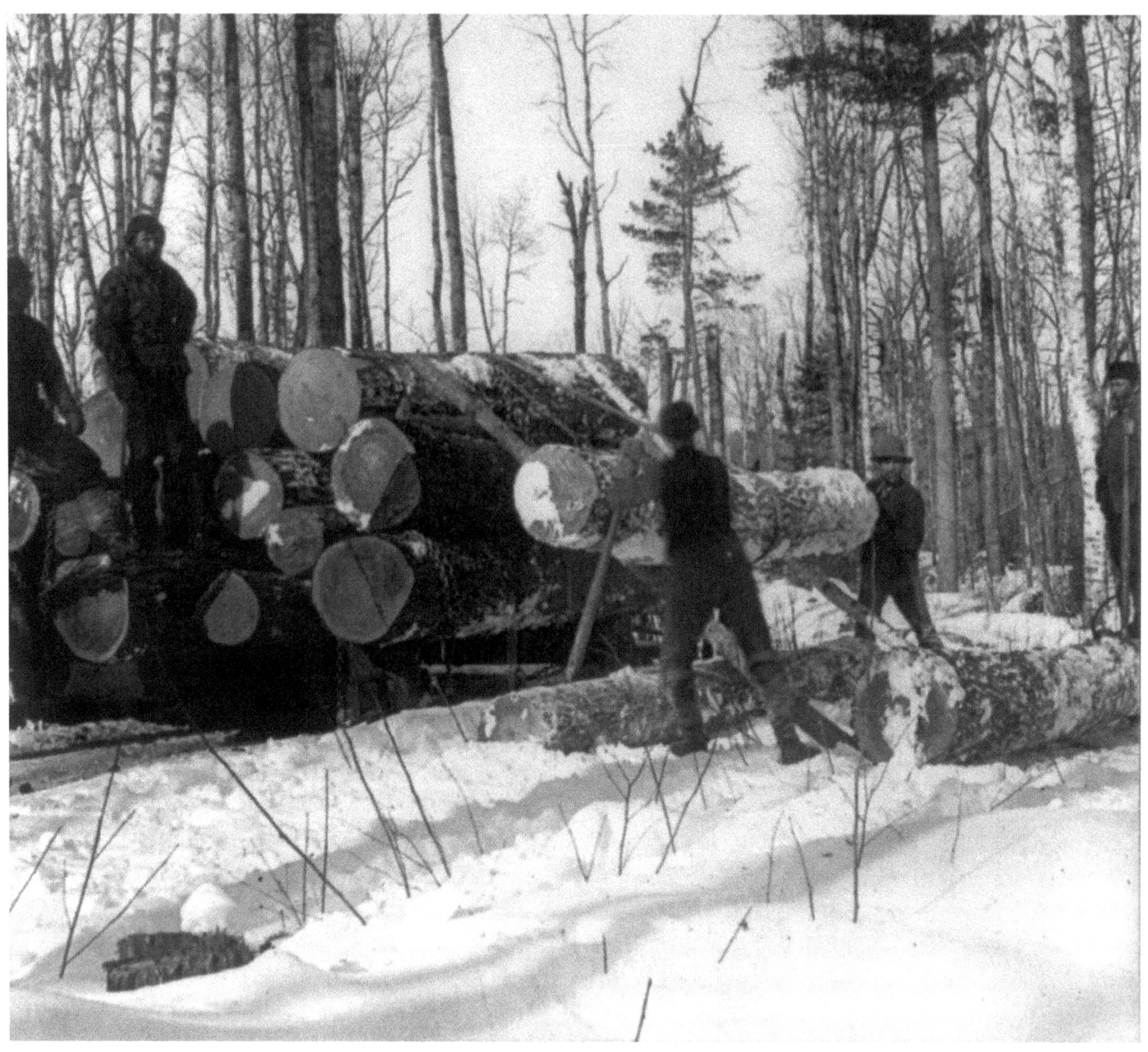

In 1915, lumberjacks use a block-and-tackle system to load felled trees onto a sleigh, to then be pulled by horses to a river or train. The work was grueling and dangerous, and many jacks were crushed trying to maneuver logs.

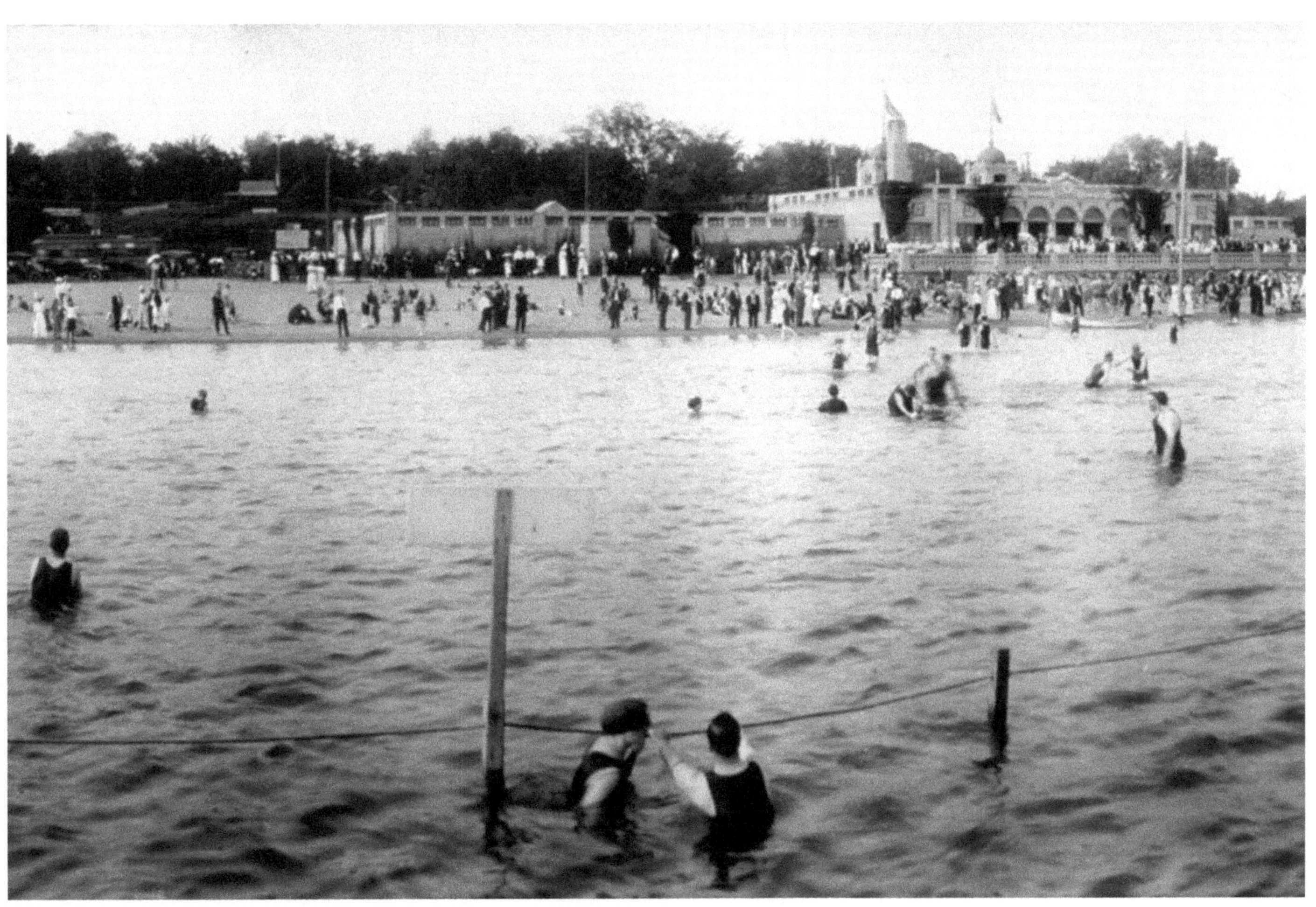

Minneapolis earned the nickname "City of Lakes" because of the abundance of lakes in the metropolitan area. Shown around 1915, Lake Calhoun, with its expansive bathhouse on the north shore, was one of the most popular swimming lakes. The beach at nearby Lake Harriet was also fashionable to frequent in the summertime.

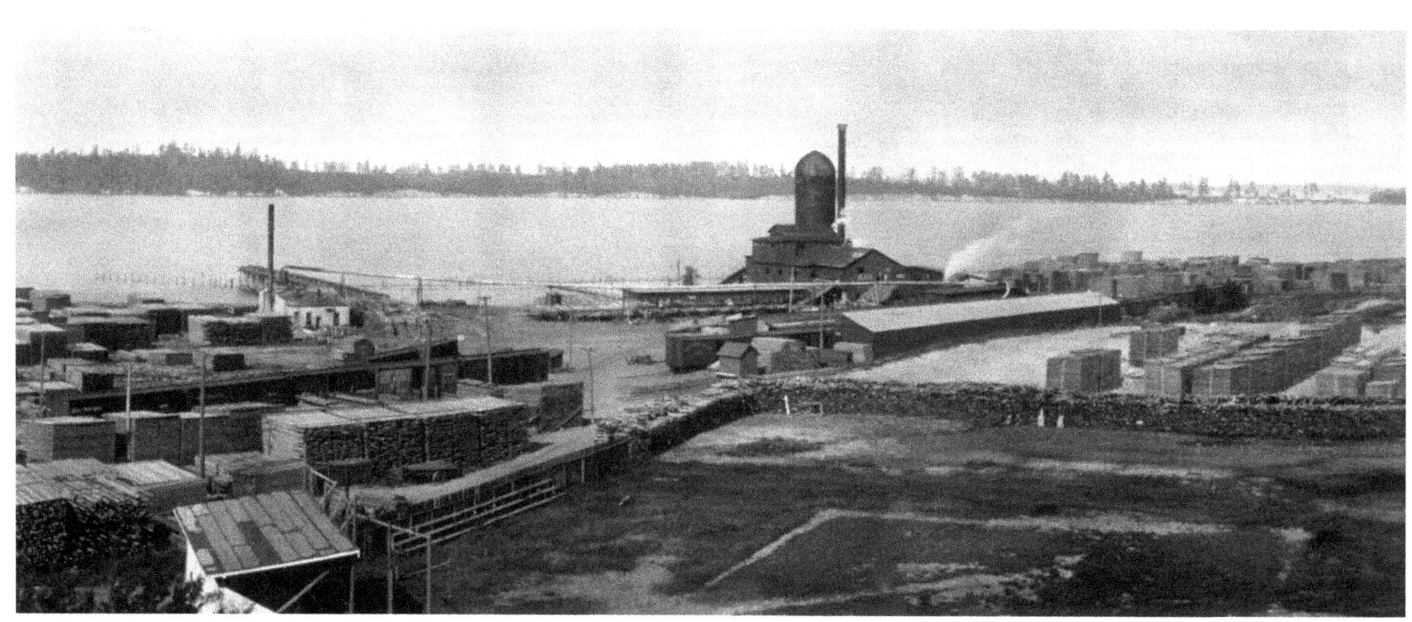

A 1915 panoramic view of the Leech Lake Lumber Company in Walker.

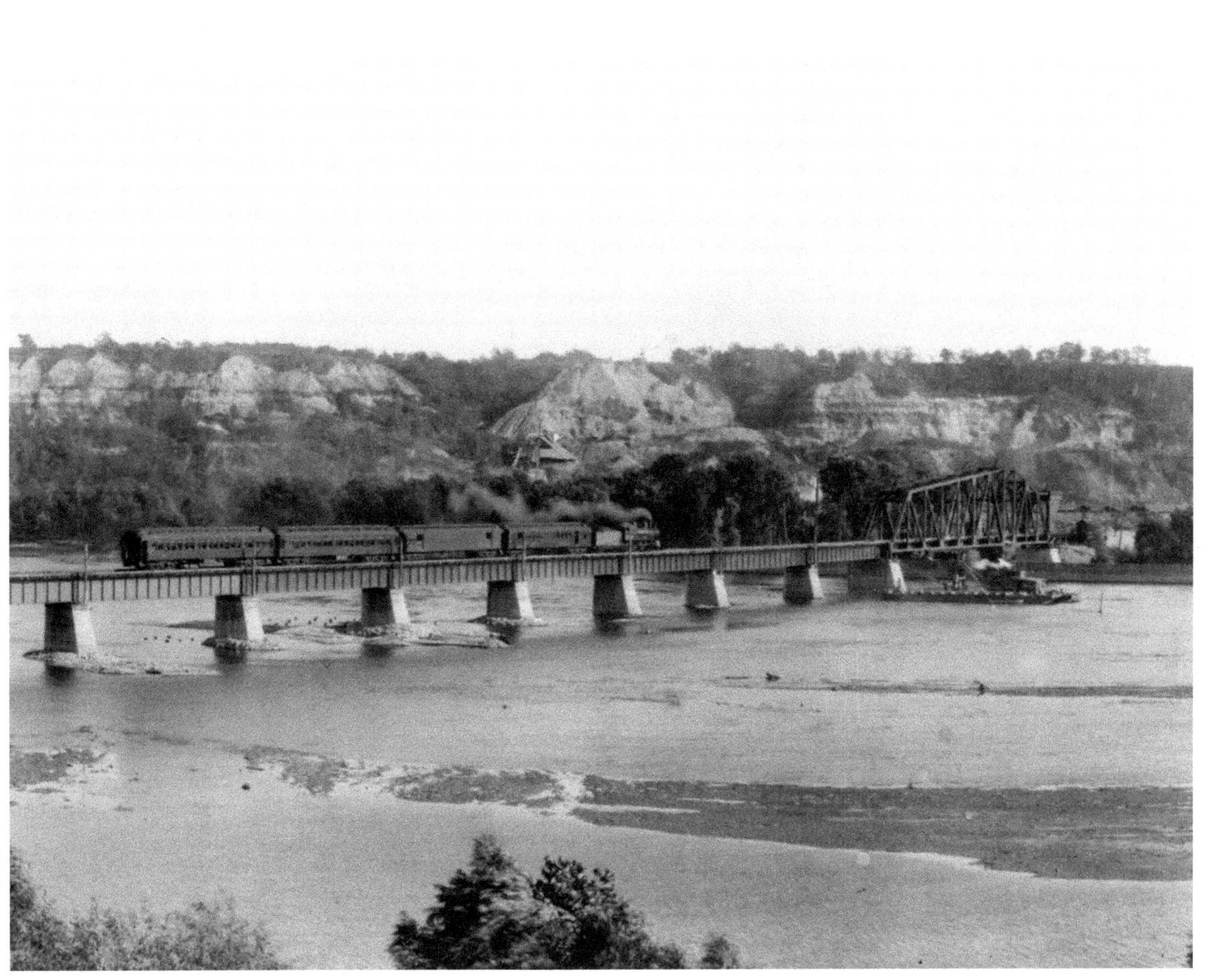

A 1916 view of a train crossing the Mississippi River at St. Paul.

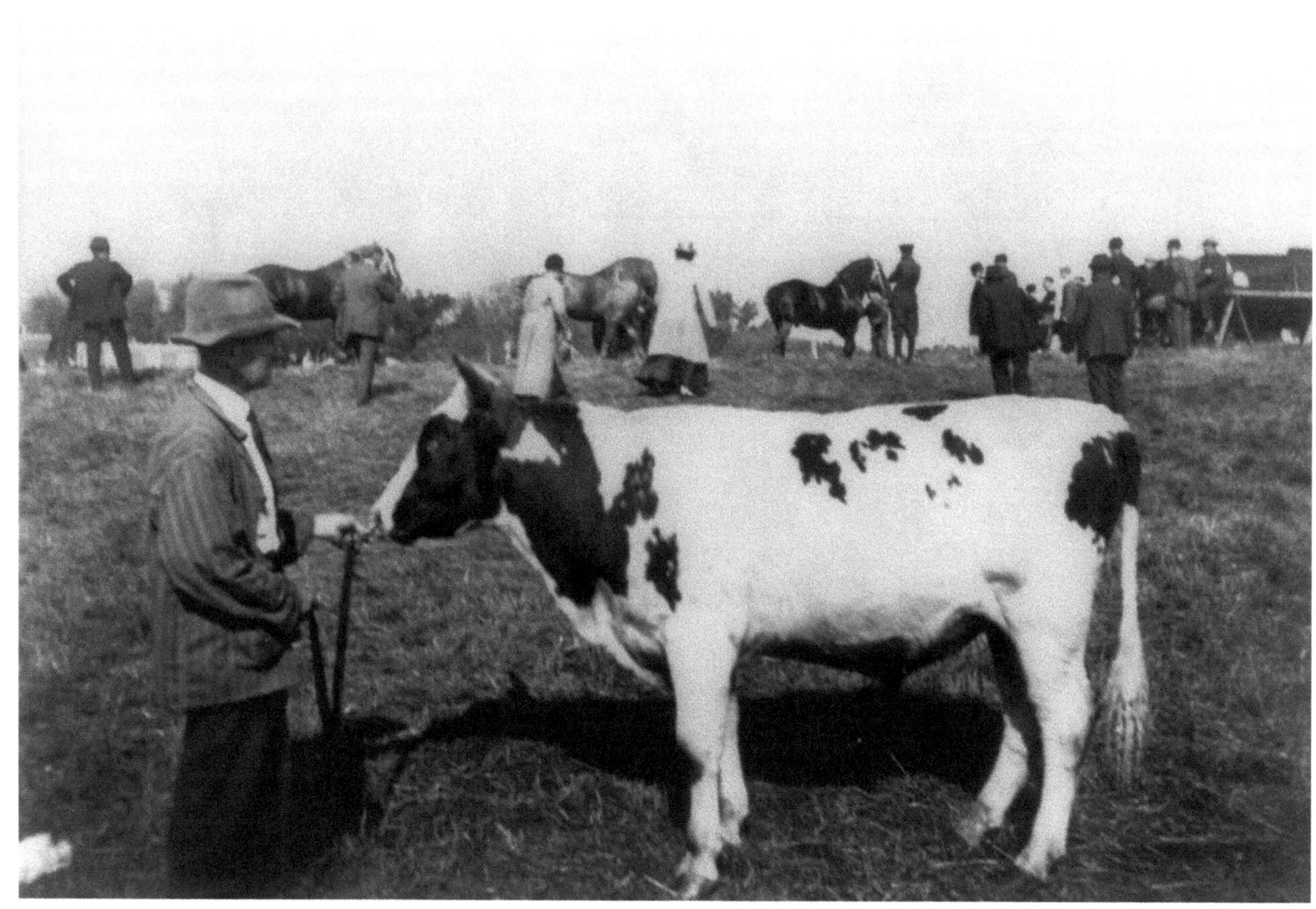

R. E. Lynch's Ayrshire bull takes the top prize at the Sherburne County Fair in 1916.

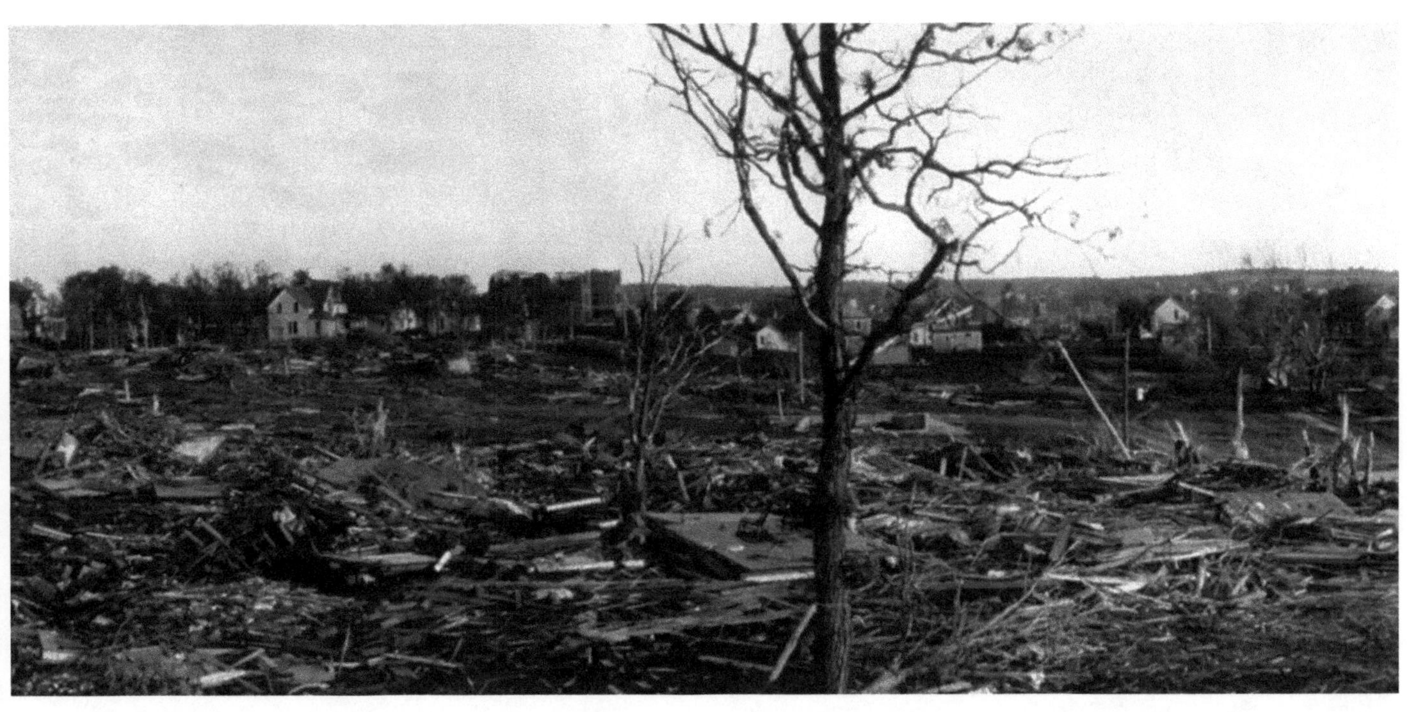

This image shows the aftermath of a deadly tornado that ripped through Fergus Falls on June 22, 1919, killing 59 people. Most of the deaths occurred in the Grand Hotel. A Great Northern passenger train was blown from the tracks, but the 250 passengers escaped without serious injuries.

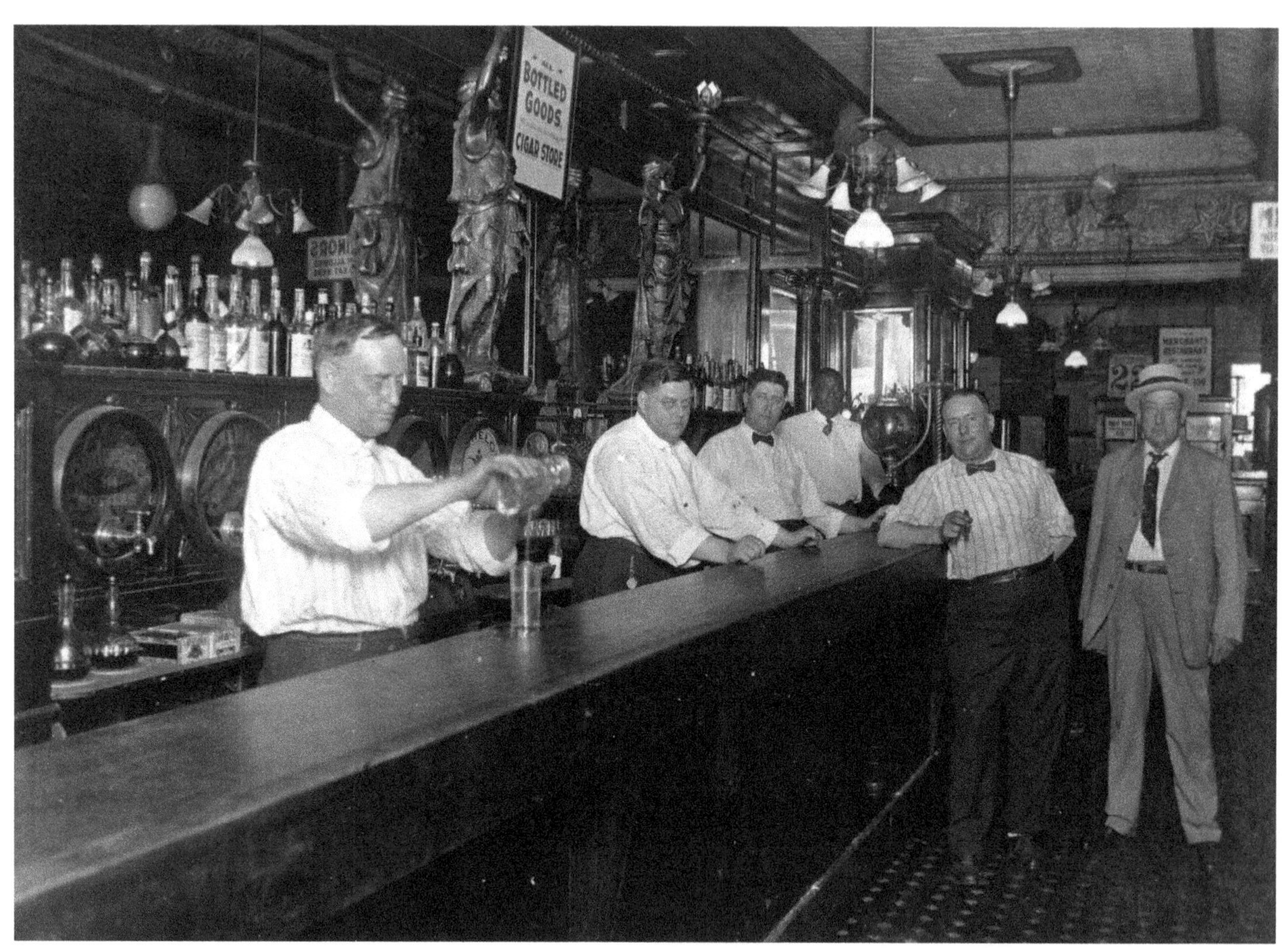


Staff bartenders, possibly at the Merchants Hotel in St. Paul, serve up "bottled goods" while they can, as Prohibition looms.

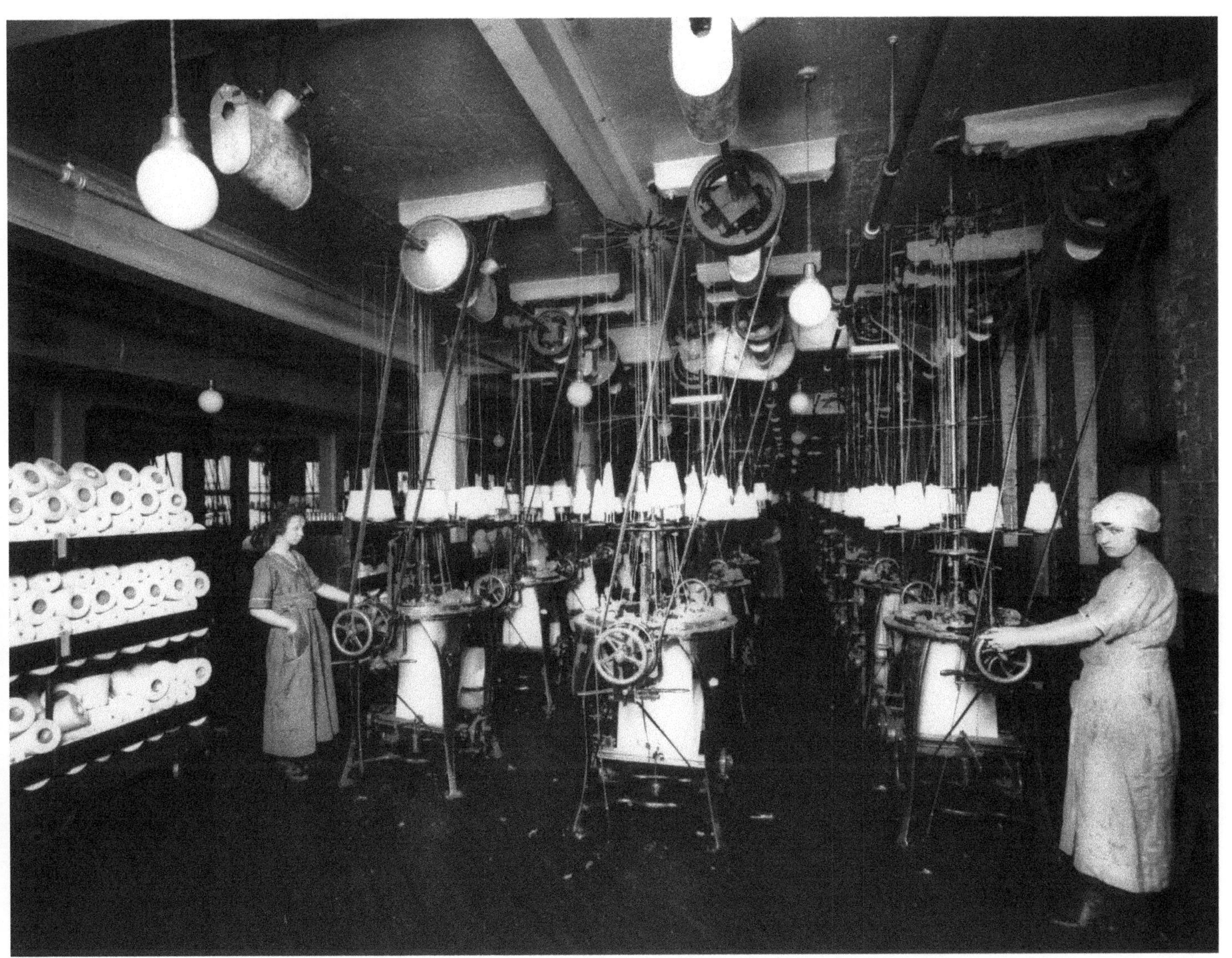

In 1920, female employees of the Munsingwear factory in Minneapolis work at the weaving machines, making underwear. The company, originally known as the Northwest Knitting Company, turned out 30,000 garments a day around the time this photo was taken. Munsingwear was also the state's largest employer of women—who made up 85 percent of the company's total workforce of 3,000 employees.

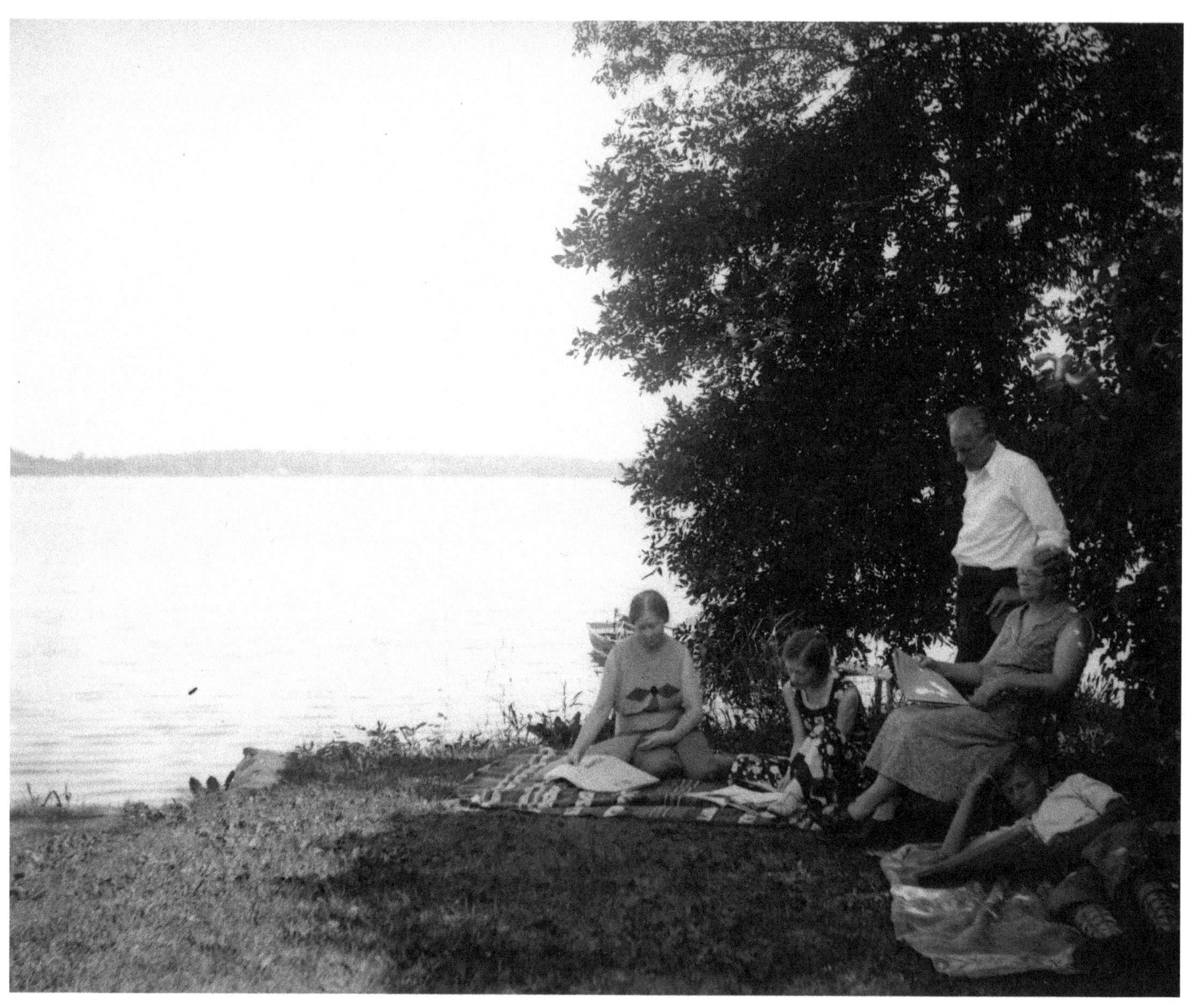

When summertime temperatures soared, Minnesotans cooled off at one of the state's many lakes, like this group did at Glen Lake in Minnetonka around 1920. While Minnesota is known to be "the land of 10,000 lakes," the actual count is 11,842.

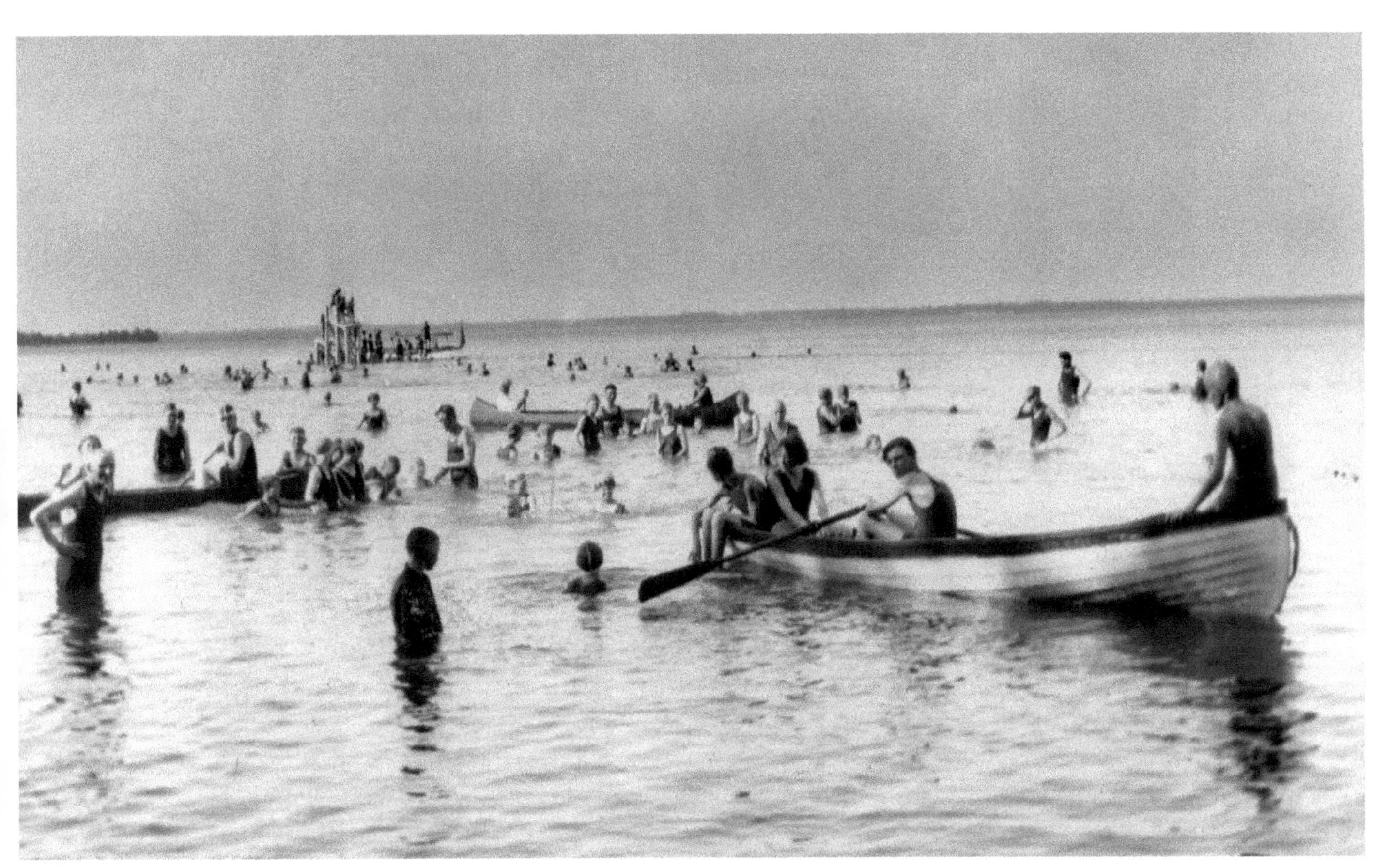

A familiar, joy-filled summertime scene at a Minnesota lake in the 1920s.

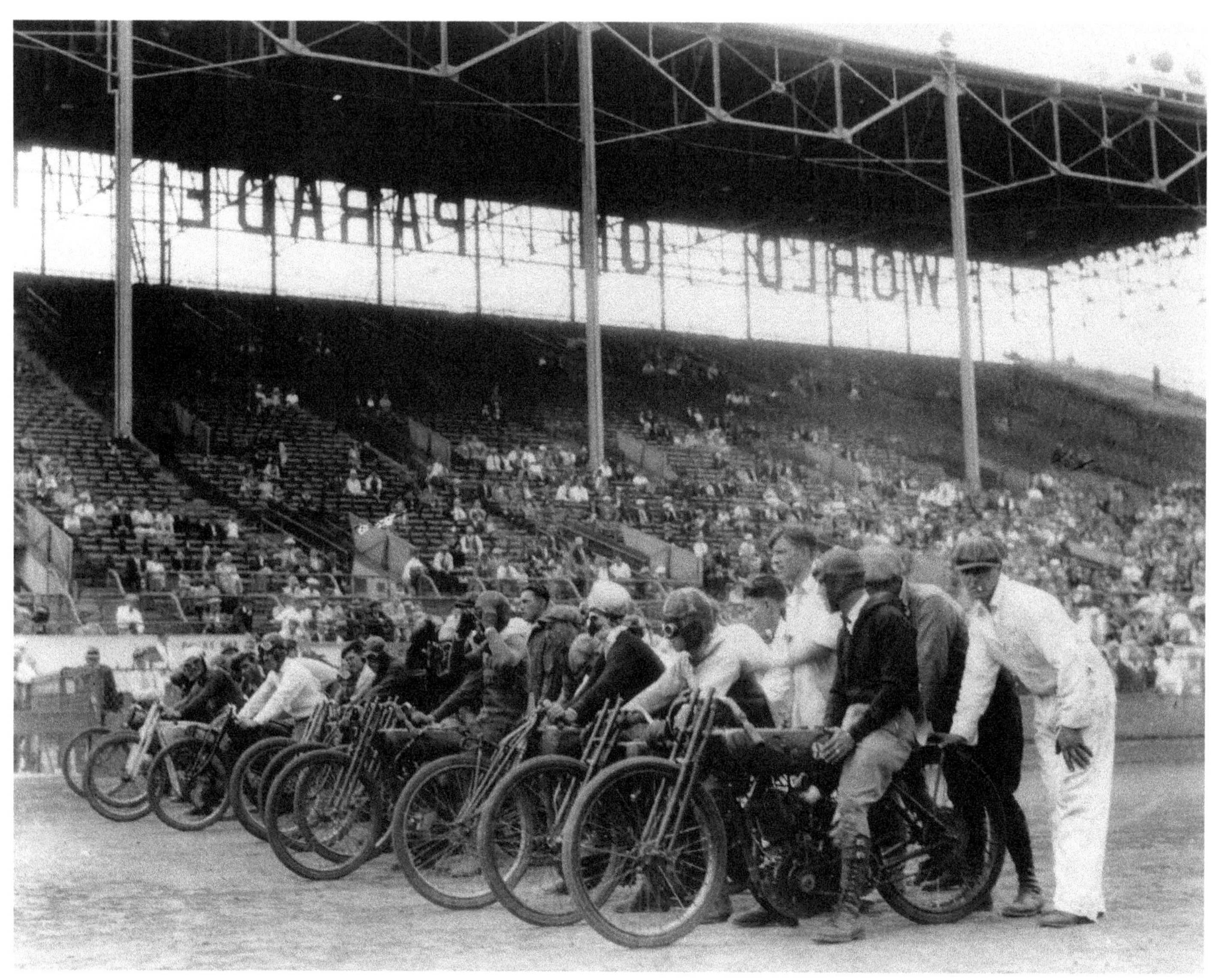

Although this motorcycle race, featured as part of the Minnesota State Fair's "World on Parade" around 1920, drew only a modest crowd, the sport was growing in popularity. In 1921, a Harley-Davidson rider became the first to win a motorcycle race with an average speed in excess of 100 miles per hour.

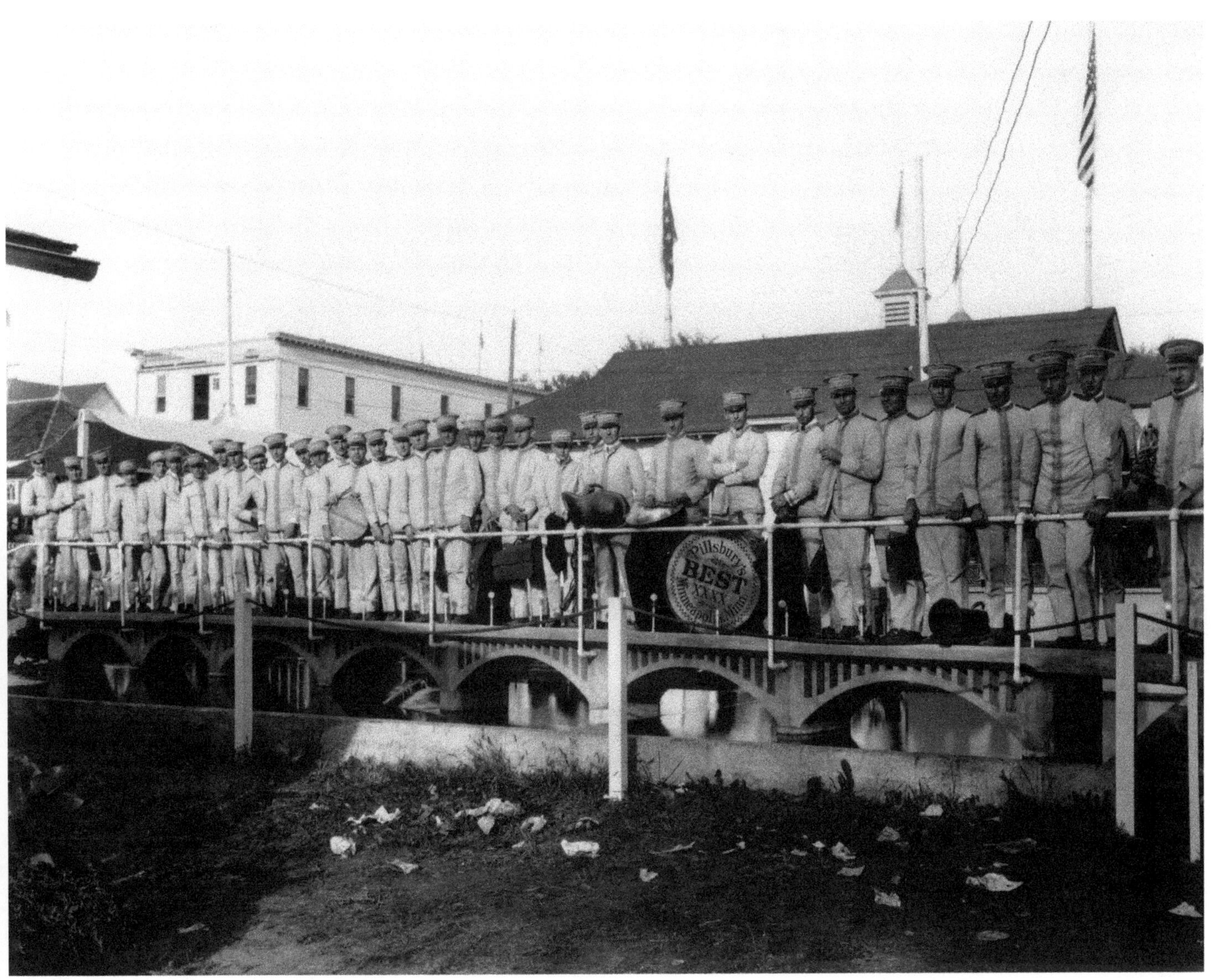


Pillsbury Company band members pose at the company's exhibit at the Minnesota State Fair in 1920. The musicians are standing on a miniature version of the Stone Arch Bridge. The bass drum advertises Pillsbury's Best Flour.

There was nothing more important to a lumberjack after 12 hours of hard, physical labor than a good meal. And the camp food was famously abundant and delicious. Lumber camp cooks such as these two were so crucial to the productivity of Minnesota camps that some earned as much as $2.50 per day—2½ times what the lumberjacks were paid.

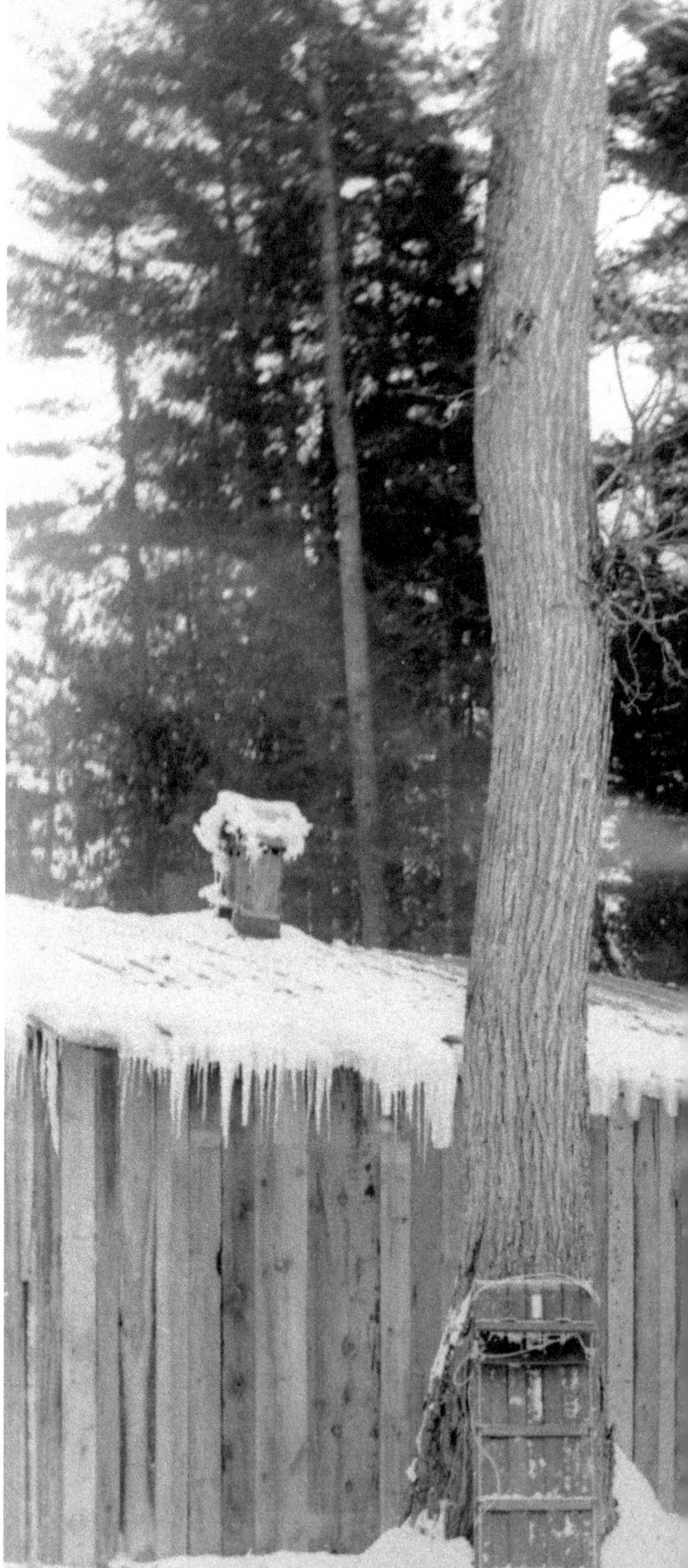

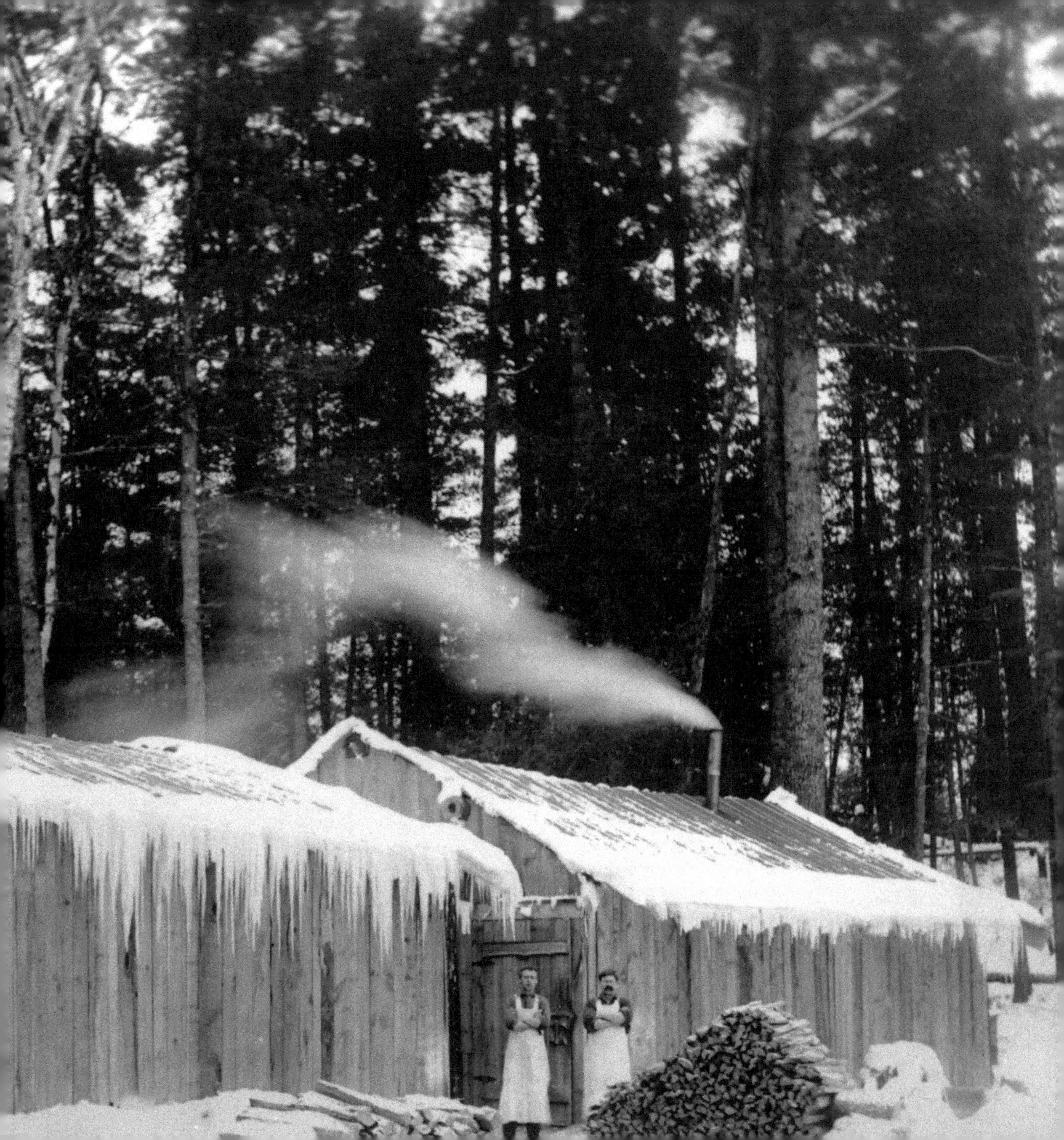

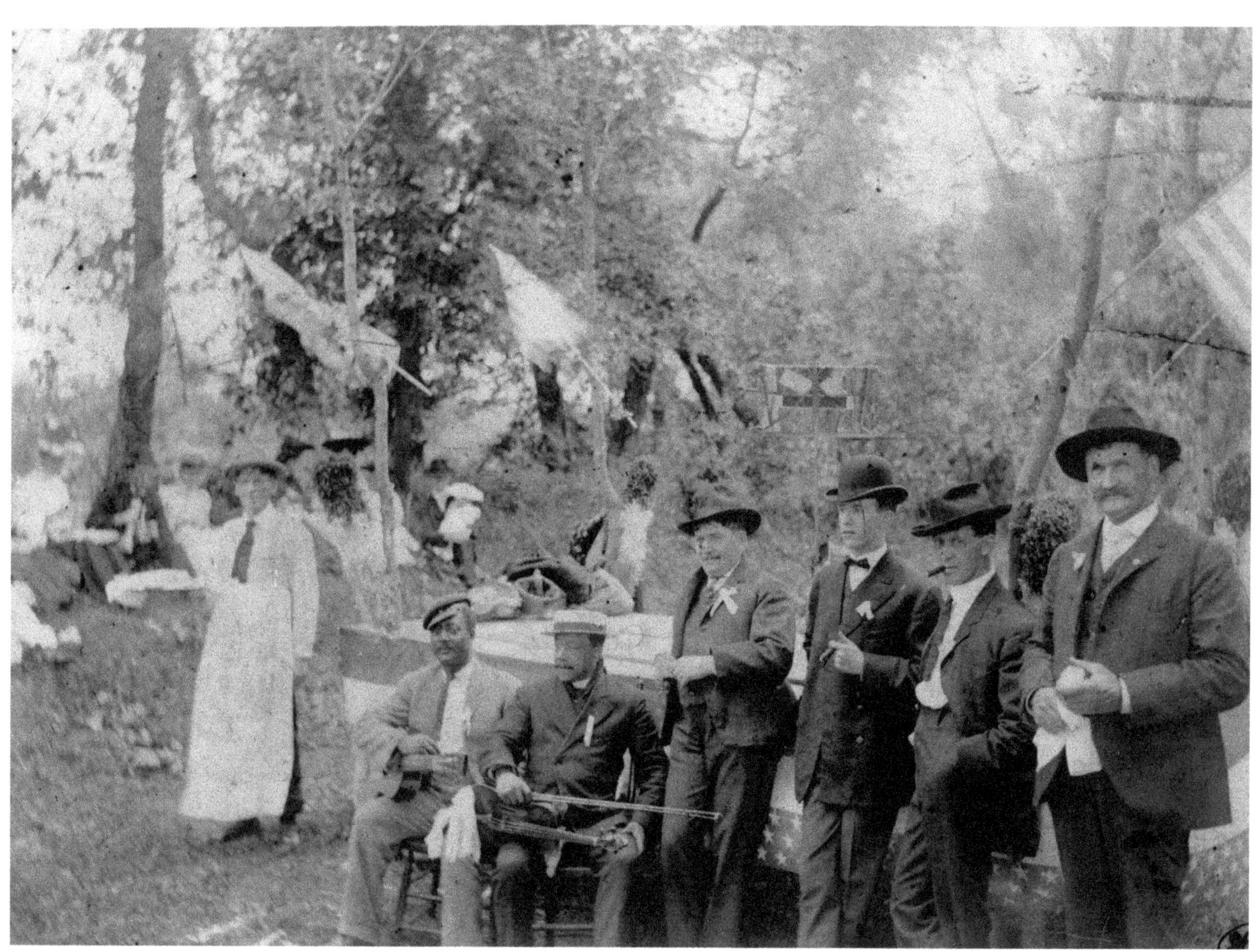

The city of Savage celebrates Independence Day around 1920 with a community picnic, complete with music. Savage is located 15 miles southwest of downtown Minneapolis. The city was originally named Hamilton, after the city in Ontario, Canada, but was renamed Savage in 1904 in honor of Marion Willis Savage, owner of the famous racehorse Dan Patch.

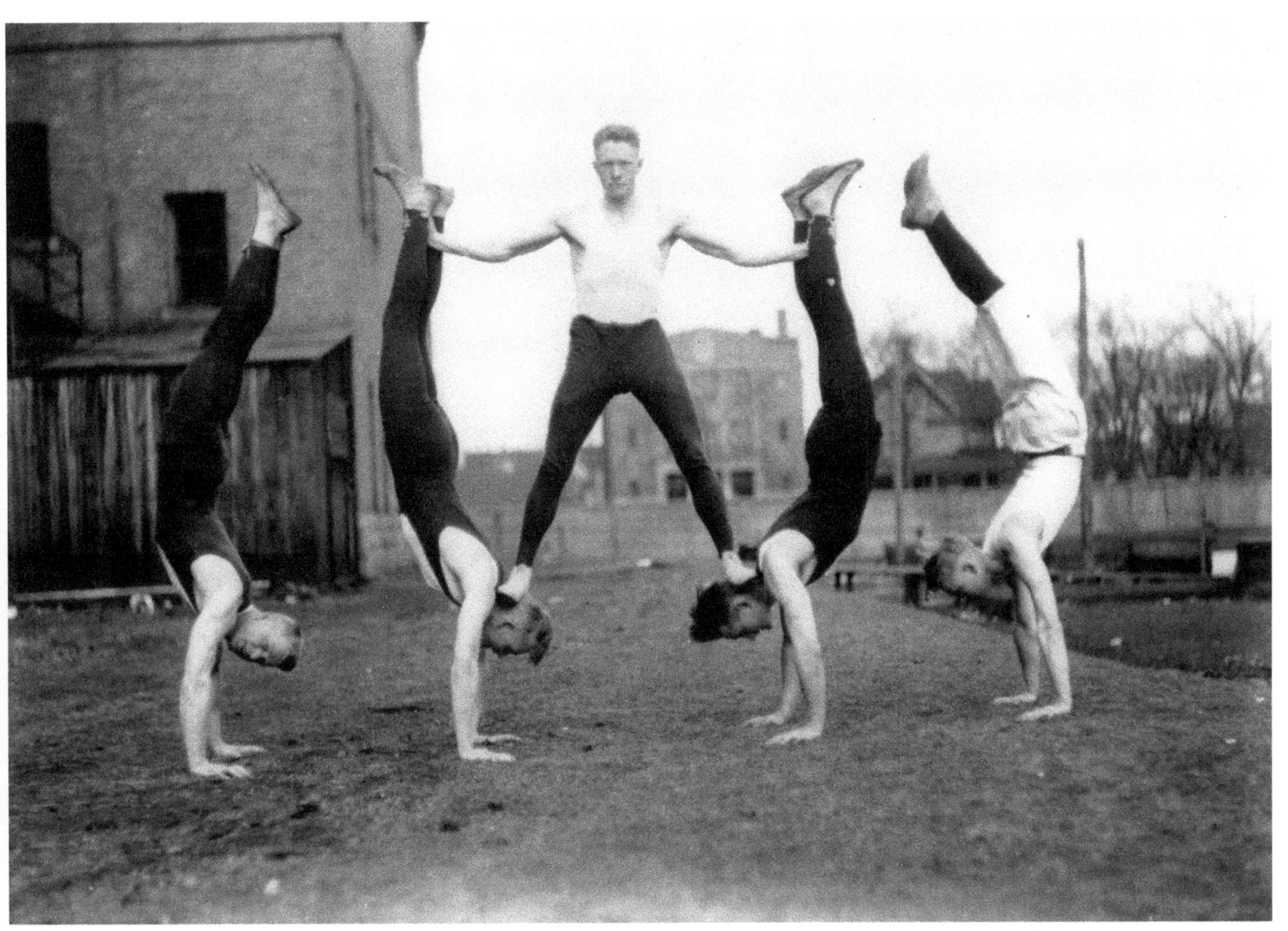

An impressive gymnastic formation and show of neck-strength, most likely by University of Minnesota students in Minneapolis, around 1920.

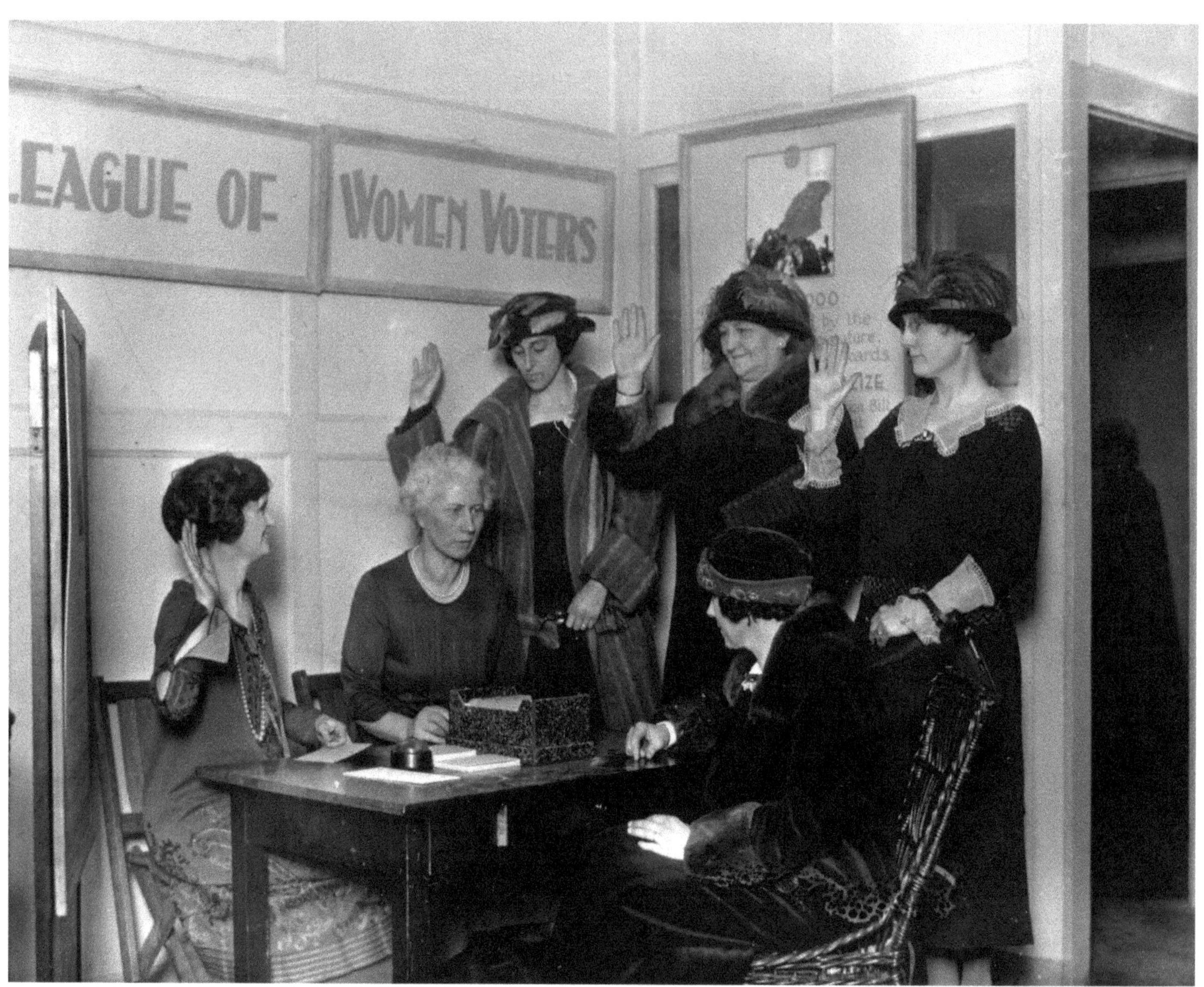


Minnesota's League of Women Voters swear in new members or register women to vote, around 1923. After the Minnesota legislature ratified the 19th Amendment, granting women the right to vote, on September 8, 1919, the Minnesota Suffrage Association dissolved, becoming the Minnesota League of Women Voters. Their purpose was to "complete full enfranchisement of women and increase effectiveness of women's votes in furthering better government."

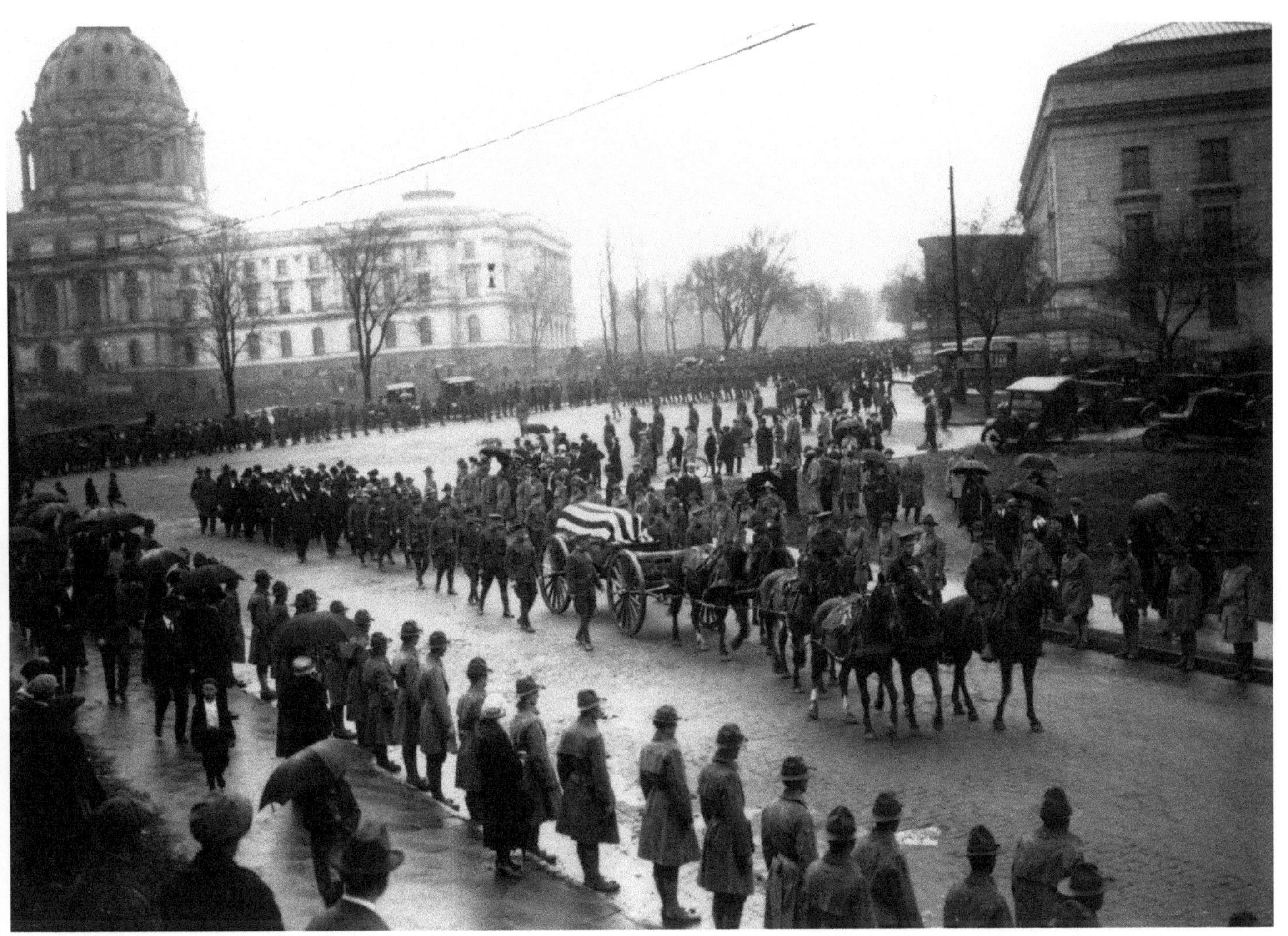

The funeral procession for politician Knute Nelson passes the former home of the Minnesota Historical Society on Cedar Street in St. Paul, May 1923. Nelson was a well-loved statesman who was born in Norway in 1842 and immigrated to Wisconsin. He was wounded and taken prisoner while serving in the Union army during the Civil War. Nelson went on to serve in the Wisconsin legislature, Minnesota legislature, U.S. House of Representatives, and U.S. Senate, and also served as governor of Minnesota.

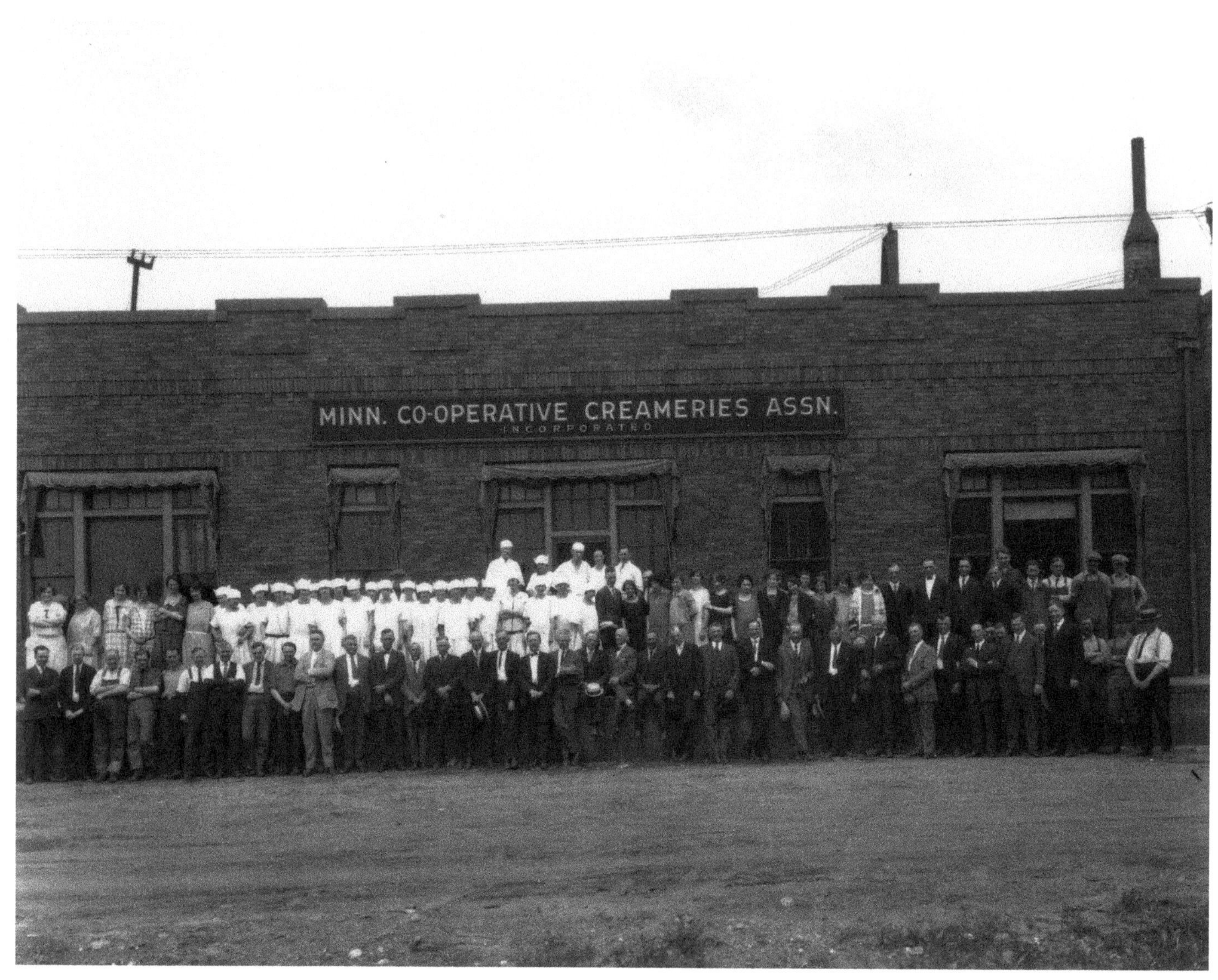


Board members, creamery workers, and other employees of the Minnesota Cooperative Creameries Association gather for a group photo in 1922. In February 1924, the cooperative announced a contest to name its butter. Two contestants tied for first place with the suggestion of "Land O'Lakes." Soon after, the company changed its name to Land O'Lakes Creameries.

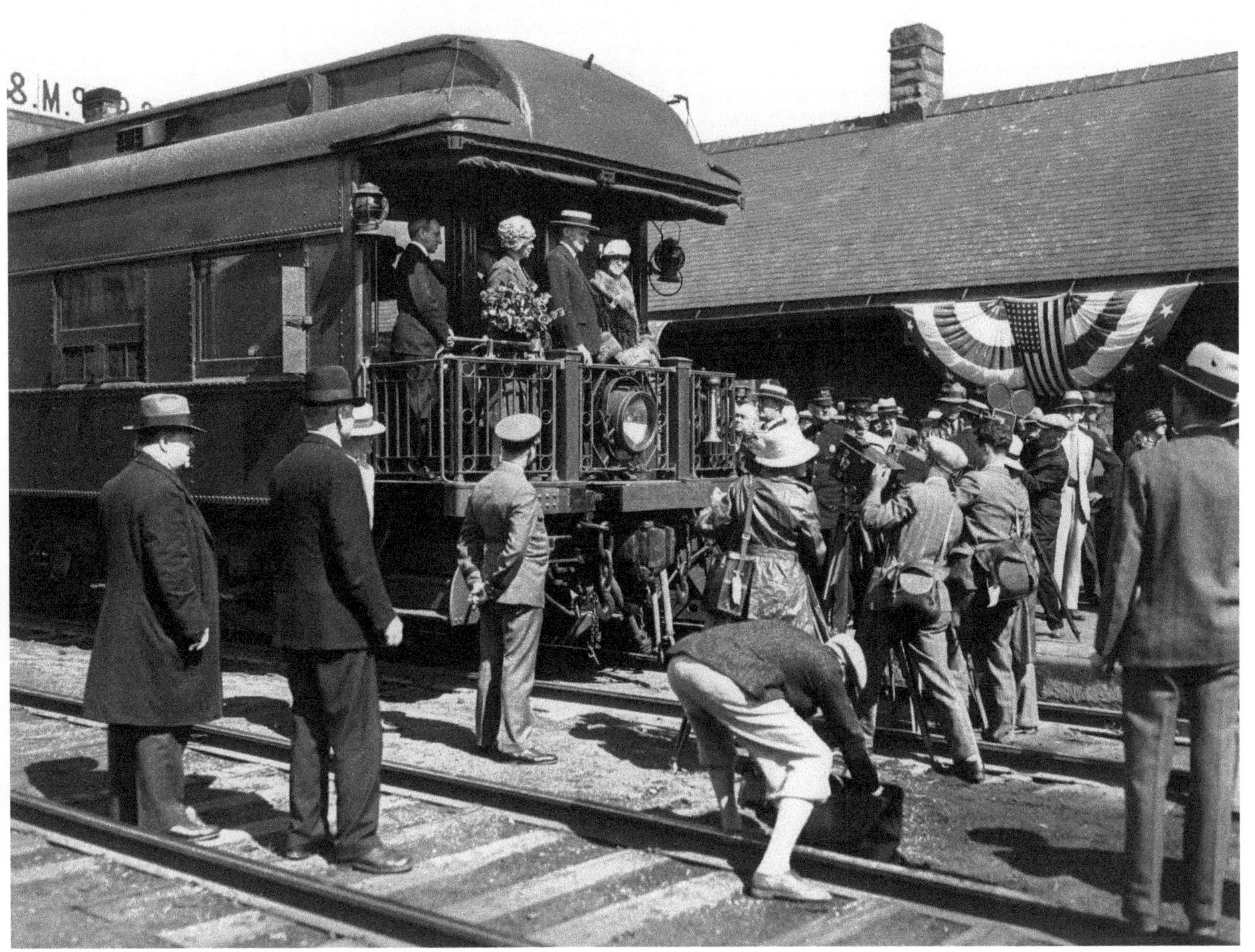

Newsreel cameramen capture Calvin Coolidge on the presidential whistle-stop campaign trail through Minnesota in 1924. When this photo was taken, Coolidge had recently lost his son to a deadly infection.

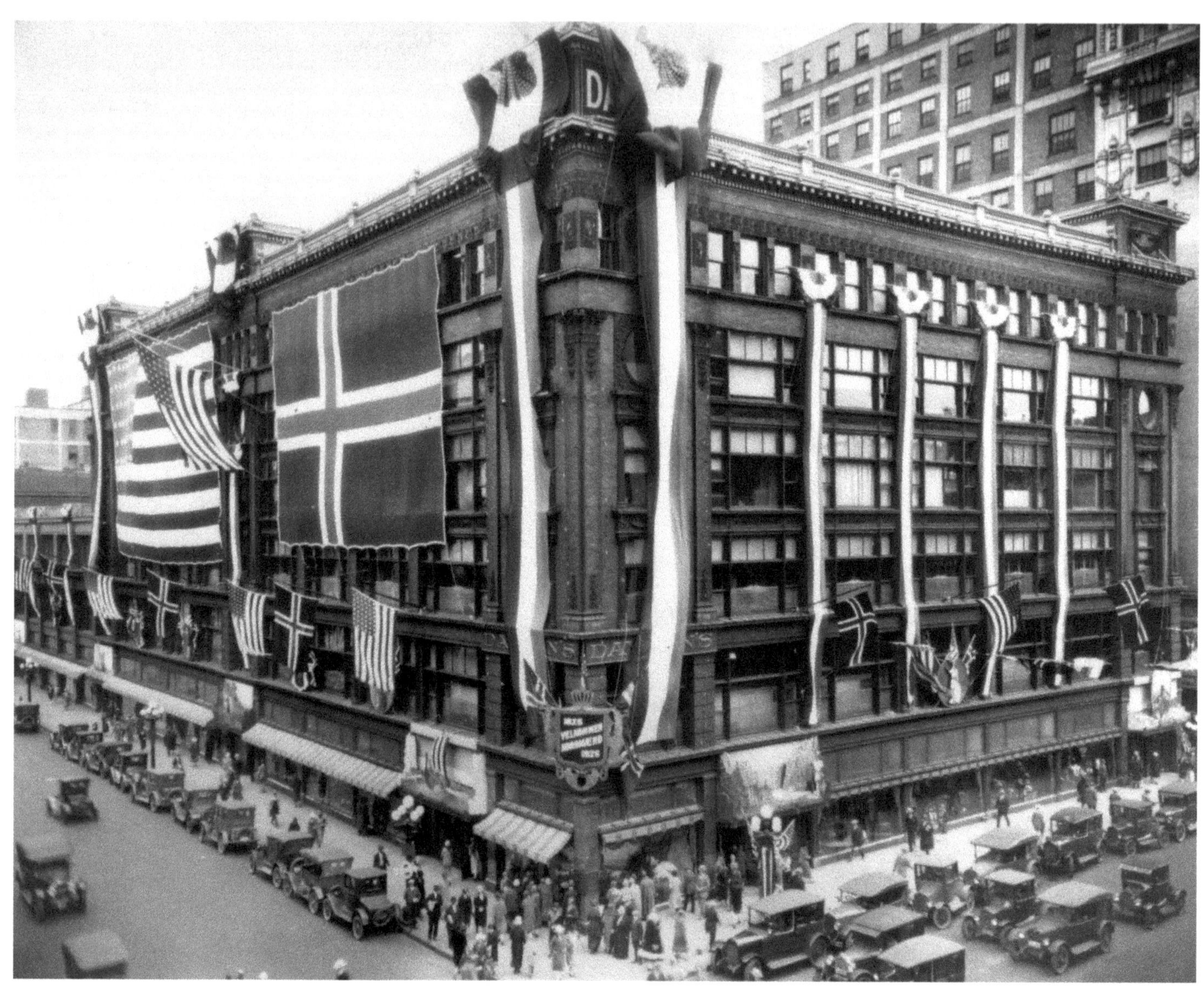

Downtown Minneapolis shoppers in 1925 gather in front of Scandinavian window displays at Dayton's Department Store. George Draper Dayton, originally a banker from Worthington, constructed this six-story building at Nicollet Avenue and Seventh Street in 1902. Dayton's Department Stores grew to be a retail icon in the Midwest.

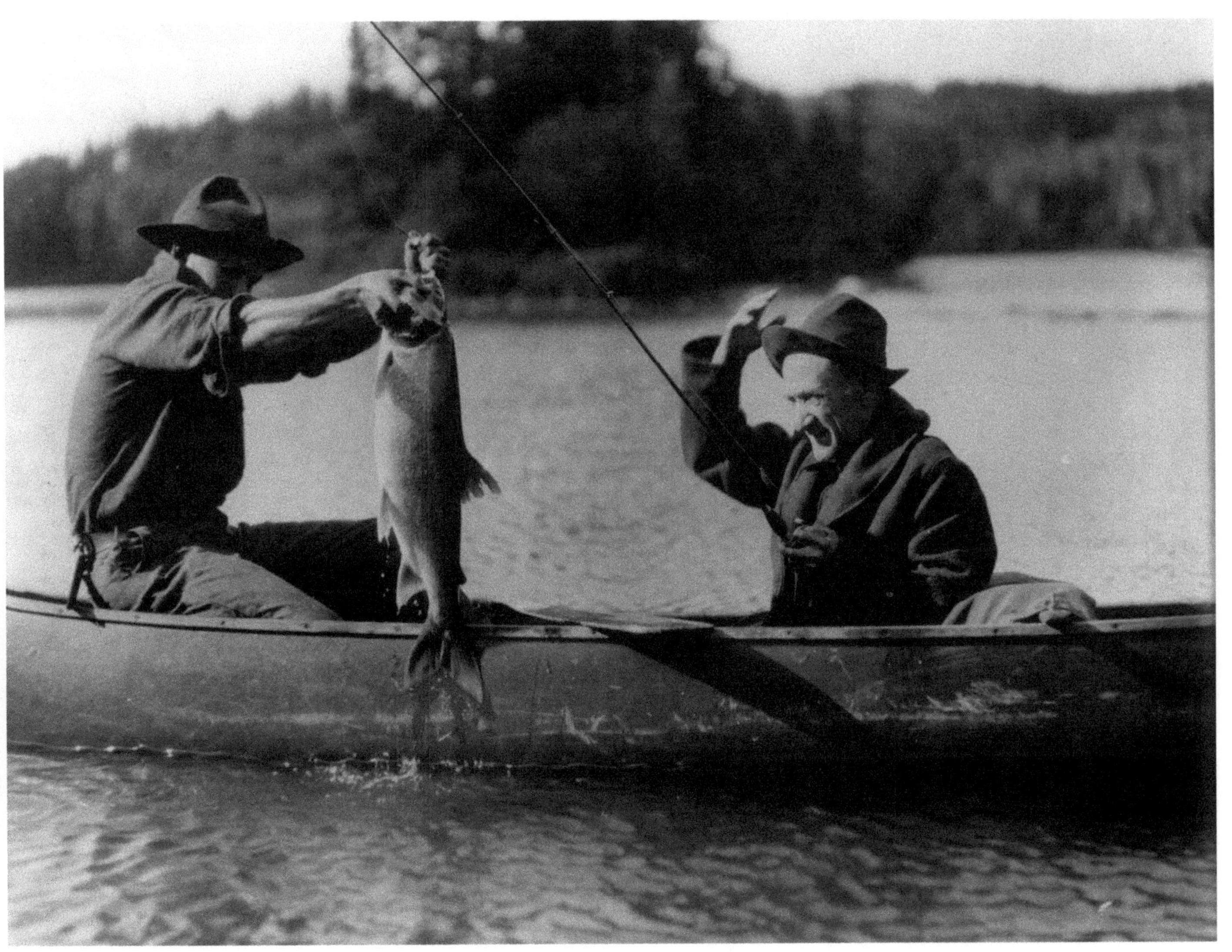

Two anglers in a canoe catch a good-sized trout from a Minnesota lake around 1925. Anglers traveled from all over the world to fish Minnesota's pristine lakes.

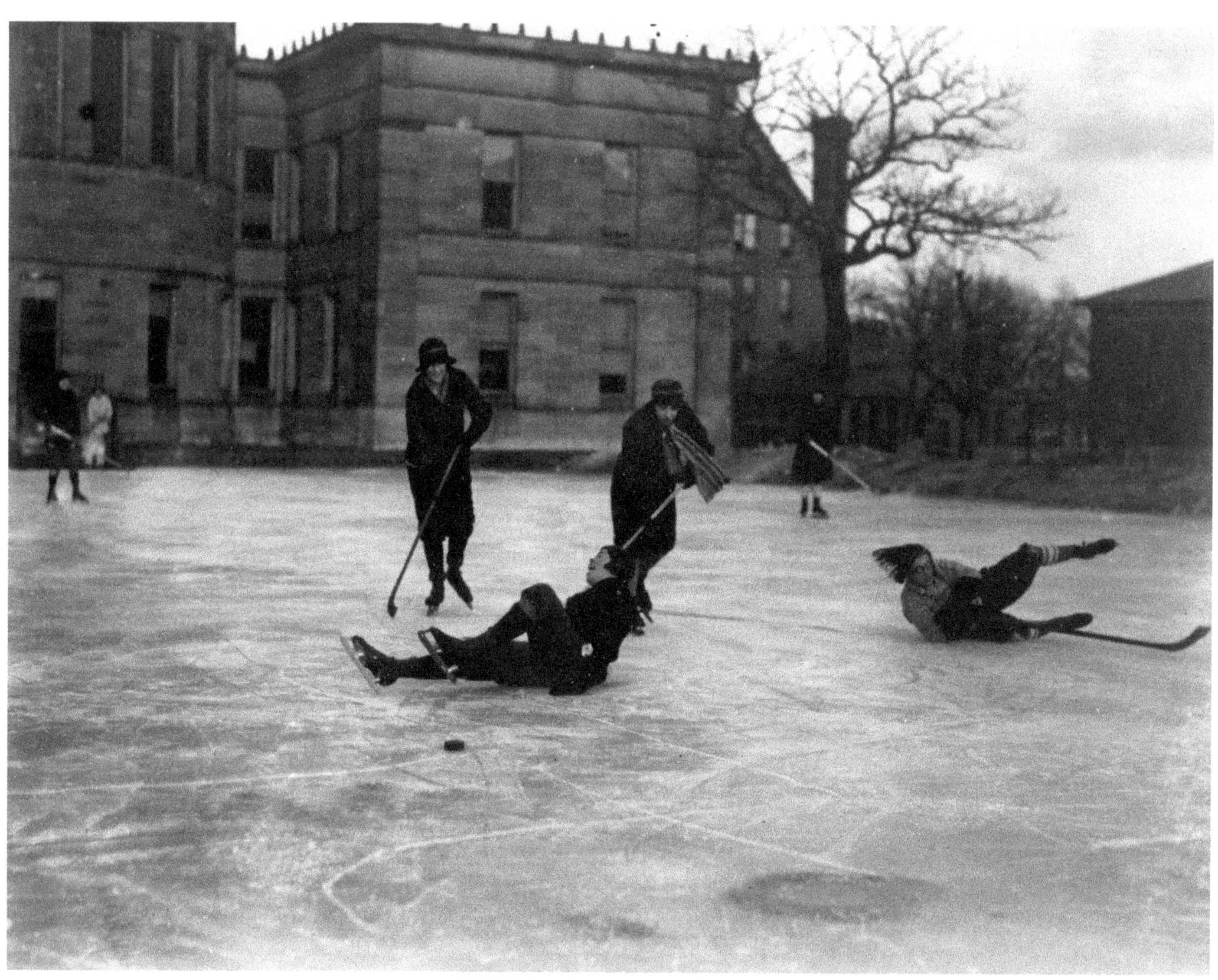

Photographed around 1925, women play hockey (and some fall trying) on a rink behind Burton Hall at the University of Minnesota's Minneapolis campus.

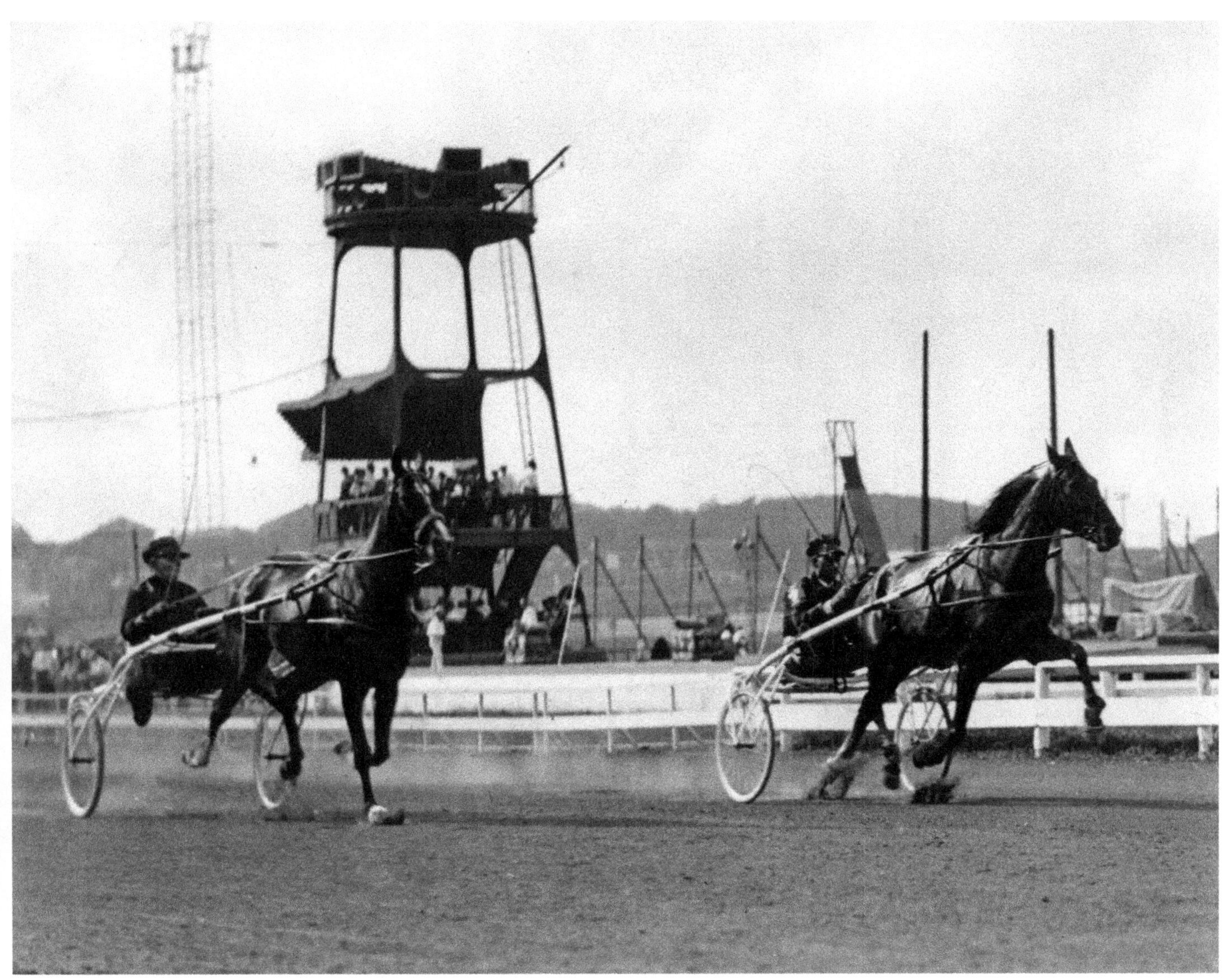

Harness racing was popularized at the Minnesota State Fair by the legendary racehorse Dan Patch, who never lost a race and set world records in the early part of the century. This photo shows harness racing at the fair in 1925. Race commentary was announced through the speakers on the judging stand. The speakers were installed by the Northwestern Bell Telephone Company and were touted to transmit a human voice five miles.

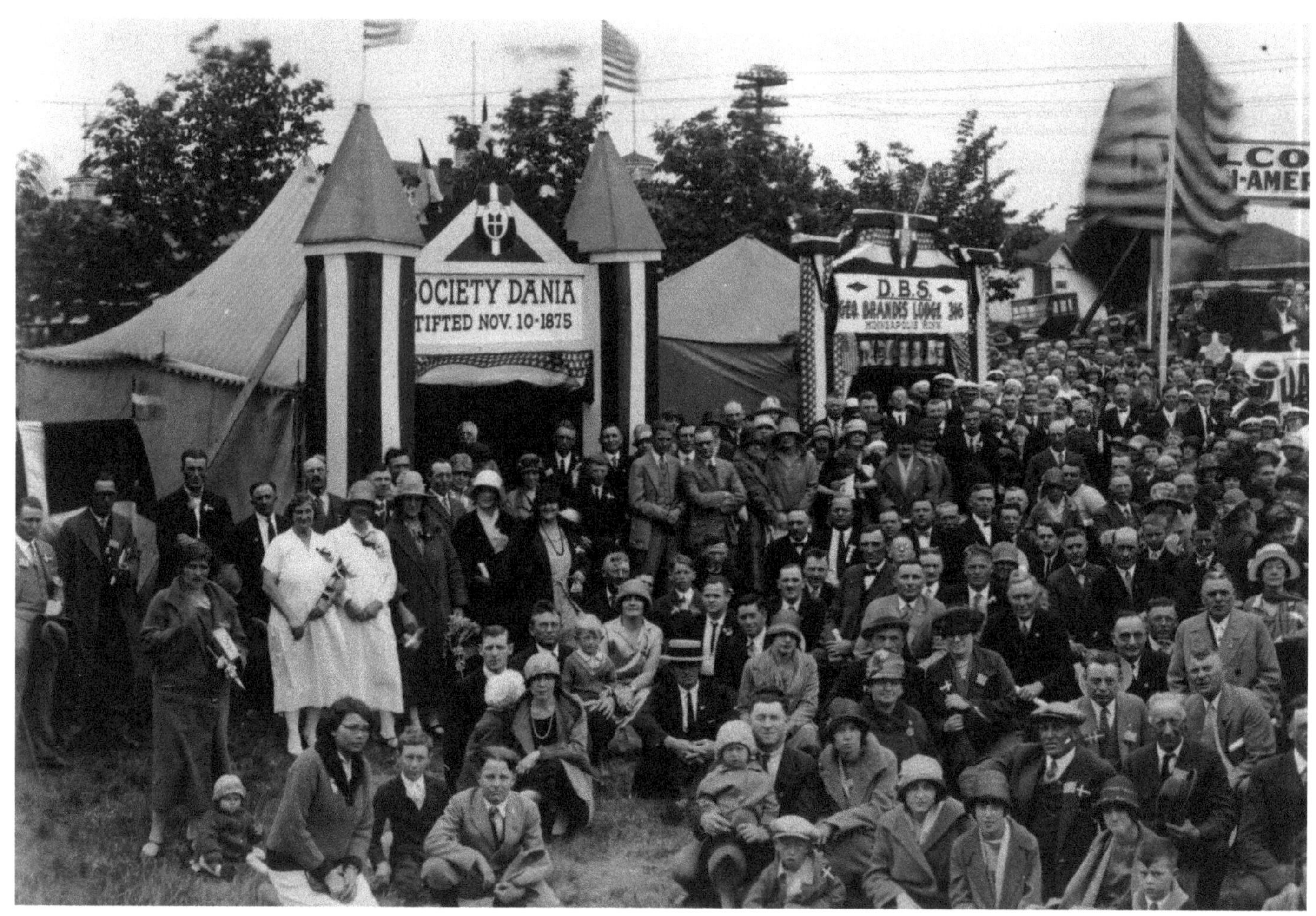


A large group poses at a Danish festival in 1926. Danes made up the third-largest Scandinavian group to settle en masse in Minnesota, behind the Swedes and Norwegians. Around the time this photo was taken, 16,904 Danish immigrants lived in Minnesota. They settled all over the state, with large pockets in Southern Minnesota.

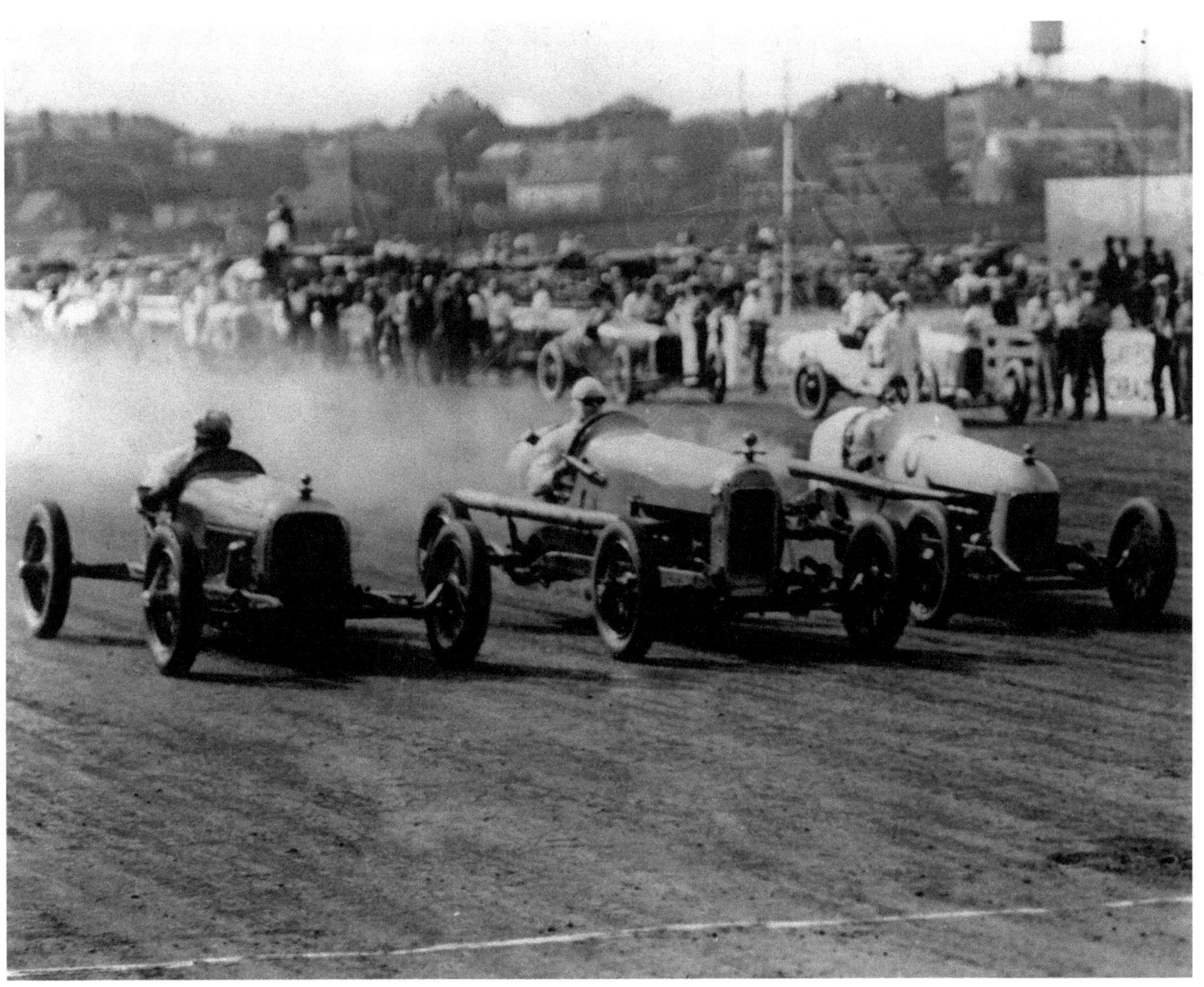

The second heat looks close in a three-mile race at the Minnesota State Fair in 1927. During the fair, autos and horses alternated days racing around the track.

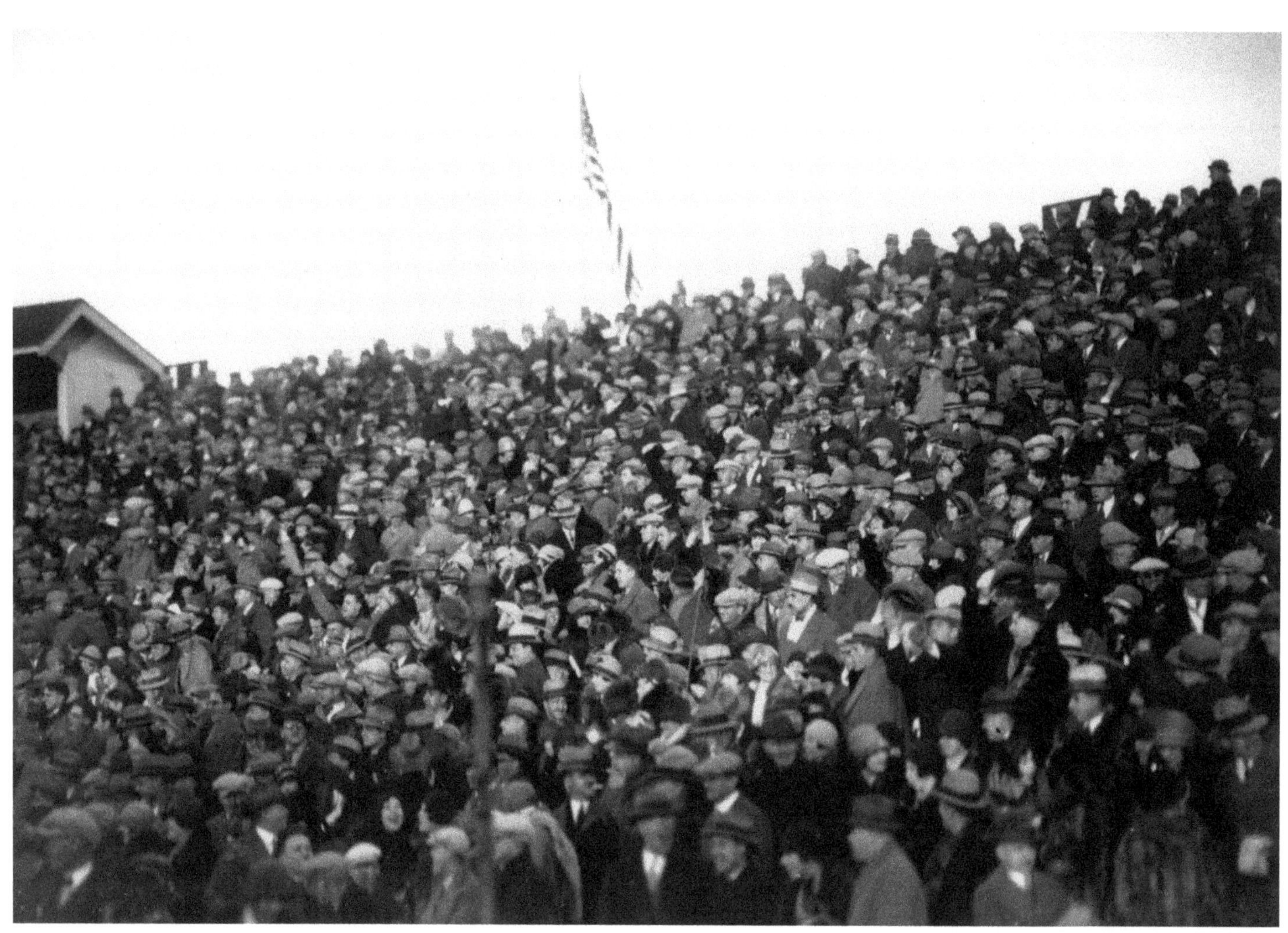

A crowd cheers on the Minnesota Golden Gophers football team at the open-air Memorial Stadium. The stadium was built in 1924 to accommodate the growing popularity of the sport in the Twin Cities.

# Depression and War

## (1930–1945)

In the wake of the stock market crash of 1929, thousands of Minnesotans lost their jobs and homes. The Great Depression took a harrowing toll on the state from border to border, with massive Iron Range layoffs, farm foreclosures, and the long drought experienced in Minnesota as throughout the Great Plains. Many communities, especially small rural towns, pulled together and reached out to one another. Without a doubt, many would have perished, if not for the kind handouts of those who had almost nothing but gave to those who had even less.

Relief came to Minnesota through the Works Progress Administration and the Civilian Conservation Corps, two of President Franklin D. Roosevelt's New Deal agencies created to put people to work improving the nation's quality of life. The numerous projects undertaken by these agencies included the building and improvement of roads, schools, and public buildings, the creation of state parks, and an initiative to help preserve the area that would later become the Boundary Waters Canoe Area. Employed by the Public Works of Art Project and the WPA Federal Art Project, Minnesota artists painted and sculptured works of art for display in public buildings.

The Farm Security Administration, initially created as part of the Resettlement Administration, stepped in to promote "rural rehabilitation" efforts in poverty-stricken rural areas of Minnesota. This controversial project resettled poor farmers on group farms for greater efficiency. The FSA eventually failed, but it lives on through documentation by the famous FSA photography program. Photographers such as Russell Lee were charged with depicting realistically the challenges of rural poverty.

A great economic boost was given to Minnesota when the United States entered the Second World War in 1941. Patriotism hit a fever pitch as thousands of Minnesotans enlisted. Wartime production of ships and artillery soared in areas like Savage, Duluth, and the Twin Cities, and thousands of Minnesota women filled factory positions, doing jobs generally thought of as "man's work."

The call of the wild was undeniable in Northern Minnesota, even during trying economic times. Camping, hiking, fishing, and canoeing were great and inexpensive forms of escape.

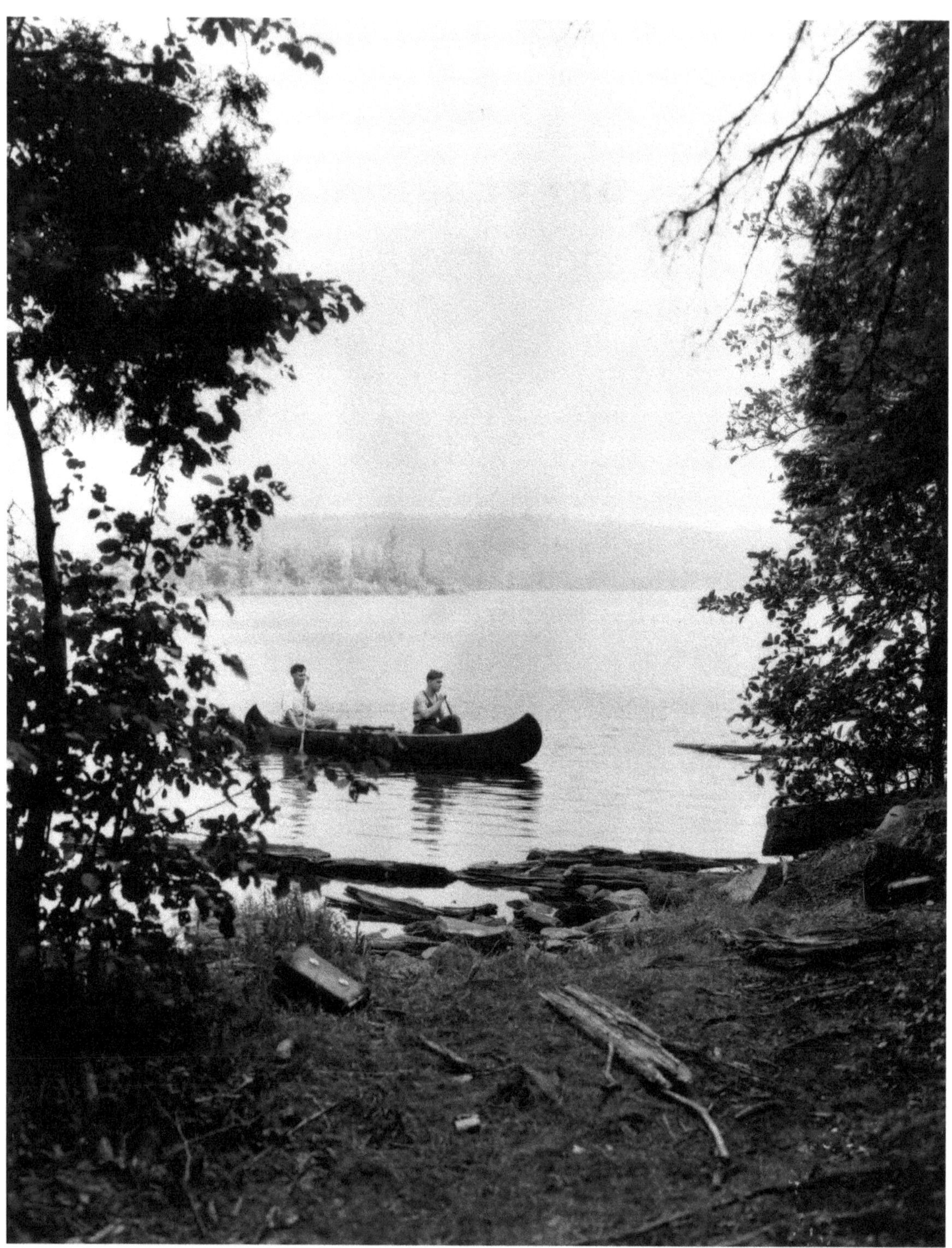

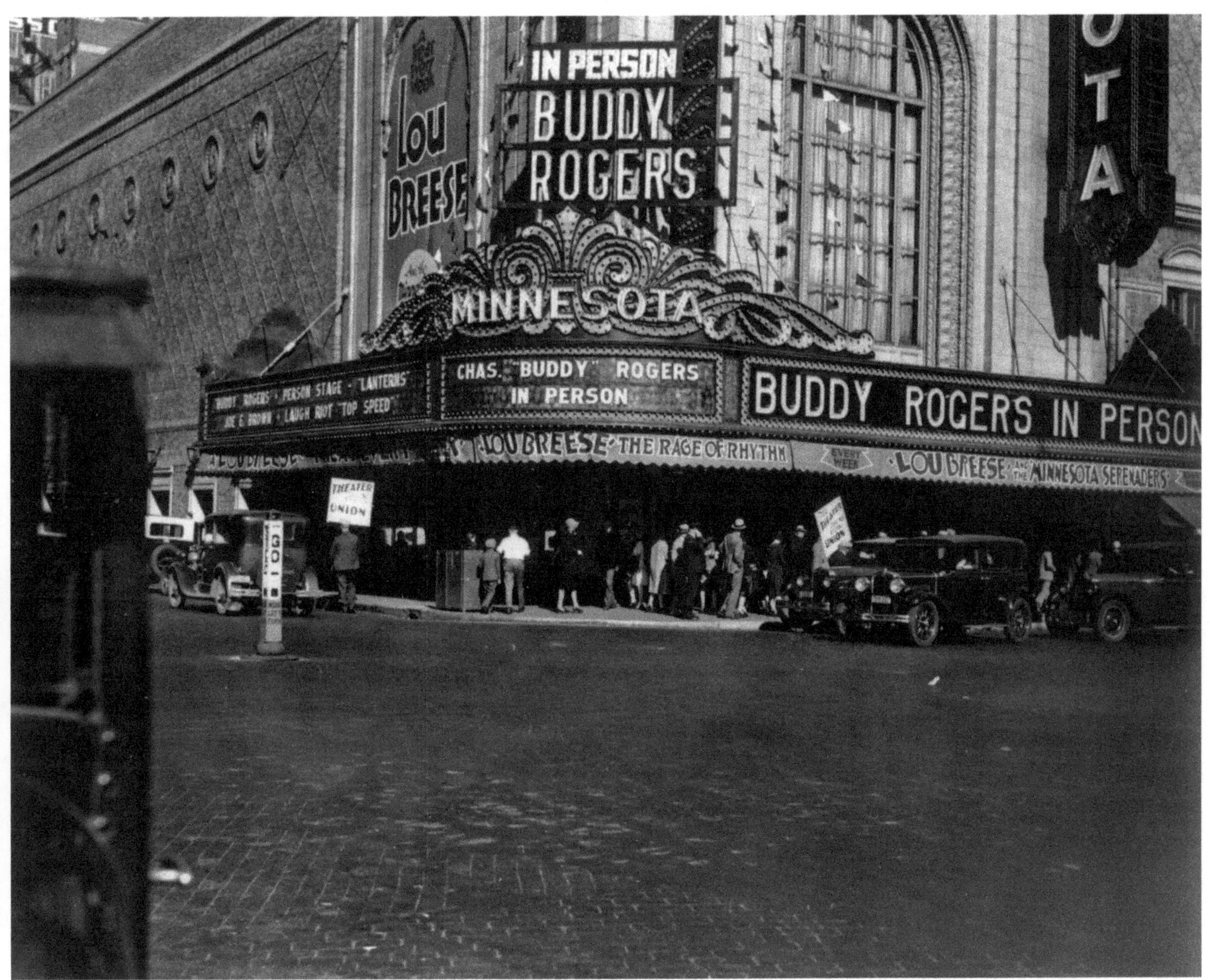


Here on September 29, 1930, the Minnesota Theater in Minneapolis is being picketed for hiring nonunion labor. Built in 1928, the 4,000-seat theater was once the fifth-largest in the country.

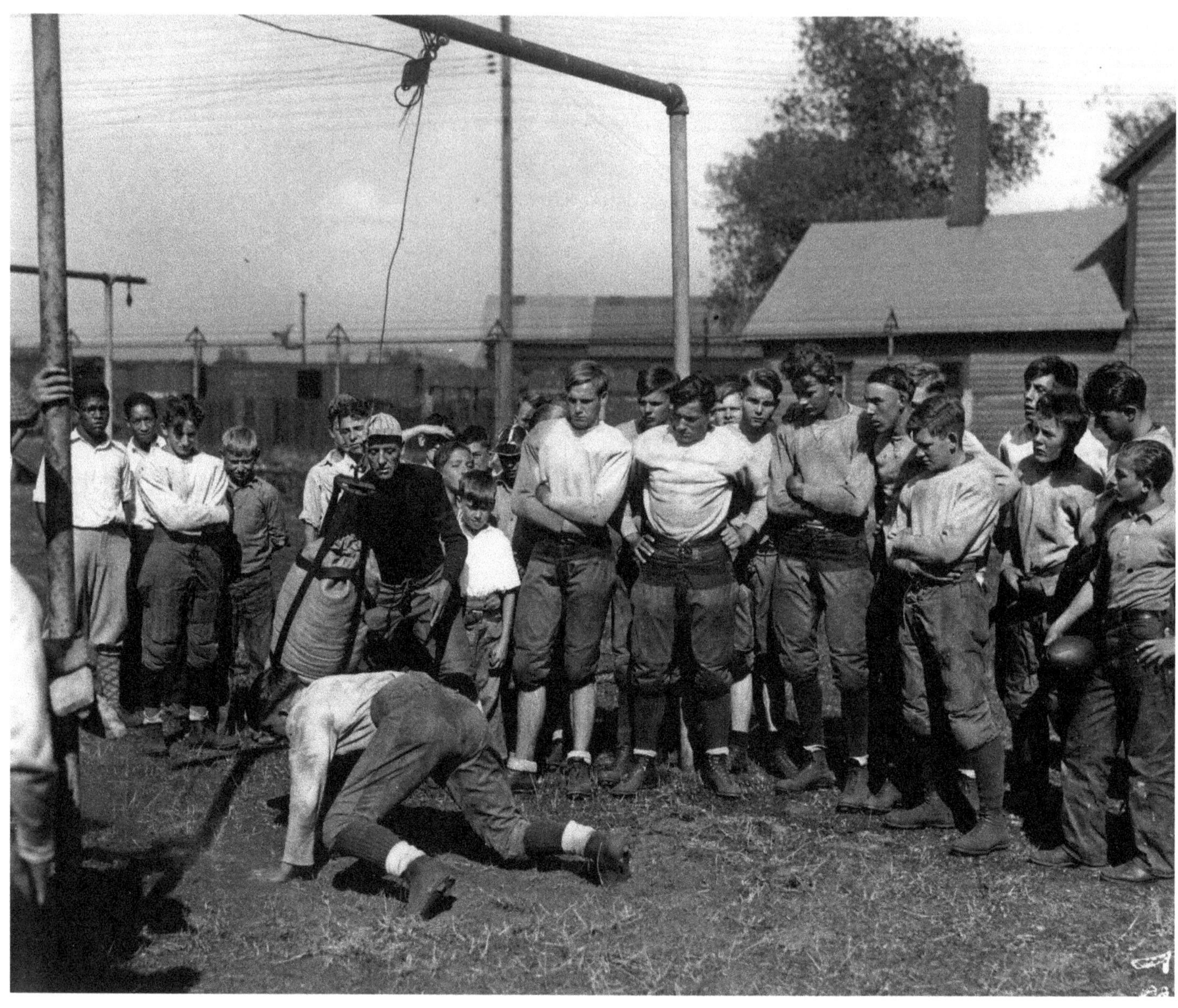

The Minneapolis South High School football team prepares for the new season in the fall of 1930. Football fever was undeniable in the Twin Cities, and many boys dreamed of becoming all-star football heroes.

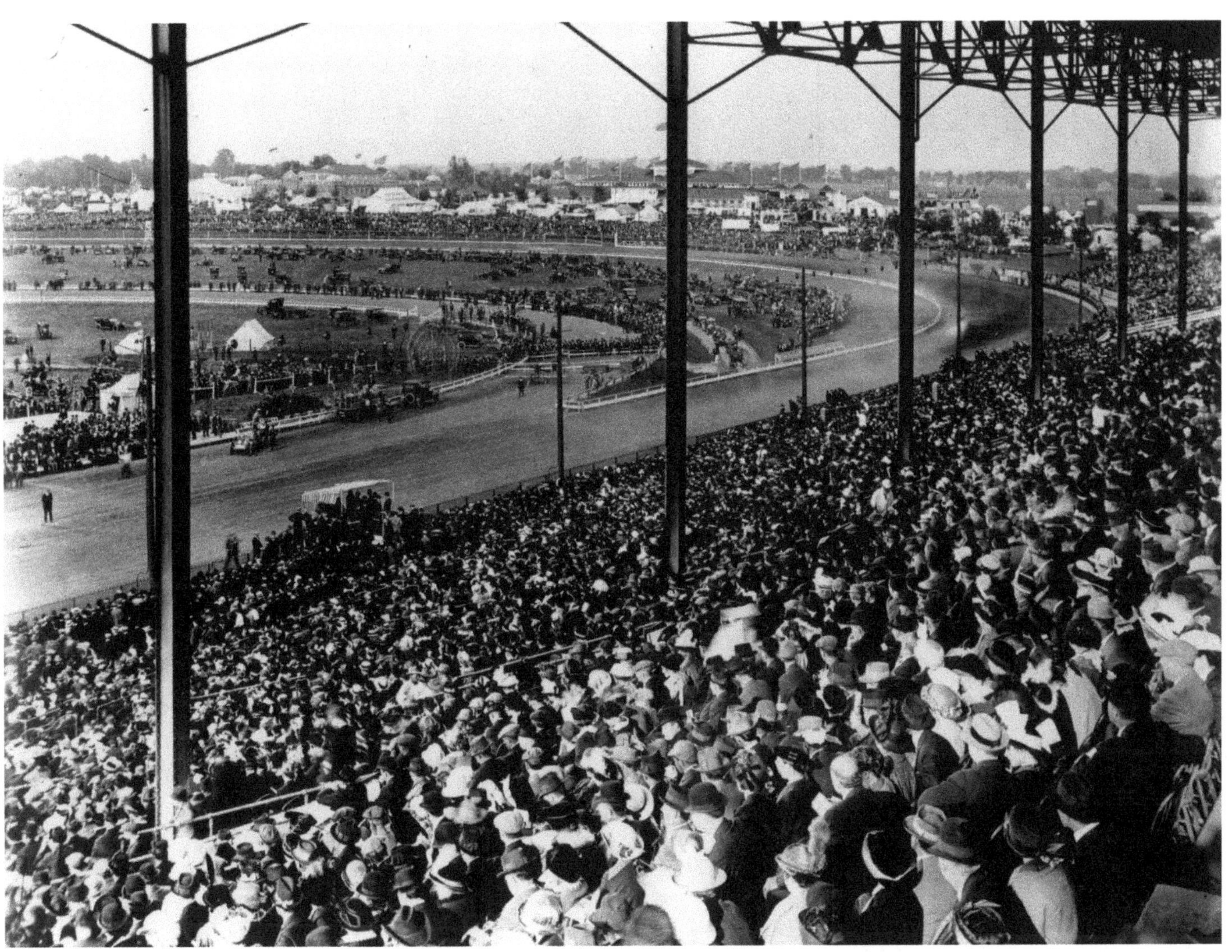

Minnesota State Fair attendees pack the grandstand around 1930. To accommodate such crowds, the original wooden grandstand was replaced in 1909 with a new brick grandstand that could seat 22,000.

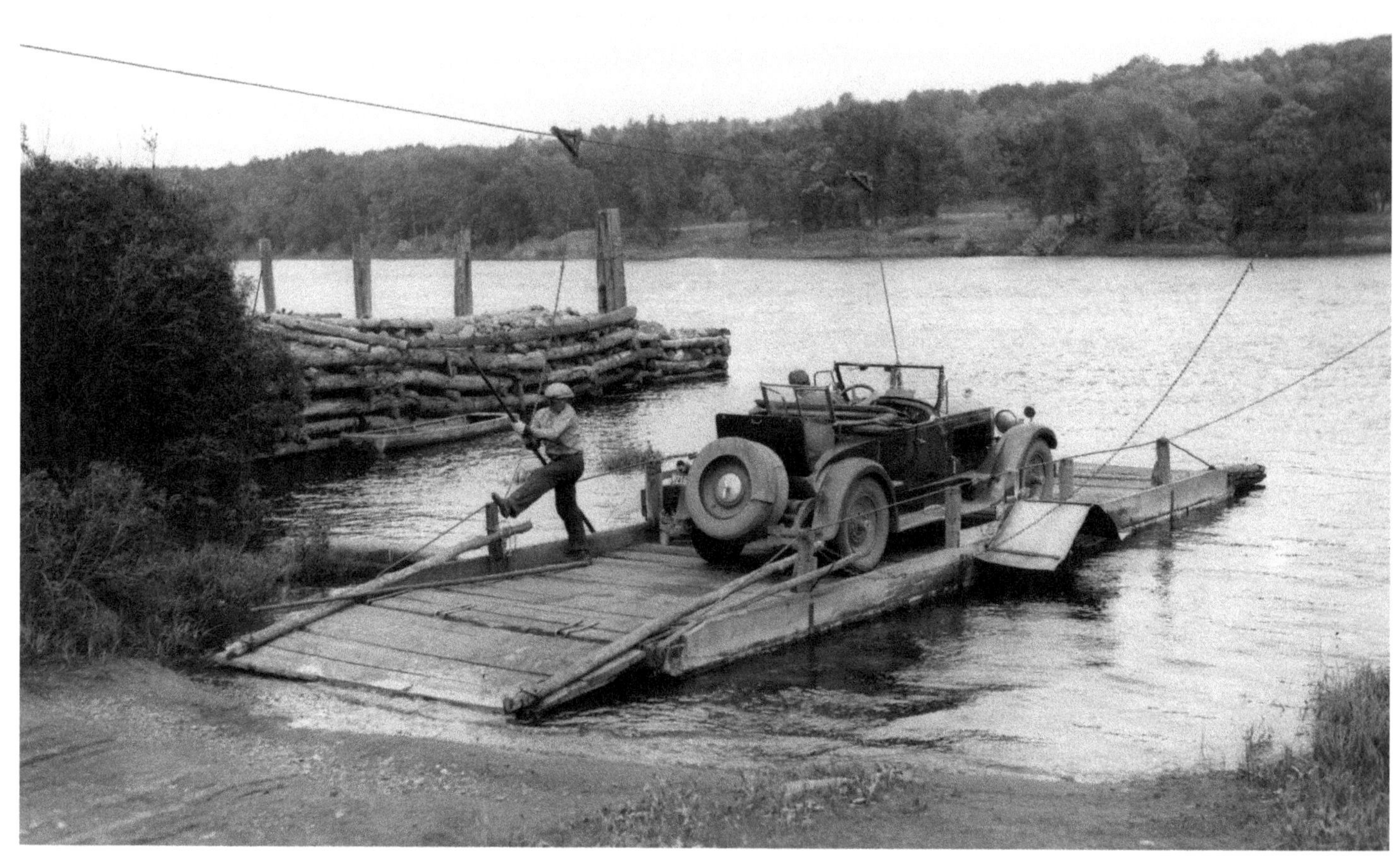

In June 1931, a man in Rush City guides a ferry carrying an automobile across the St. Croix River to Wisconsin by means of the ferry's cable system.

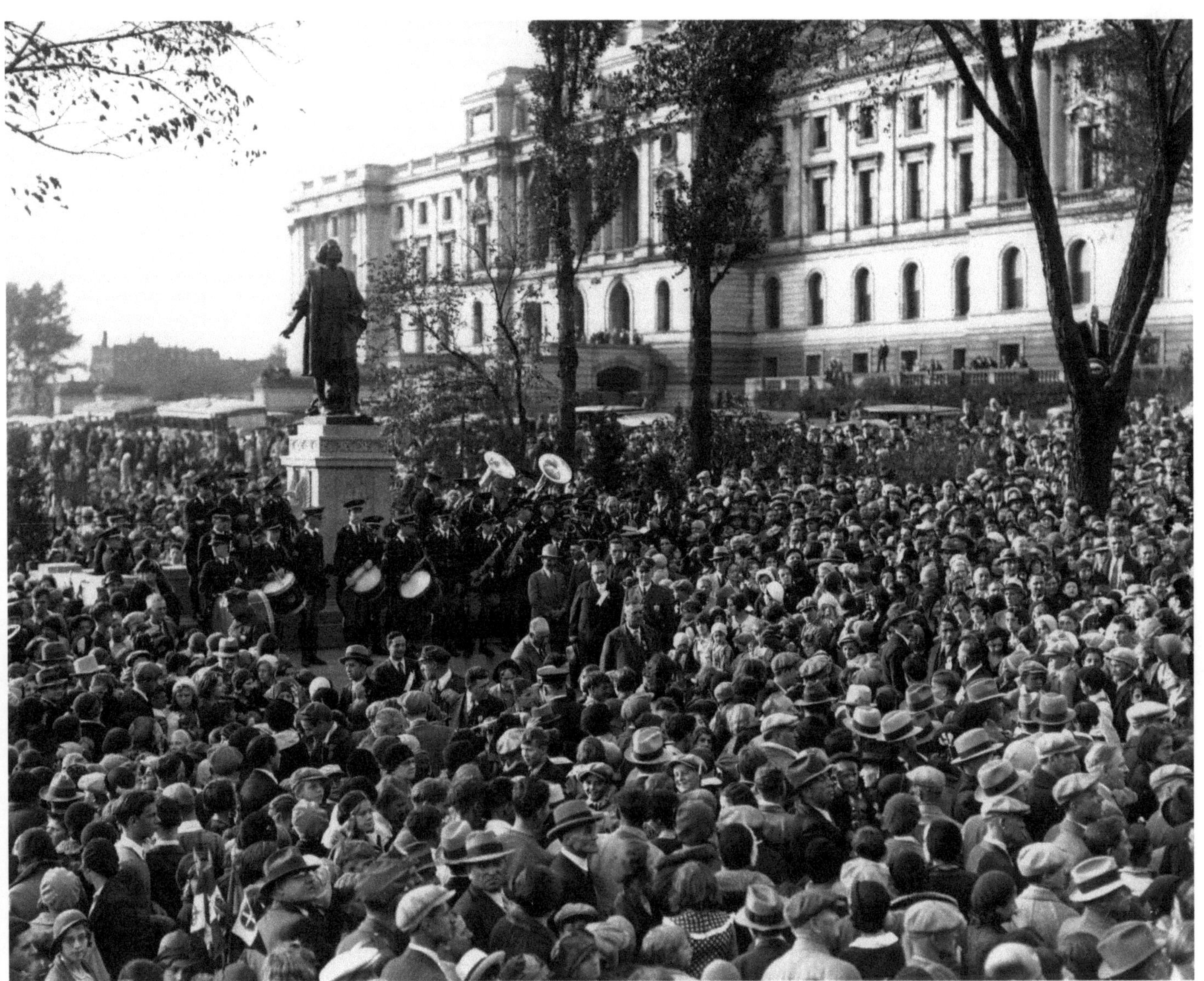

On October 12, 1931, a crowd of 25,000 gathered for the unveiling and dedication of the Christopher Columbus statue on the State Capitol grounds. The Columbus Day celebration began with a parade that made its way from Rice Park to the Capitol. The statue was a gift from the Columbus Memorial Association—a group composed of Italian societies in Minnesota.

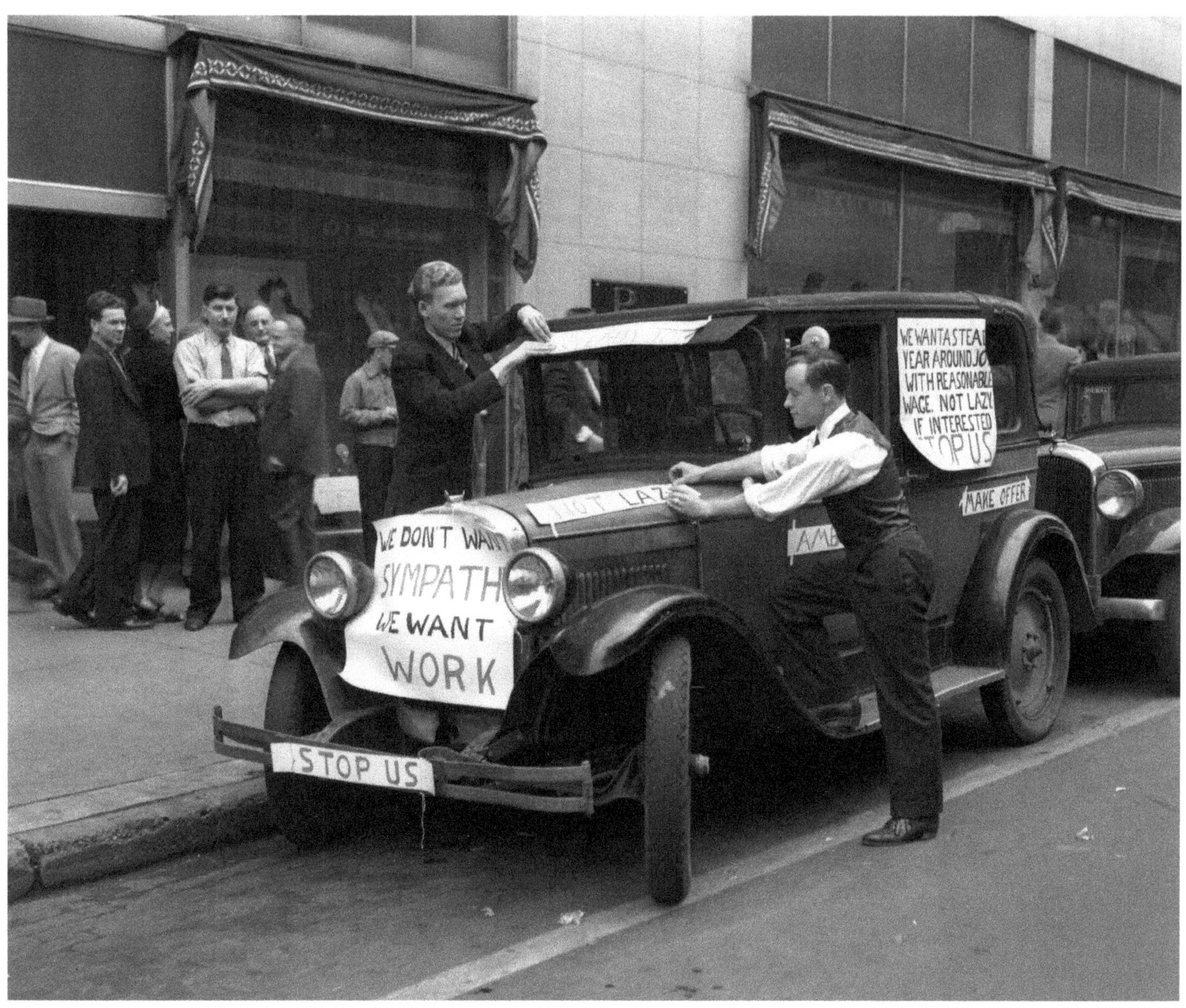


The Great Depression left millions out of work, including these two innovative Minnesota job seekers. Established in 1935, the Works Progress Administration helped alleviate some of the burden in Minnesota, as elsewhere. The WPA funded projects to improve streets, sewers, and schools. White-collar jobs also opened up—indexing newspaper articles for libraries, organizing the Health Department's birth records, updating the city assessor's plat maps, and coordinating educational programs in the arts.

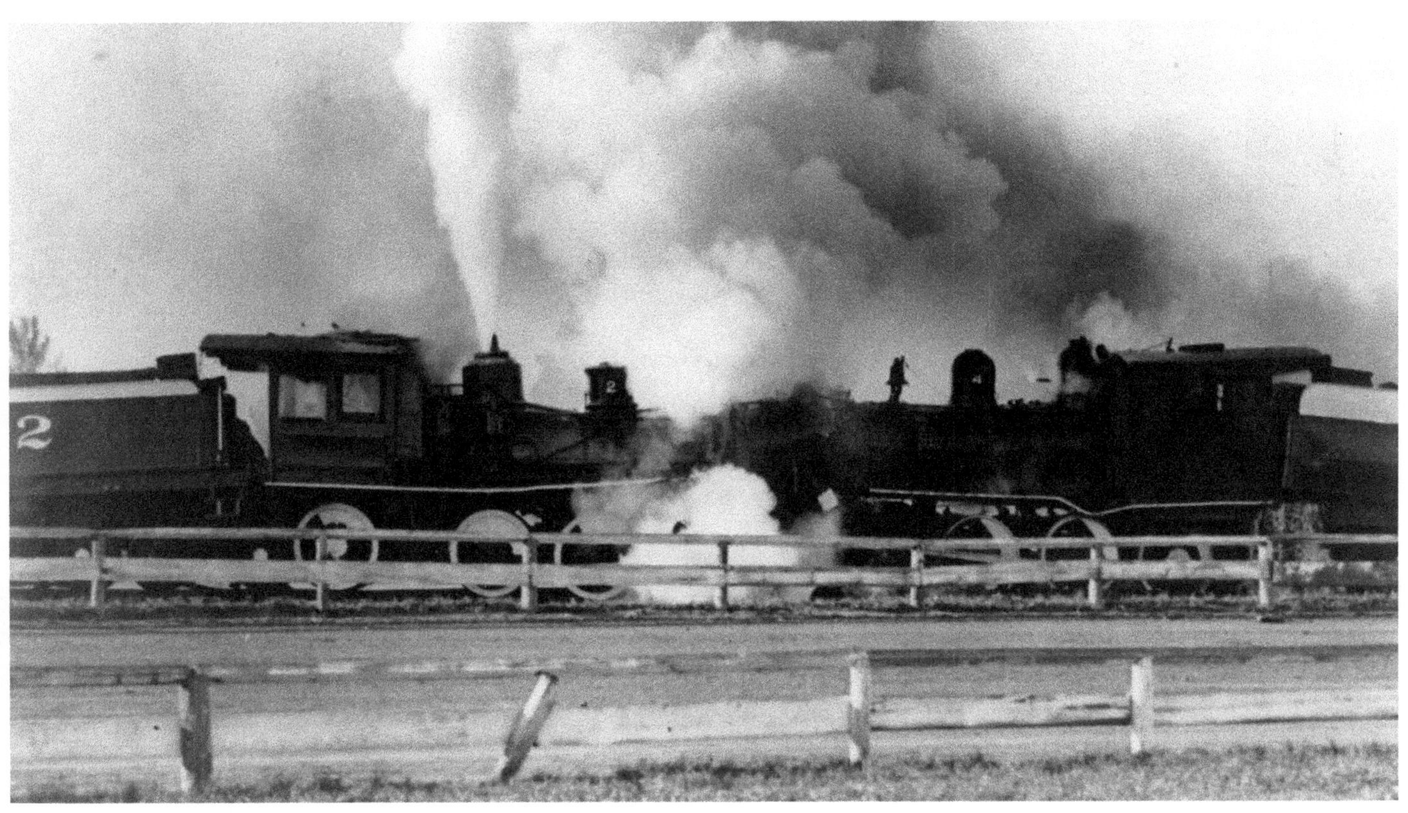


Thrill Day at the Minnesota State Fair provided another form of escapism for thousands of spectators. In 1934, the main attraction was a "Duel to the Death" train collision. The locomotives careered toward each other at a combined speed of 100 miles per hour. The engineers leaped to safety after putting the trains in motion.

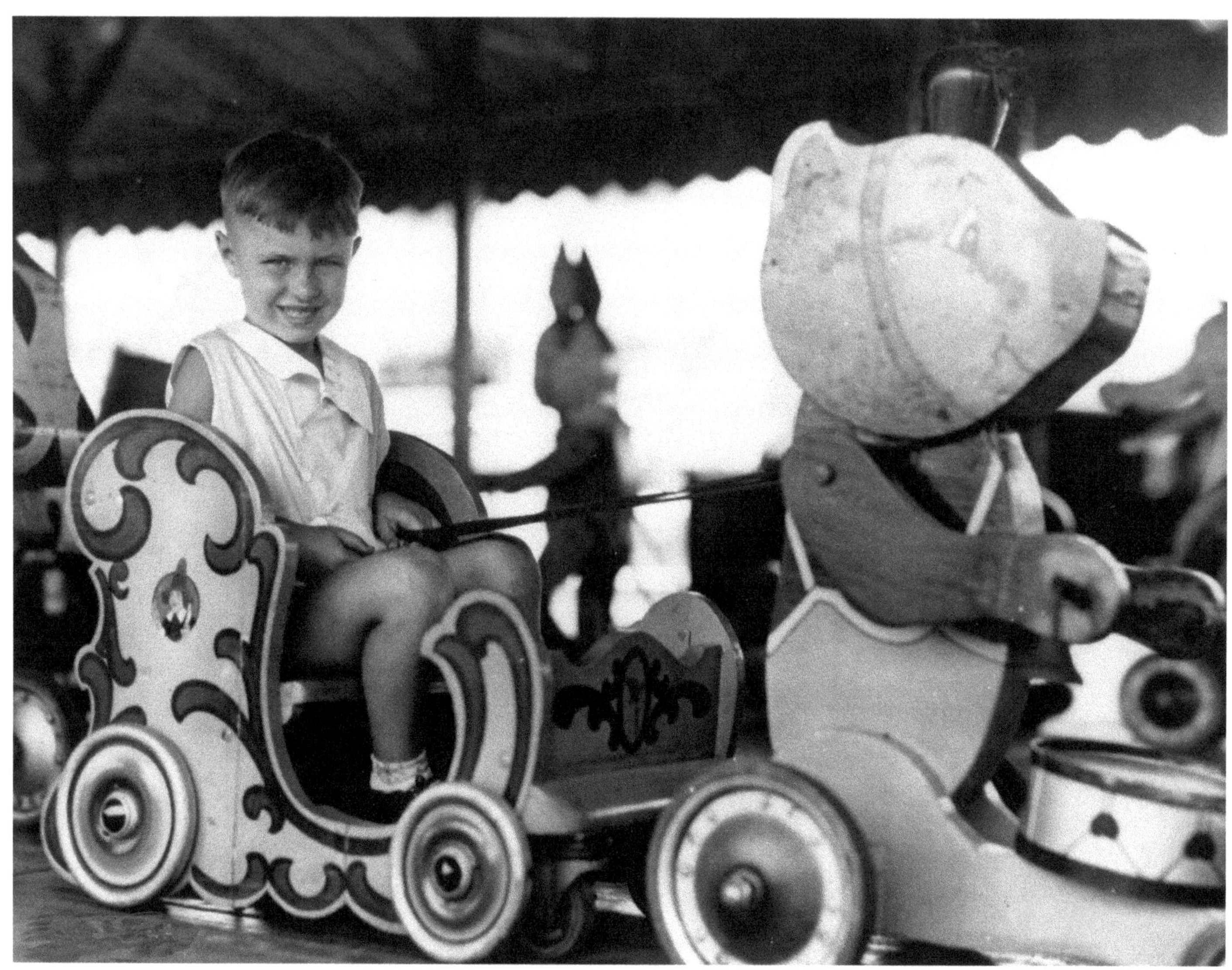

On Children's Day at the 1934 Minnesota State Fair, a boy poses on a merry-go-round ride. According to the *St. Paul Pioneer Press*, "The fair turned 75 years old in 1934 and never looked younger," due to WPA-funded projects that provided a new front grate, new buildings, new sidewalks, and extensive cosmetic improvements throughout the fairgrounds.

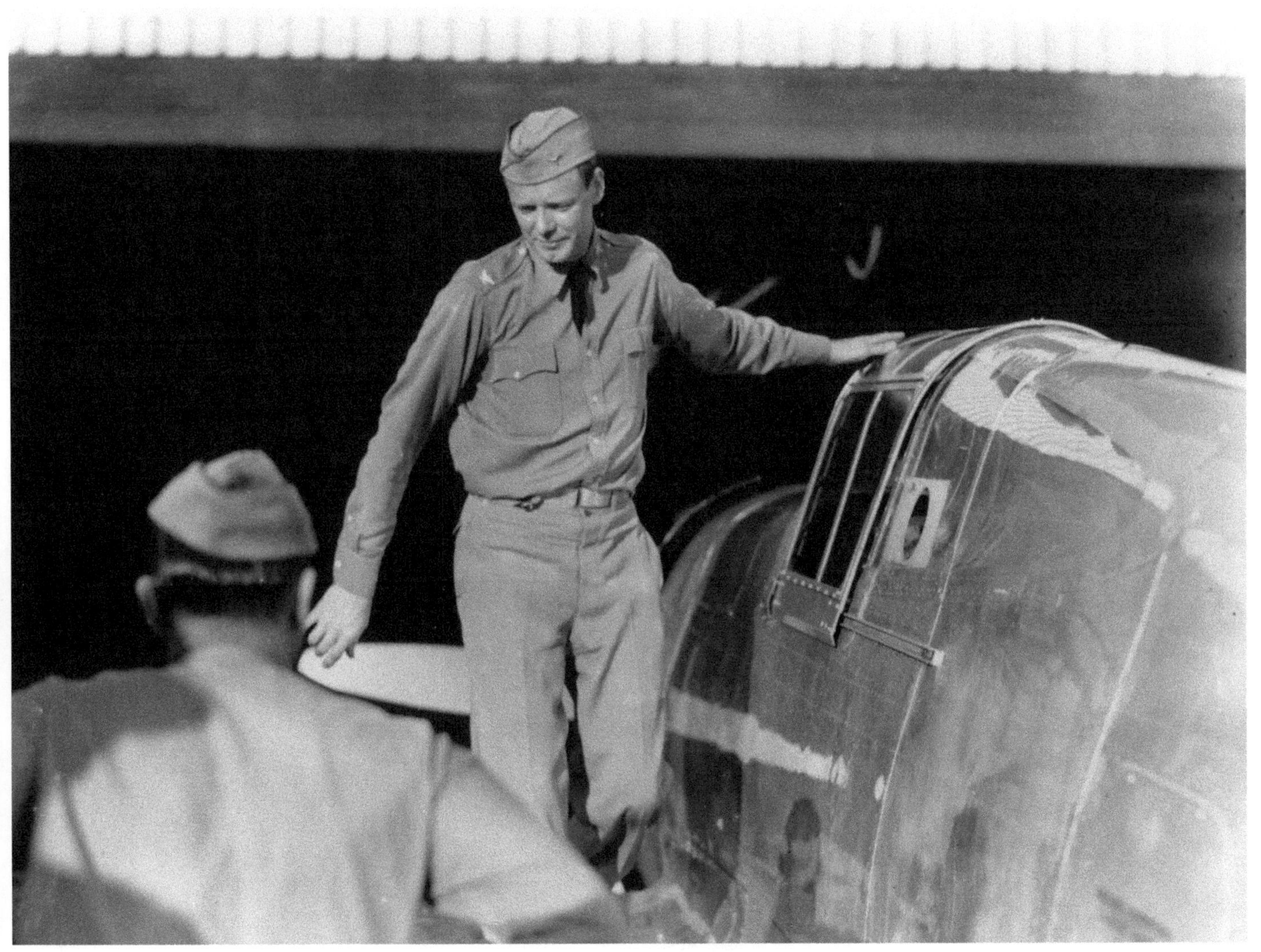

Charles A. Lindbergh visits with the men of the 109th Observation Squadron at Camp Ripley near Little Falls, around 1935. Lindbergh, famous for making the first solo nonstop flight across the Atlantic Ocean, May 20-21, 1927, grew up on a farm near Little Falls.

Two future musicians take turns trying out a baritone at the Minnesota State Fair in 1935, the first year of the fair's statewide band contest.

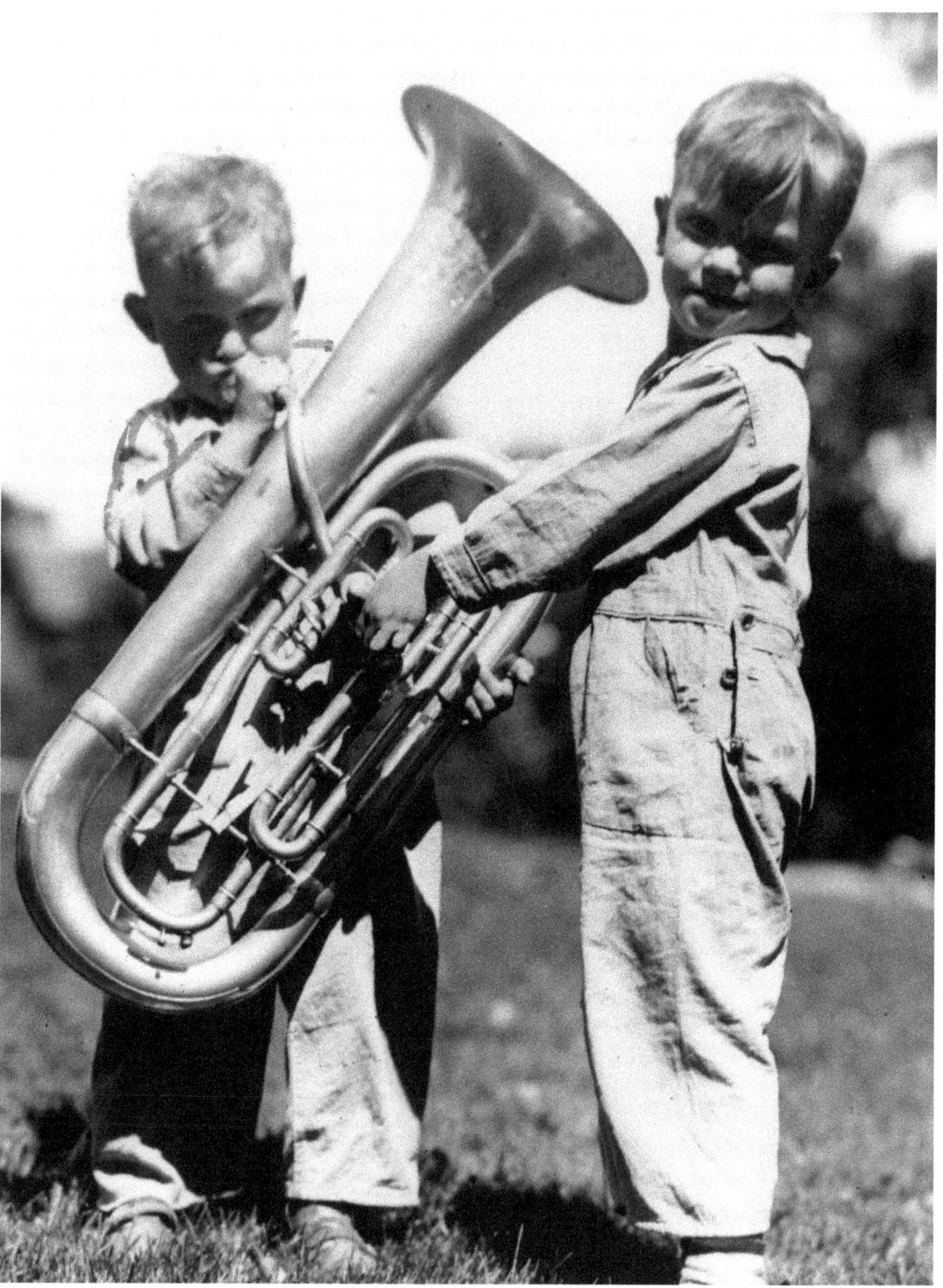

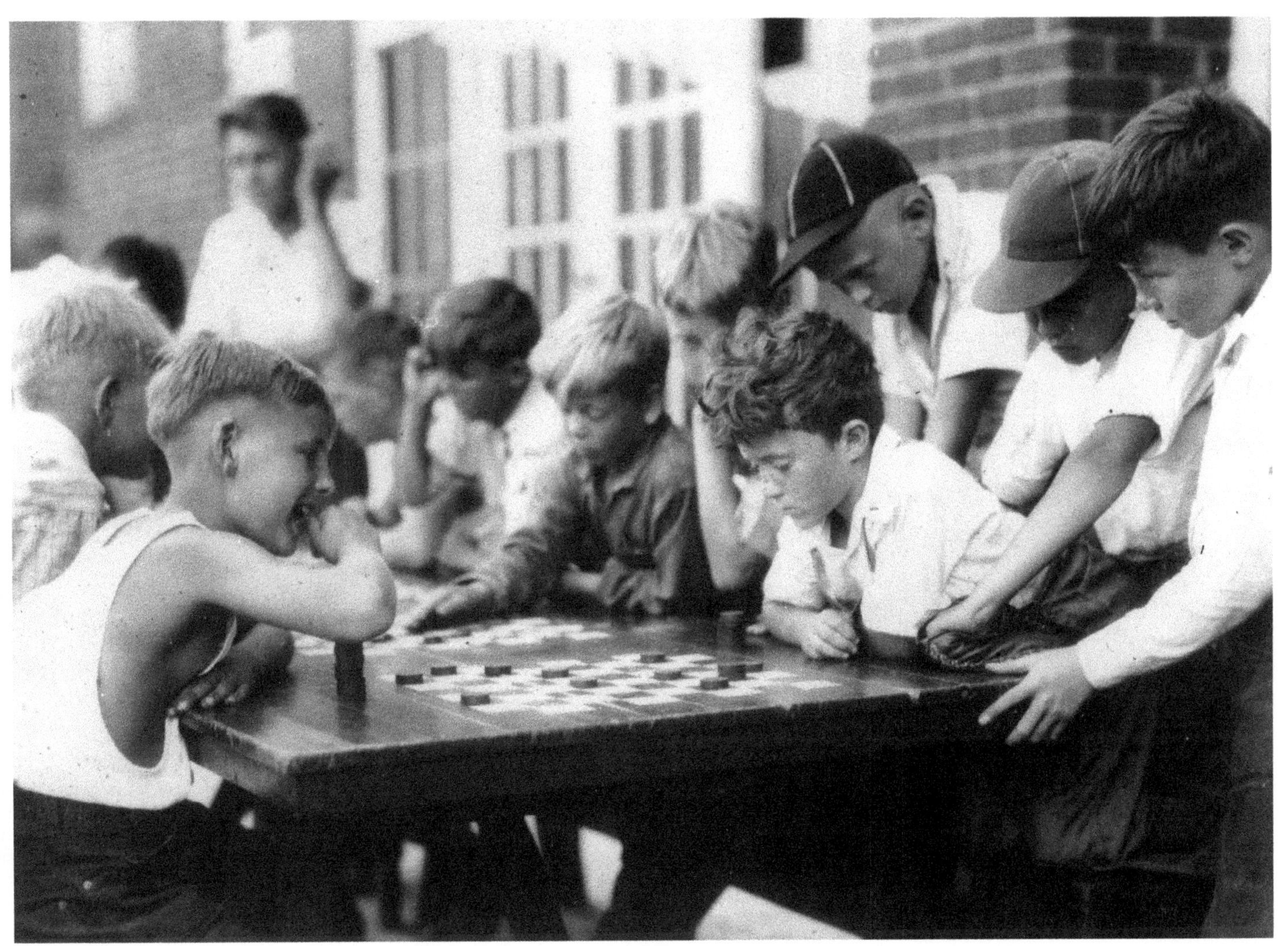

Minneapolis kids in a checkers tournament at Logan Park in 1934. The well-loved Logan Park and Community Center was central to kids growing up in this Northeast Minneapolis neighborhood. Beyond checkers tournaments, Logan Park neighborhood kids could also participate in parades, marble games, tumbling classes, plays, pageants, wood shop classes, soccer, hockey, and much more.

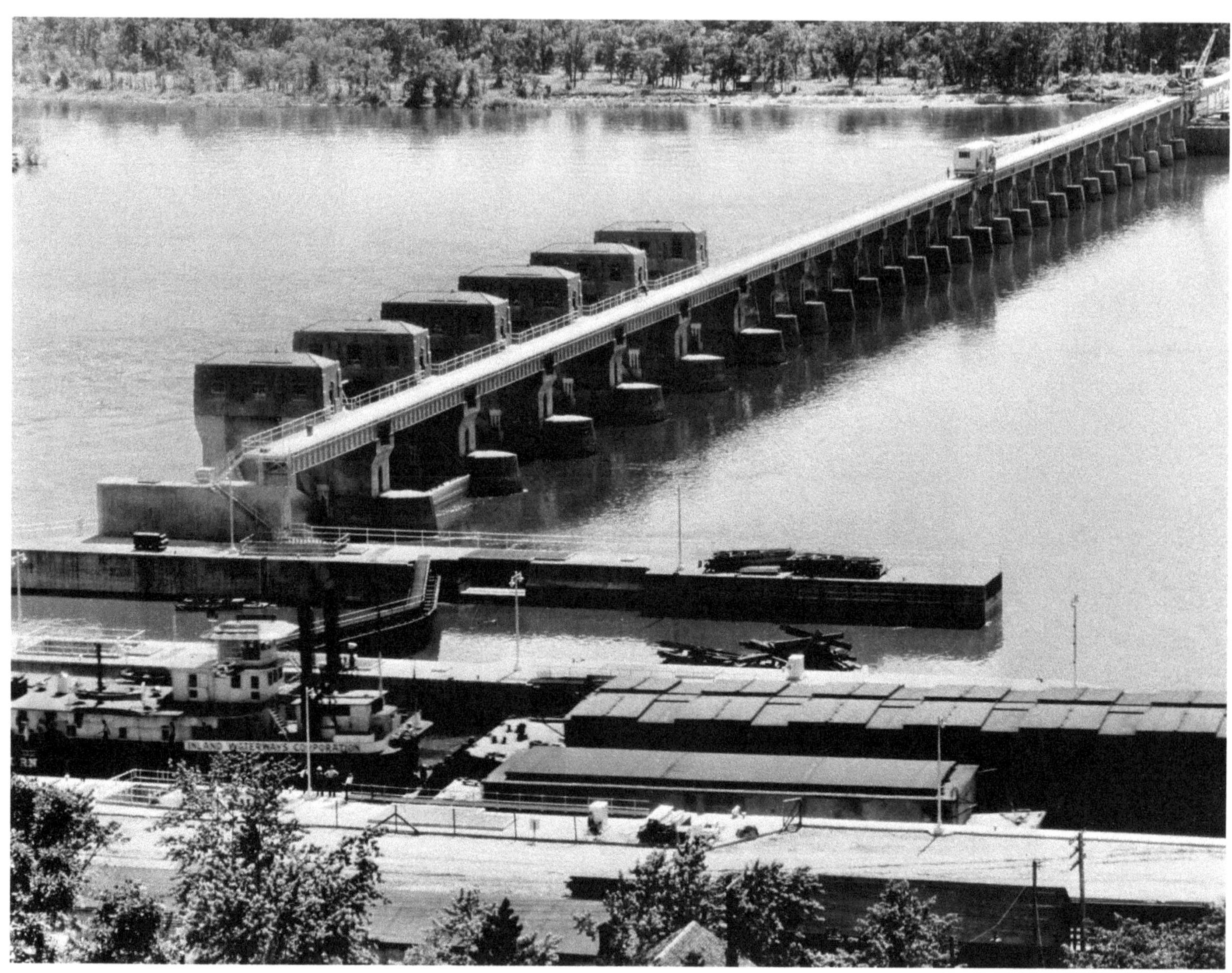


Lock and Dam Number Four on the upper Mississippi River, near Kellogg, Minnesota, and Alma, Wisconsin, as it appeared shortly after it was constructed in 1935. Building locks and dams was a dangerous affair, and several men lost their lives during construction of the facility.

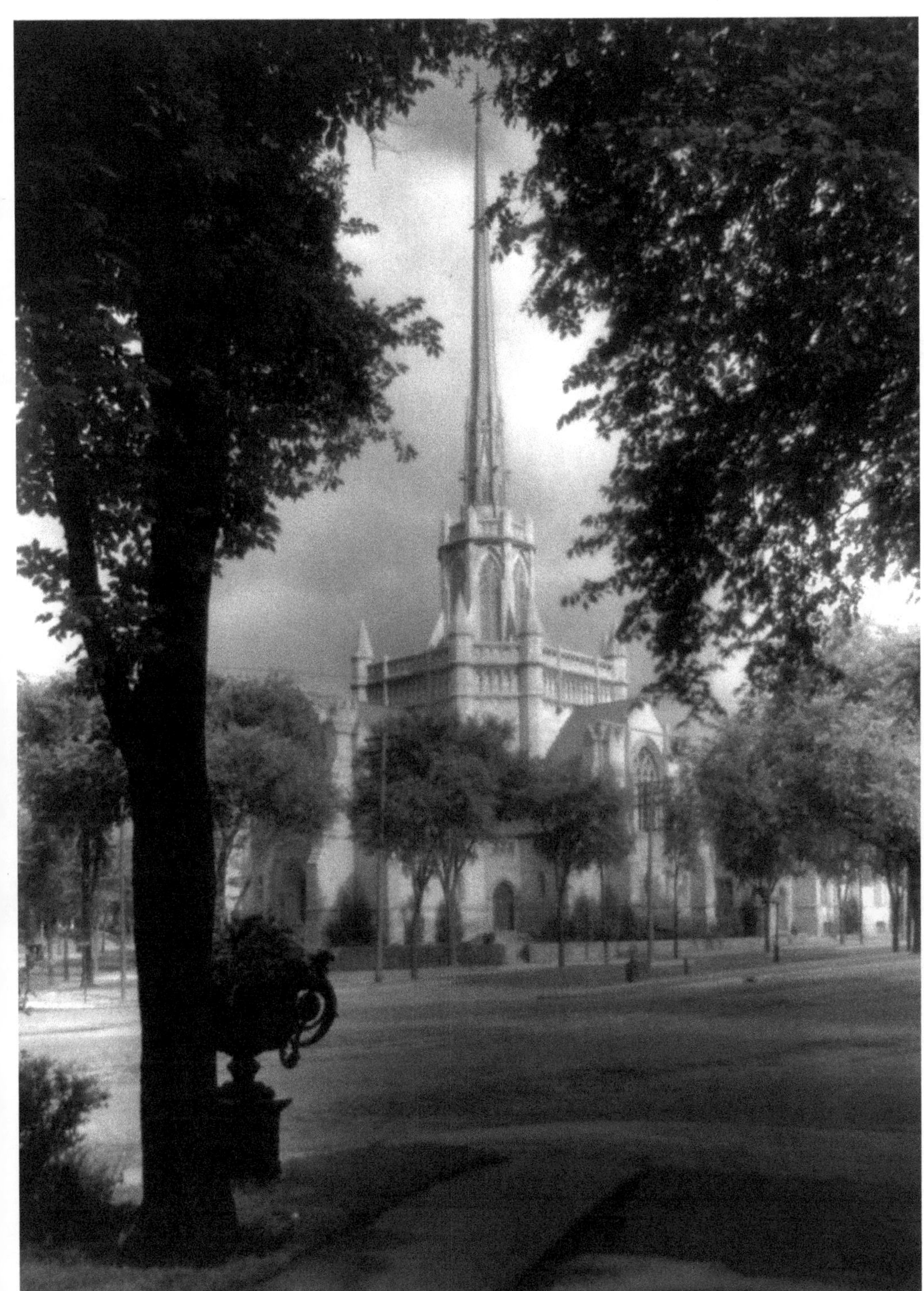

Hennepin Avenue Methodist Church, in Minneapolis, as it appeared in 1936. Minnesota lumber magnate and art collector Thomas Barlow Walker donated the land for the church (the Walker Art Center would later be built across the street). The church was formally dedicated in 1916, but worship services began in the unfinished church in 1914.

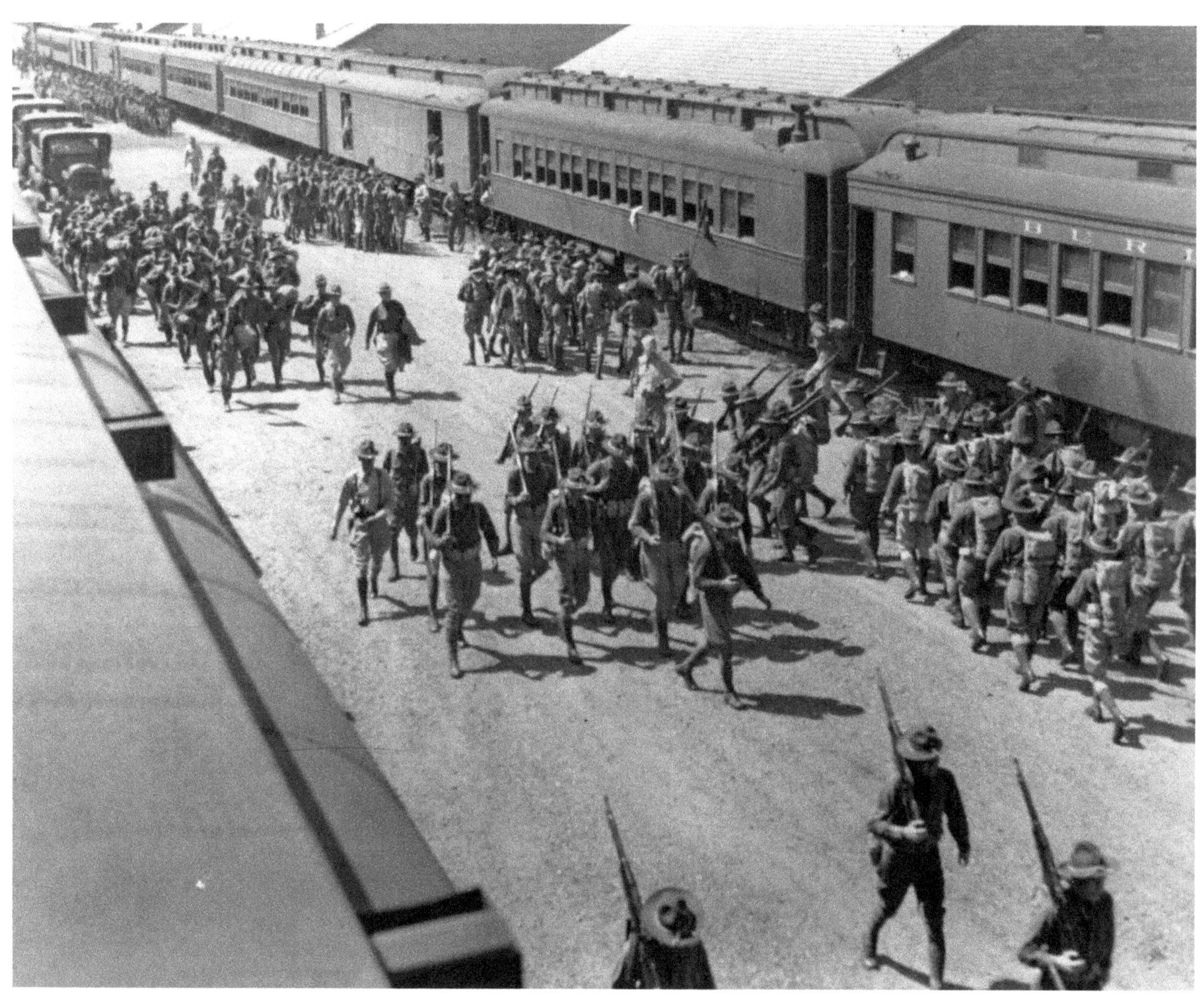

Troops disembark from trains at Camp Ripley for maneuver training in August 1937. The expansion of both the regular army and National Guard prompted the need for a large-scale field-training site such as the Minnesota Army National Guard's Camp Ripley, which opened in 1931.

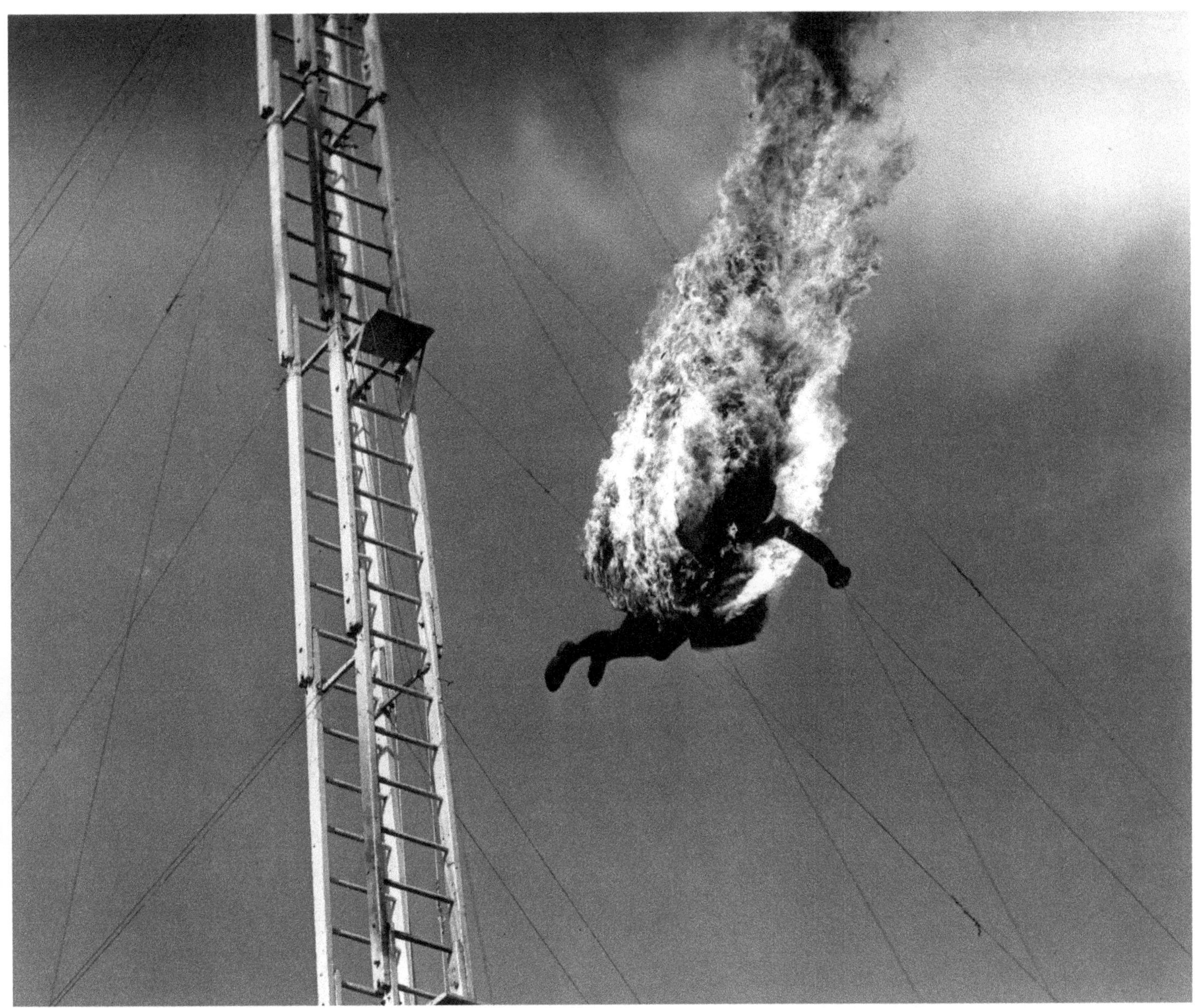

Thrill Day at the 1937 Minnesota State Fair was held on September 10 and drew record-breaking crowds. The day featured many death-defying acts, including a plane crashing into a barn on the racing track infield, an automobile crashing into a brick wall, and a diver engulfed in flames plummeting 60 feet into a water tank.

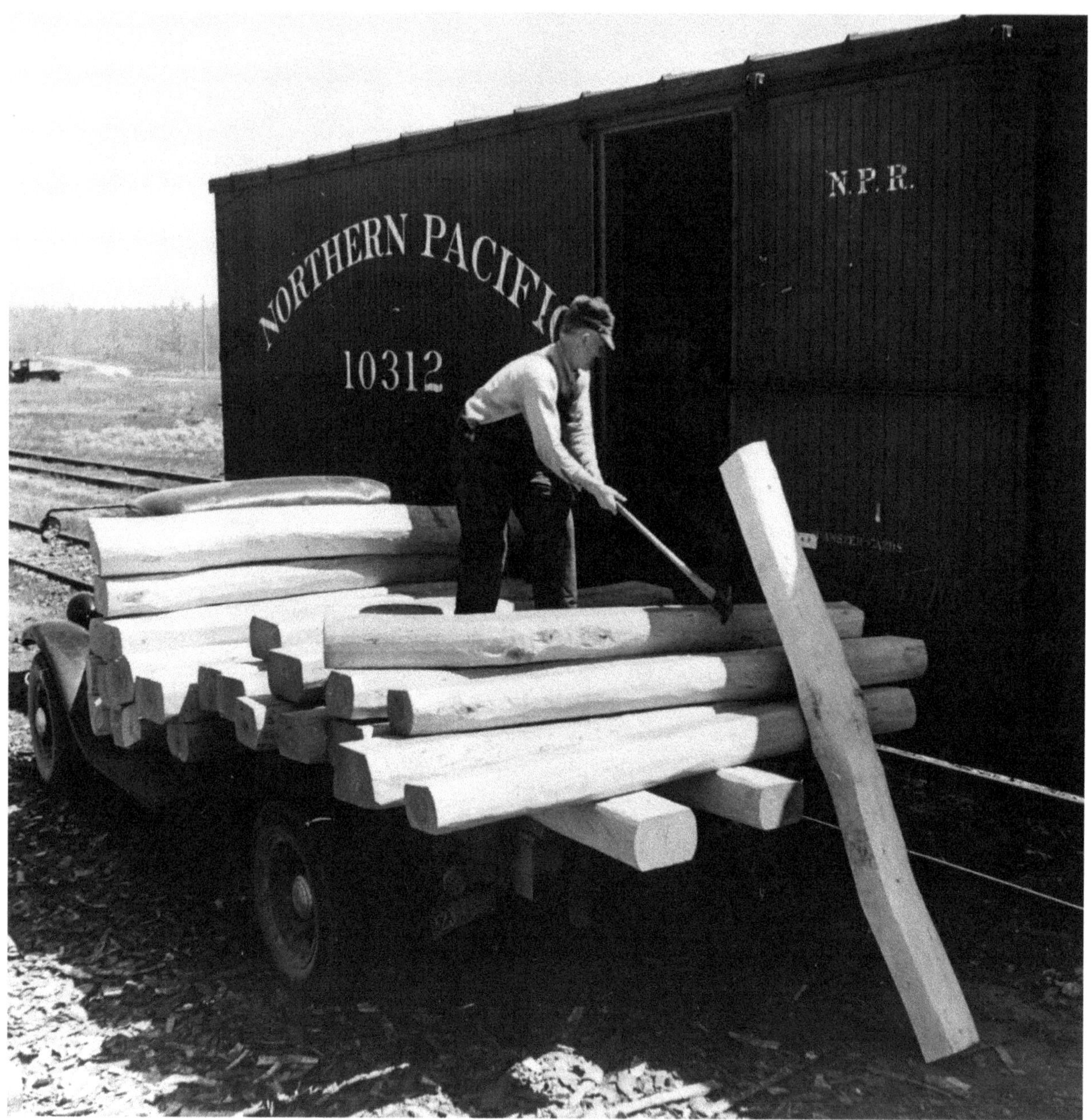


In June 1937, a man loads freshly cut railroad ties in Littlefork, near the Canadian border, as part of a Farm Security Administration program. The FSA program was originally part of a New Deal initiative to combat rural poverty by resettling poor farmers on larger group farms owned by the government.

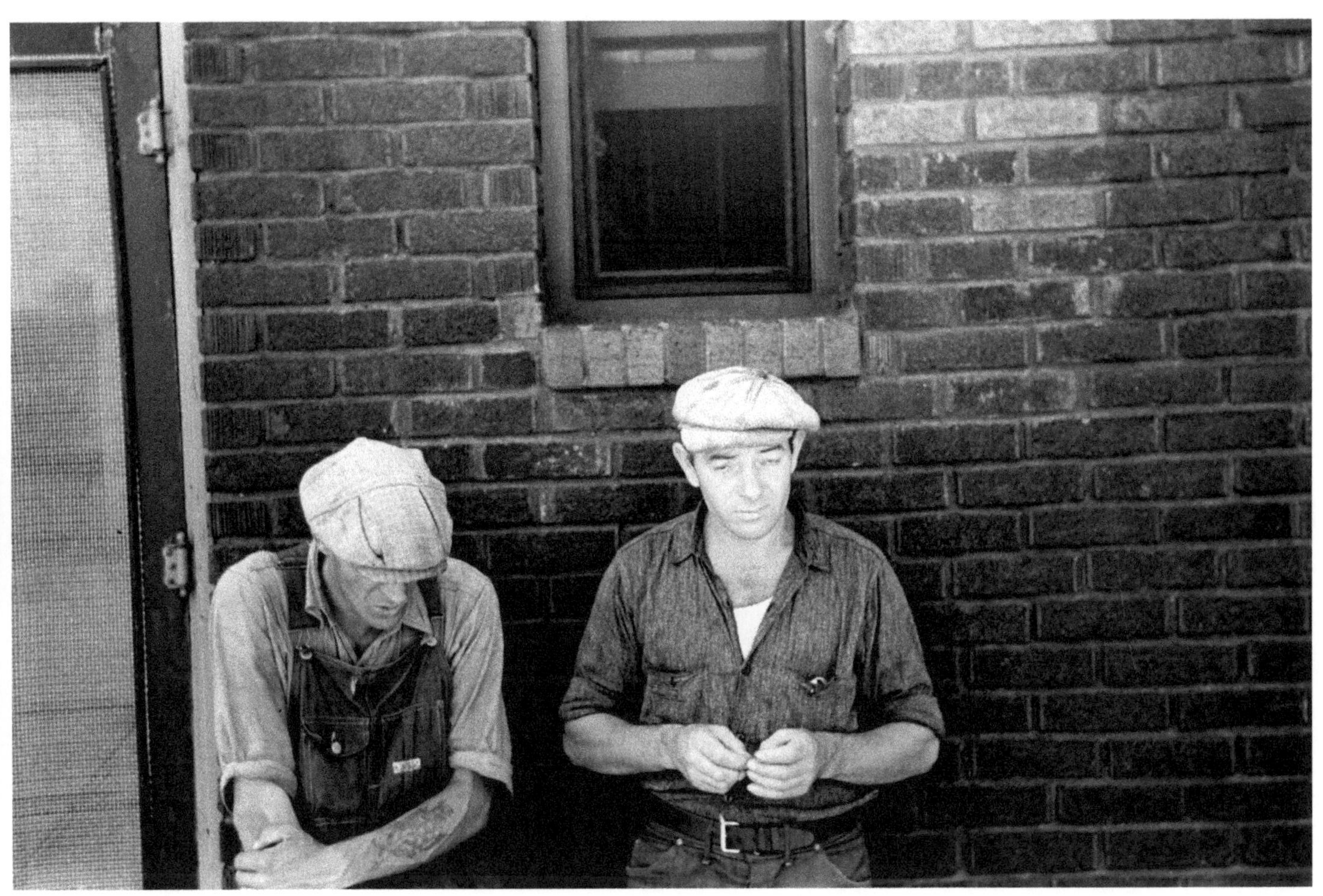

Two unemployed men in the Gateway District of Minneapolis, August 1937. Located at the convergence of Hennepin, Nicollet, and Washington avenues, the area was known for its relatively lax enforcement of vagrancy laws and as a place where day laborers could be hired. For many of the unemployed and homeless of Minneapolis, the Gateway District offered the only hope of finding any work at all.

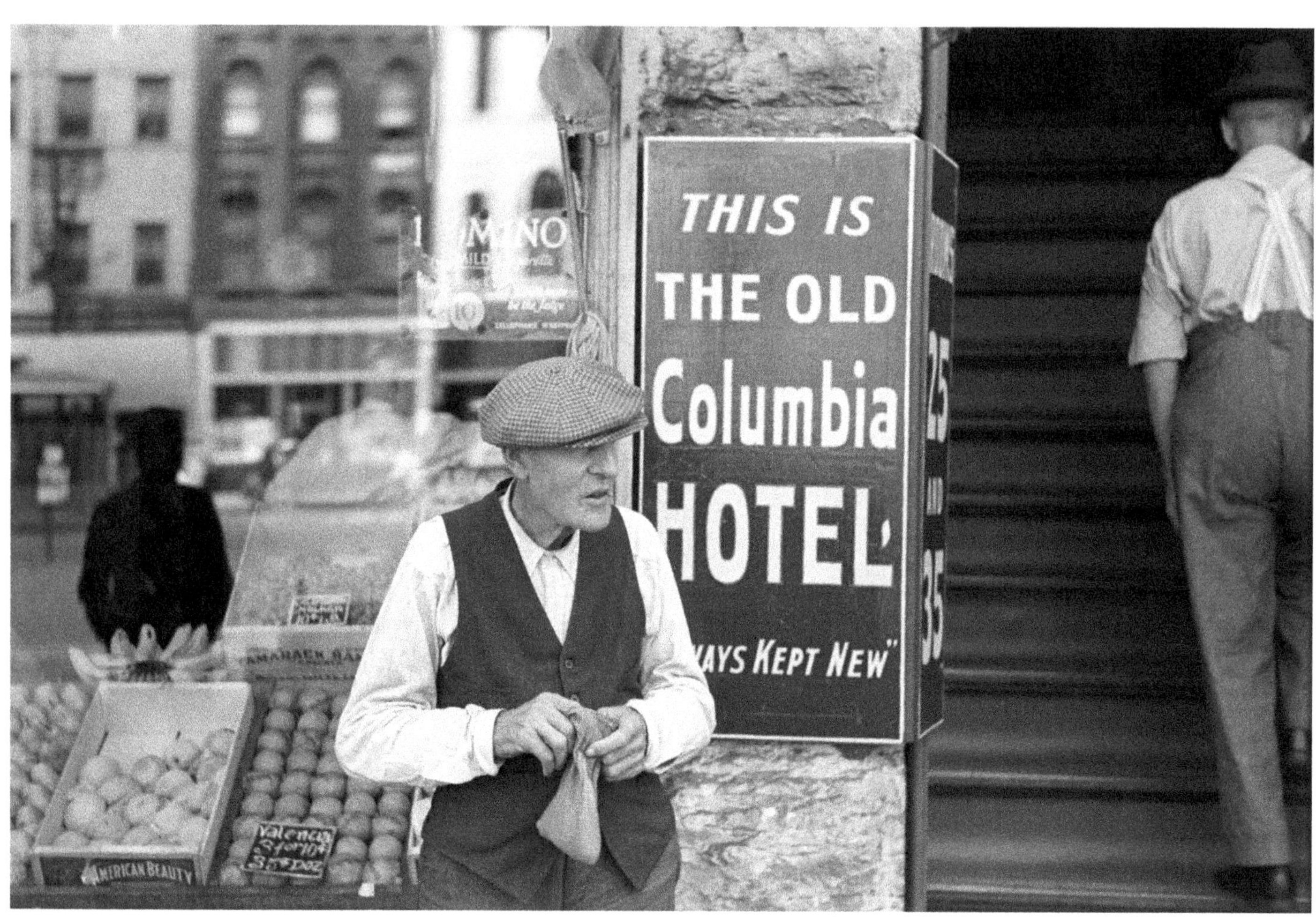


In 1937, at the height of the Great Depression, an unemployed man is pictured outside the Columbia Hotel in the Gateway District of Minneapolis.

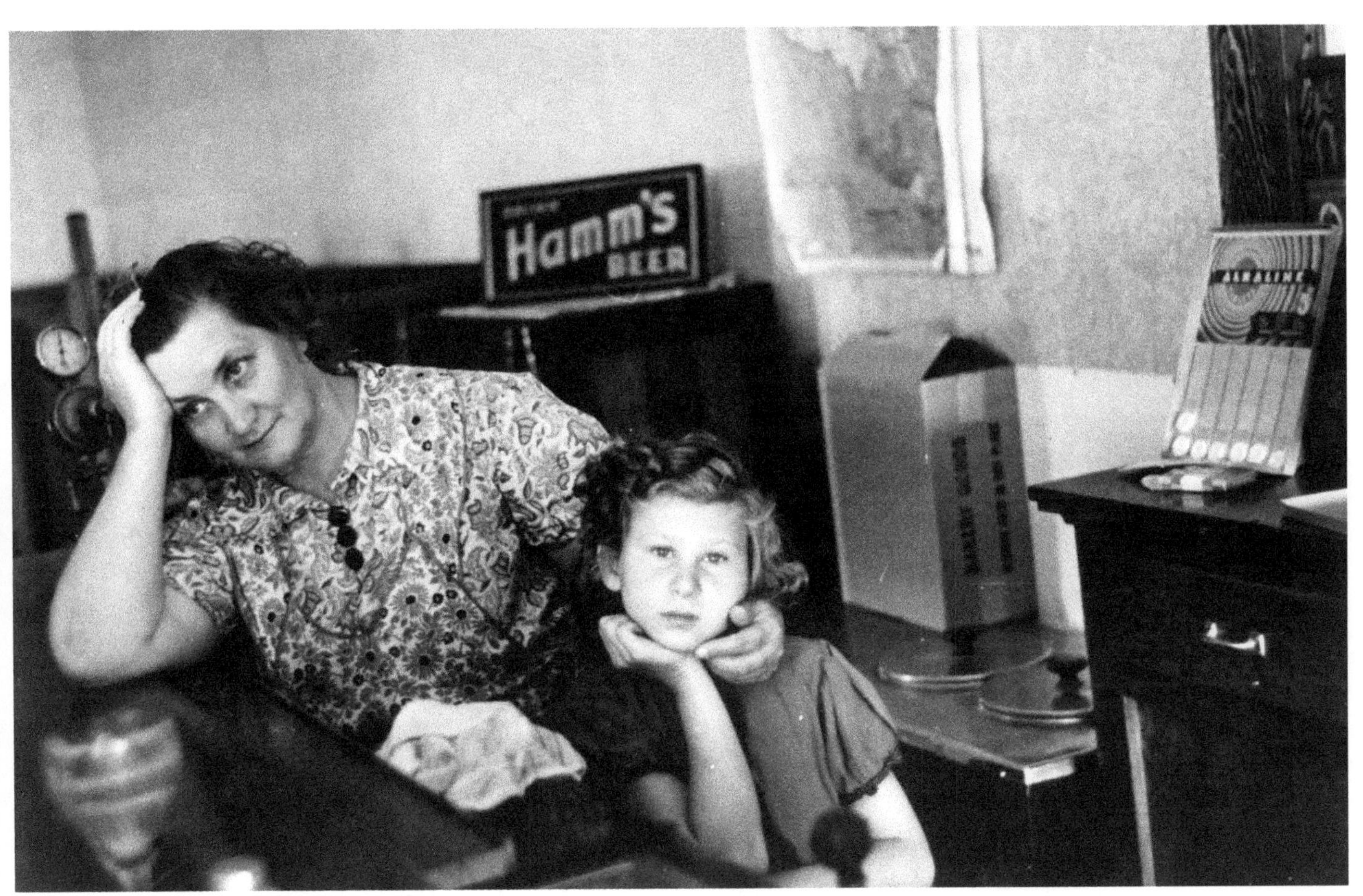


A restaurant-saloon owner and her daughter in August 1937 in Gemmell. This Northern Minnesota town was once a lucrative lumber area. Gemmell was located on the Minnesota and National Railway and boasted of many hotels, shops, and restaurants. But when the forests were depleted and the work dried up, most of Gemmell closed down.

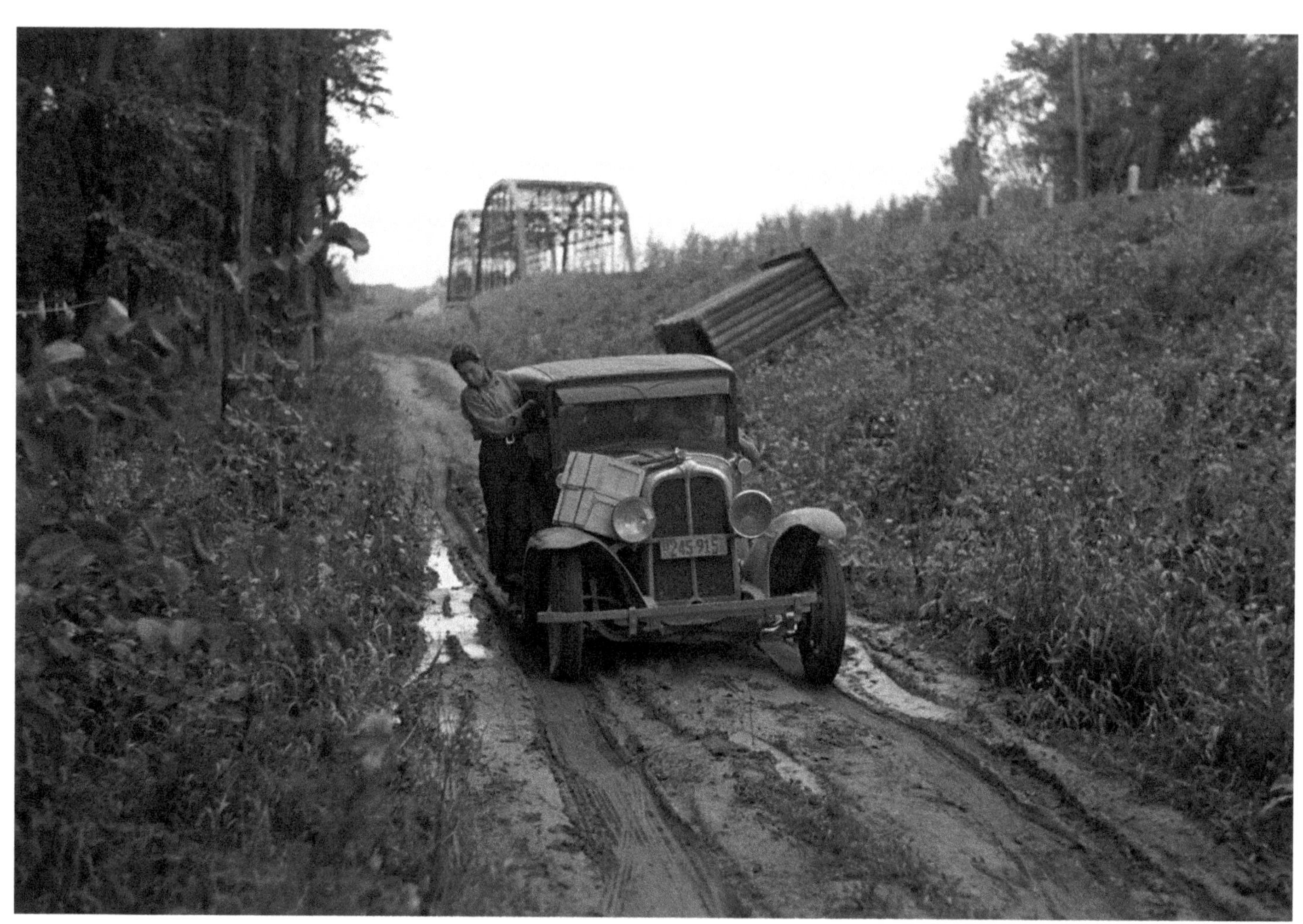

In August 1937, Ojibwe laborers from the Red Lake Indian Reservation arrive for the blueberry harvest in Littlefork, near the Canadian border. The families traveled by car and truck to previously logged areas that were giving way to impressive blueberry bush growth.

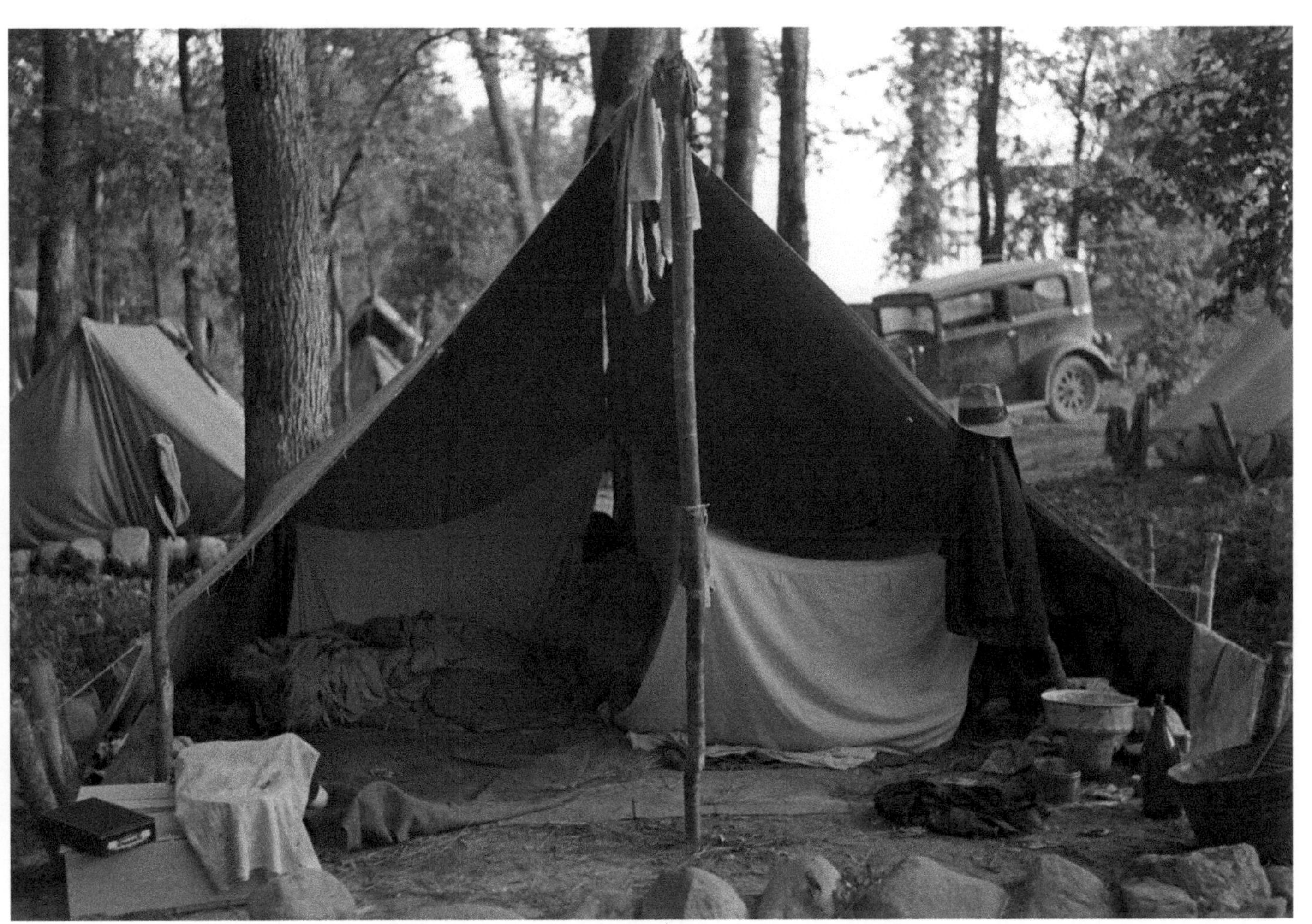

The Ojibwe blueberry pickers in 1937 camped on the north side of a river, just outside Littlefork.

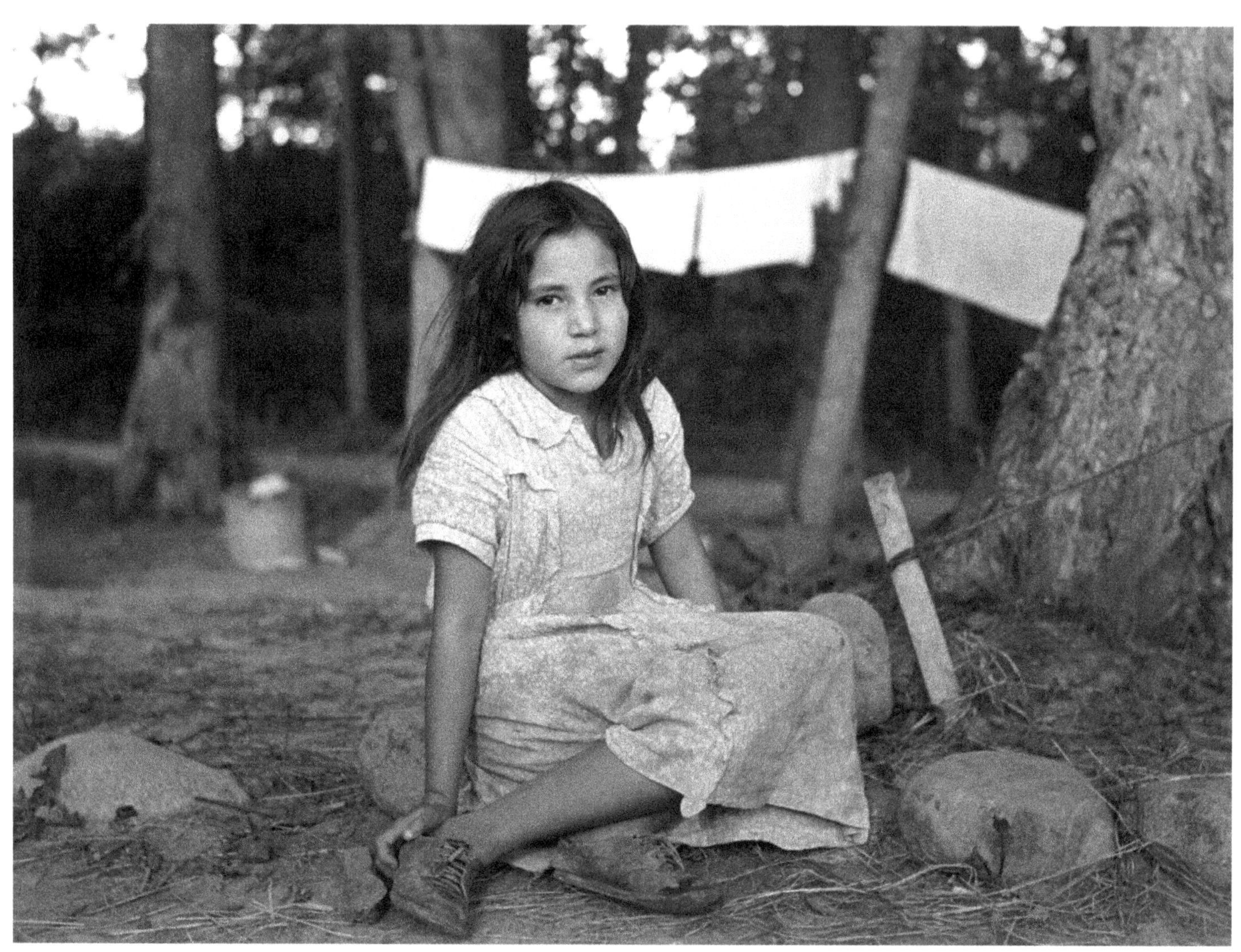

A daughter of an Ojibwe blueberry picker at their campsite near the harvest area. The pickers filled crates with blueberries and sold them for ten cents a quart to local merchants, who in turn shipped the berries by train to city markets.

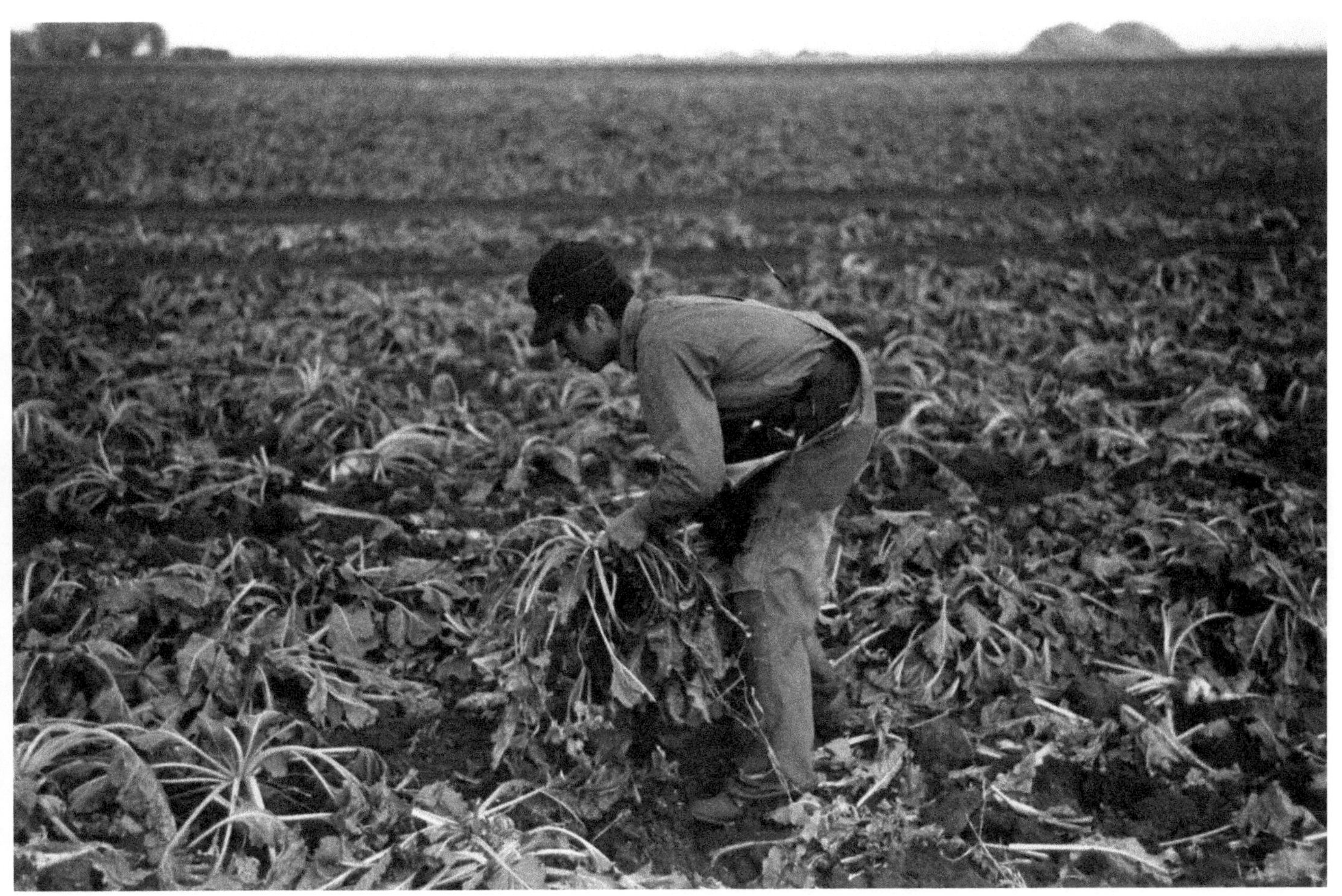

A migrant worker in the Red River Valley area of Fisher harvests sugar beets in 1937. Sugar beet laborers were often Mexican or Mexican-American and commonly referred to as *betabeleros.* Entire families often worked and traveled together. The work was labor intensive, and the wages were low.

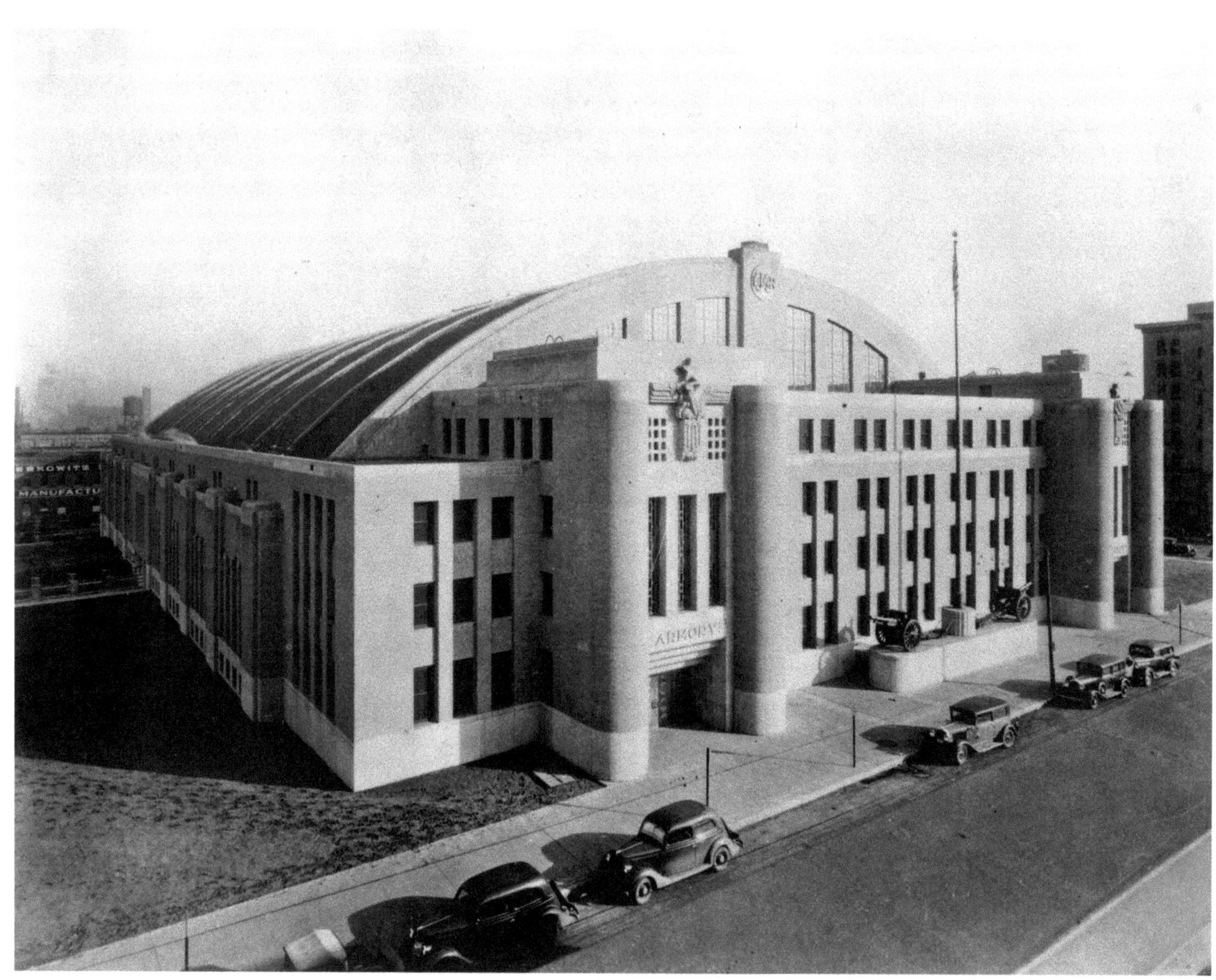


The Minneapolis Armory in 1939. Located in downtown Minneapolis, the Armory was built for the Minnesota National Guard with the aid of a grant from the Public Works Administration in 1936. At a cost of $793,000, it was the single most expensive PWA project in Minnesota. Later, the building was used for civic events and as a home court for the Minneapolis Lakers basketball team.

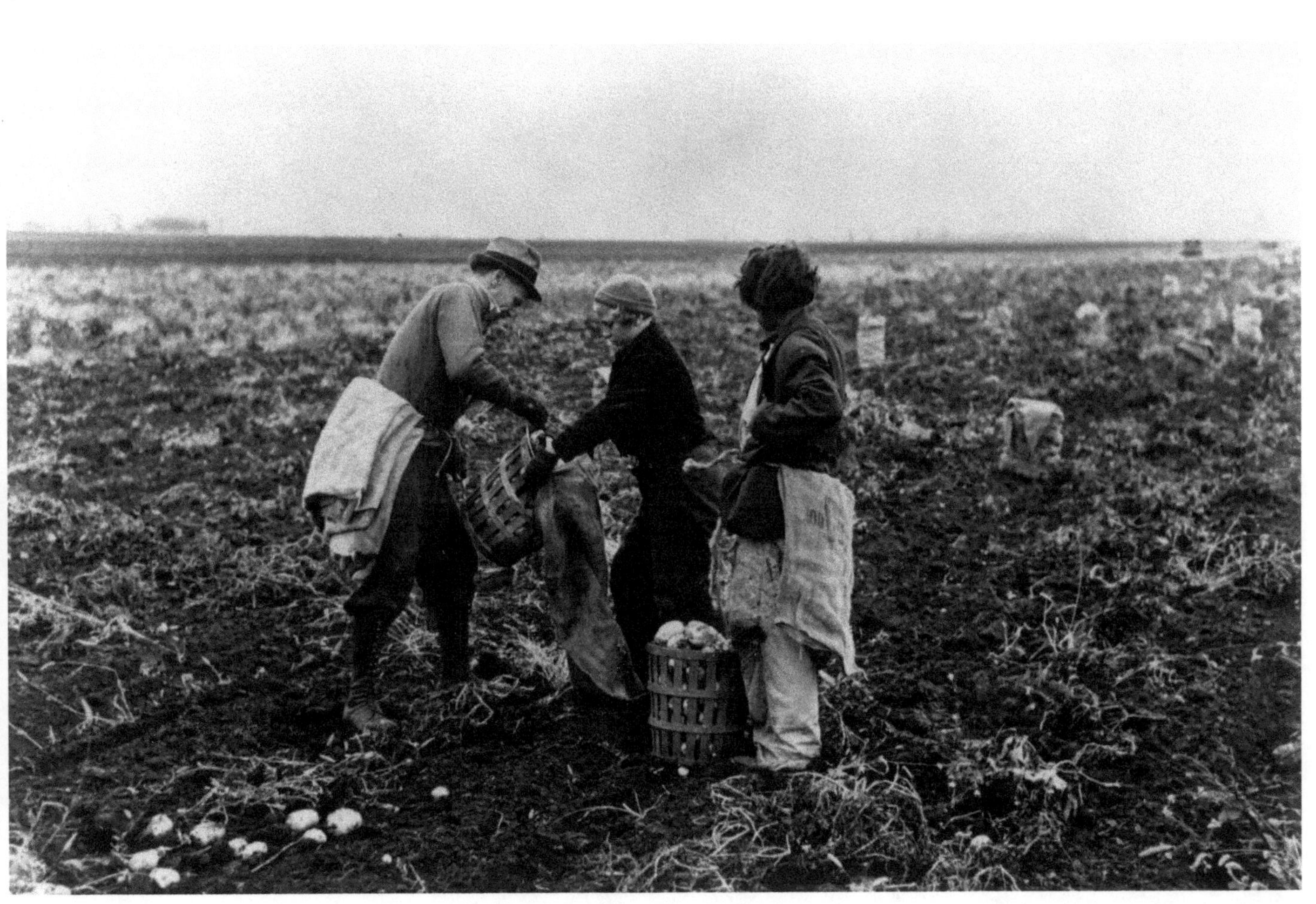

Farm laborers harvest potatoes in the Red River Valley vicinity in Northwest Minnesota, 1939. The rich soil in the area was due to the Glacial Lake Agassiz leaving behind a 20-to-30-foot-deep silt bed, ideal for growing potatoes, sugar beets, wheat, and barley.

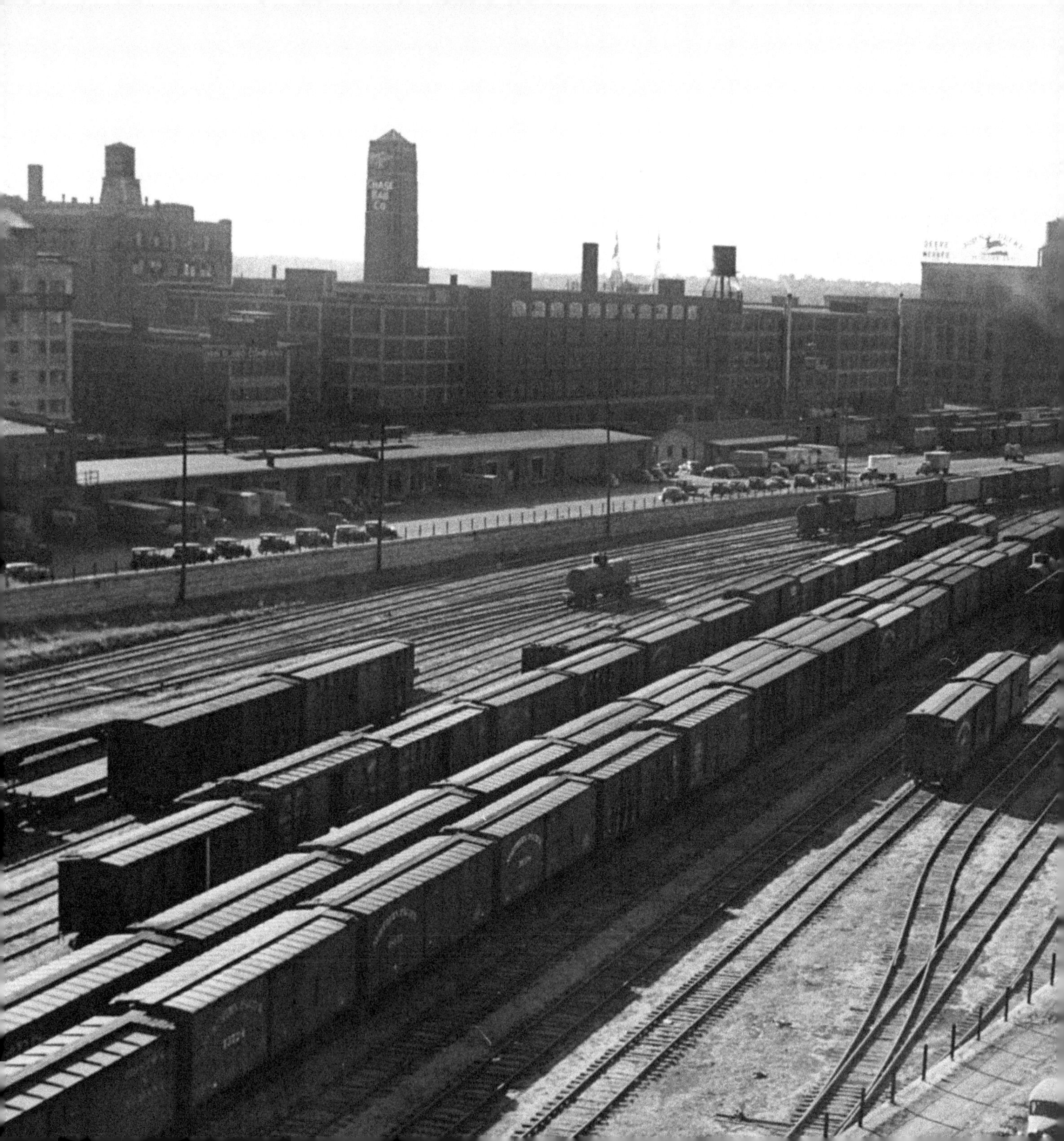
CHASE
BAG
Co

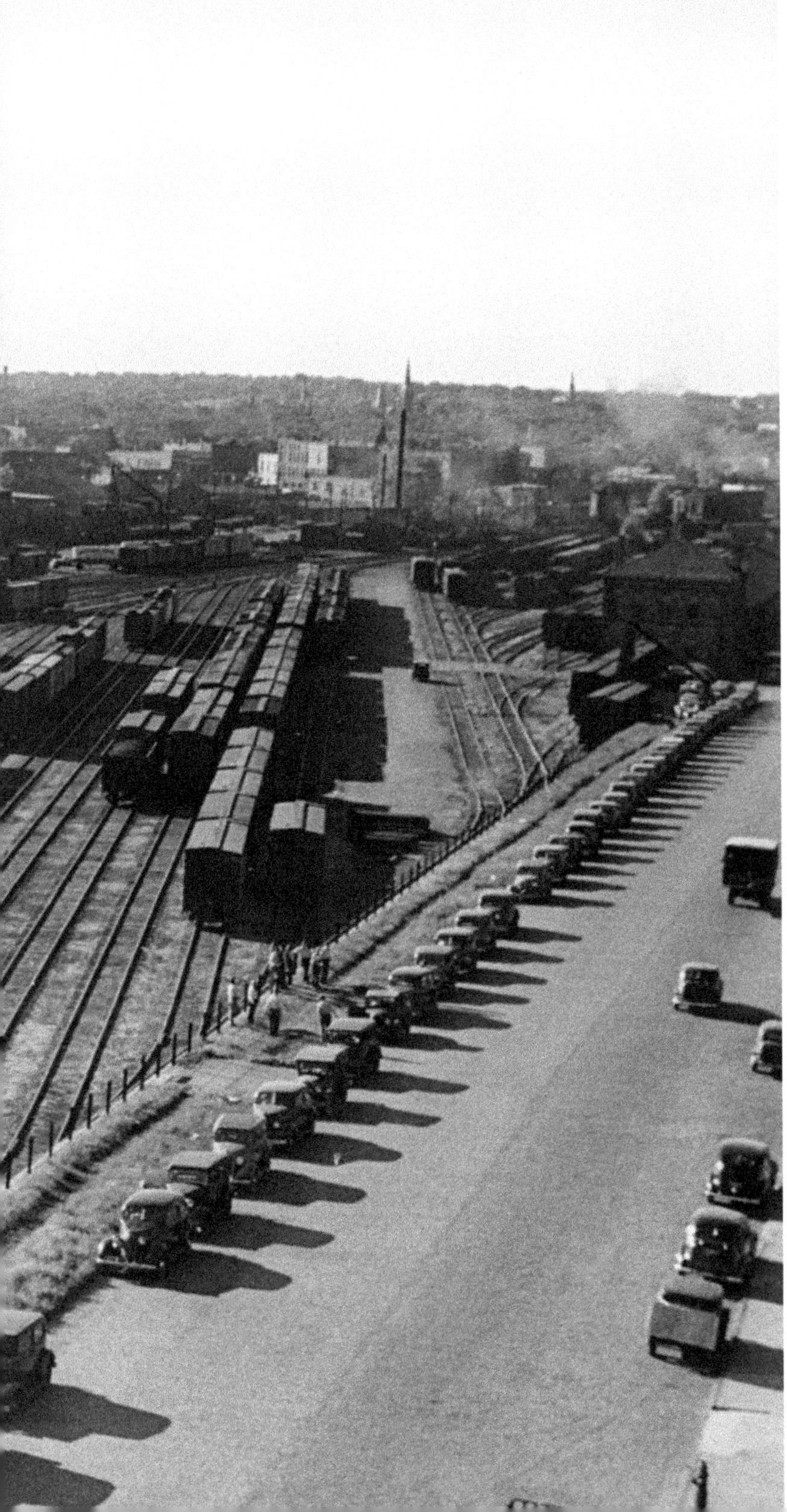

A rail yard in downtown Minneapolis, along First Street, in September 1939. The city's railroad industry helped Minneapolis and the state stay viable during the Great Depression.

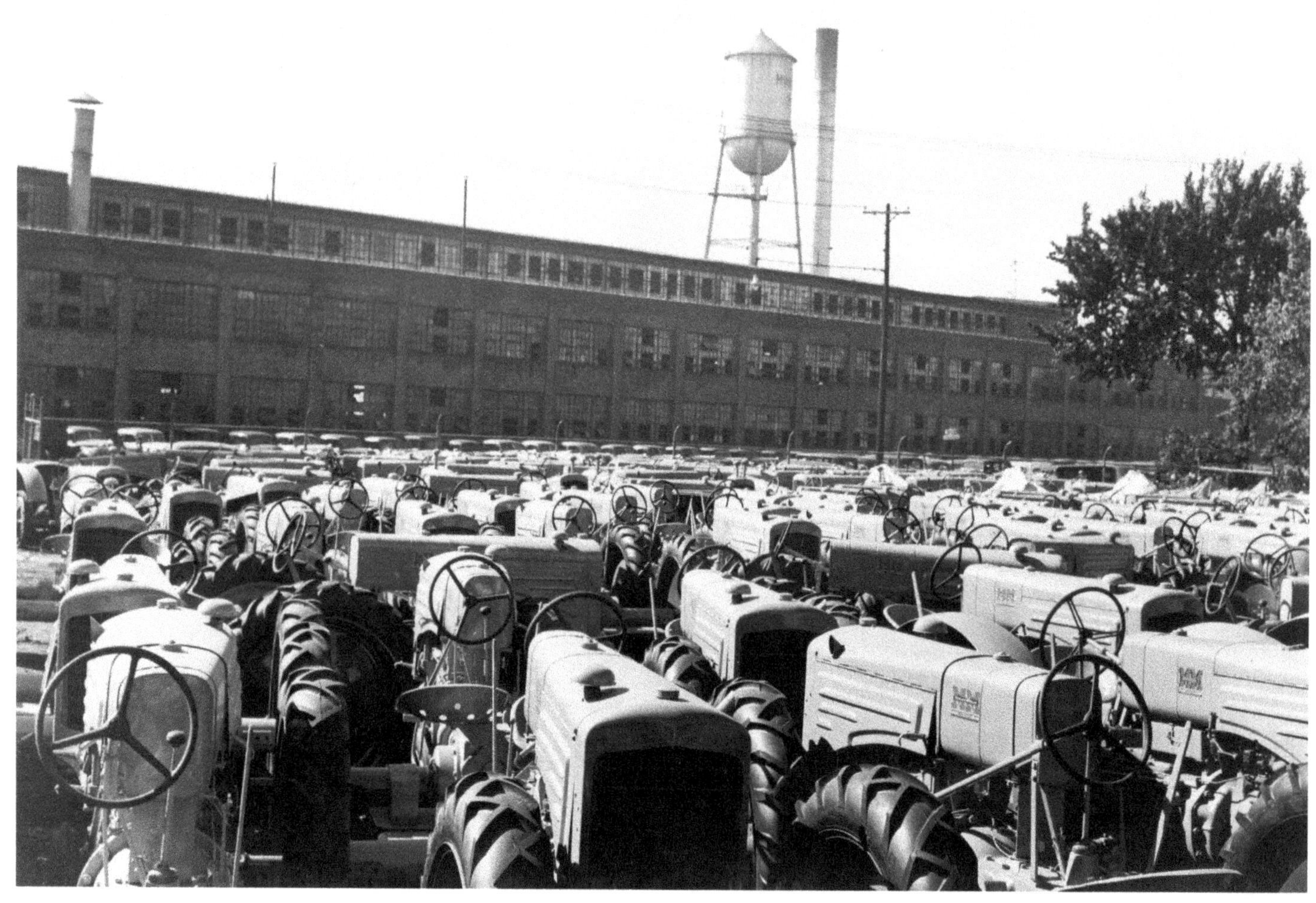

Tractors in front of the Minneapolis-Moline Company, a large tractor and machinery producer, in September 1939. Three companies—Minneapolis Steel & Machinery, Minneapolis Threshing Machine, and Moline Plow—merged in 1929 to form Minneapolis-Moline. The headquarters and a plant were located in Hopkins, with additional plants in Moline, Illinois, and on Lake Street in Minneapolis.

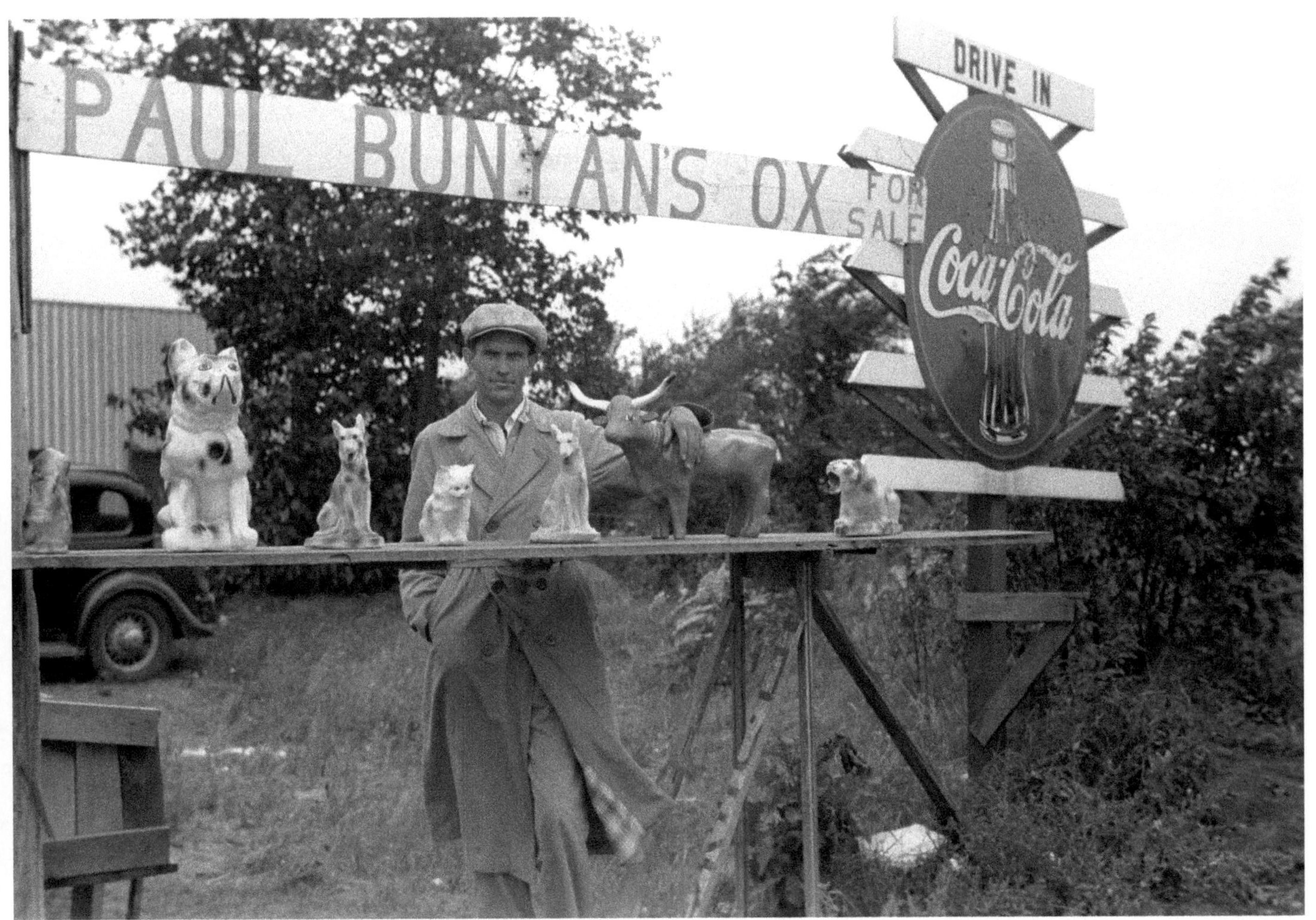


A roadside vendor near Bemidji in 1939, displaying samples of animal figurines for sale, showcases Babe, Paul Bunyan's faithful ox. According to legend, Minnesota's lakes were formed when Paul and Babe stomped across the state. Paul found Babe wandering around, lost and cold amid the snowdrifts of the "Winter of Blue Snow." Babe was so cold that he turned blue like the snow and stayed that way even after warming up.

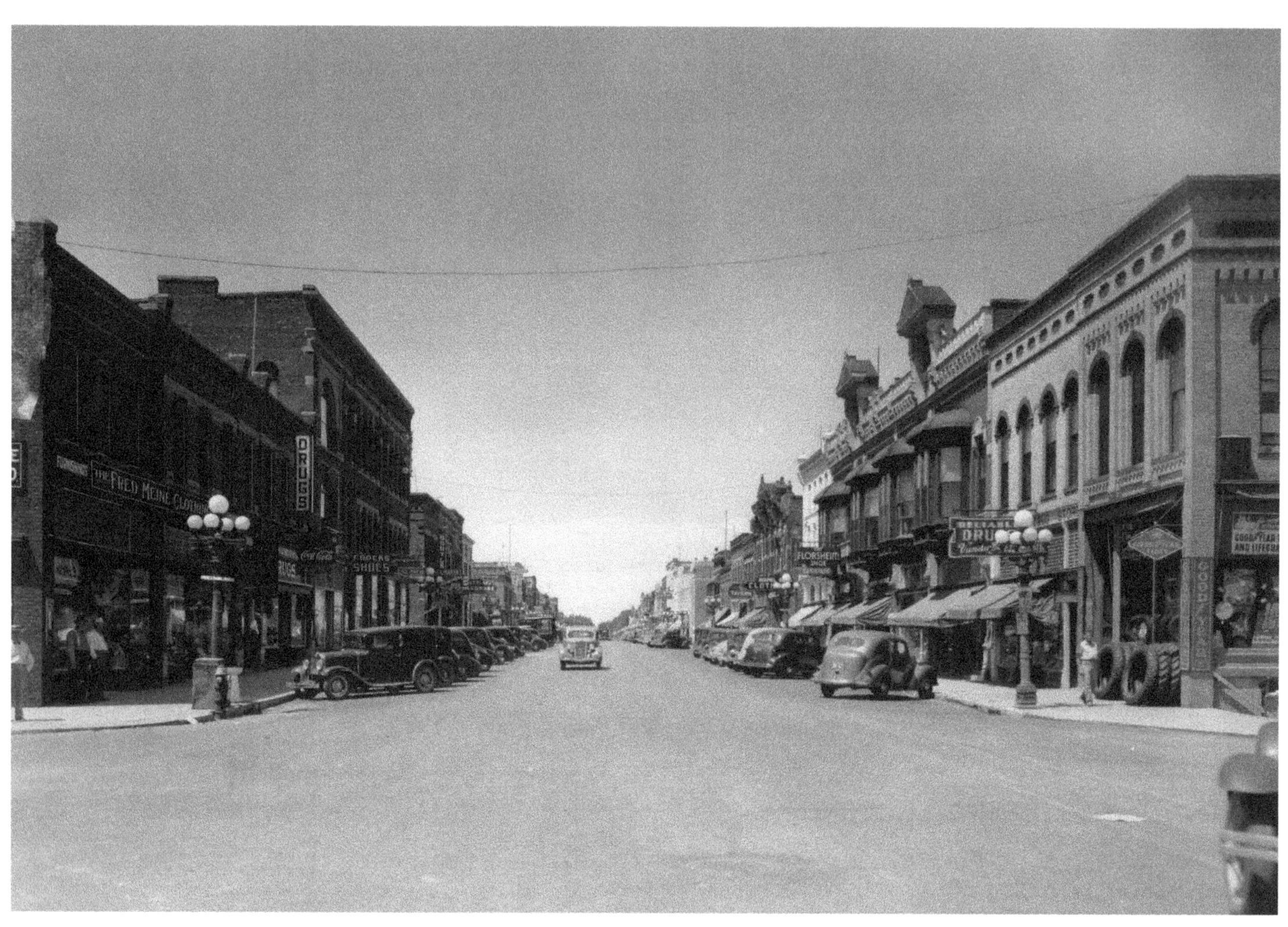


The Minnesota Street business district in New Ulm, around 1940. While business was slow all over New Ulm during the Great Depression, in 1940 the city's creamery industry reported significant gains.

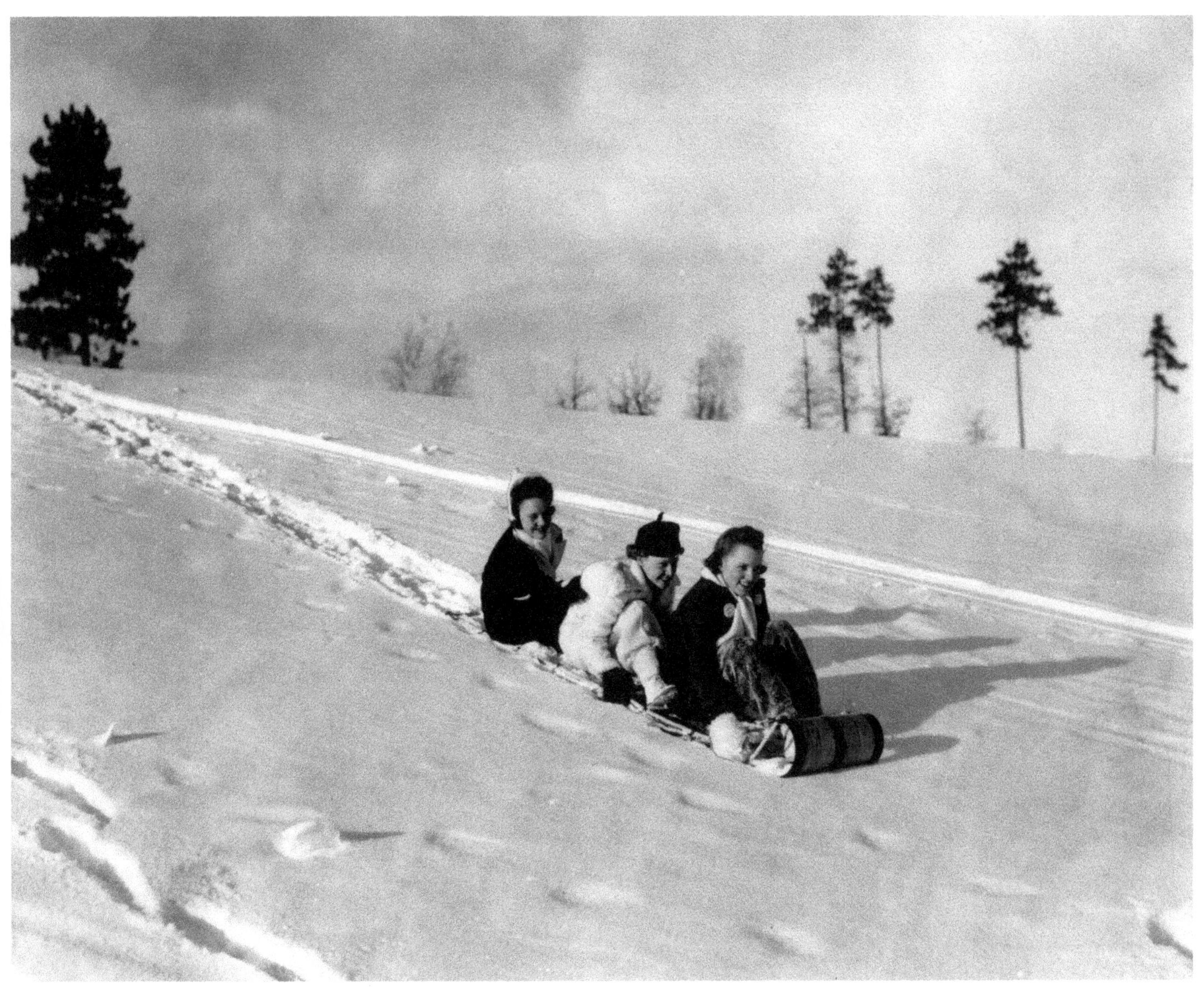

Three girls toboggan down a snow-covered hill in Minnesota around 1940. For most Minnesota kids, long, cold winters did not signal the end of outdoor fun. Kids of all ages enjoyed snowshoeing, skiing, ice-skating, sledding, and occasional snowball fights mixed with making snow angels.

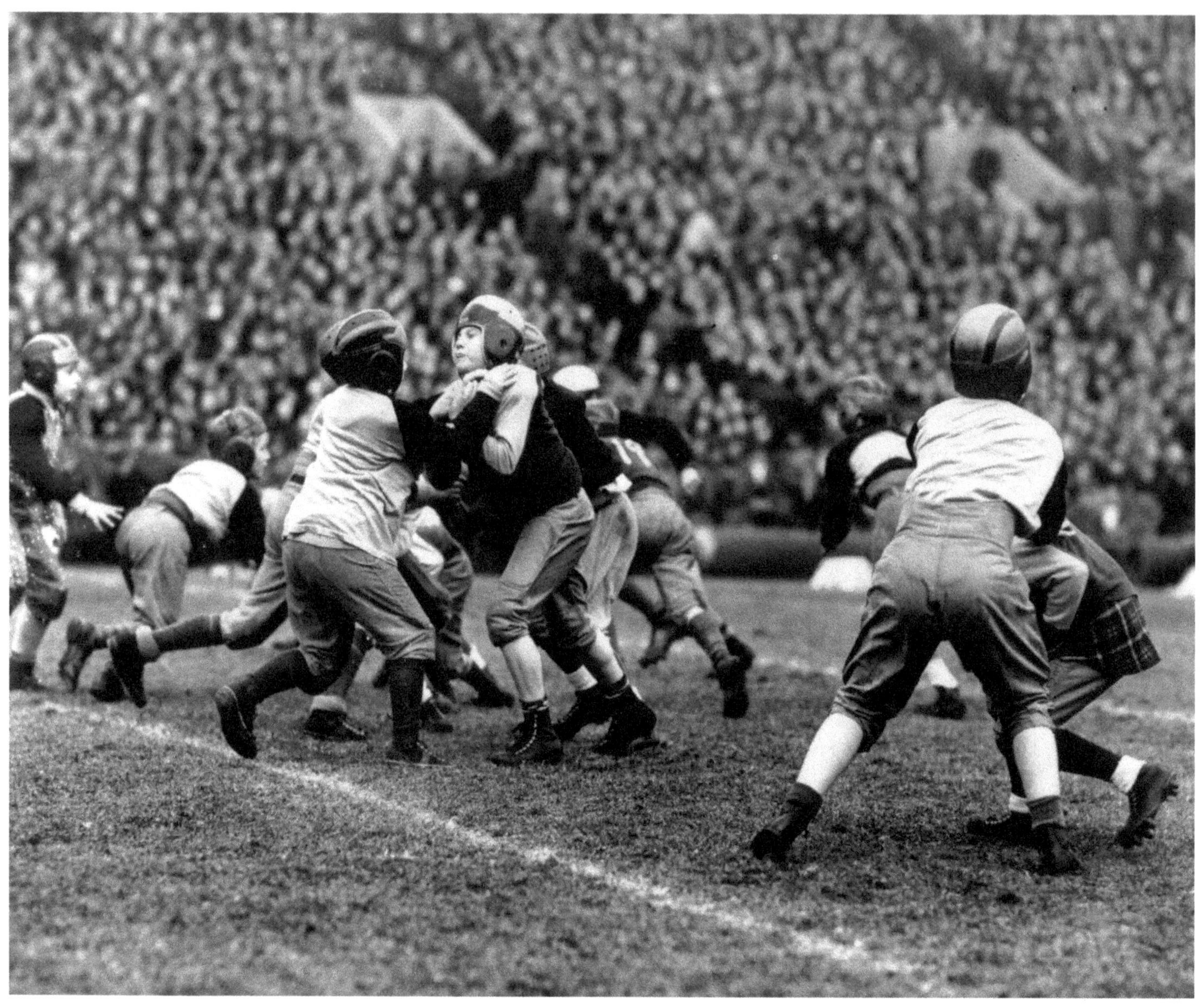

Two youth football teams got the opportunity to play for a University of Minnesota Gophers football crowd as the halftime show during a Memorial Stadium game in the 1940s.

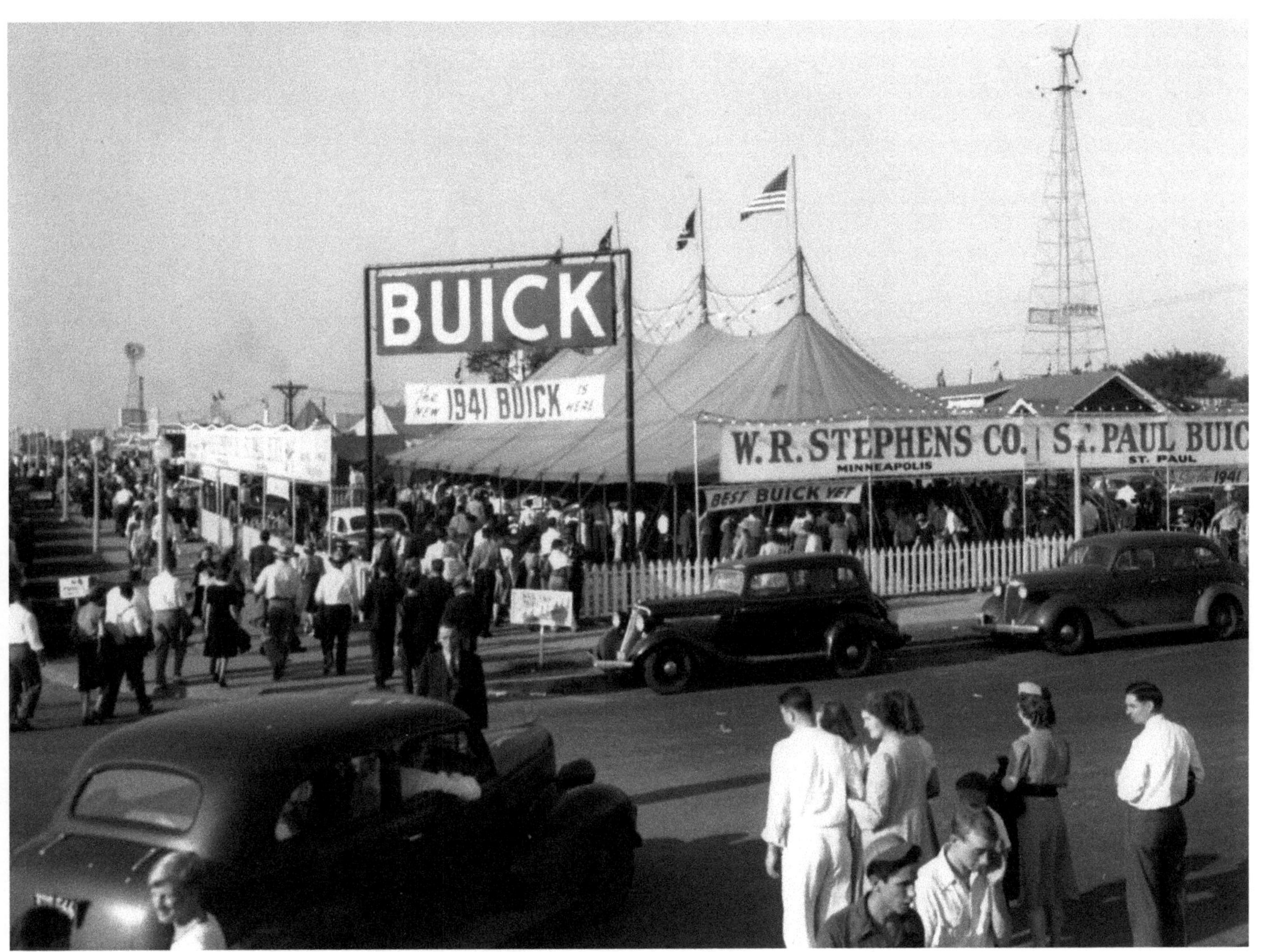


In 1941, a few months before the United States entered World War II, fairgoers packed the Stephens Buick tent at the Minnesota State Fair. The average cost for a Buick at that time was around $1,314. The admission price to the fair had dropped to 25¢.

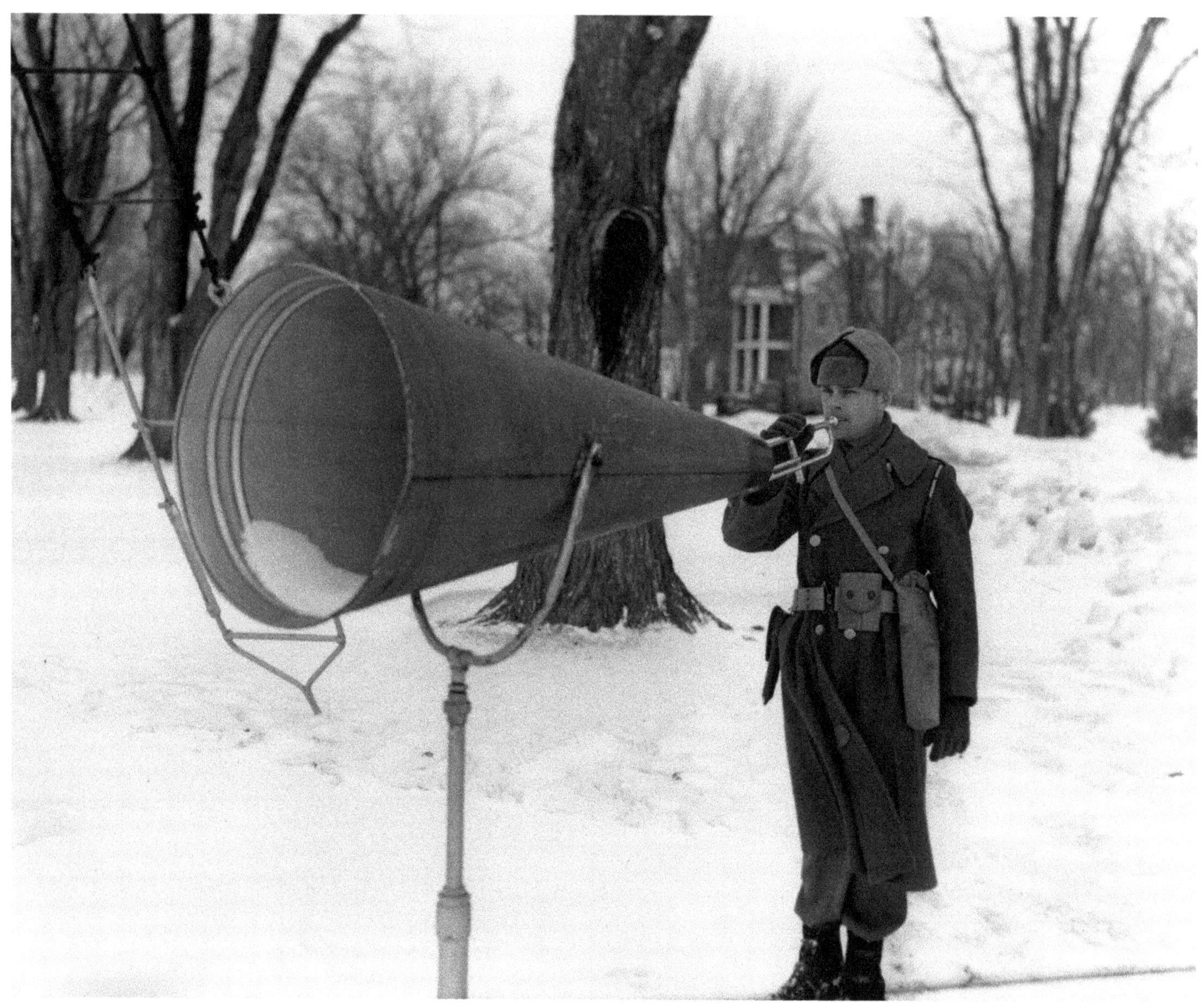

A soldier at Fort Snelling during the winter of 1941 plays a bugle into a mammoth megaphone. During the war, Fort Snelling served as an important reception center for newly drafted recruits, who were tested to determine physical and mental fitness before being assigned to training camps. In total, 300,000 recruits were processed through Fort Snelling during the war years.

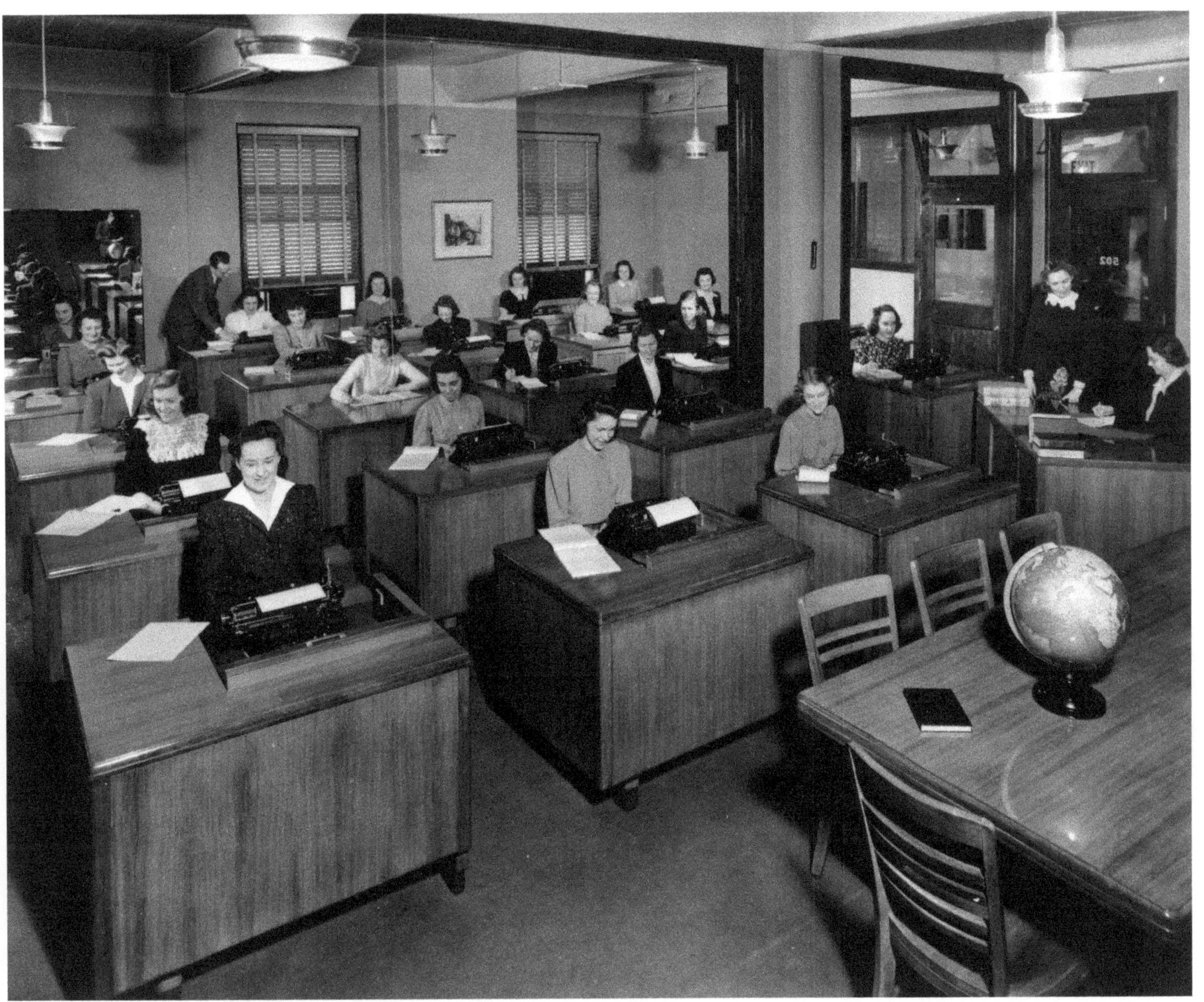

A classroom at the Minnesota School of Business in Richfield in May 1941. The women are likely training for secretarial and bookkeeping positions. Professor Alexander R. Archibald, formerly of Dartmouth College, founded the school in 1877. The school's first location was a three-room building at Third and Marquette in Minneapolis, where Professor Archibald taught bookkeeping, shorthand, English, and penmanship.

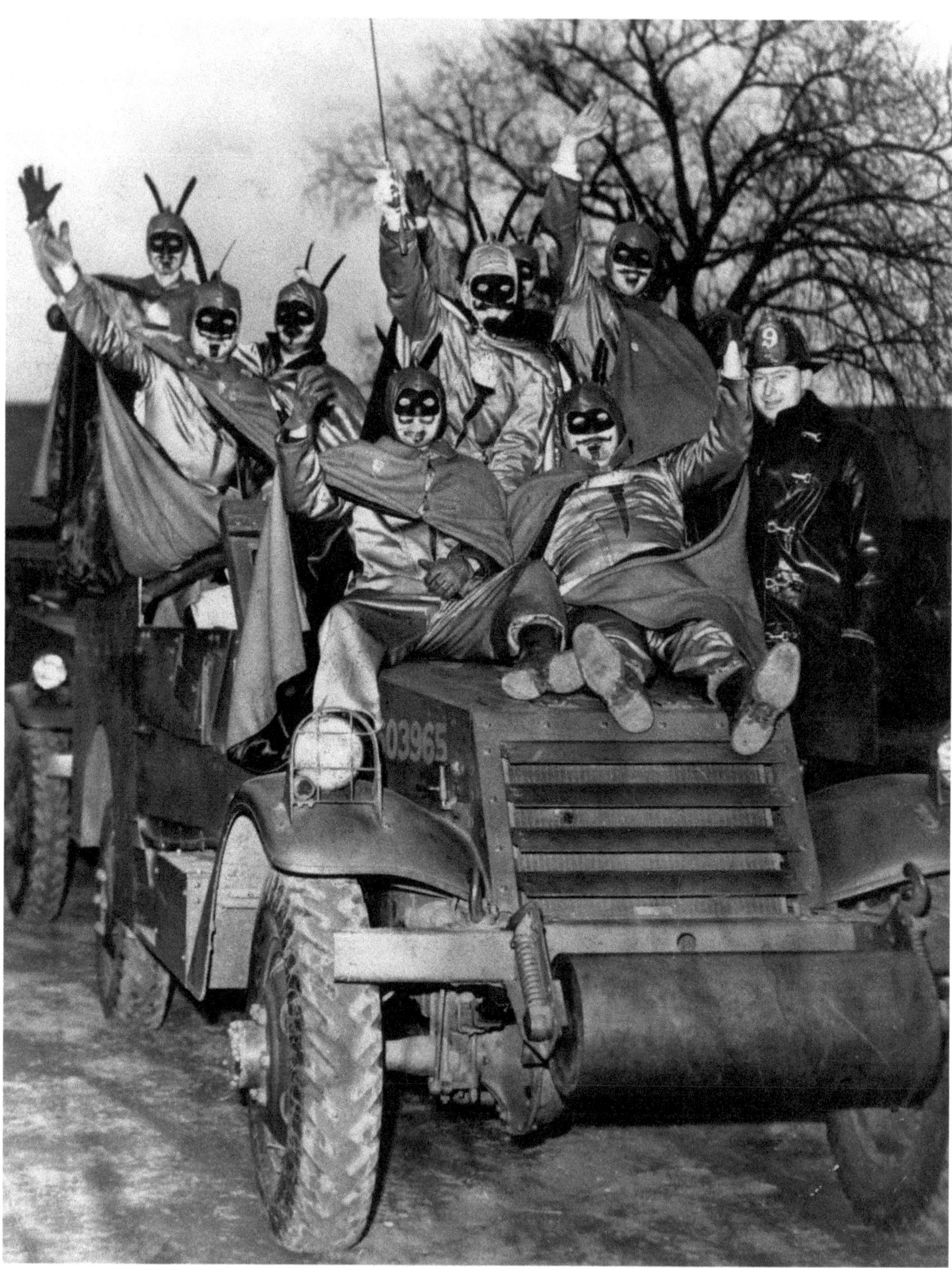


Vulcan Rex VIII, his Vulcan Krewe, and a firefighter in the St. Paul Winter Carnival parade in 1942. The Vulcans have a long history of mischief-making and mythic battling, dating to St. Paul's first Winter Carnival in 1886. Originally, there was just one Vulcan, known as the Fire King, who battled King Boreas and his royal family throughout the carnival. But in 1940, Vulcan Rex VI recruited friends, and the rest is history.

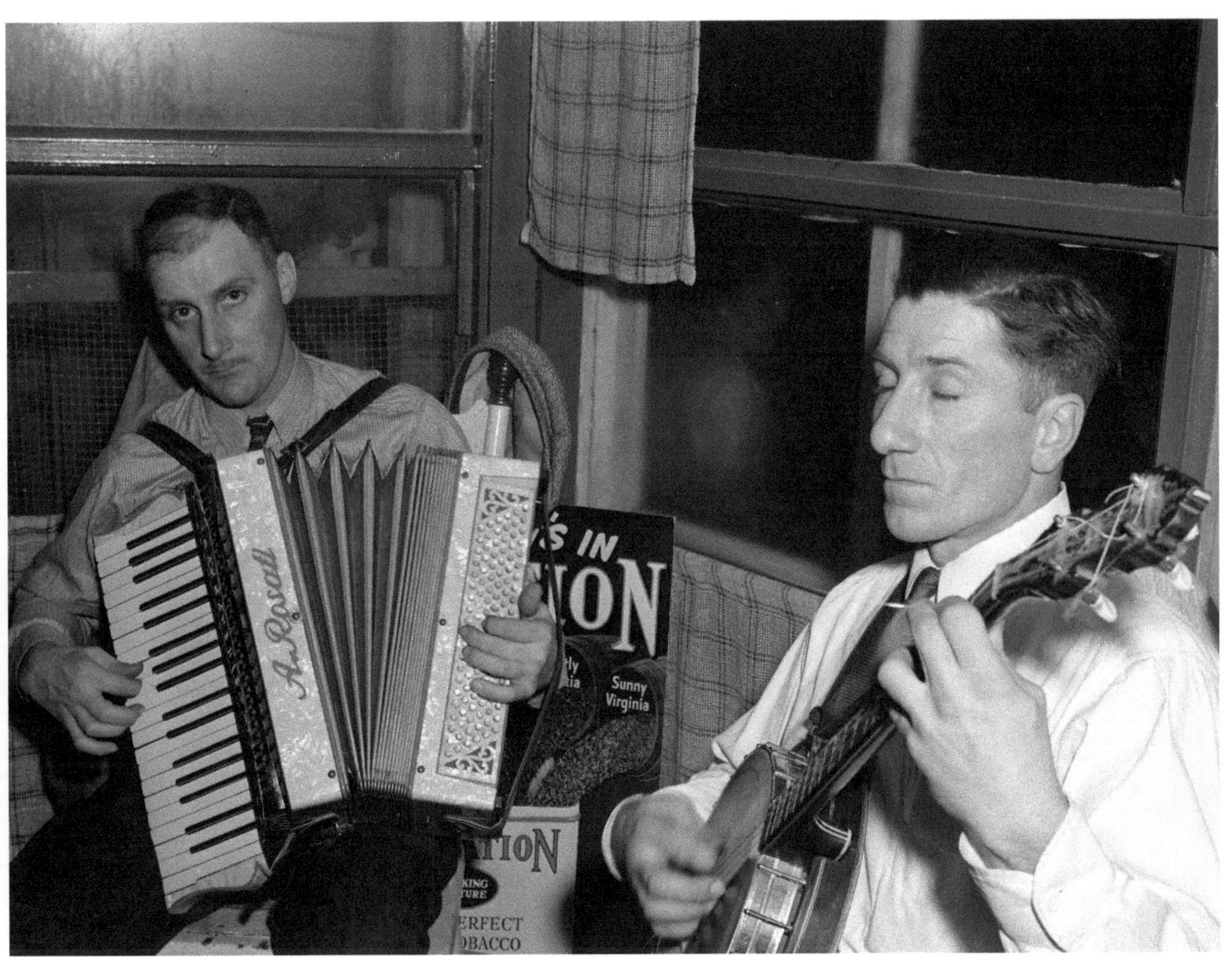


Wielding accordion and banjo, two Meeker County farmers supply the music for a dance at a crossroads store in February 1942.

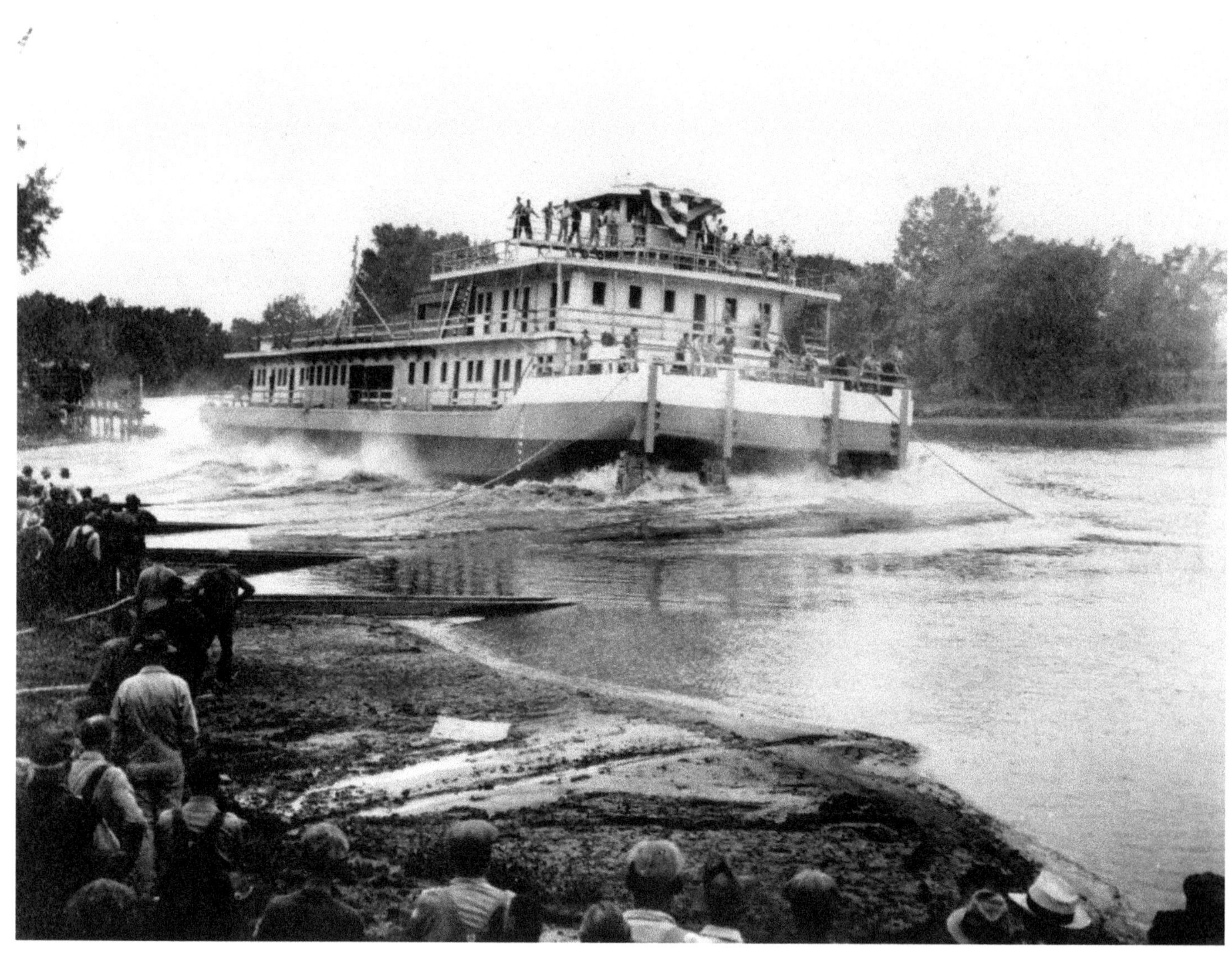

Onlookers watch the launching of *Quarter* at Port Cargill in Savage. In 1942, Cargill Incorporated contracted with the U.S. Navy to build six ocean-going tankers. The company constructed Meadowland Shipyard and changed the name of Hamilton Landing to Port Cargill. To launch the ships, 14 miles of the Minnesota River were dredged from Savage to the Mississippi River confluence. About 3,500 people were employed during peak production, resulting in construction of 18 auxiliary oil and gas carriers, and 4 tugboats.

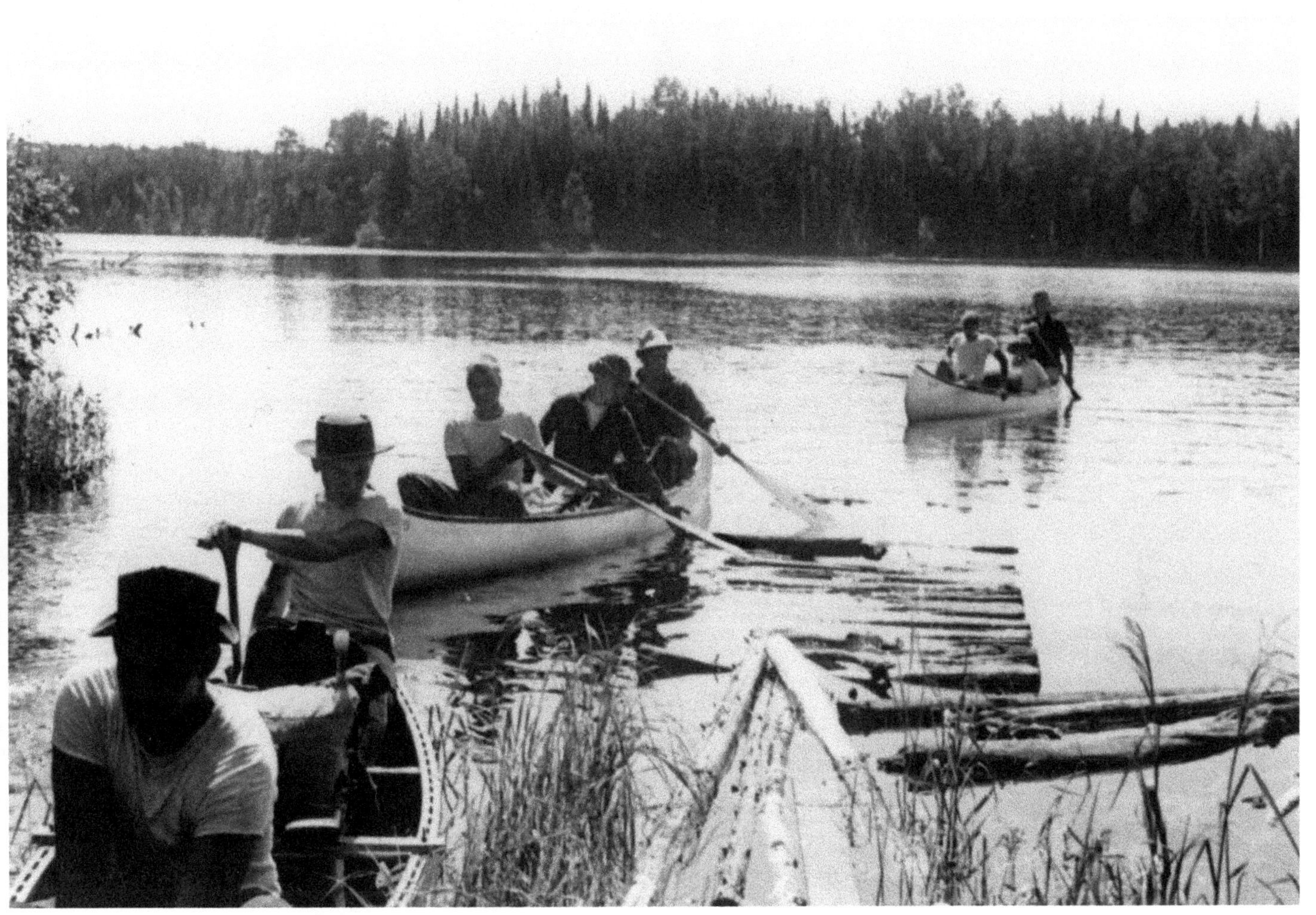

A canoeing party near a portage at Basswood Lake in 1943. This area would later be a protected wetland known as the Boundary Water Canoe Area.

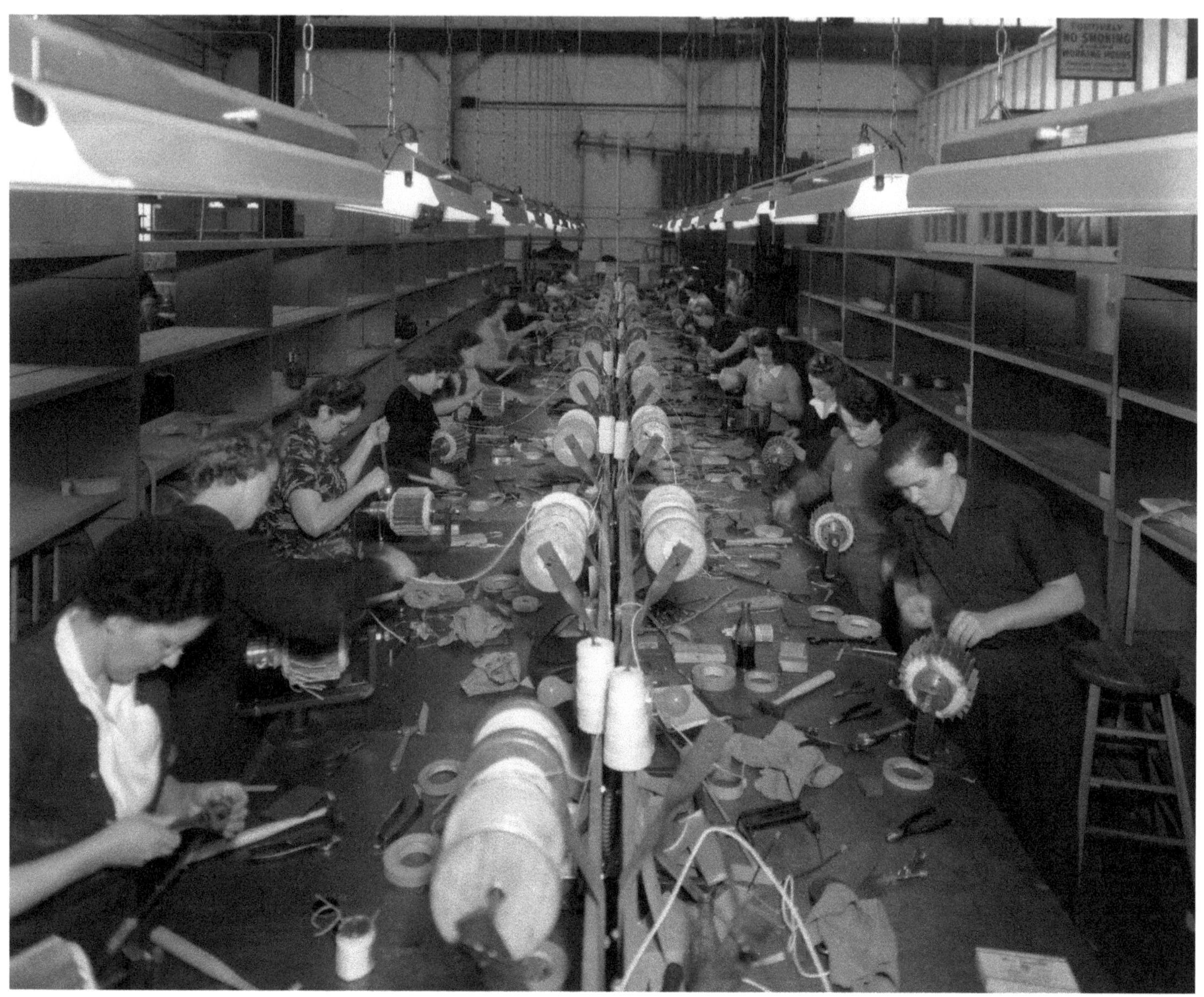


The wartime increase in production and the shortage of male labor meant that employers had to recruit and train women for positions traditionally filled by men. These wartime workers are winding armatures at the D. W. Onan and Sons plant near the University of Minnesota.

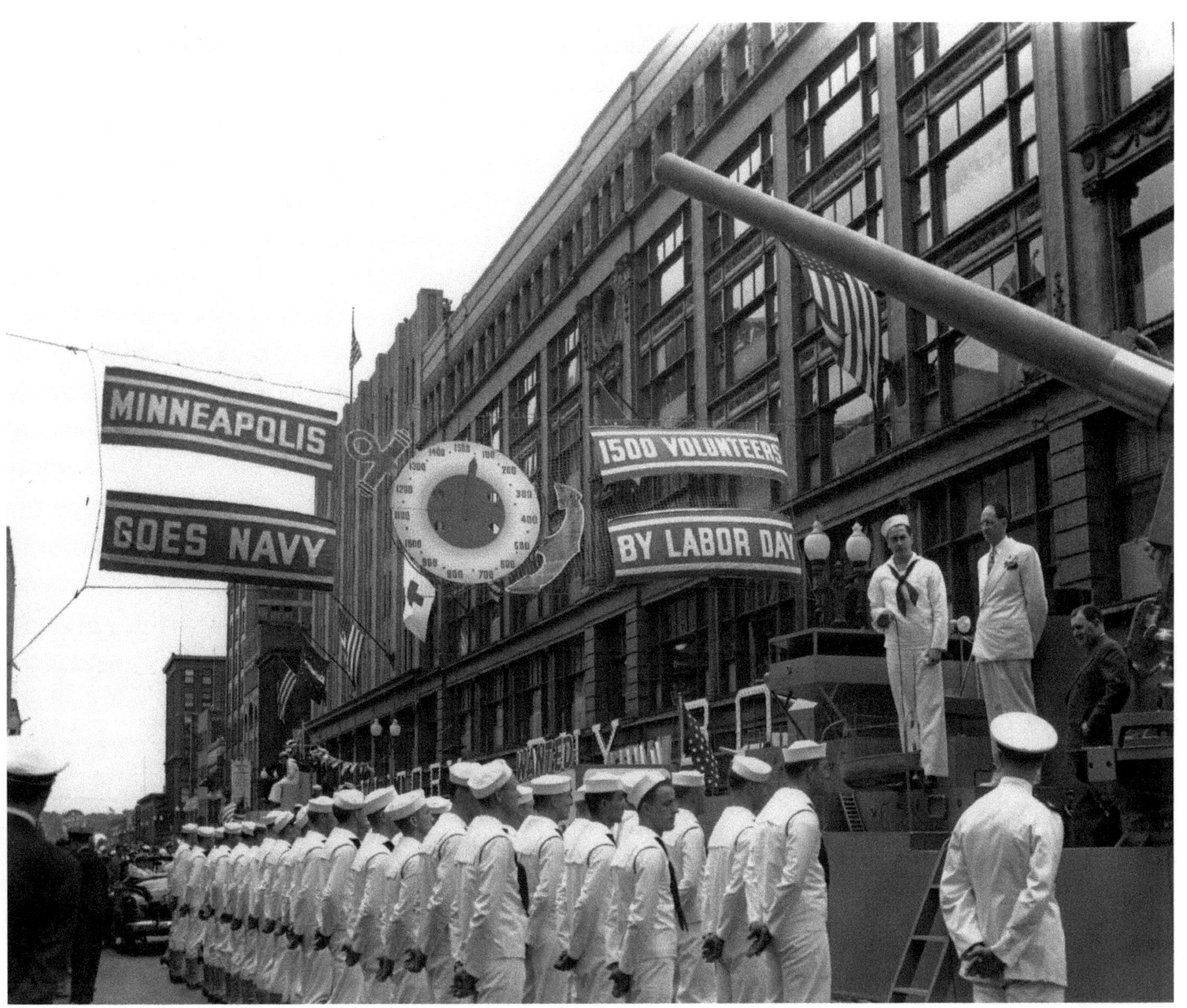


In a great show of patriotism and pageantry, the Navy recruited in downtown Minneapolis in the months following U.S. entry into World War II.

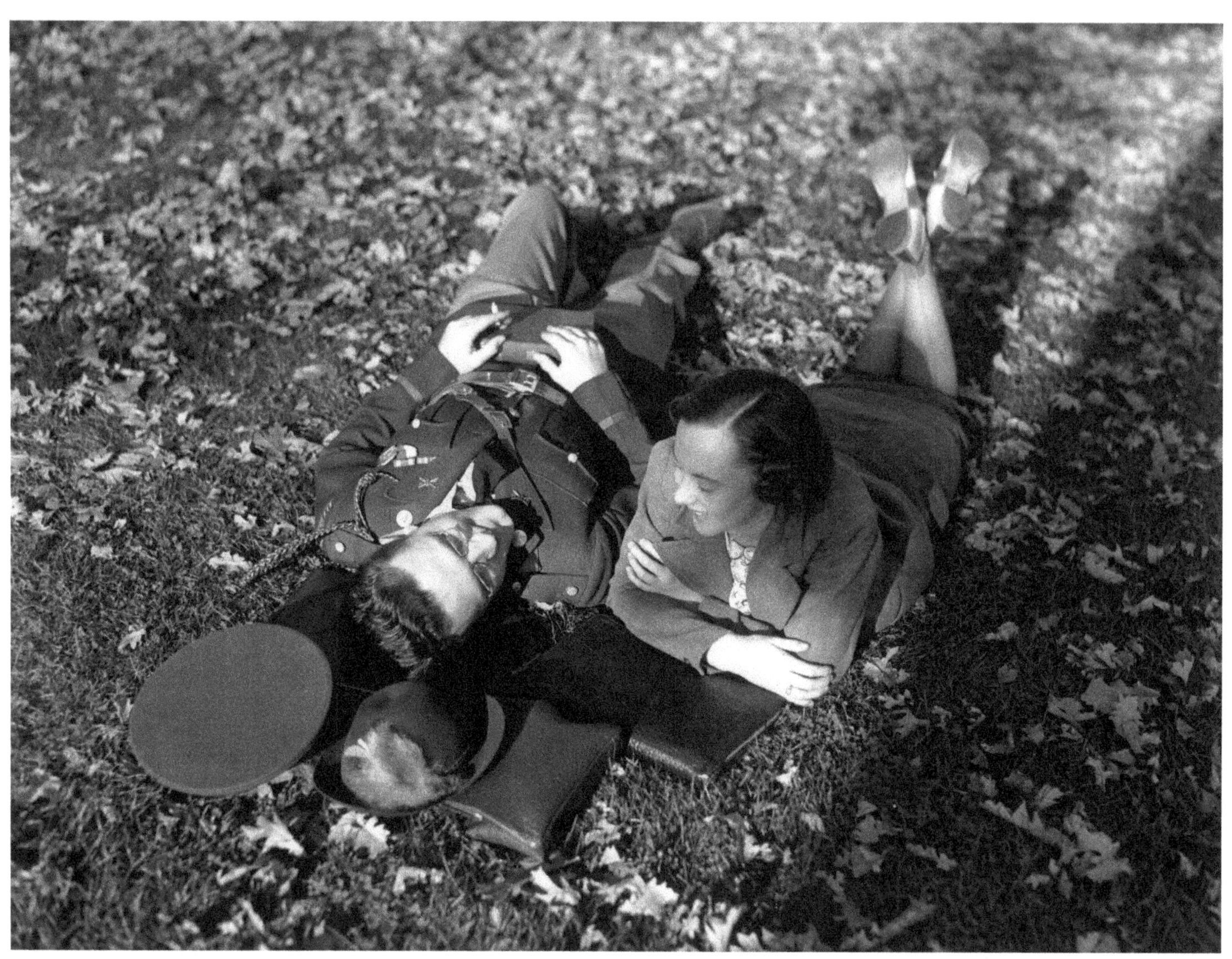

The quintessential image of a World War II soldier and his "gal back home." The soldier, on leave, is home in Minnesota for a short visit.

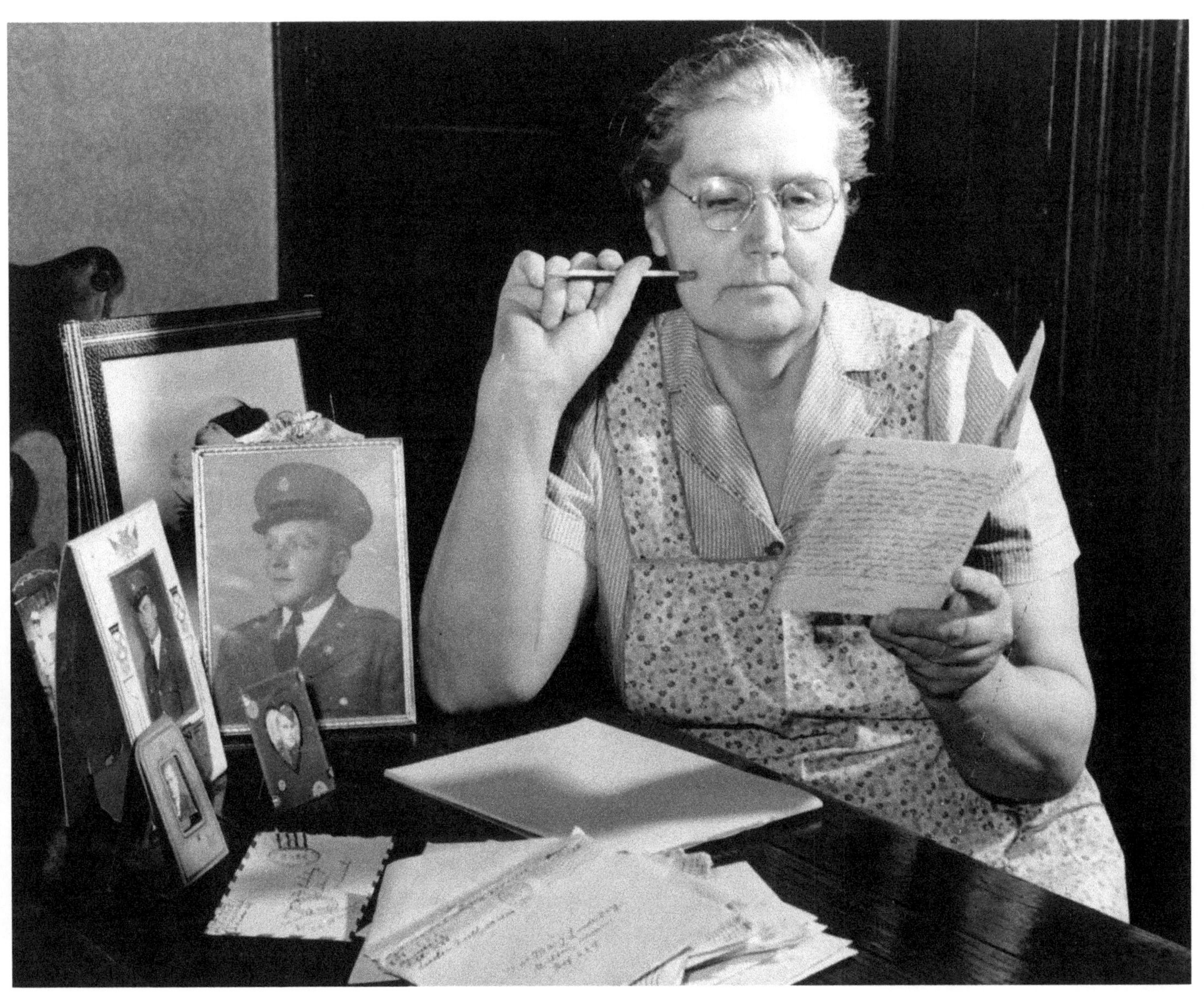

A Minnesota mother sits and reads a letter from her son who is fighting overseas in 1943.

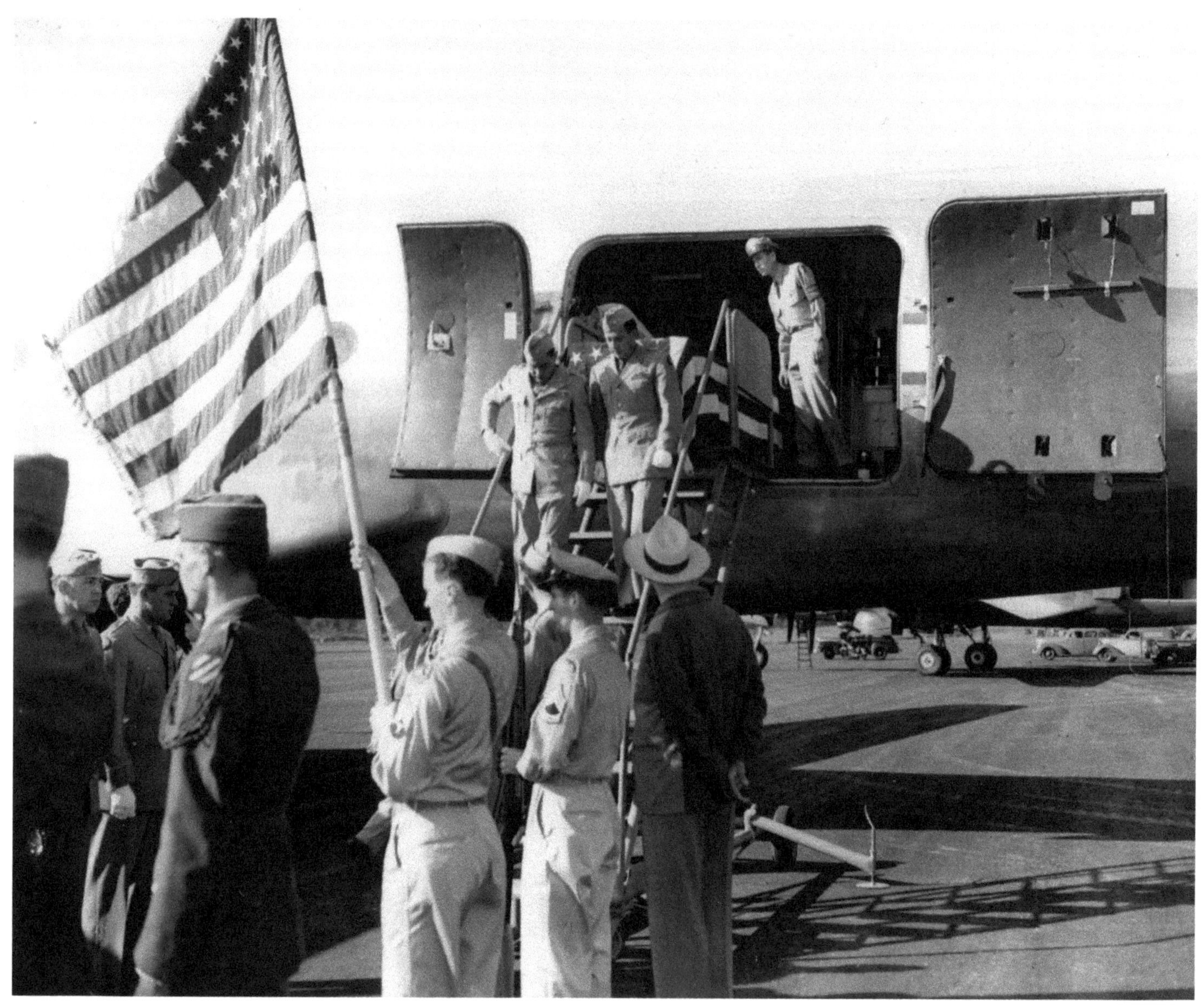

In August 1945, the body of Major Richard Bong, a World War II Medal of Honor recipient, was flown to Duluth to be buried in nearby Poplar, Wisconsin. A Wisconsin native, Bong shot down at least 40 Japanese planes during World War II, making him the United States' highest-scoring air ace. He died during a test flight in Burbank, California, when the plane's fuel pump malfunctioned.

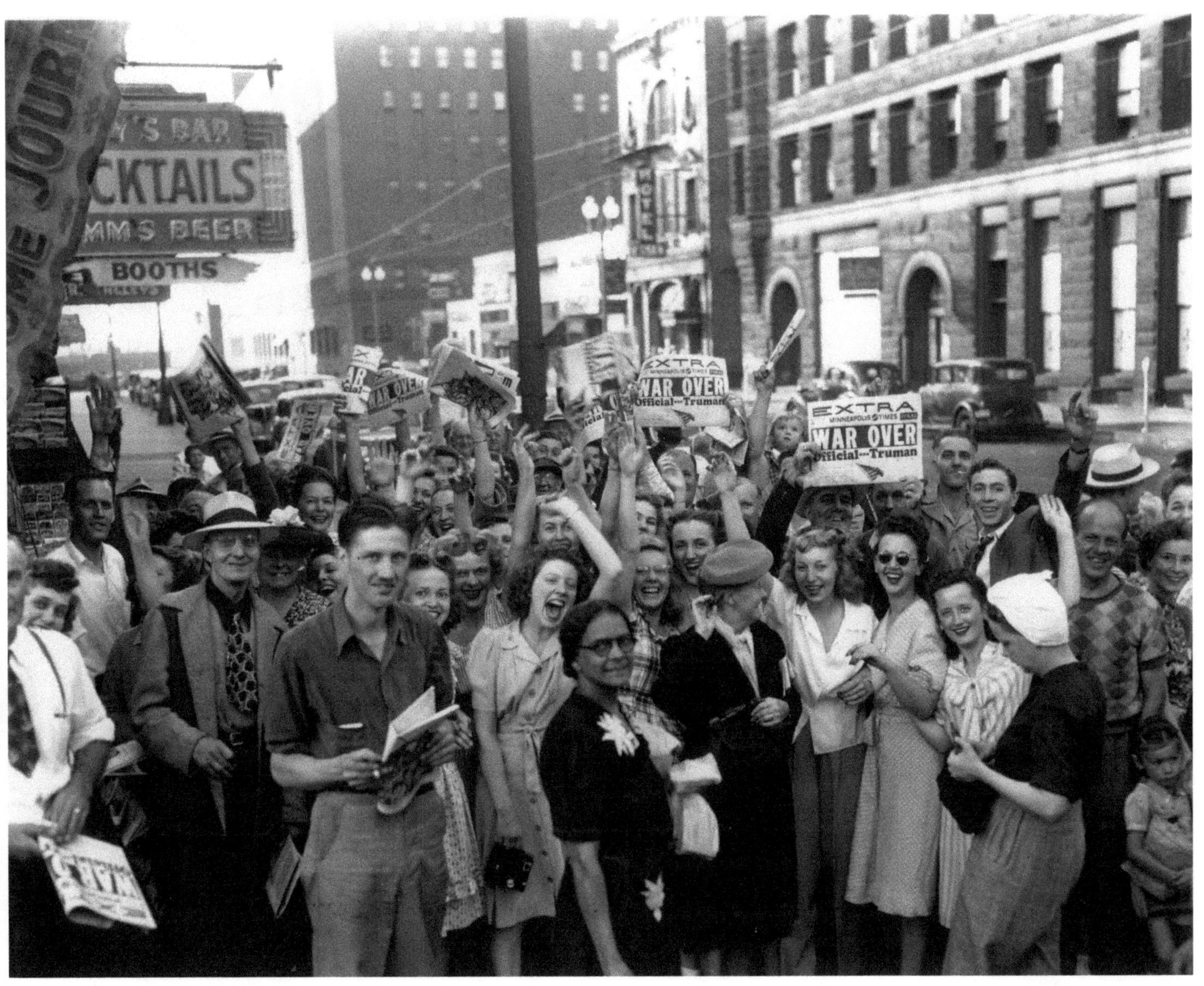


With newspapers held aloft, a crowd in downtown Minneapolis celebrates victory over Japan and the end of World War II on August 15, 1945. All across the state, Minnesotans celebrated V-J Day with singing, drinking, and dancing. Some celebrations in the downtowns of the Twin Cities spanned several days and nights.

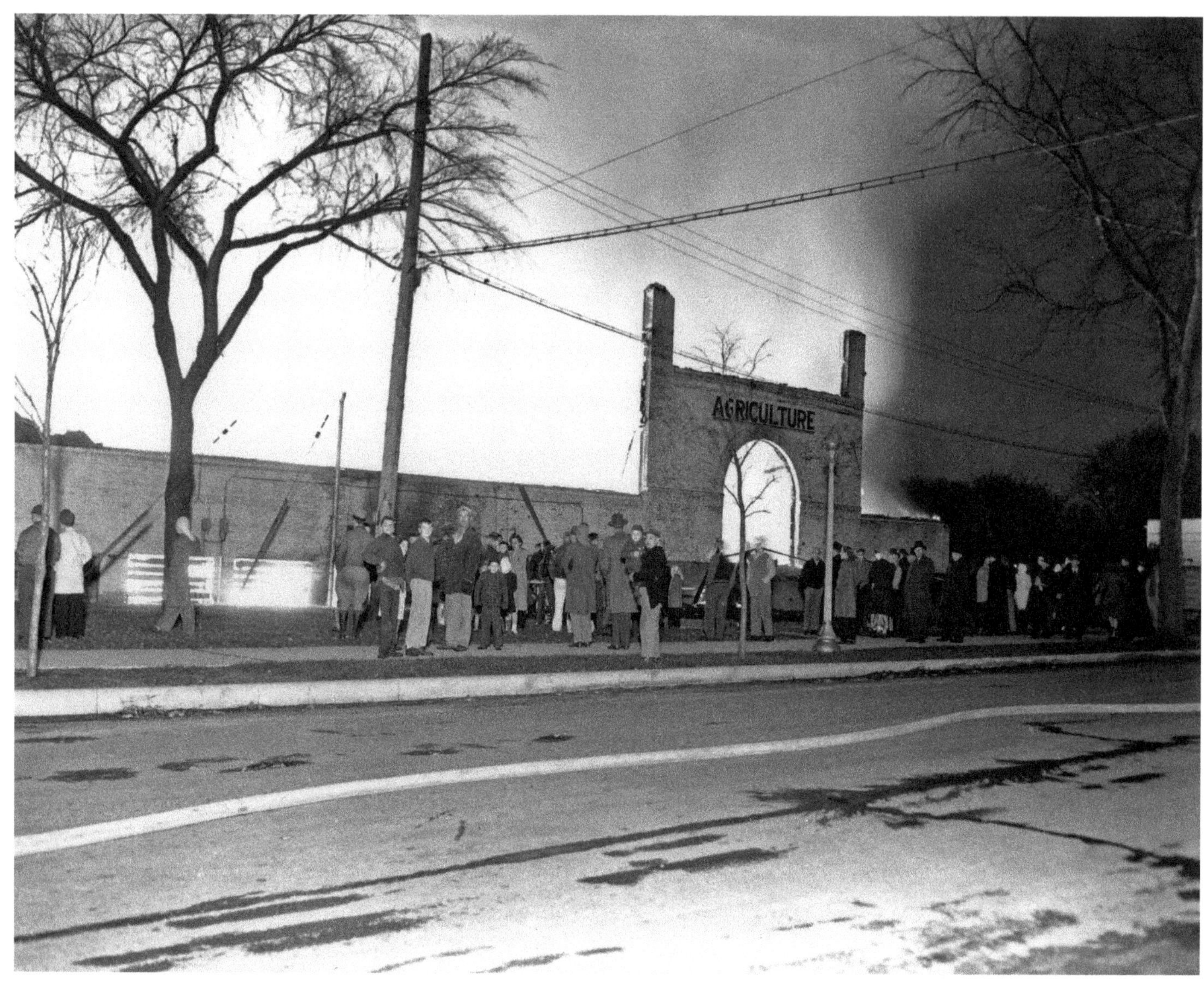


On November 10, 1944, crowds turn out to watch the fire department attempt to put out a fire engulfing the Agriculture Building on the Minnesota State Fairgrounds. The fire completely destroyed the building. Built in 1885, the Agriculture Building was the first structure on the fairgrounds.

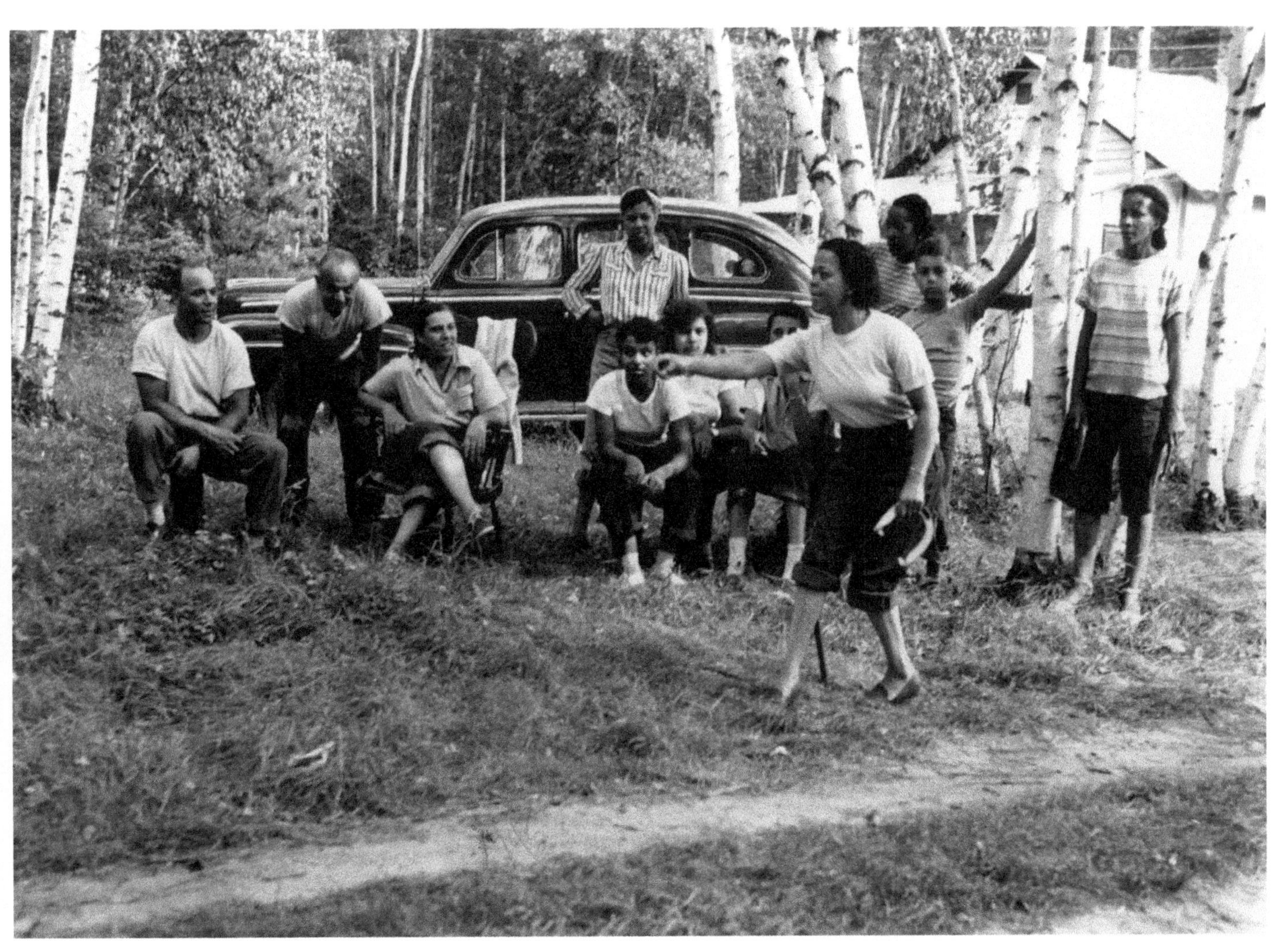

Minnesota families play horseshoes at a Twin Cities Reel and Trigger Club picnic on Labor Day in 1945.

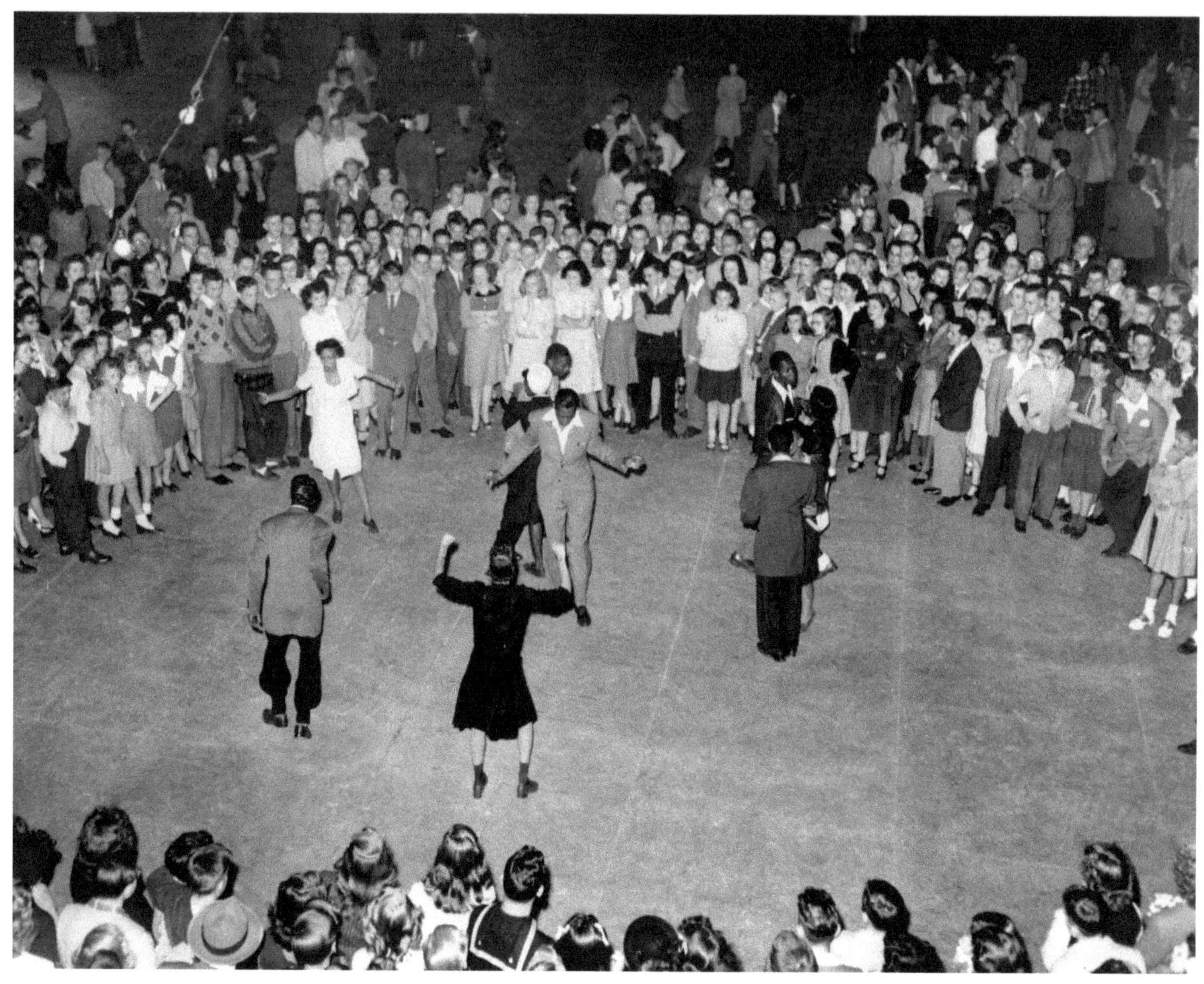

A crowd of teens, most of whom are white, stand back and watch as African American couples dance the jitterbug at the 1945 Harvest Moon Ball at the St. Paul Auditorium.

# Modern Minnesota

## (1946–1969)

When World War II ended, servicemen and servicewomen came home, women on the home front left their wartime jobs, and many people settled down to start families. However, in Minnesota, a major housing crisis kept young couples from finding places of their own. Temporary housing—Quonset huts made of prefabricated, corrugated, galvanized iron—was established on the Minnesota State Fairgrounds, and in West St. Paul and North Minneapolis, until demand could meet supply.

In 1949, the state proudly celebrated the Minnesota Territory Centennial with numerous parades, reenactments, pageants, and concerts, then did it all again in 1958 to mark the 100-year anniversary of Minnesota's statehood.

A new optimistic era began, yet the cold war threat of nuclear annihilation was a constant reminder to many that they could lose everything they had fought so hard for during the war. Bomb shelters were built, schoolchildren learned to "duck and cover" in the event of an enemy attack, and people stockpiled goods, just in case.

Minnesotans built new suburbs, businesses, highways, hospitals, schools, libraries, and shopping centers. However, the state's progress left a scarred landscape and transformed cityscapes, with entire neighborhoods, farmlands, and beautiful buildings wiped out in the name of modernity.

Manufacturing and technology experienced enormous growth in the postwar era, with Minnesota companies producing the latest in computers and medical devices. Agriculture also flourished and diversified. With the richest deposits depleted on the Iron Range, it looked as though the mining industry in Minnesota would experience a fate similar to lumber. However, new manufacturing plants were created to process taconite ore, keeping mining a viable state industry.

Minnesotans were called into service again in Korea and Vietnam, and more than 1,700 soldiers from the state gave their lives in the two conflicts. But as the 1960s progressed, many Americans weren't quick to support more war. When Dr. Martin Luther King, Jr., spoke at the University of Minnesota in 1967, he urged the crowd of 4,000 to raise their voices in protest against the Vietnam War. King also spoke of the fulfillment of the promise of equality, and expressed his belief that it was not too late for peace at home, and around the world.

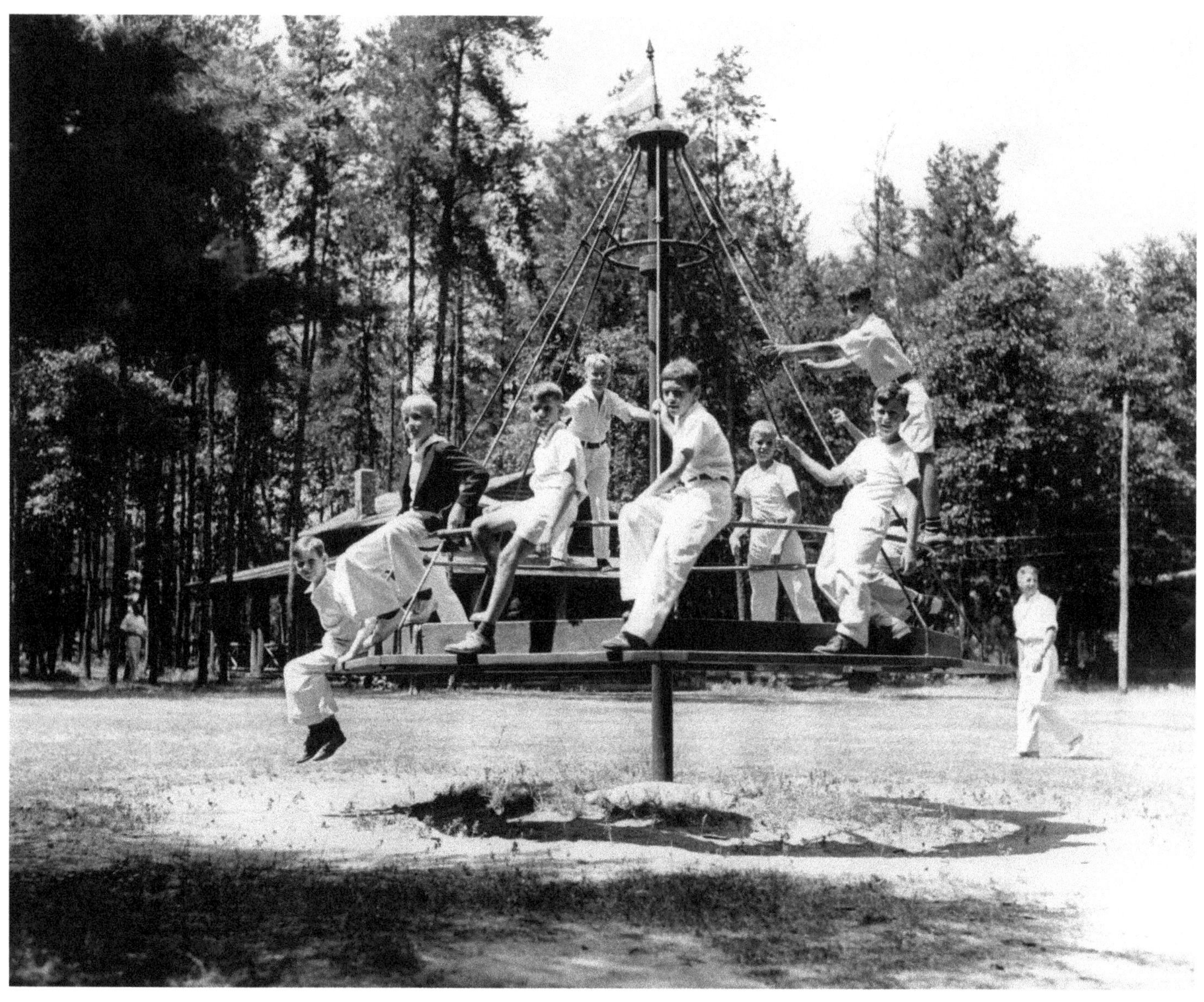

After the war, life began anew. Children born before or during the war enjoy the playground equipment at a Northern Minnesota resort.

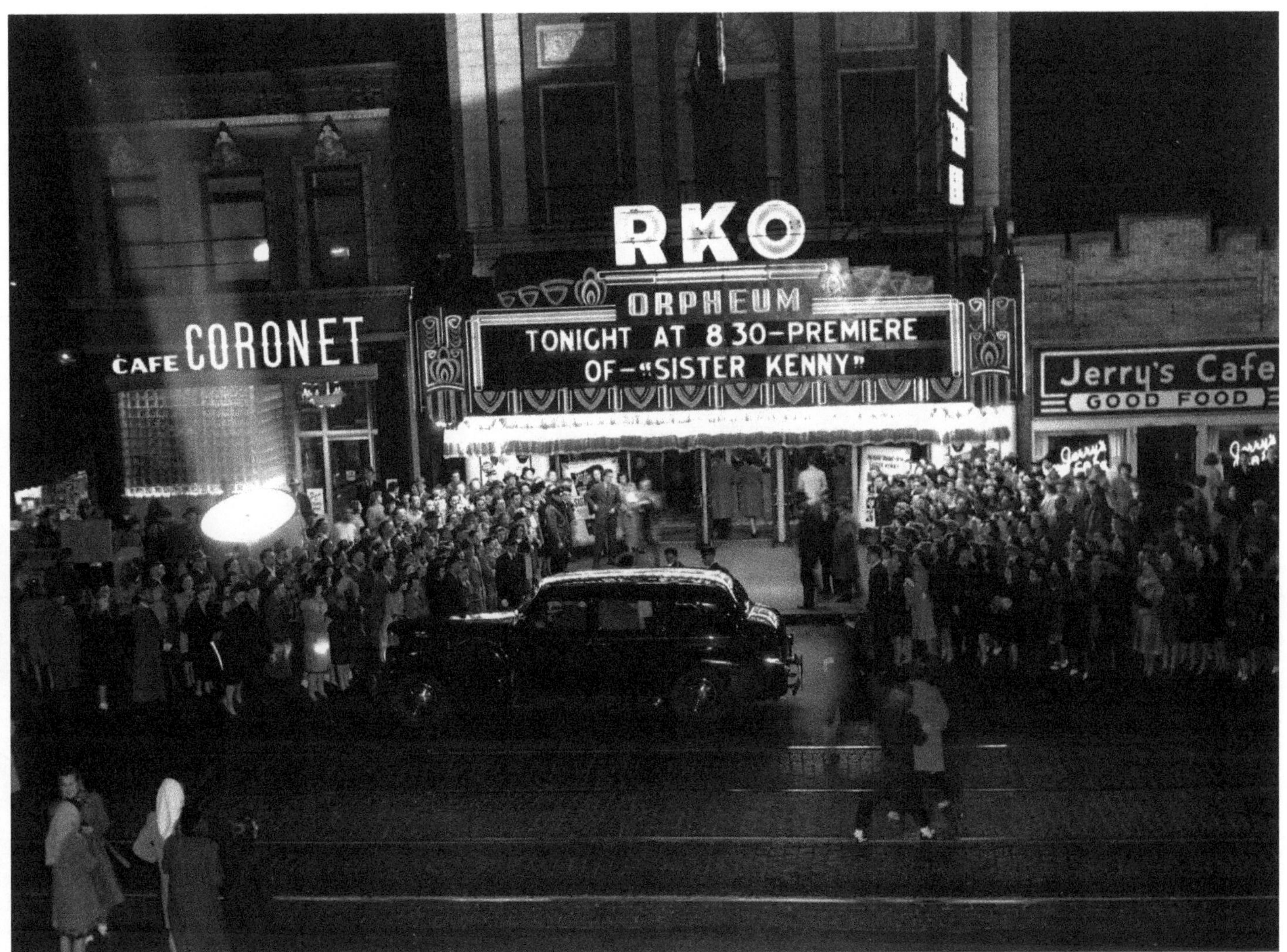


The premiere of the film *Sister Kenny* at the Orpheum Theater in Minneapolis in 1946. The movie was based on the life of Sister Elizabeth Kenny, who discovered a revolutionary treatment for infantile paralysis. She came from Australia to Minnesota in 1940 and established the Sister Kenny Institute, which opened its doors in Minneapolis in 1942. Rosalind Russell portrayed her in the film.

The Christmas tree in the governor's office reception room at the Minnesota State Capitol is decorated in 1946. Edward J. Thye's tenure as governor was about to end, with Luther W. Youngdahl prepared to take office on January 8, 1947.

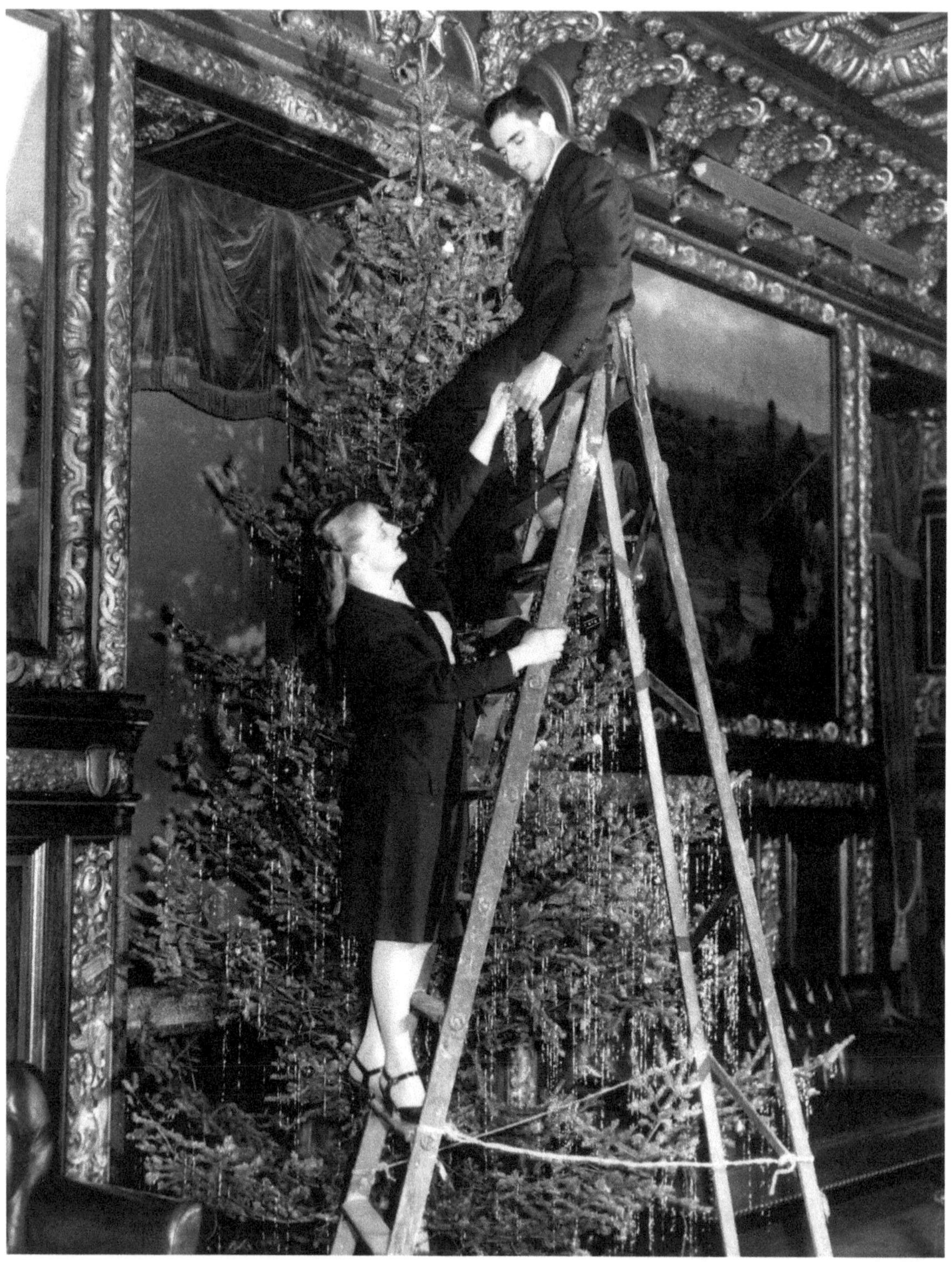

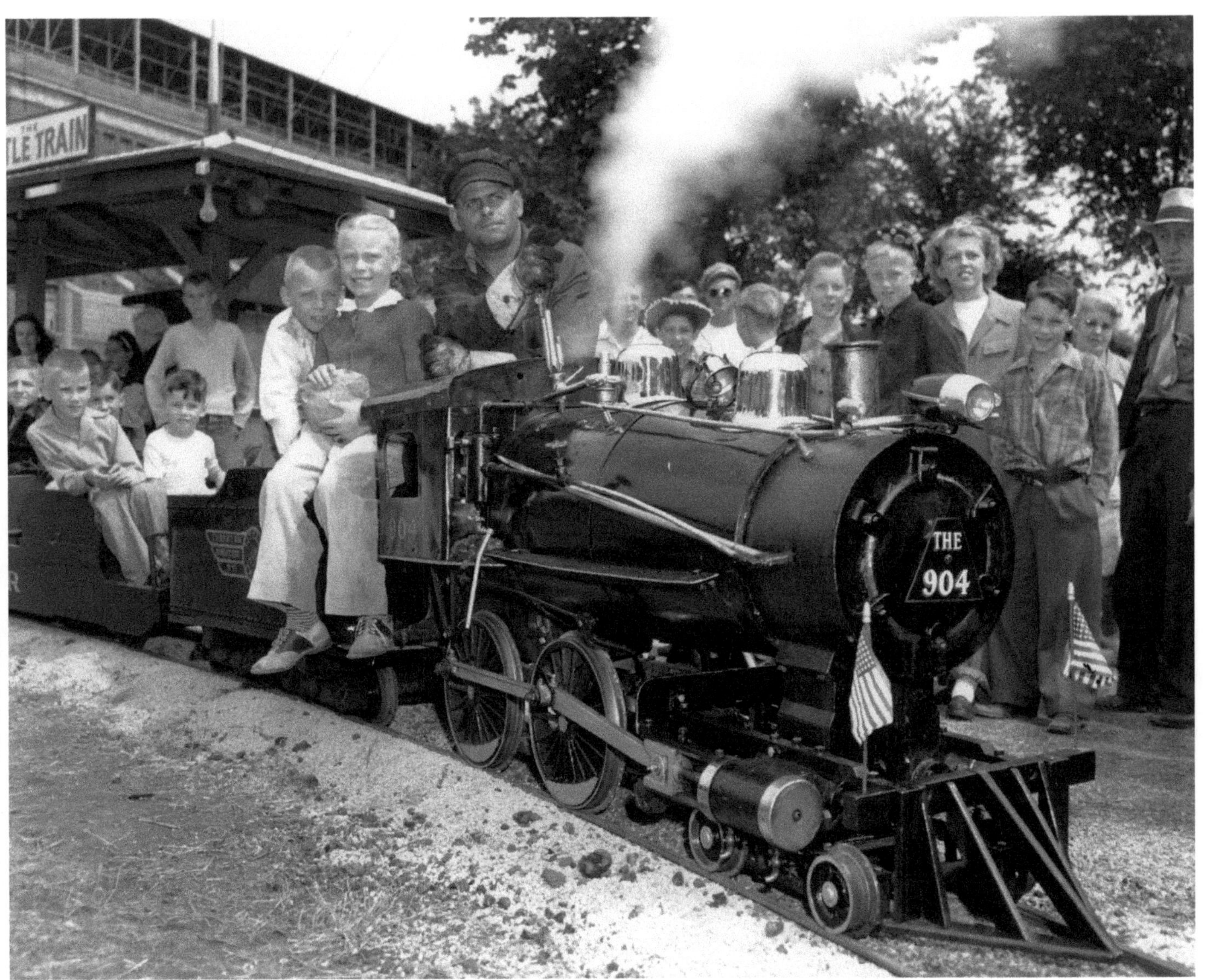


The engineer blows the whistle as a group of children prepare for an excursion on the popular Little Train at the Minnesota State Fair in 1947.

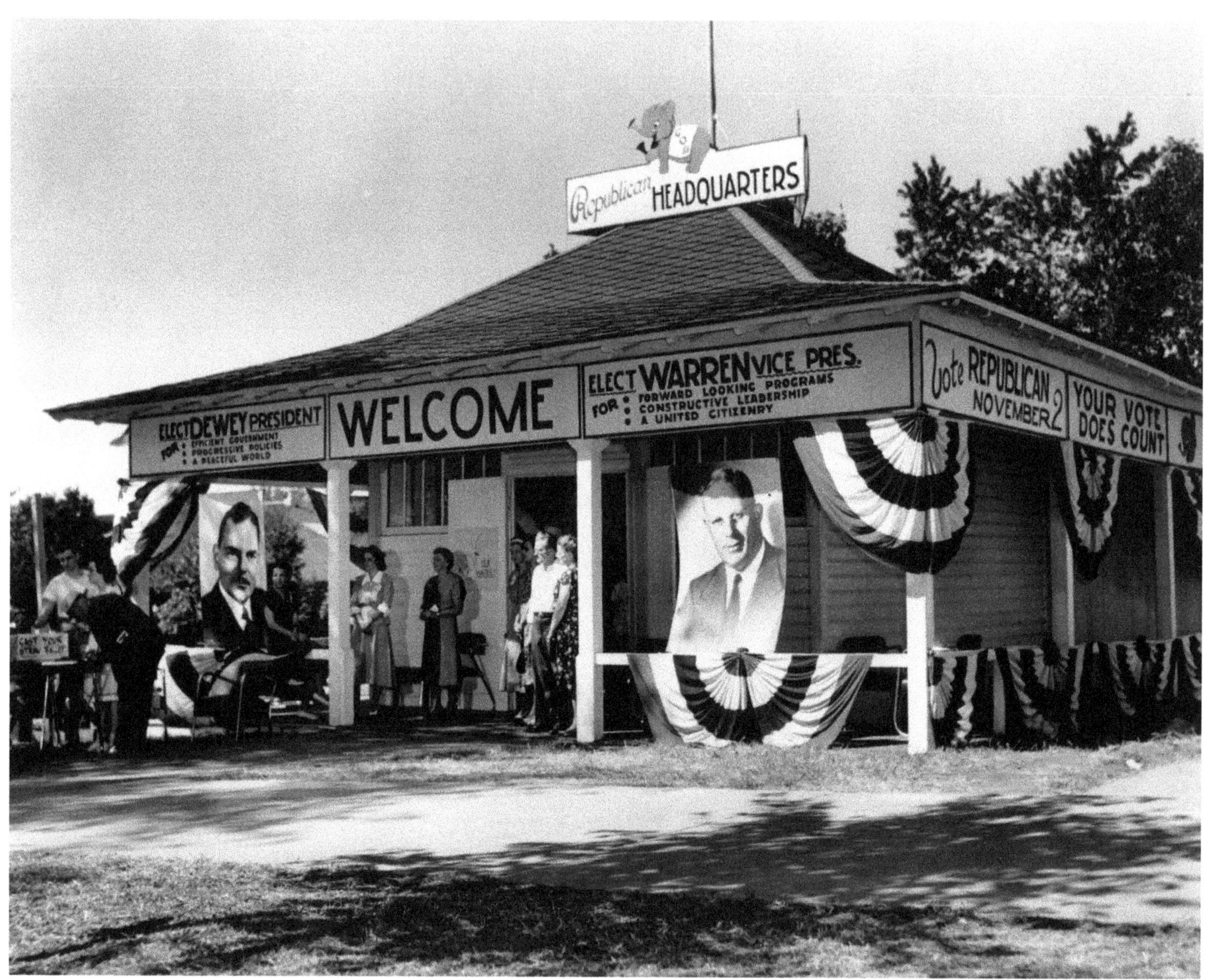


Republican headquarters for the Dewey-Warren ticket in 1948 at the Minnesota State Fair. From the early days, politicians were at home at the fair, campaigning and delivering speeches. Two presidents, Coolidge and Hayes, spoke to packed crowds at the grandstand, and Vice-president Theodore Roosevelt introduced his famous line "Speak softly and carry a big stick" at the fair in September 1901. Less than two weeks later, President McKinley was assassinated and Roosevelt became president.

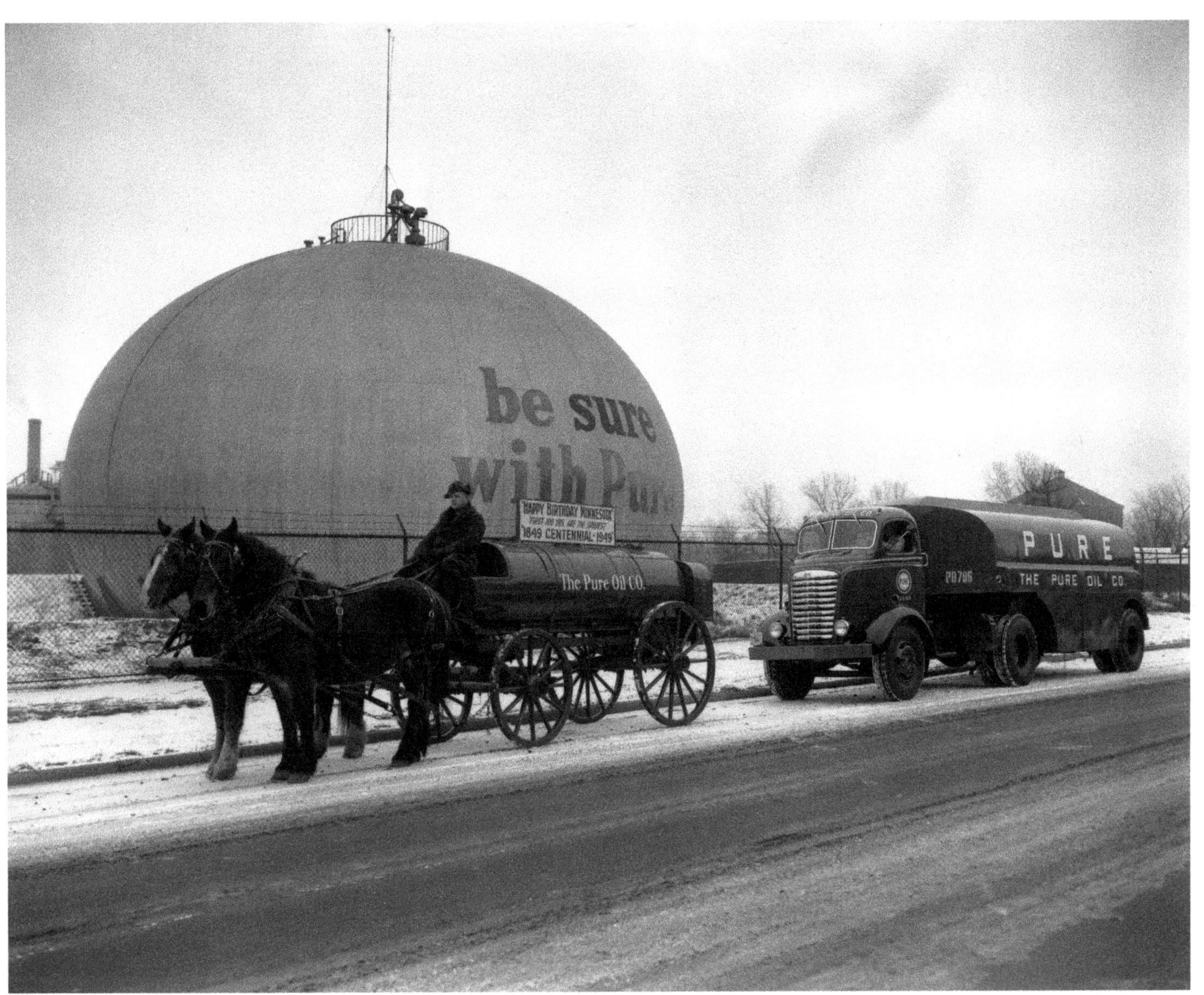


The Pure Oil Company kicks off celebration of the Minnesota Territory Centennial on December 31, 1949, with two modes of transportation, symbolic of how much Minnesota had changed in 100 years.

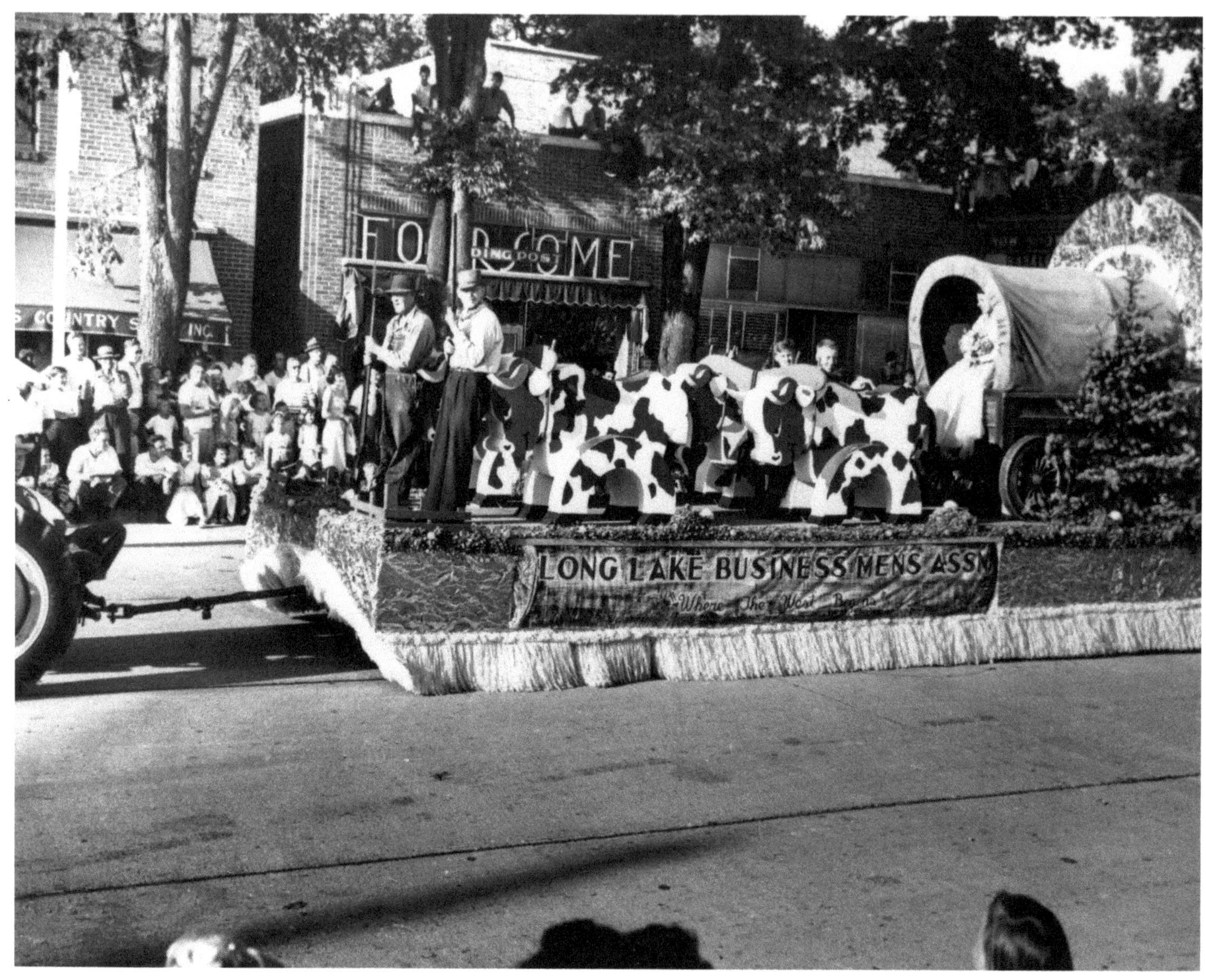


The Long Lake Business Men's Association float parades through Wayzata during the Minnesota Territory Centennial celebration in 1949. Some of the best parade viewing was from the rooftops of this Lake Minnetonka destination.

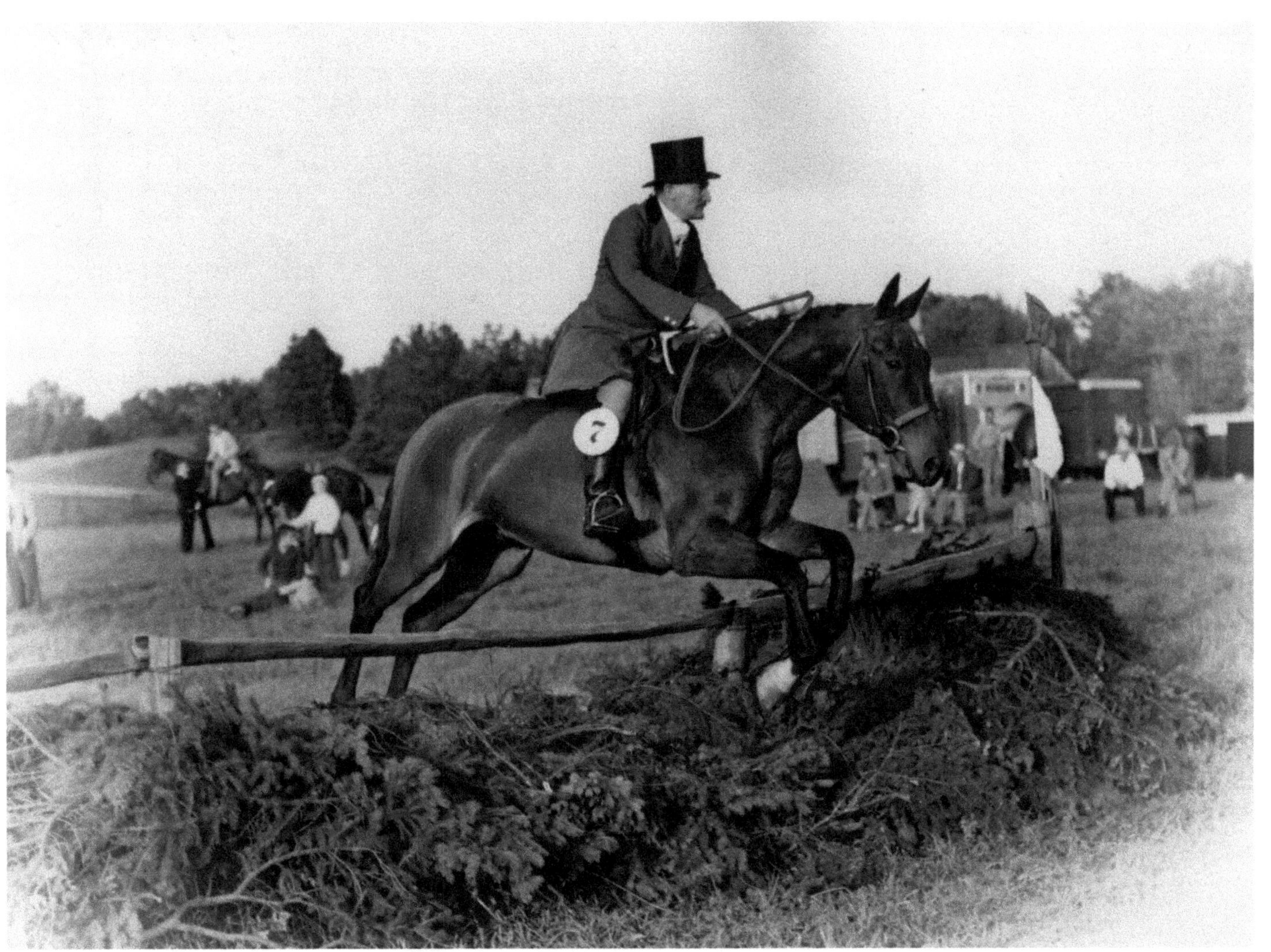

University of Minnesota faculty member Colonel Ralph M. Bitler and his horse Sun Valley compete in an equestrian event around 1949.

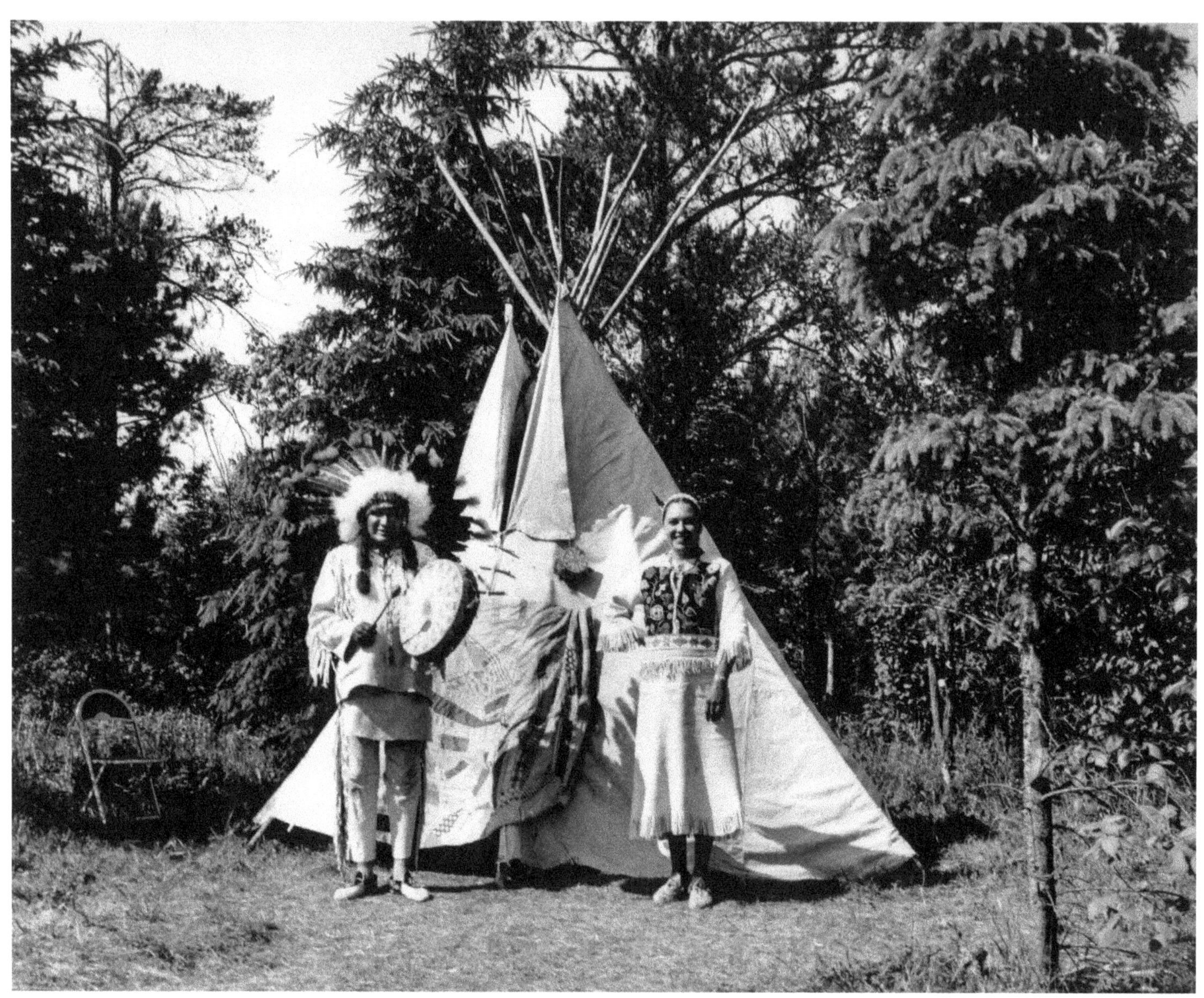

A Native American couple poses in front of a tepee at Itasca State Park during the Minnesota Territory Centennial pageant. The headwaters of the Mississippi River are inside Itasca State Park.

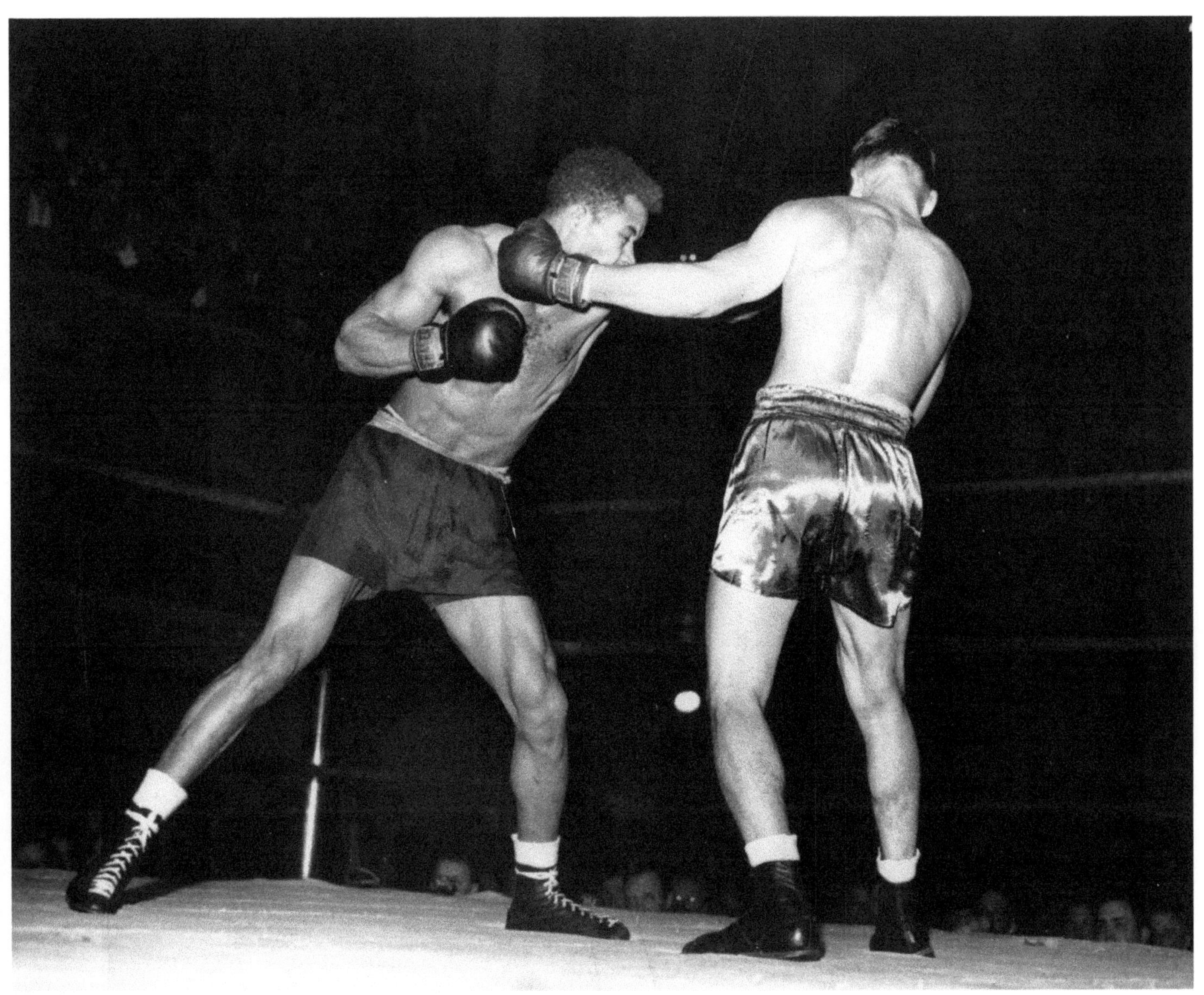

Pudgy Thurston, on the left, takes on an opponent in a 1950s boxing match. This event was an activity of the Hallie Q. Brown Settlement House, which served St. Paul's African American community. Organized in 1929 (though its origins date to 1908), the settlement house offered a host of classes, including art and athletics. Similarly, the Phyllis Wheatley House served the African American community in Minneapolis.

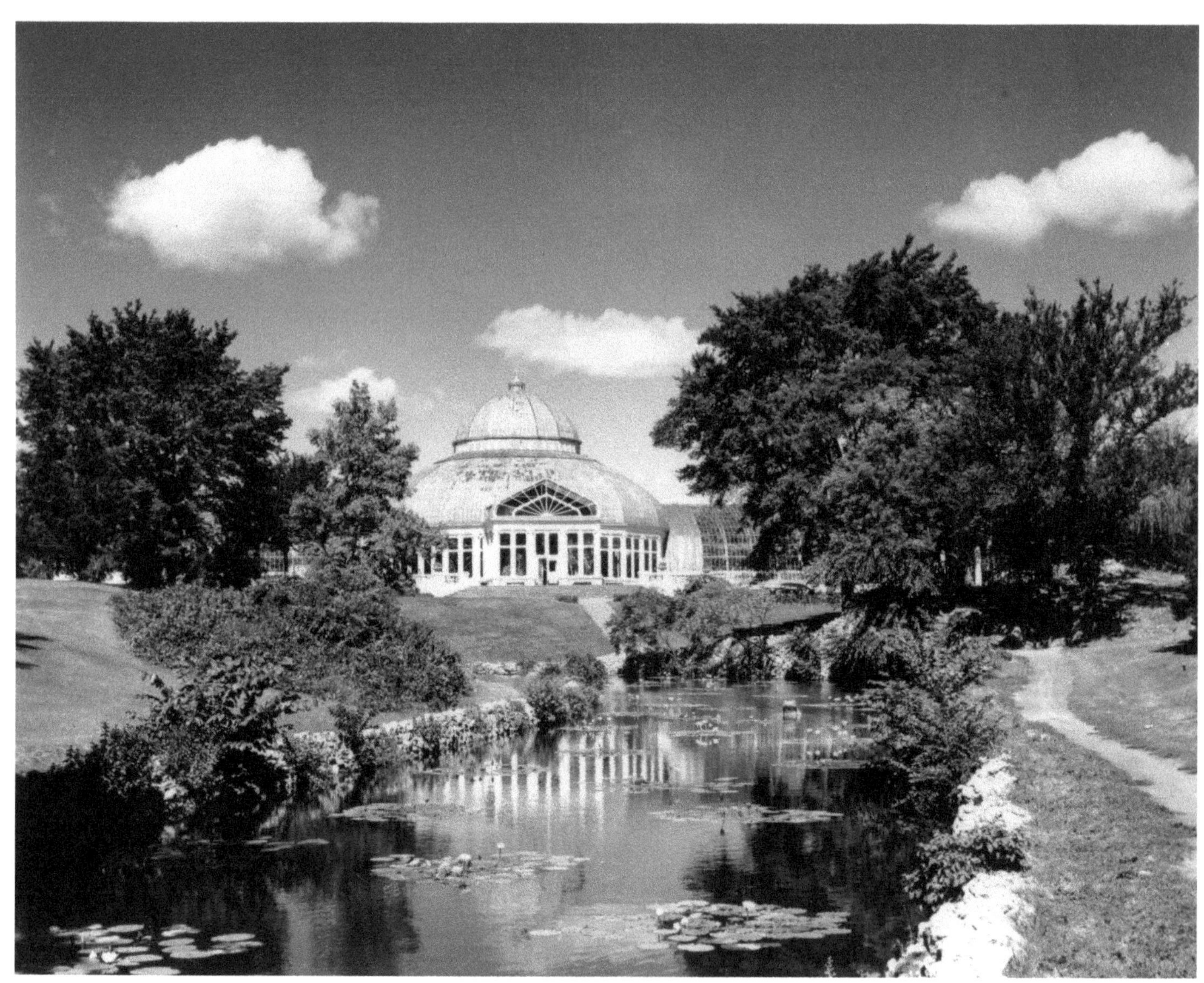

St. Paul's Como Conservatory, as it appeared around 1950. The glass-enclosed garden housed exotic plants and flower shows year round. The Conservatory is part of a picturesque area by Lake Como that was preserved by the city to develop into a "landscape park" for "physical and moral sanitation."

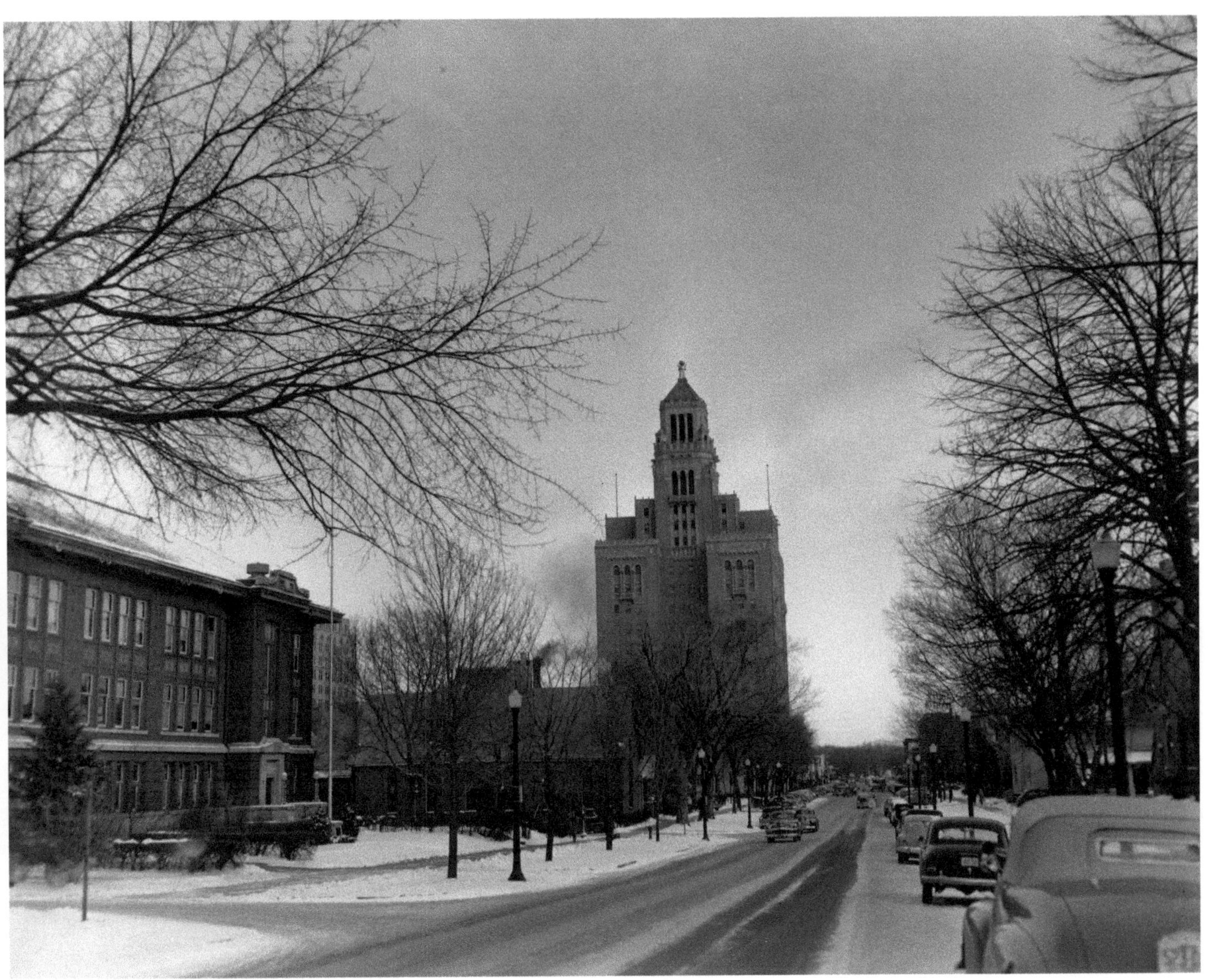

World-renowned Mayo Clinic (the tall building at center) in Rochester in January 1950. William Worrall Mayo, a doctor from England, settled in Rochester in 1863 and started a practice. His two sons joined in the 1880s. The Mayos invited other doctors to join their practice, a new concept at the time, leading to the establishment of Mayo Clinic in 1907.

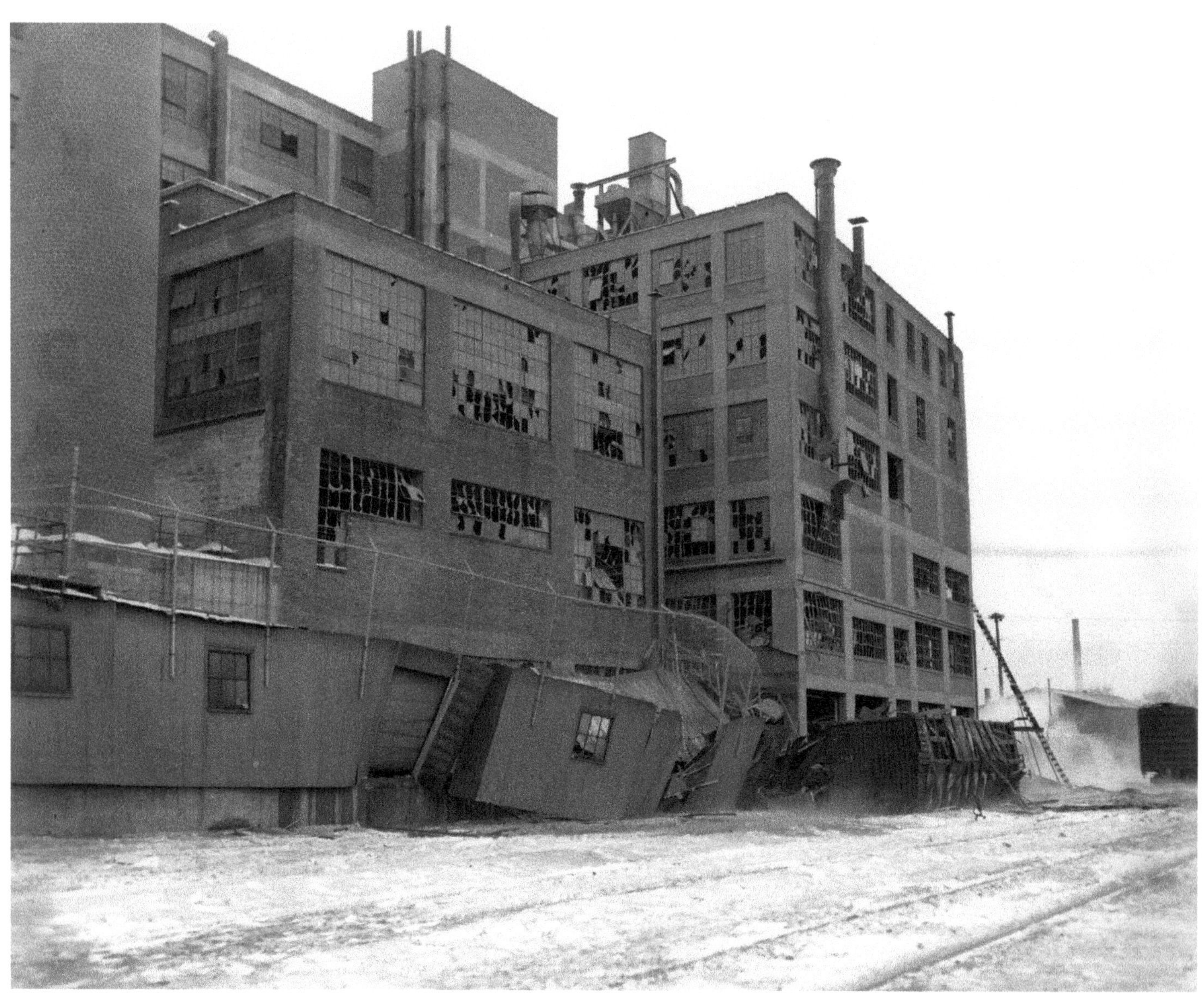

On February 8, 1951, the Minerals Building at the 3M plant in St. Paul exploded due to a butane leak. Fifteen employees died and 49 were injured in the explosion.

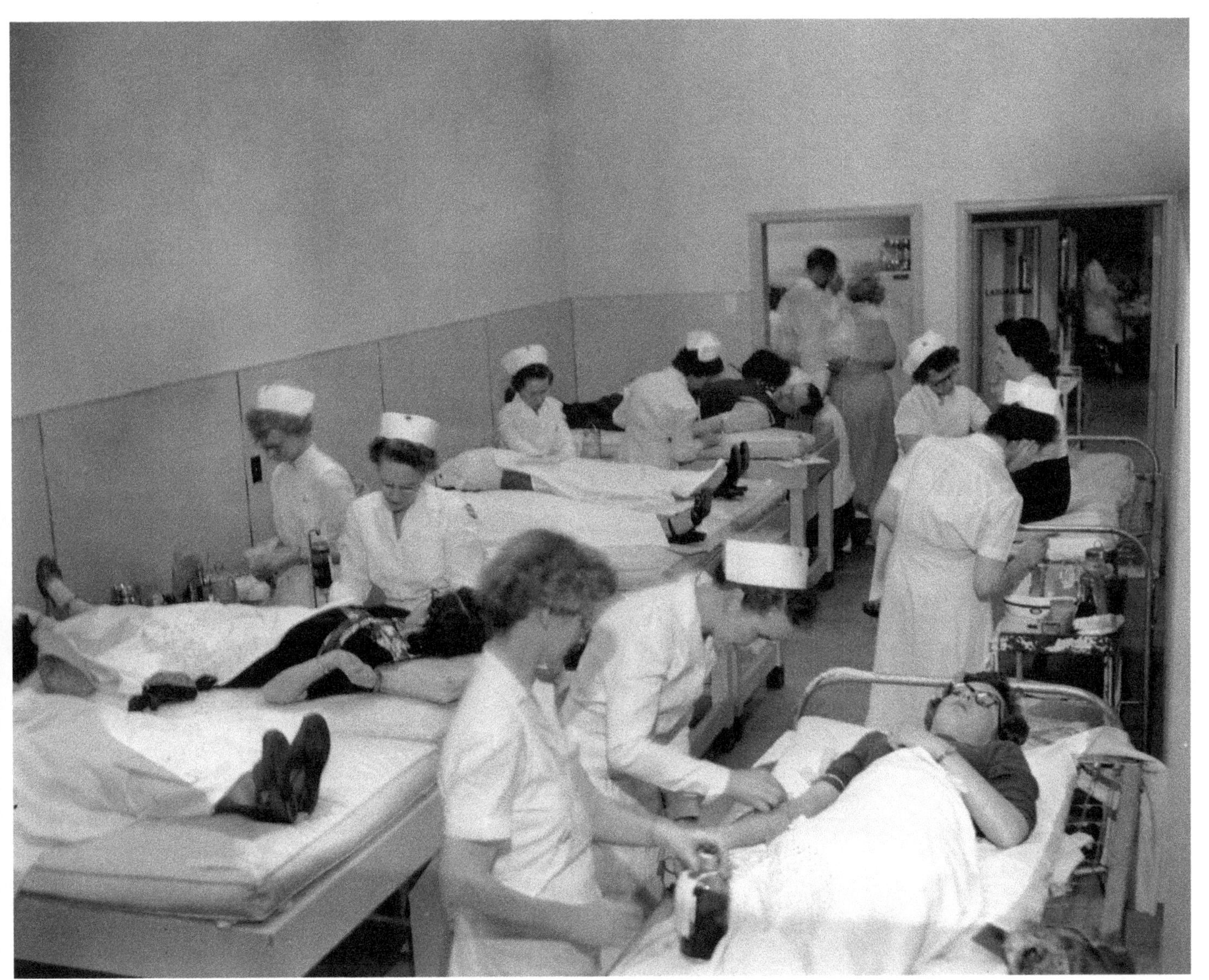

After the explosion at the 3M plant on February 8, 1951, employees were treated at various hospitals around the Twin Cities.

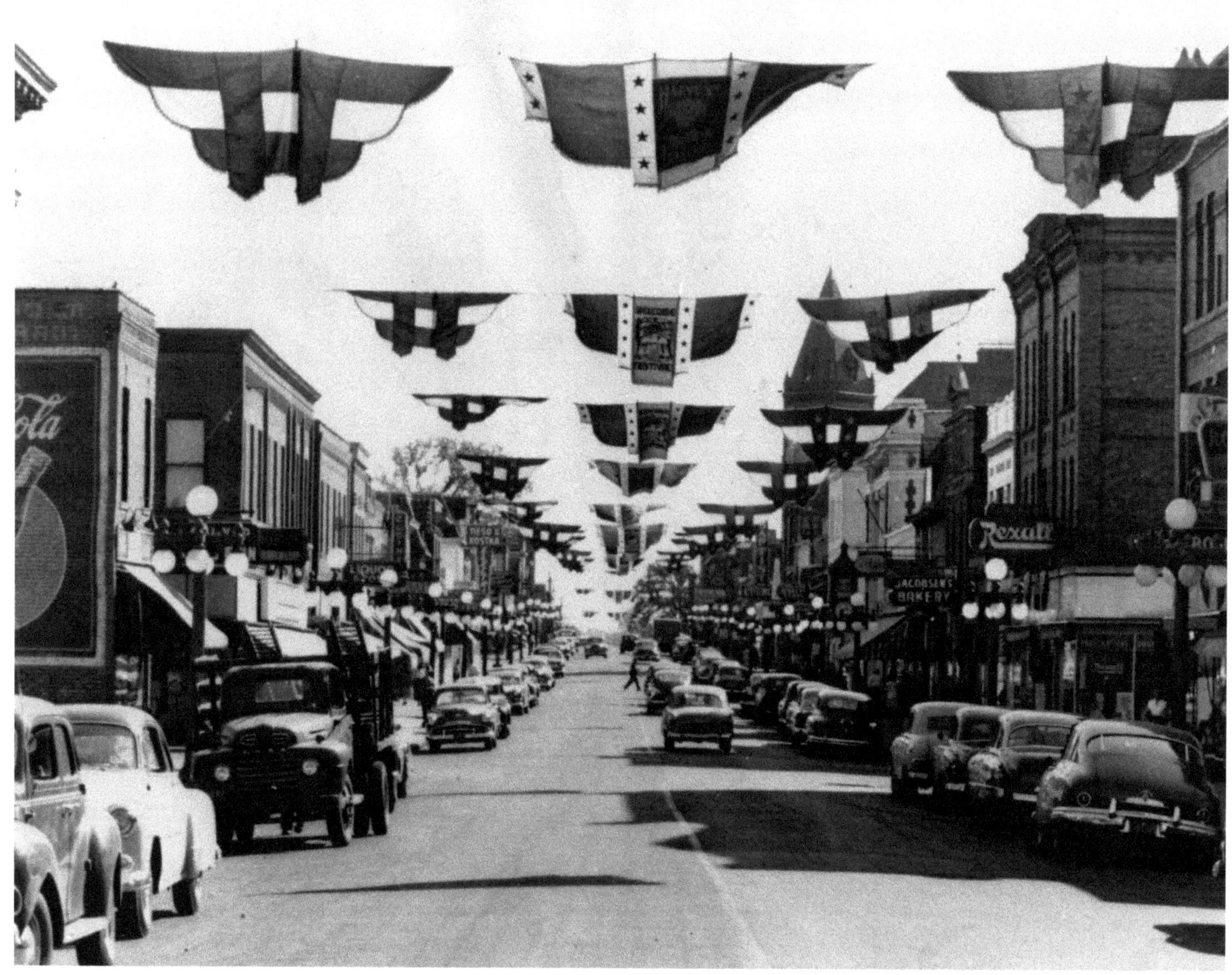


Payne Avenue on the East Side of St. Paul decorated in 1952 for the annual Payne Avenue Harvest Festival. East Side merchants looking to drum up more business founded this festival in 1906. The festival and community were deeply rooted in the East Side's Italian, Mexican, Swedish, and German roots, evident in the mom-and-pop shops along Payne Avenue.

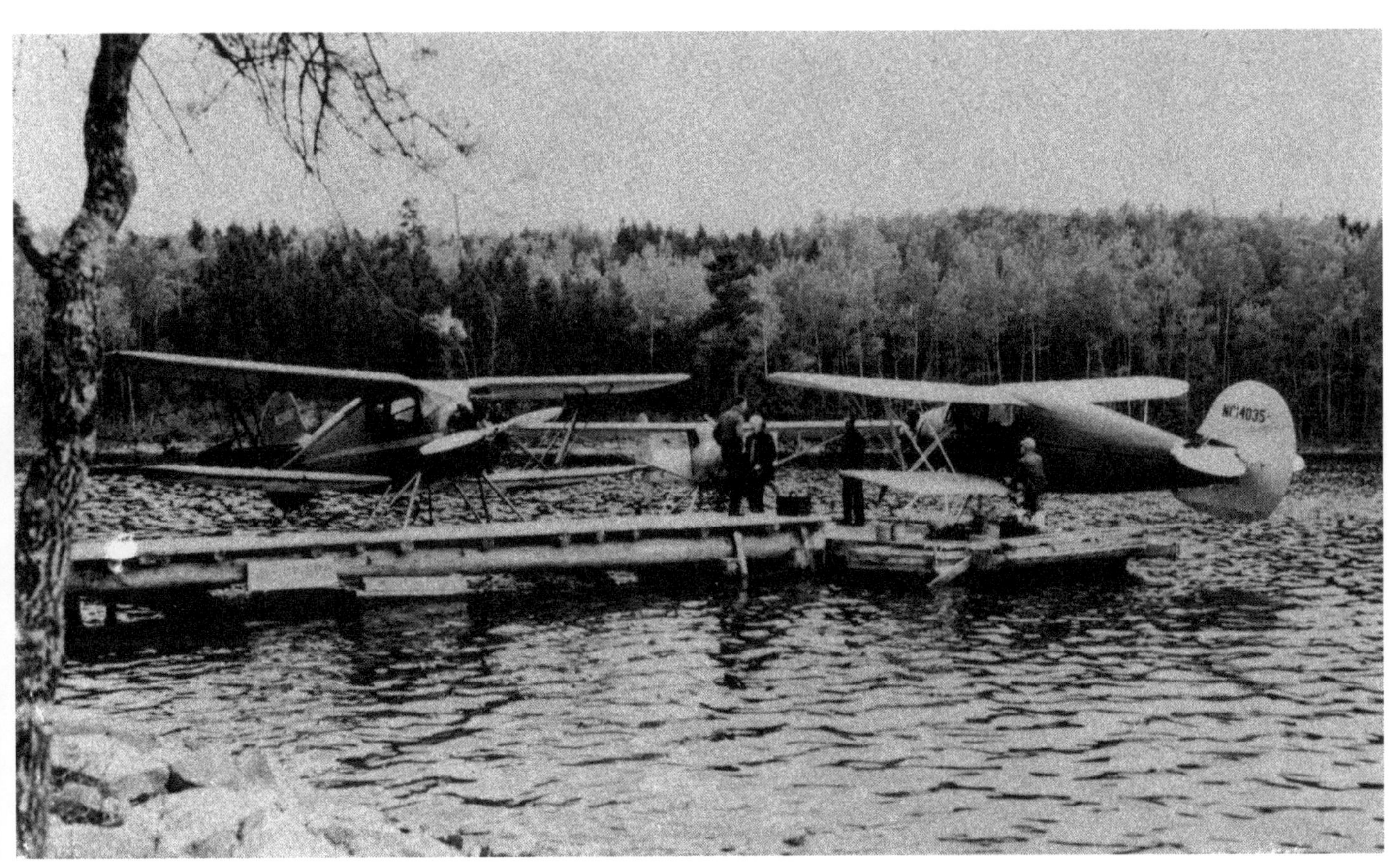


A postcard of the planes that provided access to remote fishing camps in Northern Minnesota and Canada. Taken in Ely, this photograph shows fishermen headed to Crooked Lake.

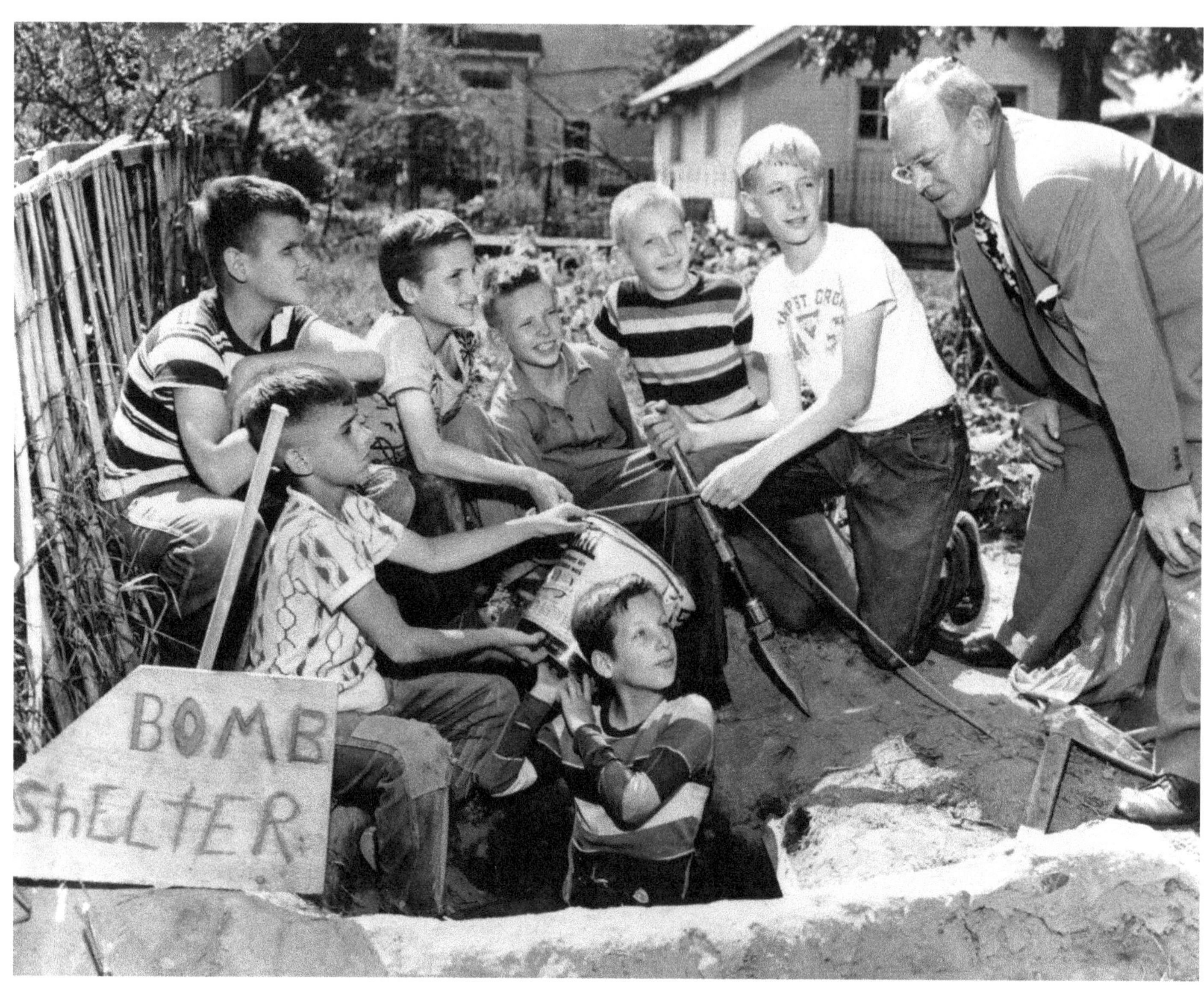


In America in 1952, the cold war threat of nuclear weapons popularized the notion that building a bomb shelter could save lives in the event of an enemy attack. In this image from a civil defense campaign, Minnesota boys have traded in their fort house to dig a backyard bomb shelter.

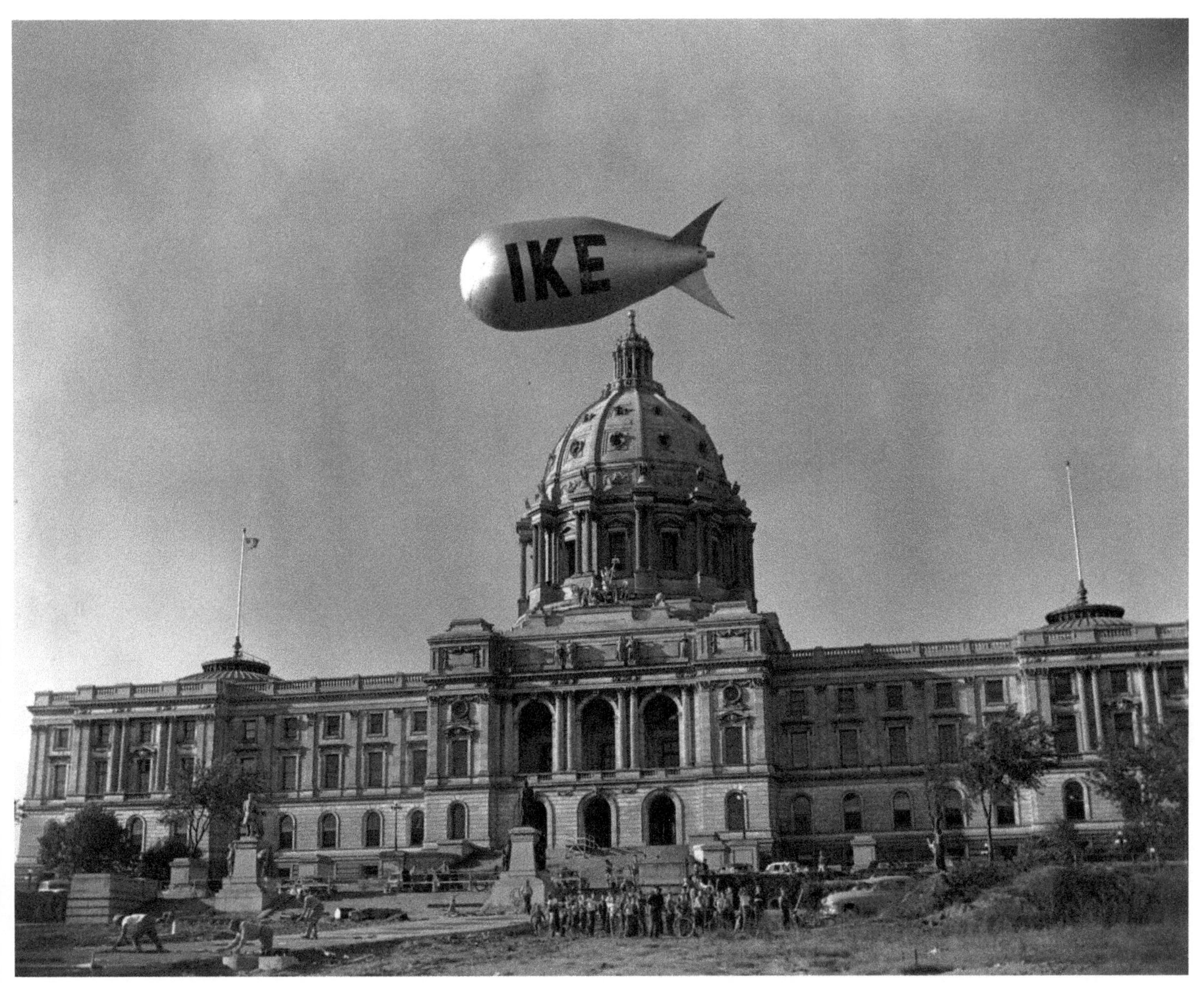


On September 15, 1952, a 35-foot "Ike" dirigible flew over the Minnesota State Capitol in St. Paul. The next day, a crowd of 12,000 turned out to hear presidential candidate Dwight D. Eisenhower speak there.

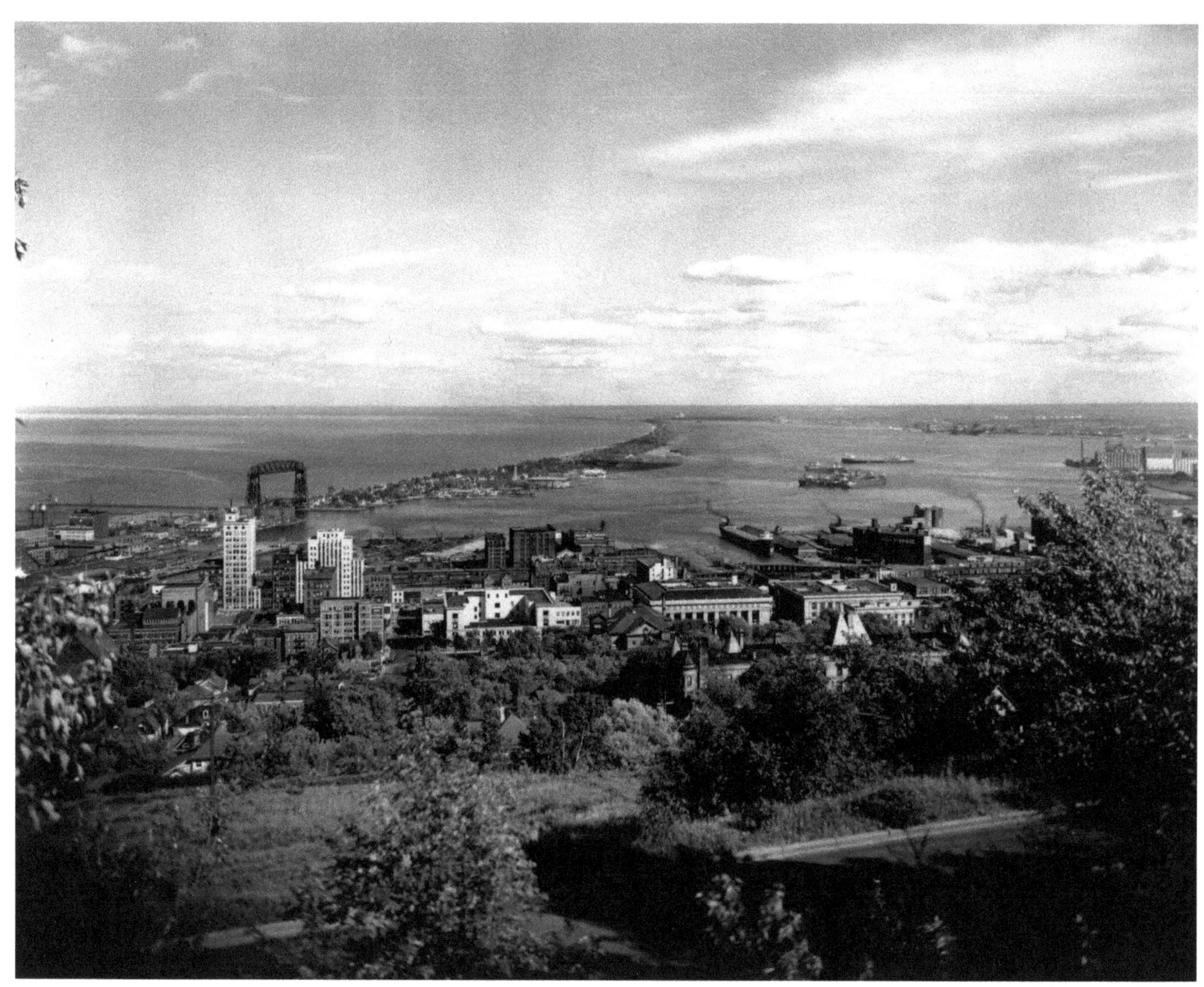

A bird's-eye view of the Duluth-Superior Harbor, ships, the Aerial Lift Bridge, and Minnesota Point (Park Point) in 1952. After the war, Duluth experienced a major boom in population and significant growth that steadily continued to 1960.

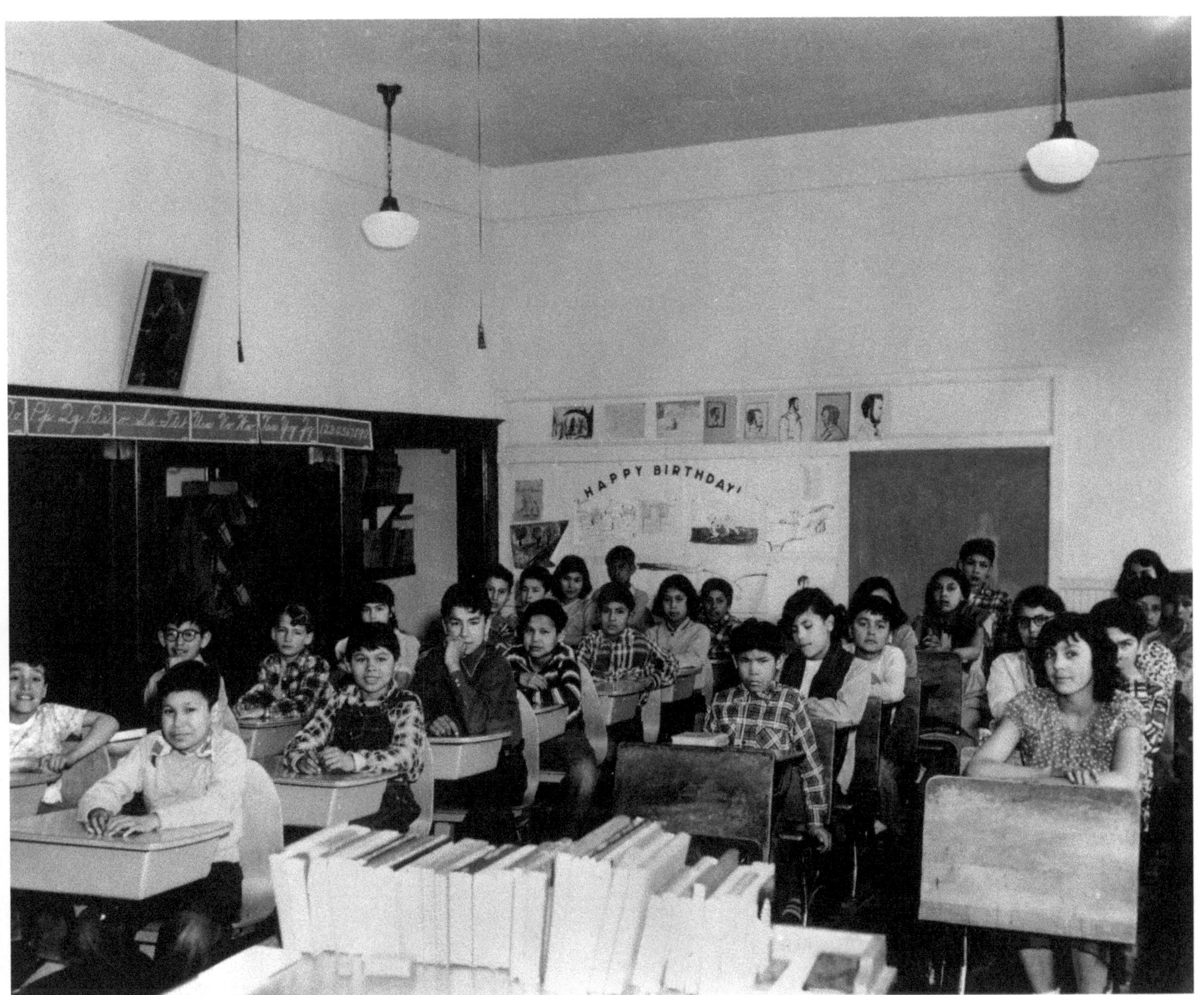


Red Lake Elementary School fifth and sixth graders sit at their desks in front of drawings of President Lincoln around 1953. The school is located on the Red Lake Indian Reservation, about 35 miles north of Bemidji. While this image suggests Lincoln is being honored on his birthday, he is often regarded by American Indians as a controversial president for his sanctioning the mass execution of 38 Dakotas following the U.S.-Dakota War, though he commuted the sentences of nearly 300 others.

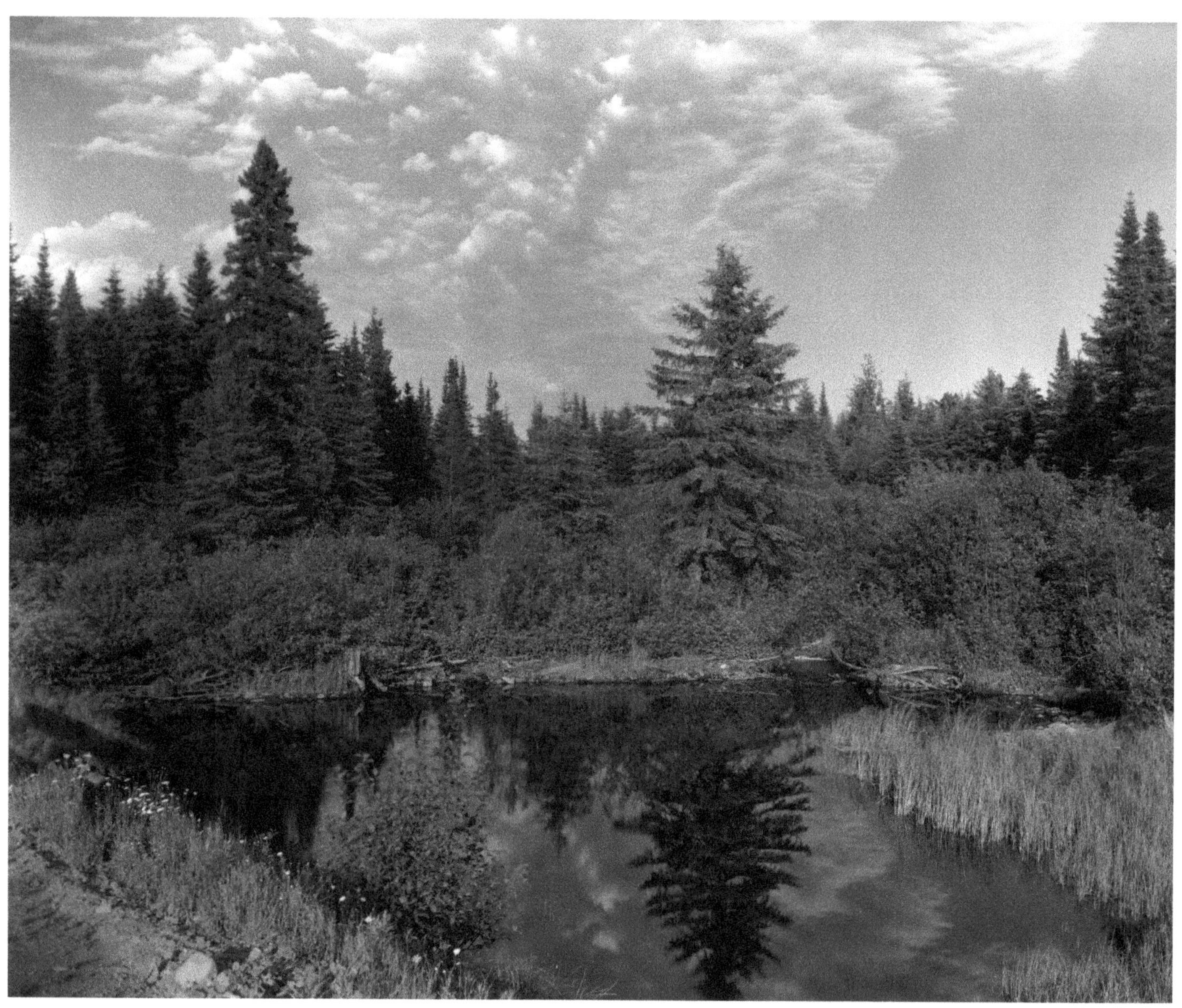

Northern Minnesota is famous for picturesque forest scenes, such as this one photographed in 1953. However, aggressive logging almost depleted the state's abundant pine forests. One extraordinary section of mature forest, known as the "Lost Forty" in the Chippewa National Forest, remains. A mapping error by a government land survey in 1882 caused the virgin pine to be untouched by loggers. The Lost Forty is actually 144 acres of red and white, 350-year-old pine.

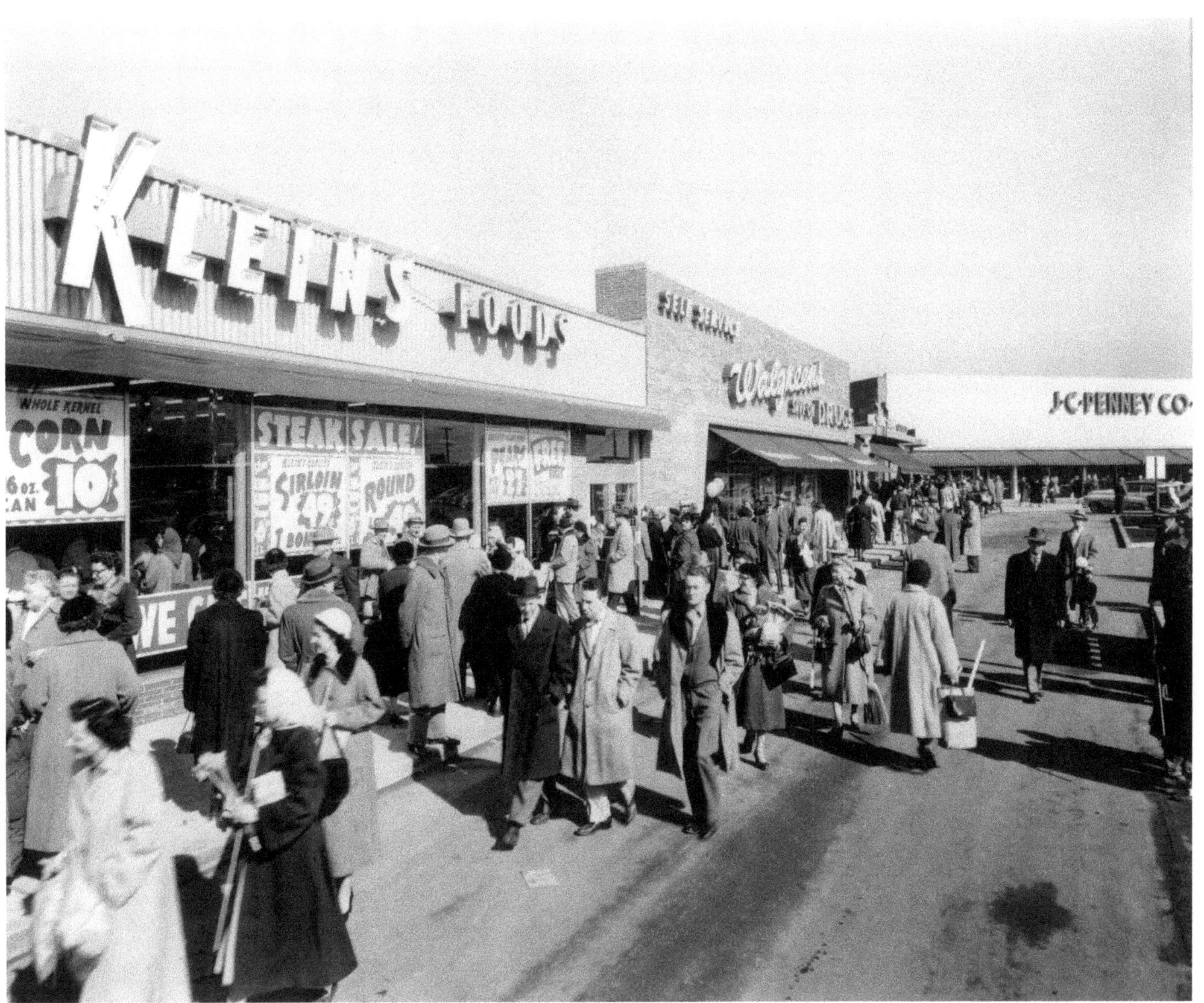


Shoppers flock to the Hub Shopping Center in Richfield on February 25, 1954, to patronize stores like Klein Foods, Walgreen's Drugs, and J. C. Penney. The Hub had 32 shops in all and was the largest shopping center in the Twin Cities. The new concept of one-stop-shopping strip malls had great appeal in the expanding suburbs of the Twin Cities.

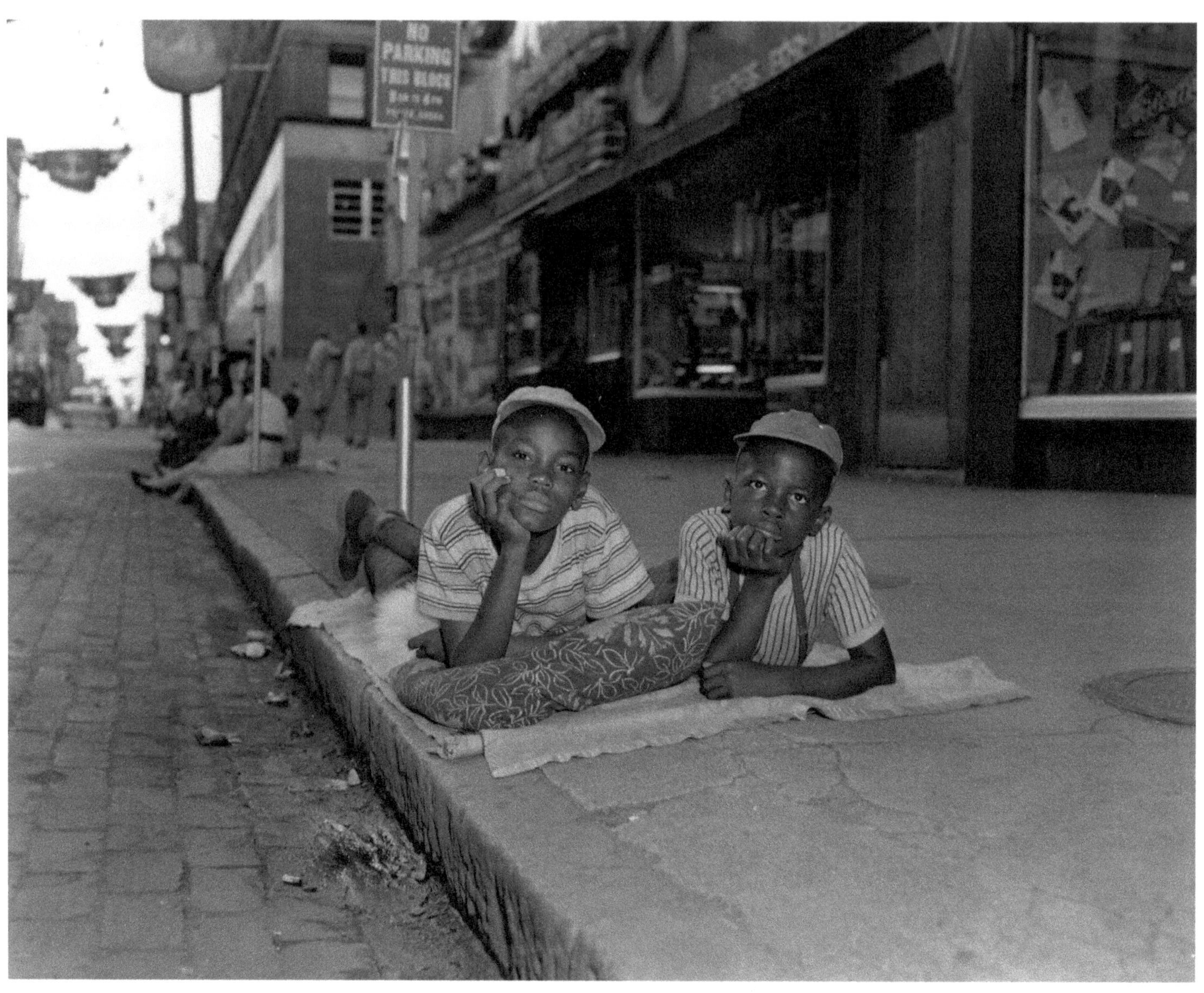


Two Minneapolis kids got up early on a Saturday morning in July 1954 to get the best viewing spot for the 15th annual Aquatennial parade. Among marching bands and floats, the parade featured 75 clowns in such famed outfits as "Clown Fire Department" and "Clowns in Jalopies." The 1951 Aquatennial boasted a visit from the Lone Ranger.

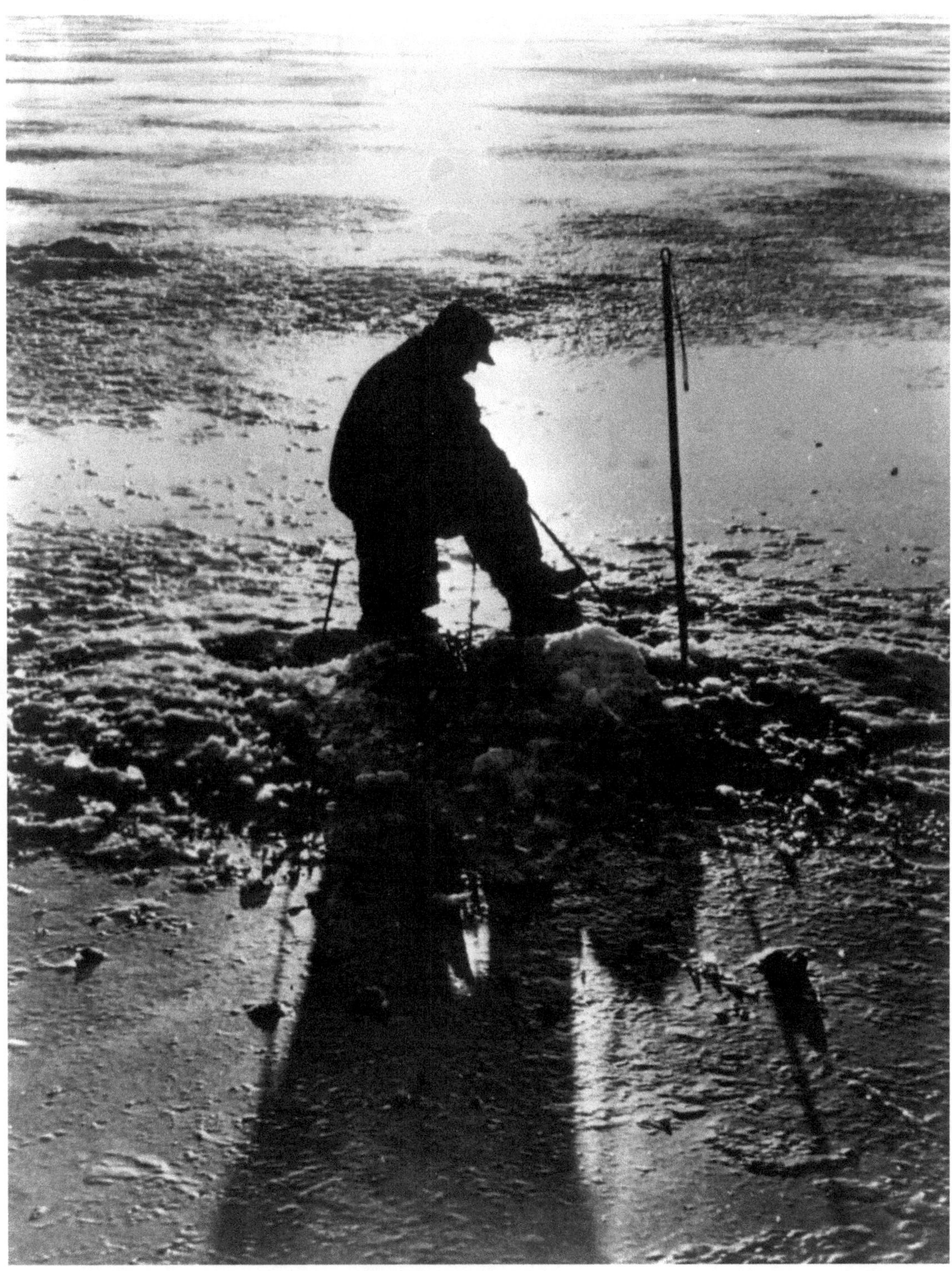

A lone fisherman casts a long shadow over a frozen lake in Minnesota. By the 1950s, ice fishing was a time-honored tradition, one that likely started when early pioneers observed Ojibwe Indians ice fishing.

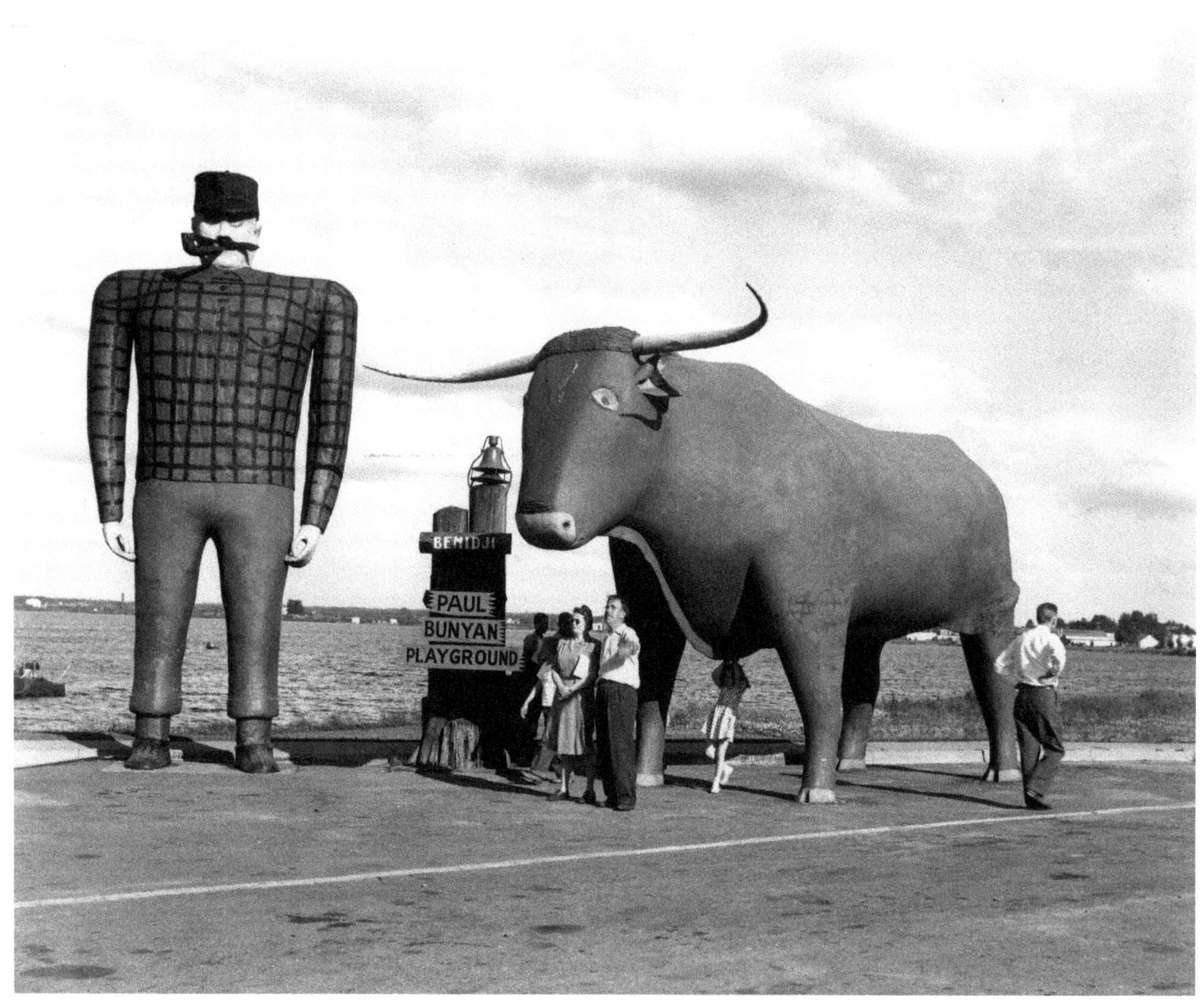


In 1955, tourists pose at the Paul Bunyan Playground in Bemidji, with the mythical giant of the lumber camps and his faithful companion, Babe. The statues were built by the Dickinson Lumber Company to coincide with the opening of the Bemidji Winter Carnival in 1937. Paul Bunyan's origins can be traced through oral narratives to actual incidents that occurred in lumber camps but were exaggerated to the point they became tall tales.

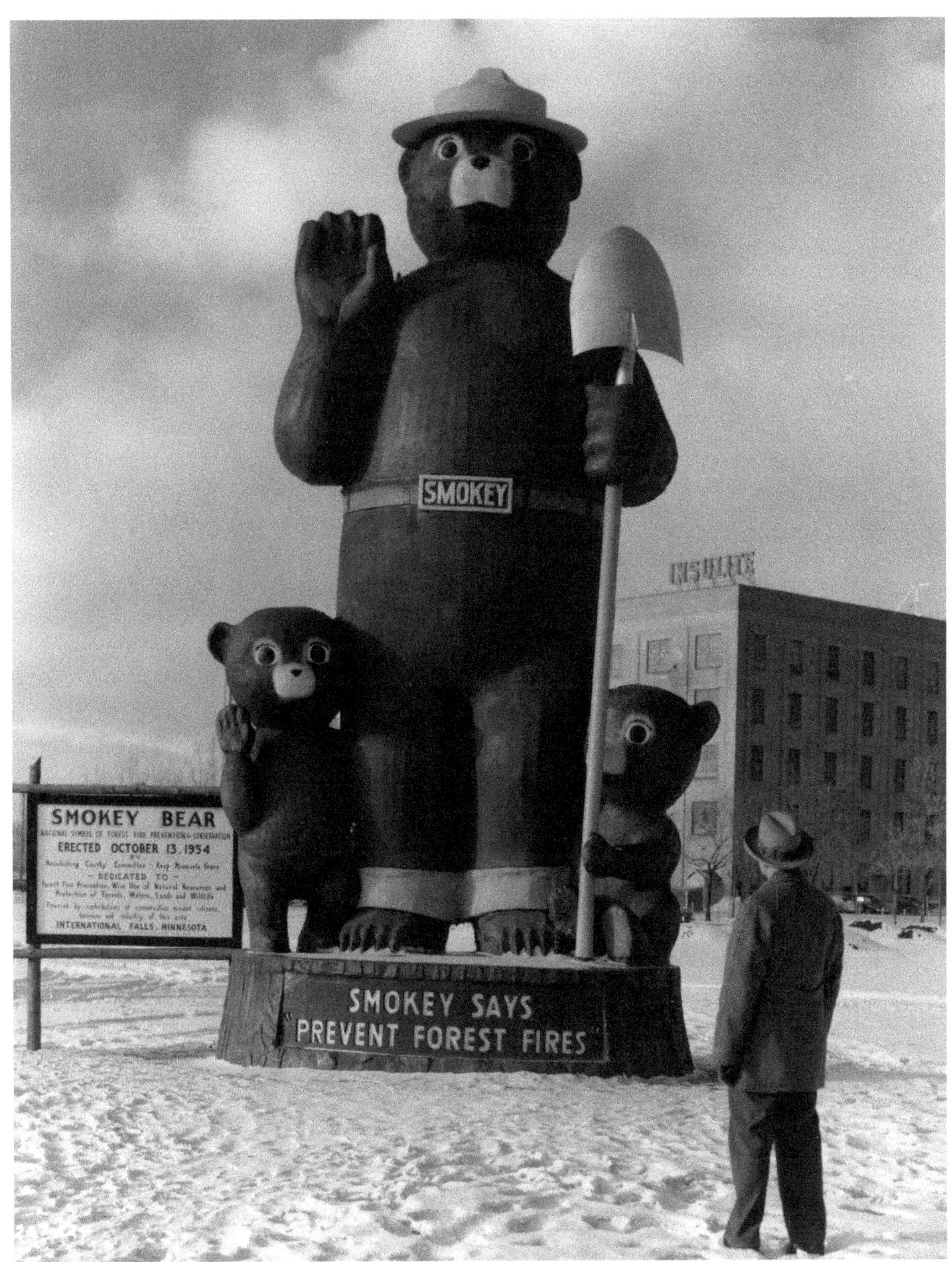


In addition to its claim as the coldest spot in 48 states, International Falls has the largest Smokey Bear statue in the entire country. Standing 26 feet tall, Smokey protects two bear cubs while reminding everyone to prevent forest fires. The statue was erected in 1954 by Koochiching County's Keep Minnesota Green Committee.

The Minneapolis Lakers take on the Detroit Pistons around 1955. Previously, the Lakers were known as the Detroit Gems. In 1947, a group of Minneapolis businessmen fronted by Sid Hartman purchased the team, moved them to Minneapolis, and renamed them. Led by center George Mikan, the Minneapolis Lakers were the NBA's first dynasty, winning five titles in six seasons from 1948-49 through 1953-54. In 1960, the franchise relocated to Los Angeles.

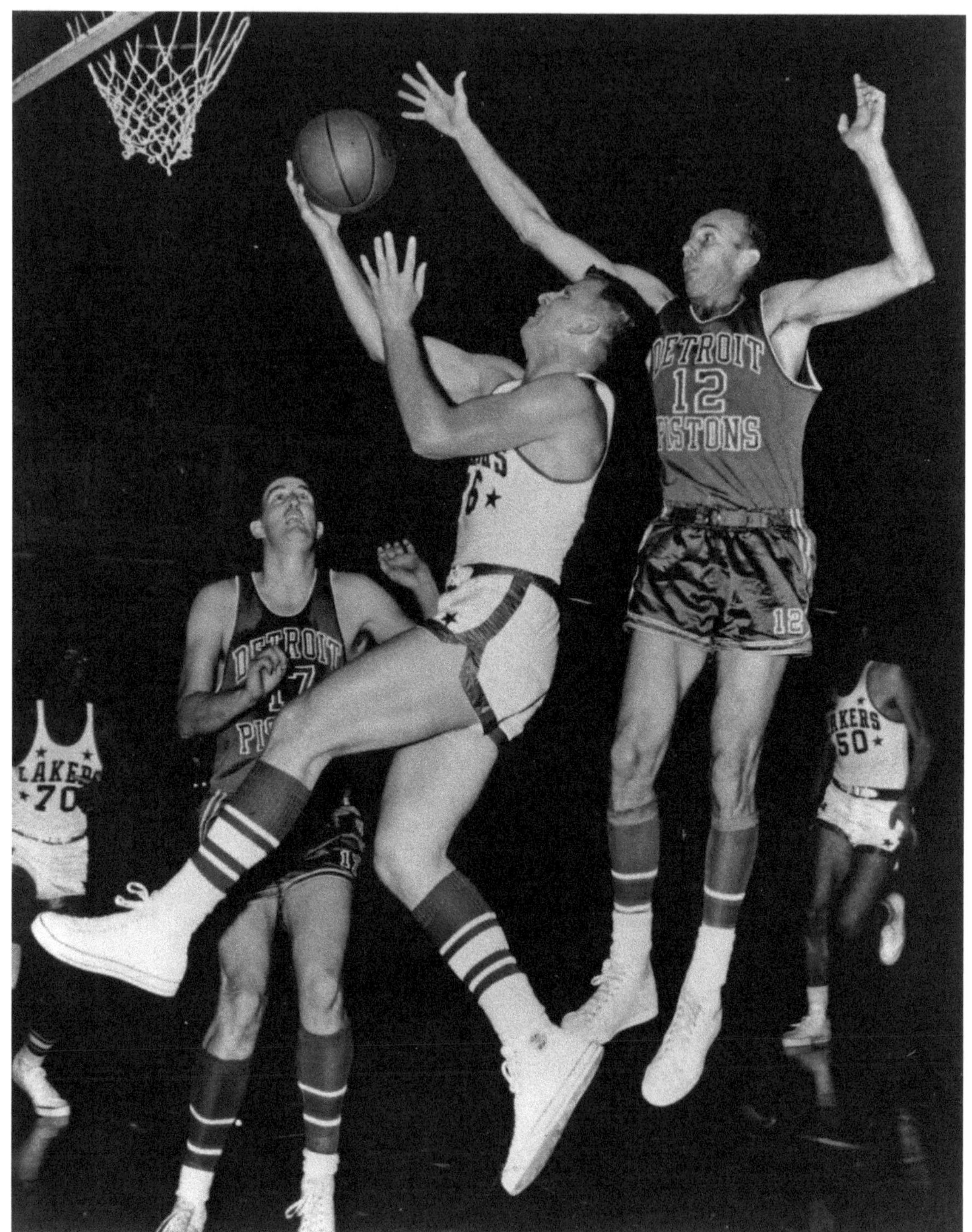

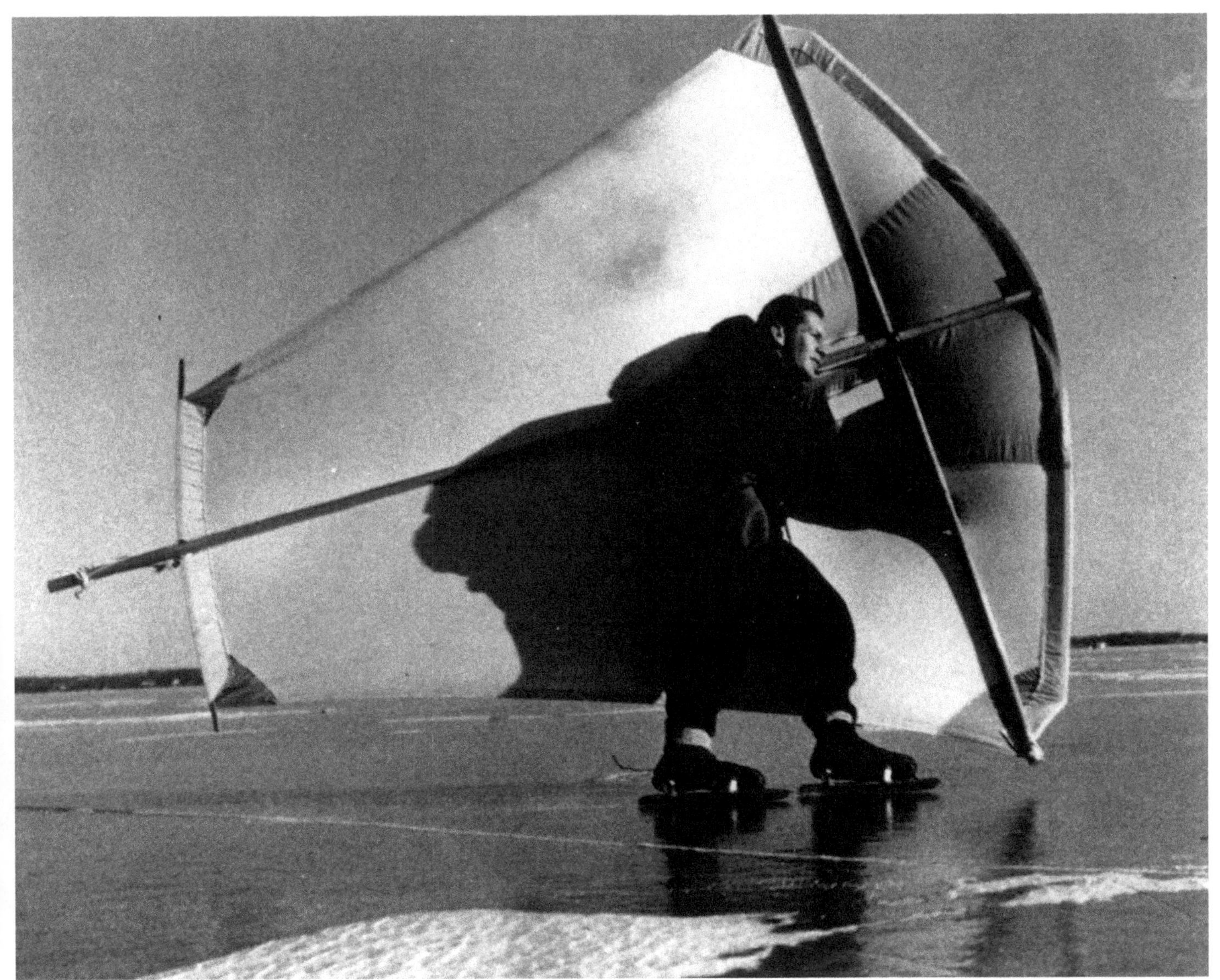

This man is skate sailing across a frozen Minnesota lake in the 1950s. Ice fishing and skating are certainly more popular sports, but skate sailing enthusiasts have a long history of taking advantage of Minnesota's long winters.

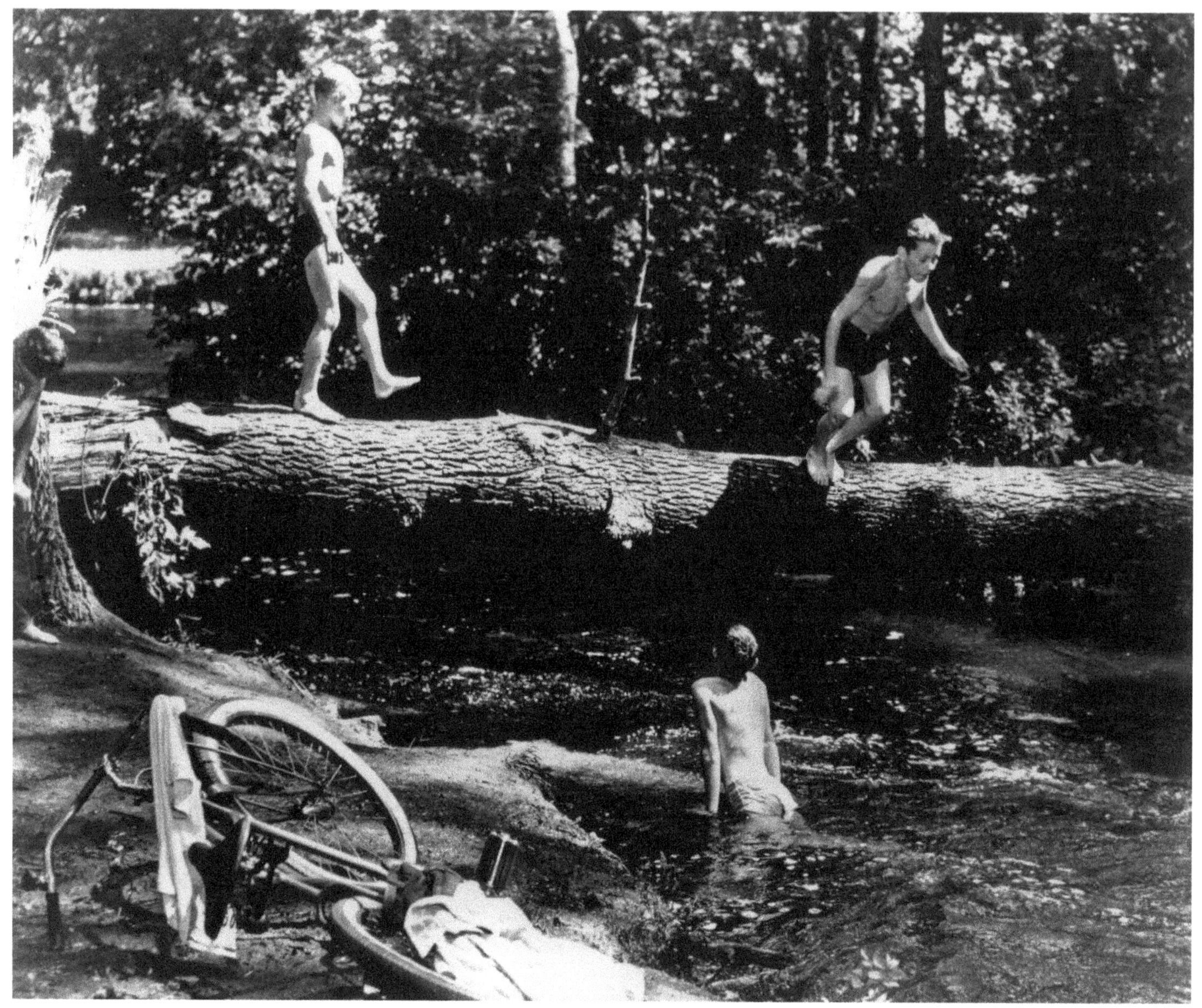

These Minnesota boys rode their bikes down to the "old swimming hole" around 1955, where a fallen tree made a fine diving platform. This photo was one of many taken to showcase the good life in Minnesota for the upcoming Statehood Centennial celebration.

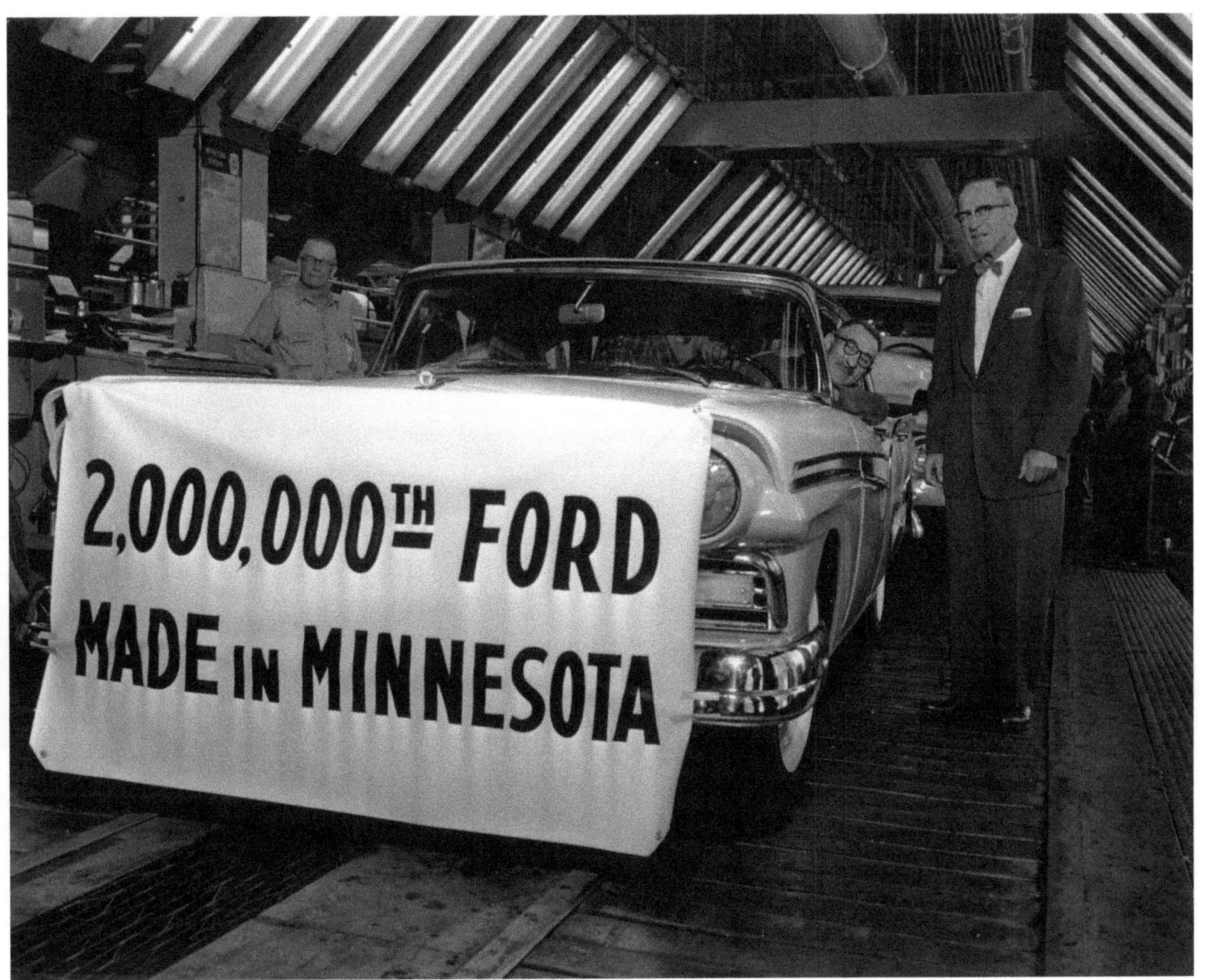


On October 6, 1956, the Ford automobile plant in St. Paul celebrated the completion of its two-millionth Ford. The plant was built in 1924, mainly because the inexpensive hydropower of the Mississippi River appealed to Henry Ford.

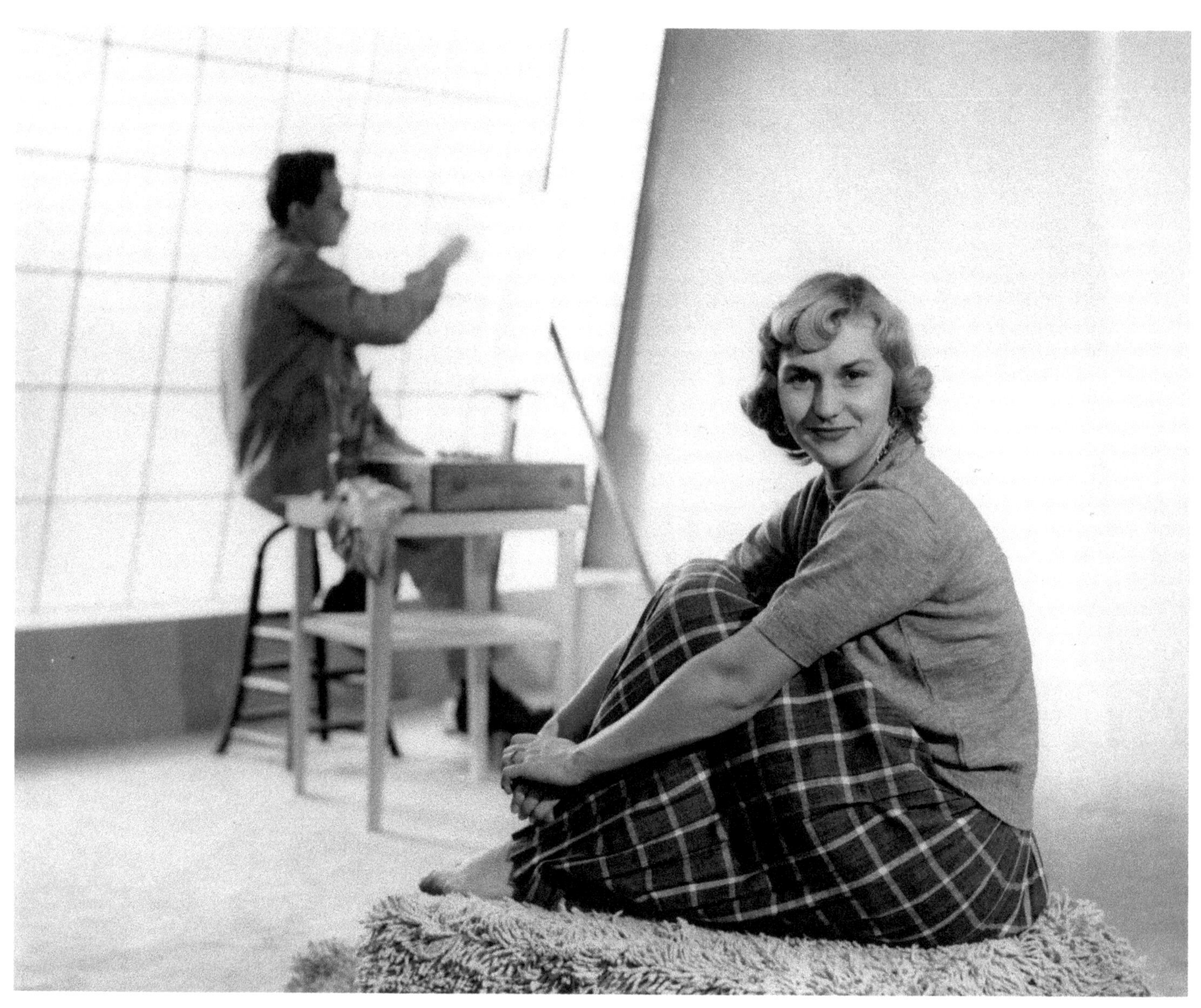

A model in 1956 poses for the camera and artist Jim Jackson in the Reid H. Ray Film Industries building on Ford Parkway.

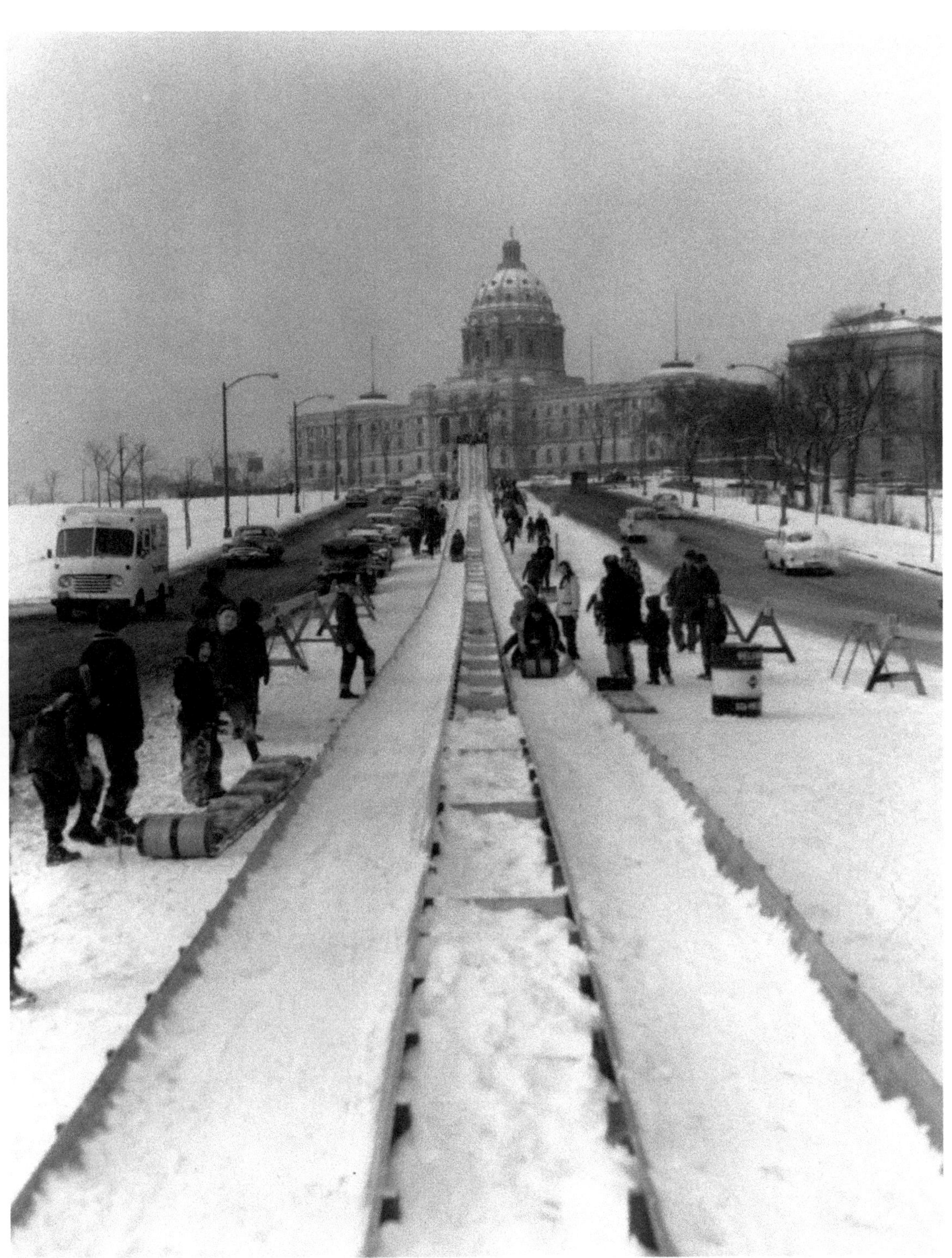

St. Paul Winter Carnival participants enjoy the double toboggan slide and view of the Capitol in 1957.

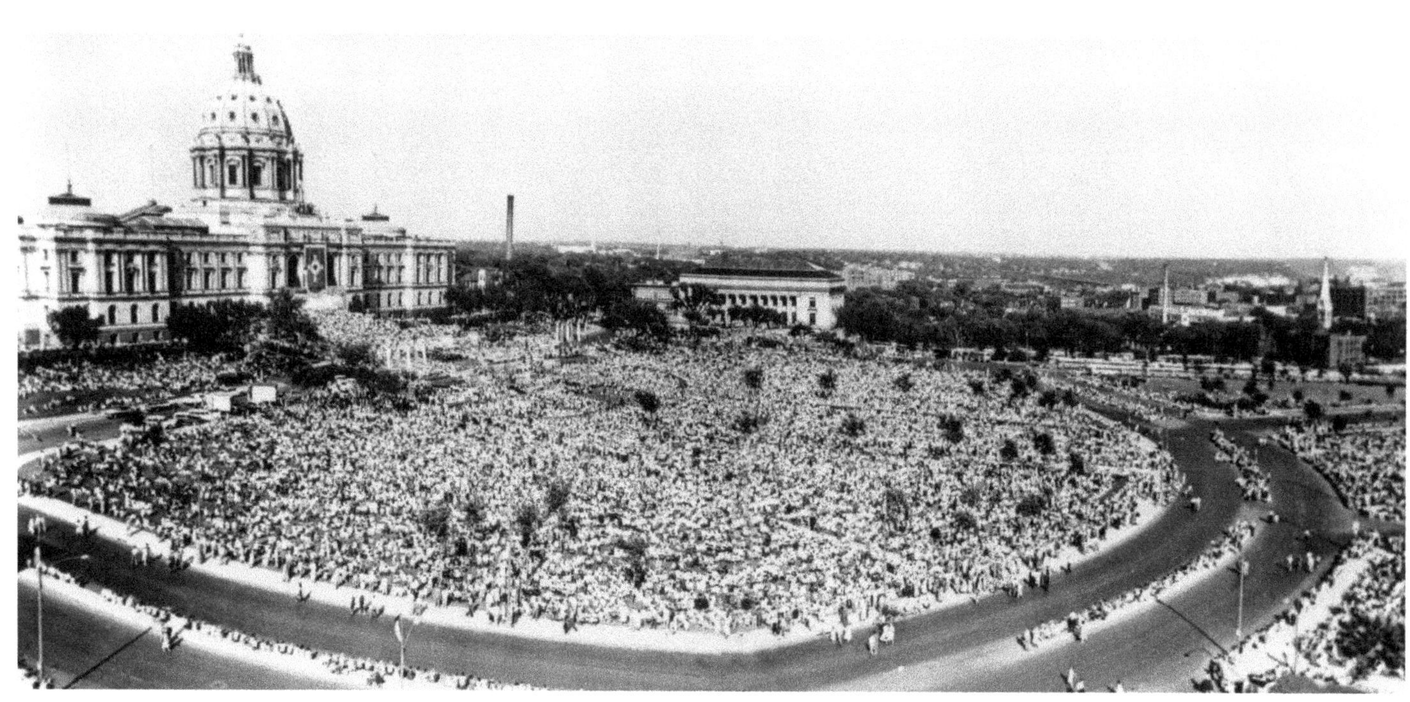

The closing festival service for the Third Assembly of the Lutheran World Federation took place at the State Capitol mall on August 25, 1957. This event made history, with over 100,000 Lutherans participating from all over the world.

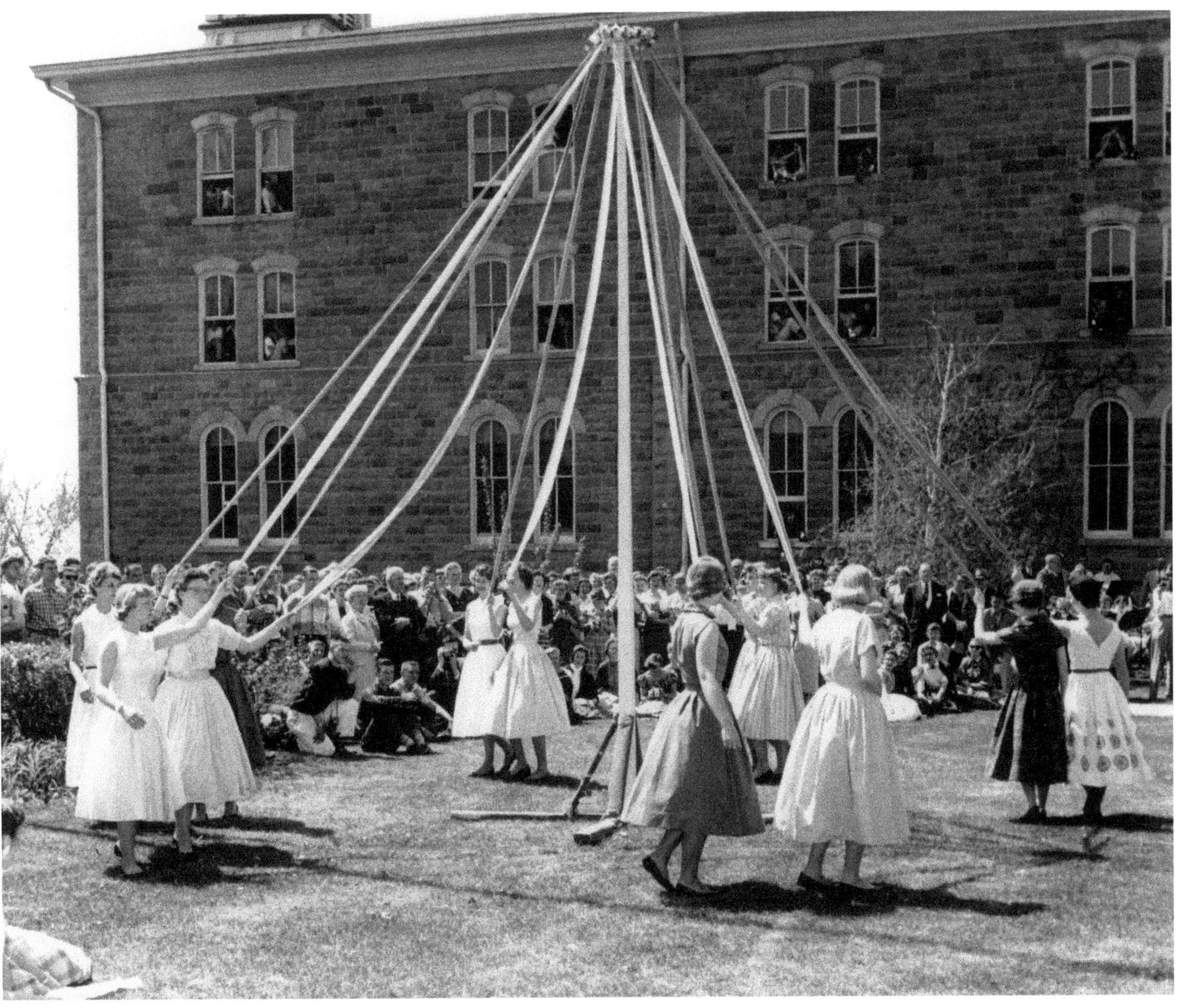

Students at Gustavus Adolphus College in St. Peter in 1958 celebrate the Minnesota Statehood Centennial with a traditional Maypole dance. The building in the background is Old Main, the first building to be constructed on the campus in 1876.

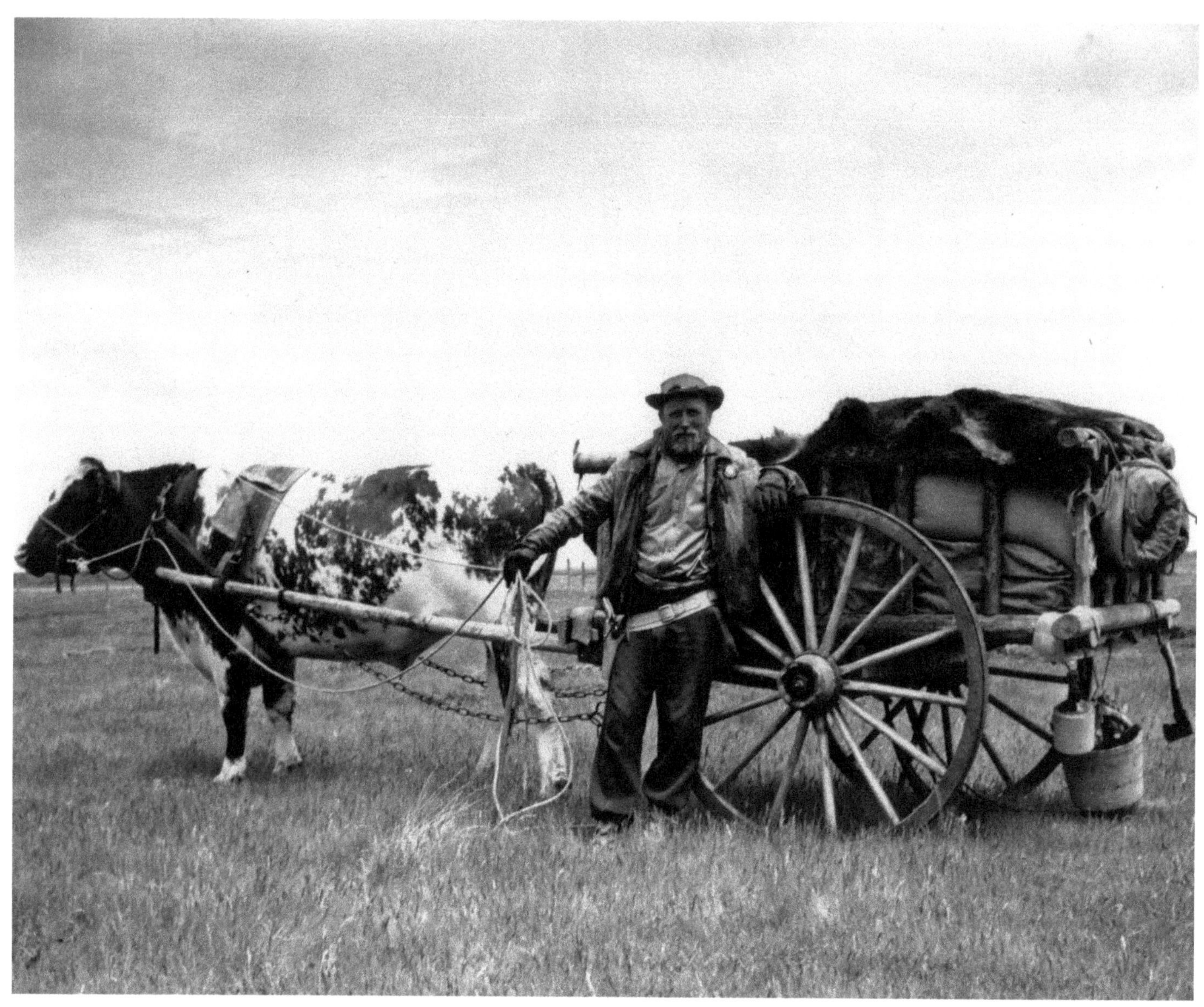

On July 10, 1958, Minnesota farmer Delmar Hagen left Pembina, North Dakota, with an ox and a two-wheeled wooden cart to reenact a Red River oxcart drive. Forty-five days later he arrived in St. Paul to help kick off the Minnesota State Fair and Centennial Exposition.

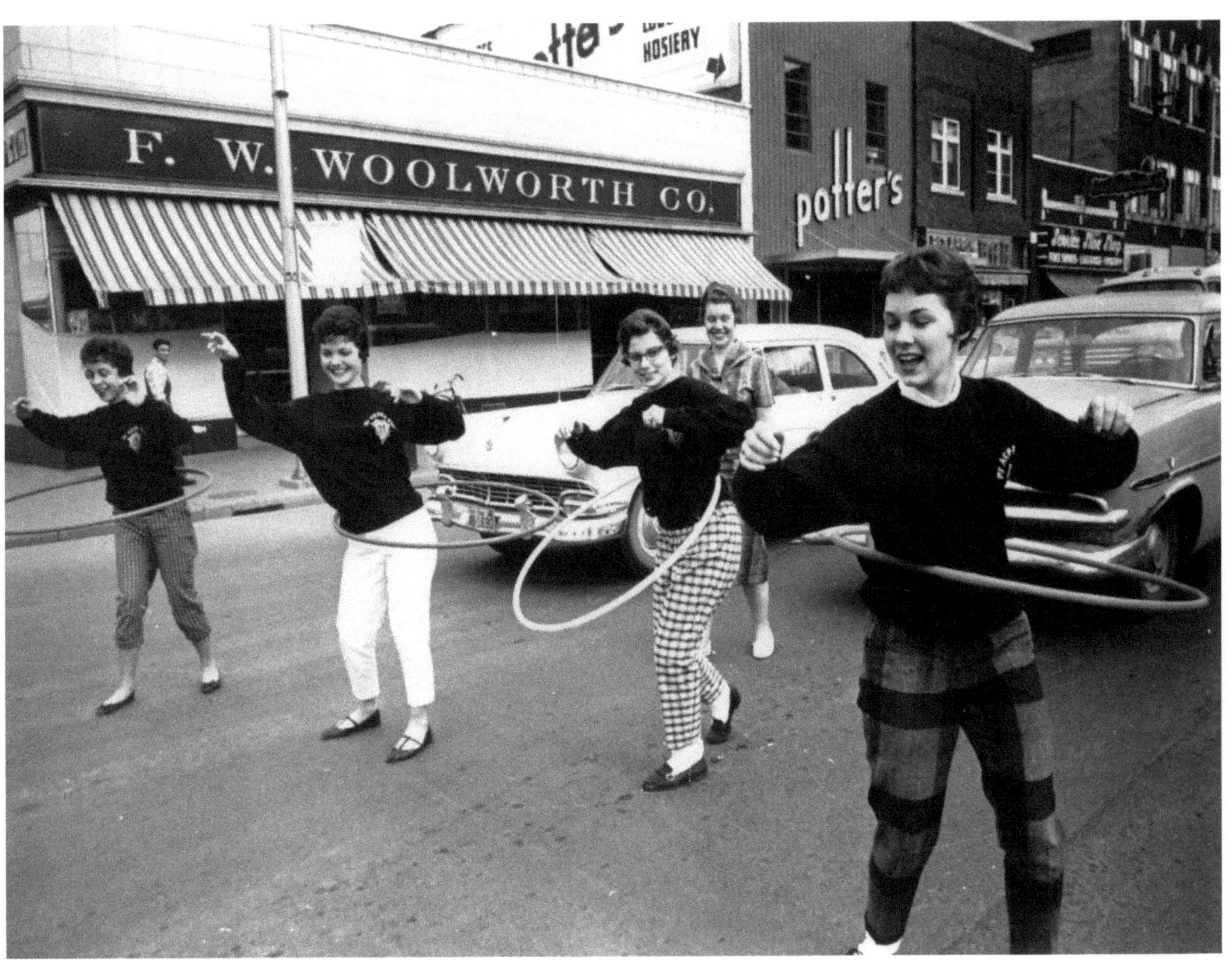


In the late 1950s, Wham-O Hula Hoops were sweeping the nation, and Minnesota was no exception. Young people showed off their Hula Hoop skills in contests and exhibitions—like these young women in front of the F. W. Woolworth store in 1959.

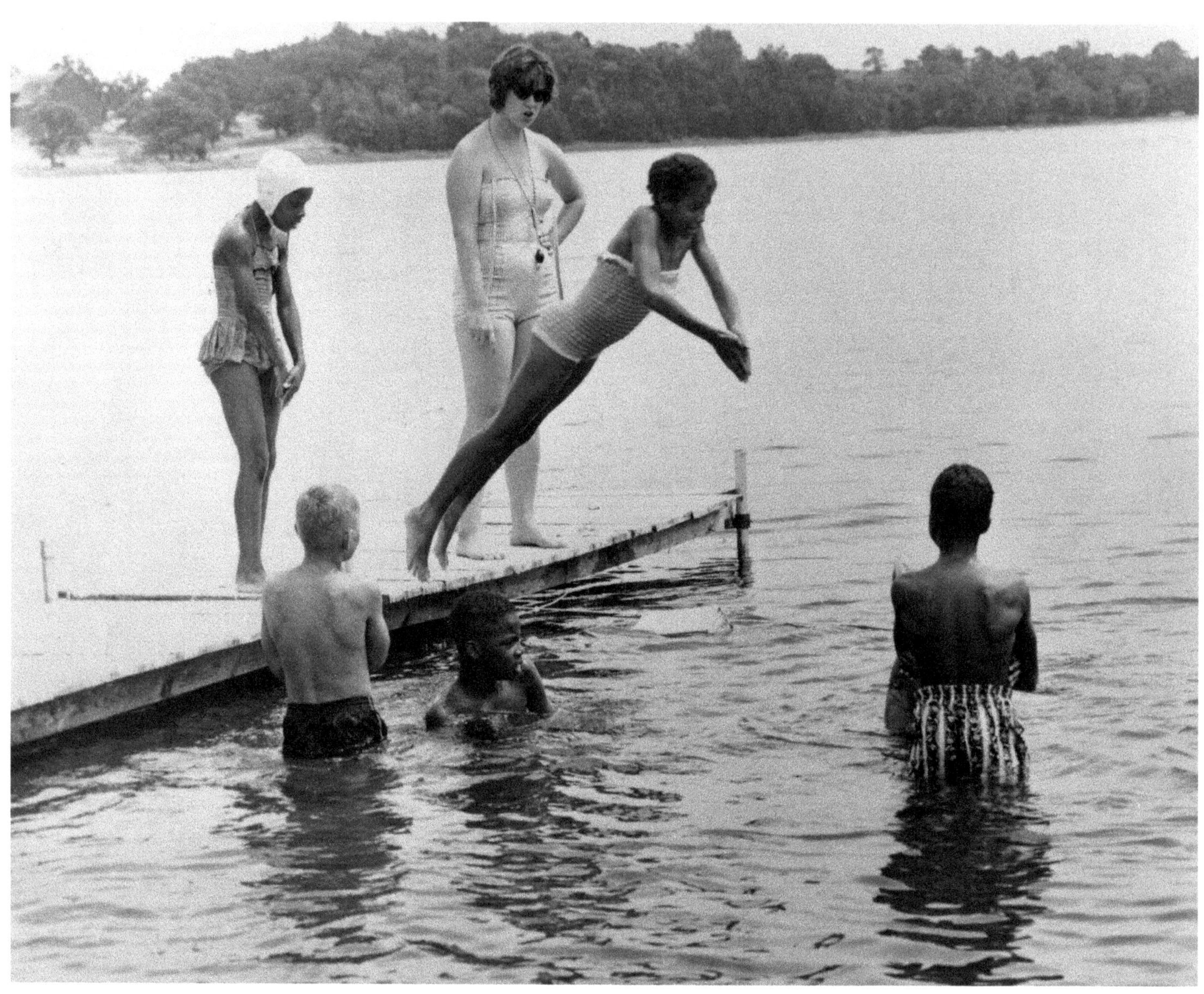

Kids take swimming lessons at a Hallie Q. Brown summer camp around 1960. Although the Hallie Q. Brown Settlement House (now the Hallie Q. Brown Community Center) was established in 1929 to serve the needs of African Americans in St. Paul, it has long followed a policy of offering its services to people of all races.

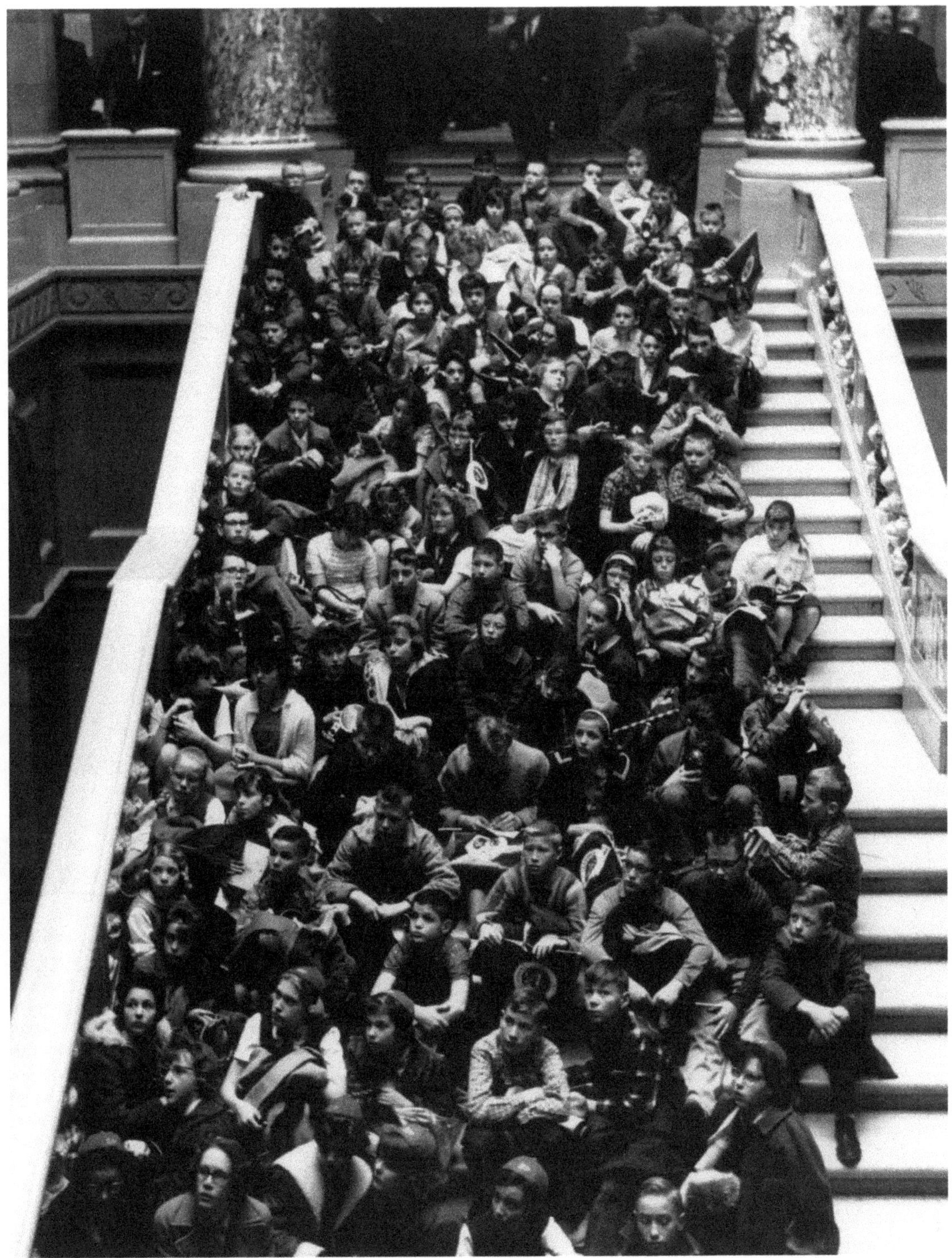

Leaving an aisle open for legislators to pass, schoolchildren gather for a photograph on the main staircase at the State Capitol around 1960. The Capitol is still a popular field-trip destination for Minnesota schoolchildren.

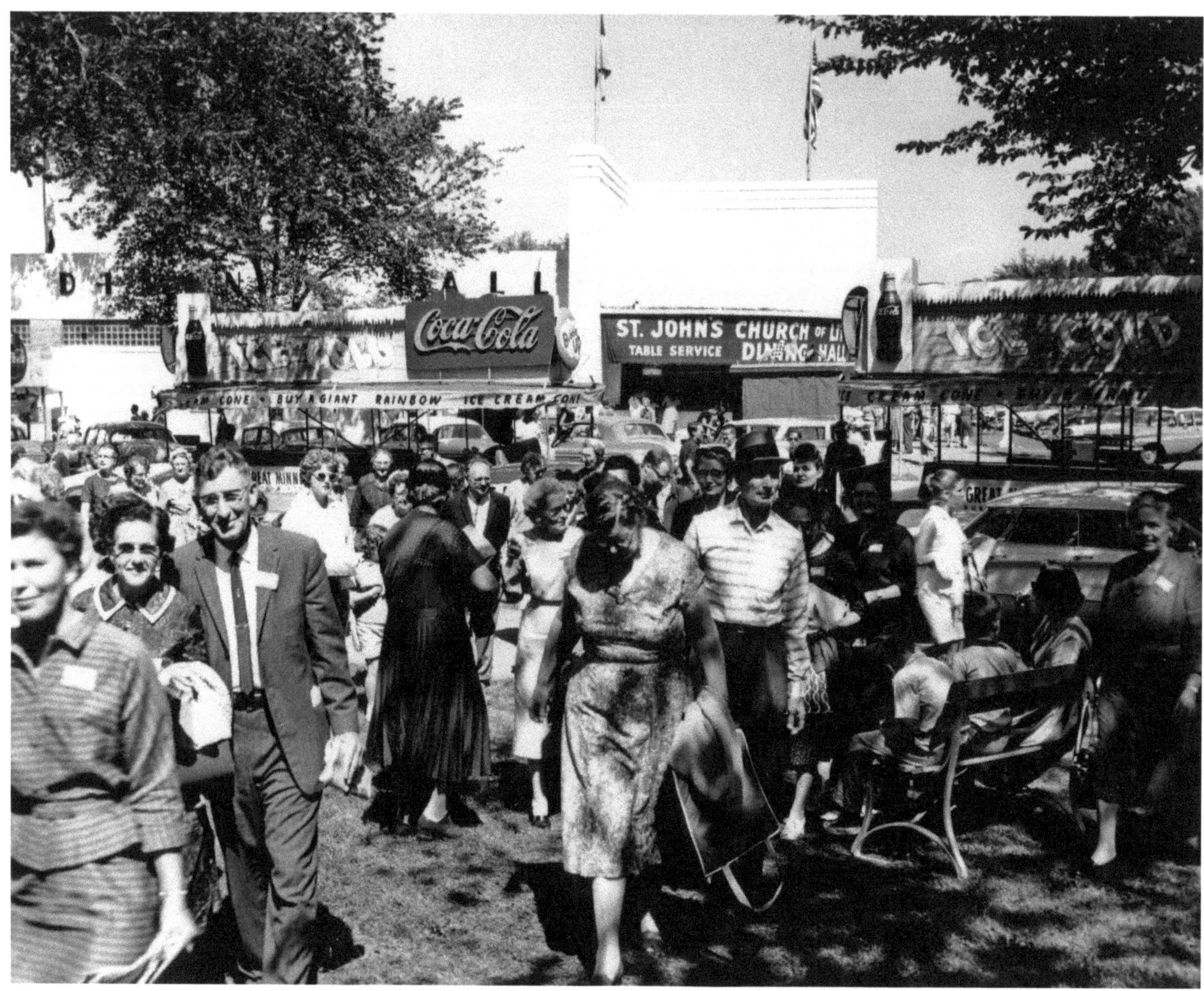


In 1960 the Minnesota State Fair set aside this day to recognize the state's elementary school teachers. It appears they couldn't have hoped for better weather for the occasion.

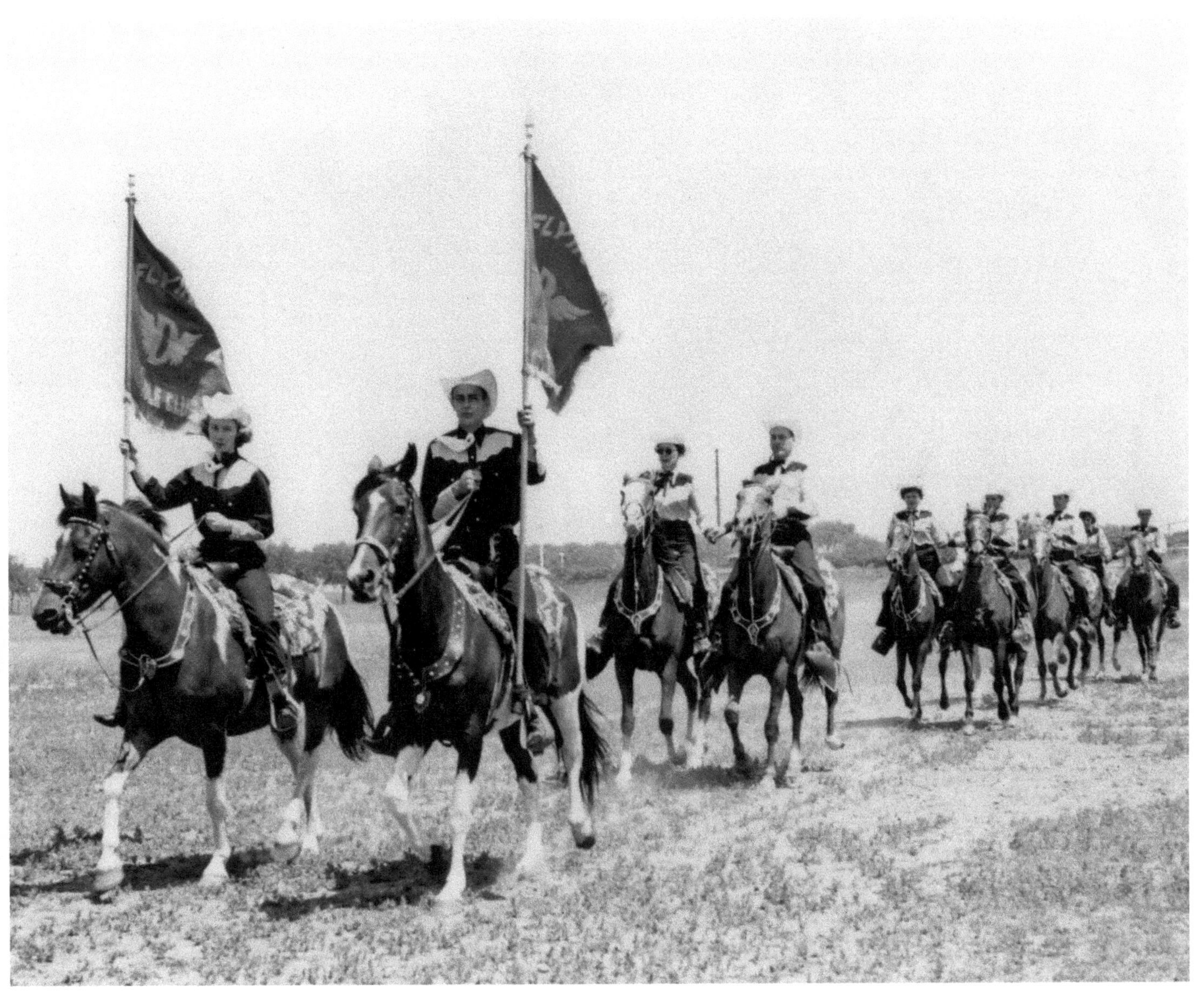

Couples promenade on horseback around 1960. Some say square dancing on horses was designed to allow young people to get close to one another, but not too close.

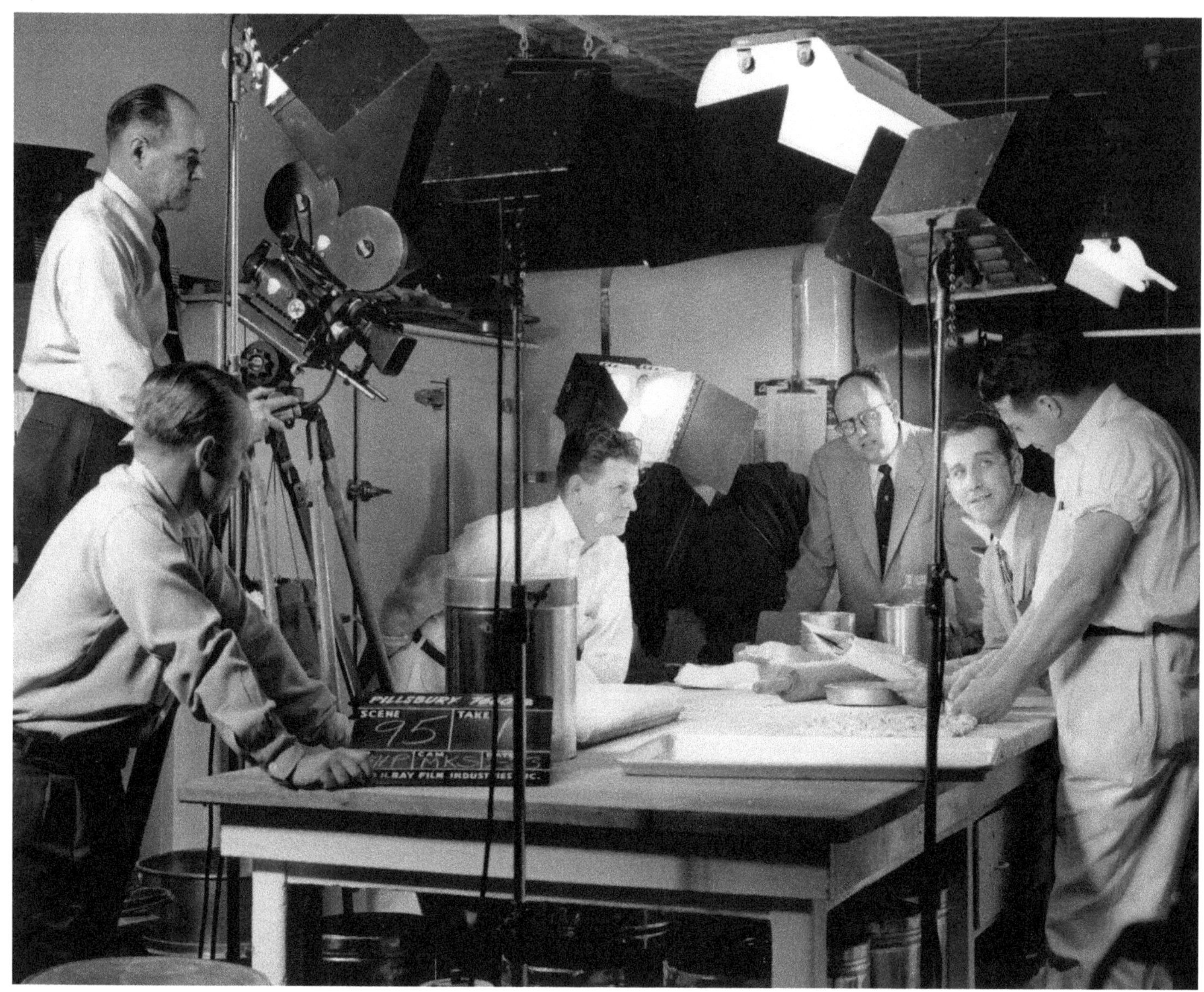


A behind-the-scenes photo from a 1960 television shoot at the Pillsbury test kitchens in Minneapolis. The production crew was from Reid H. Ray Films in St. Paul. At the time, Pillsbury and General Mills were major rivals, competing for the same consumer dollars. Pillsbury's answer to General Mills' iconic Betty Crocker was to create the most famous baking competition ever, the Pillsbury Bake-Off. Decades later, the two companies merged.

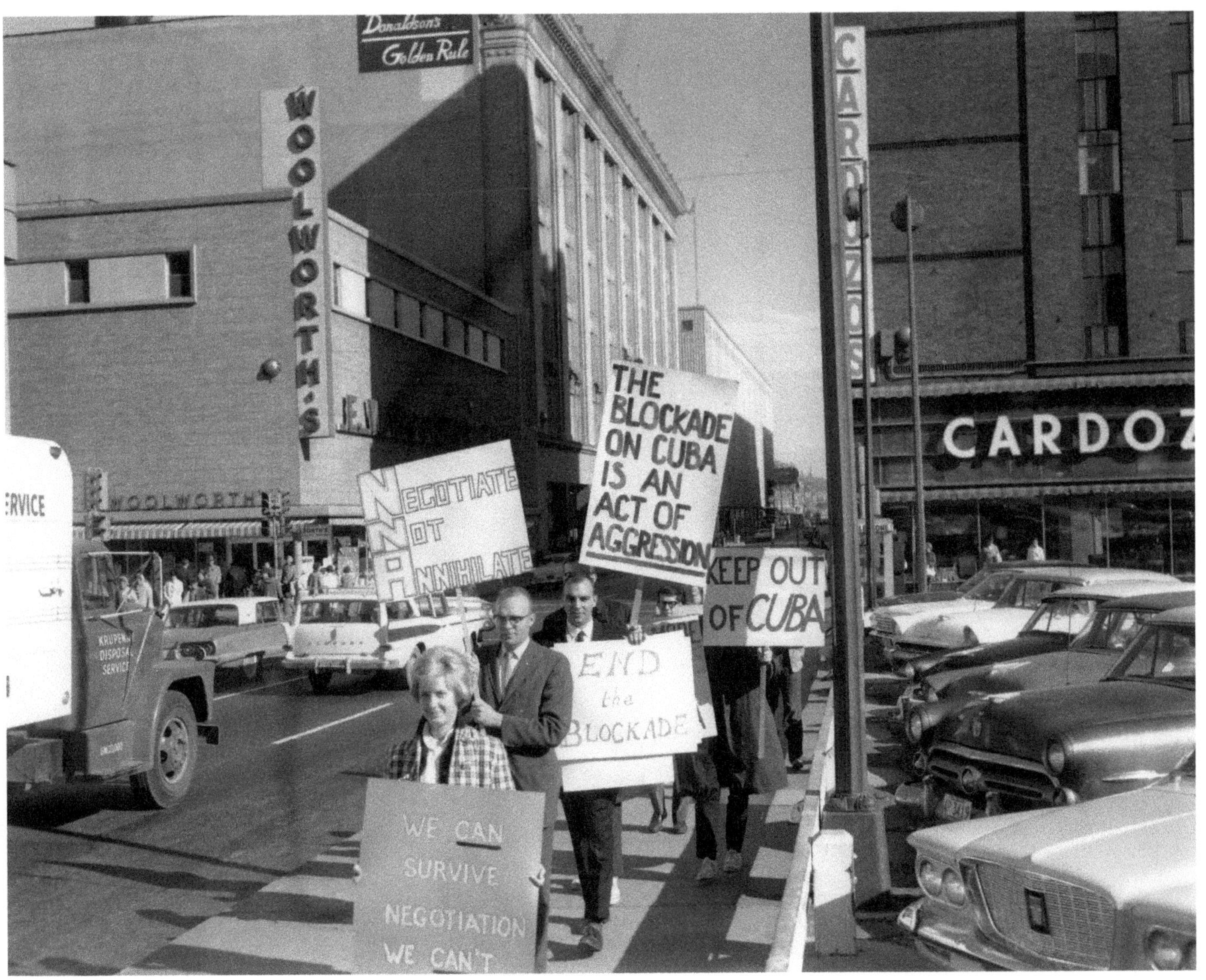


Protesters in downtown St. Paul speak out against the U.S. naval quarantine of Cuba during the height of the Cuban missile crisis of October 1962. The crisis, with its potential for nuclear war, was set in motion when U.S. intelligence discovered Soviet missile sites being built in Cuba, and responded with the quarantine and with demands for the sites' removal. The protest took place October 27—one day before the crisis ended.

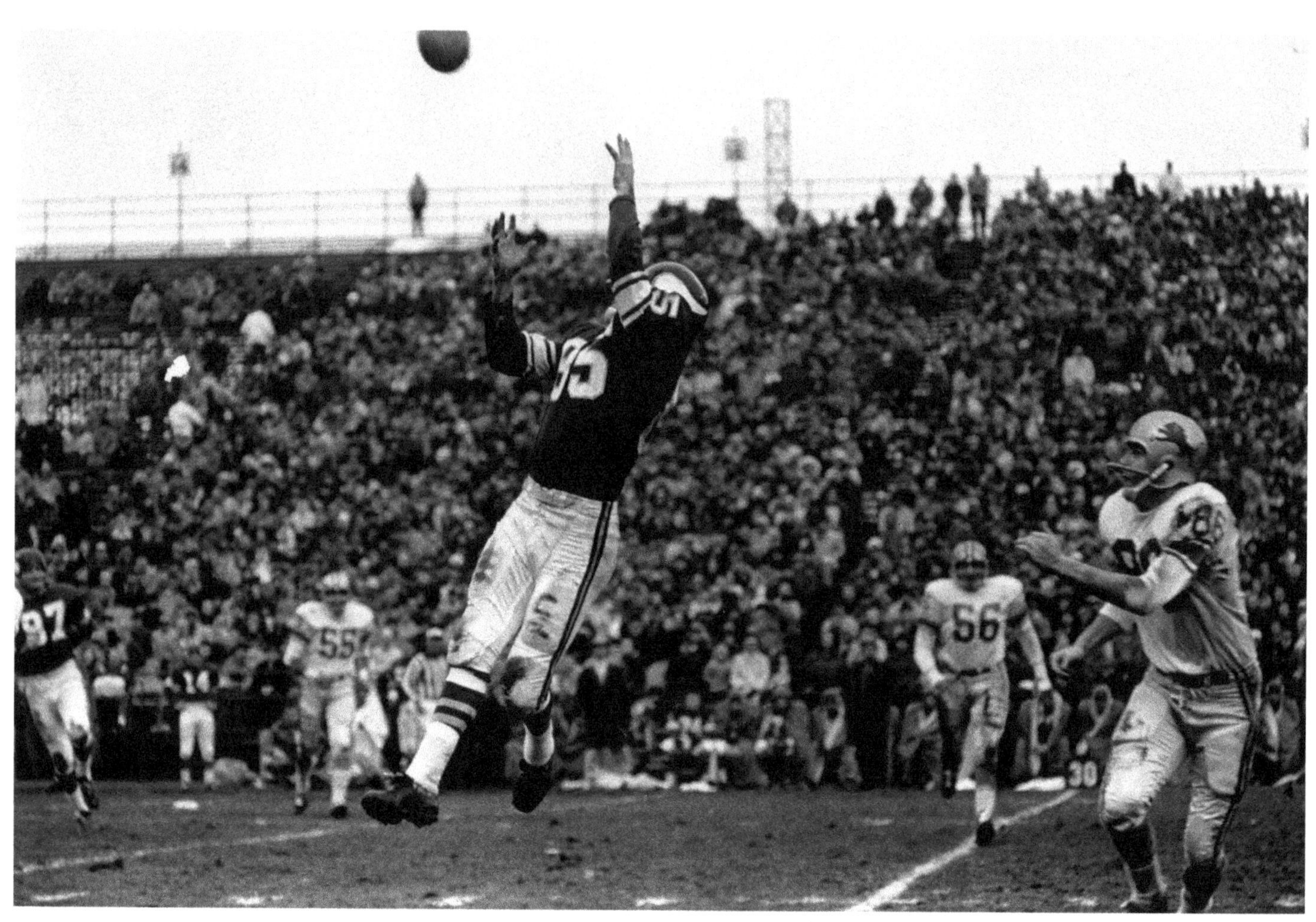

Paul Flatley of the Minnesota Vikings catches a pass against the Detroit Lions at Metropolitan Stadium on November 24, 1963, two days after President John F. Kennedy was assassinated. Having consulted with White House press secretary Pierre Salinger, Commissioner Pete Rozelle of the NFL decided the day's games should be played, but he later regretted the decision. The Vikings won 34 to 31.

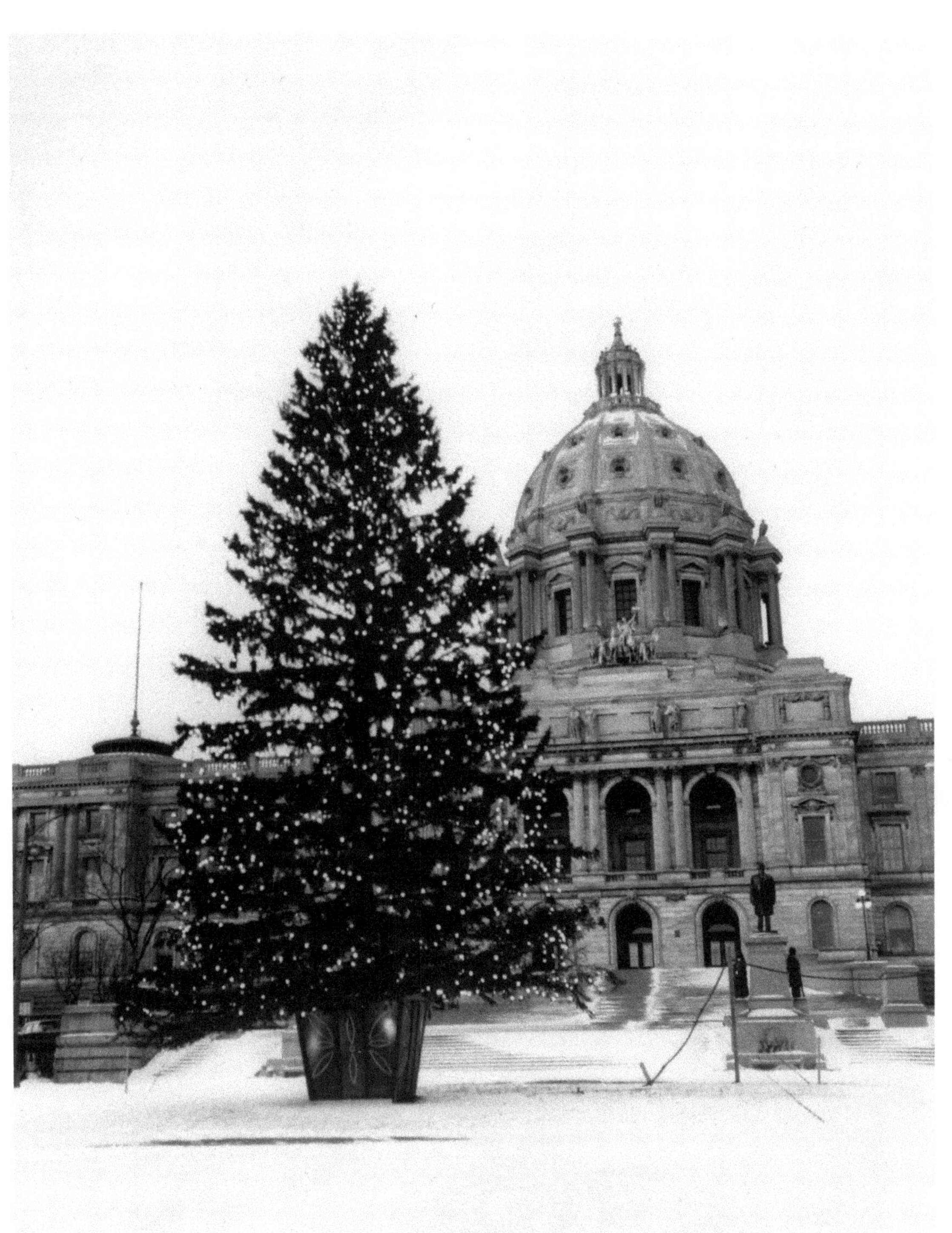

The traditional lighted Christmas tree in front of the State Capitol in 1963.

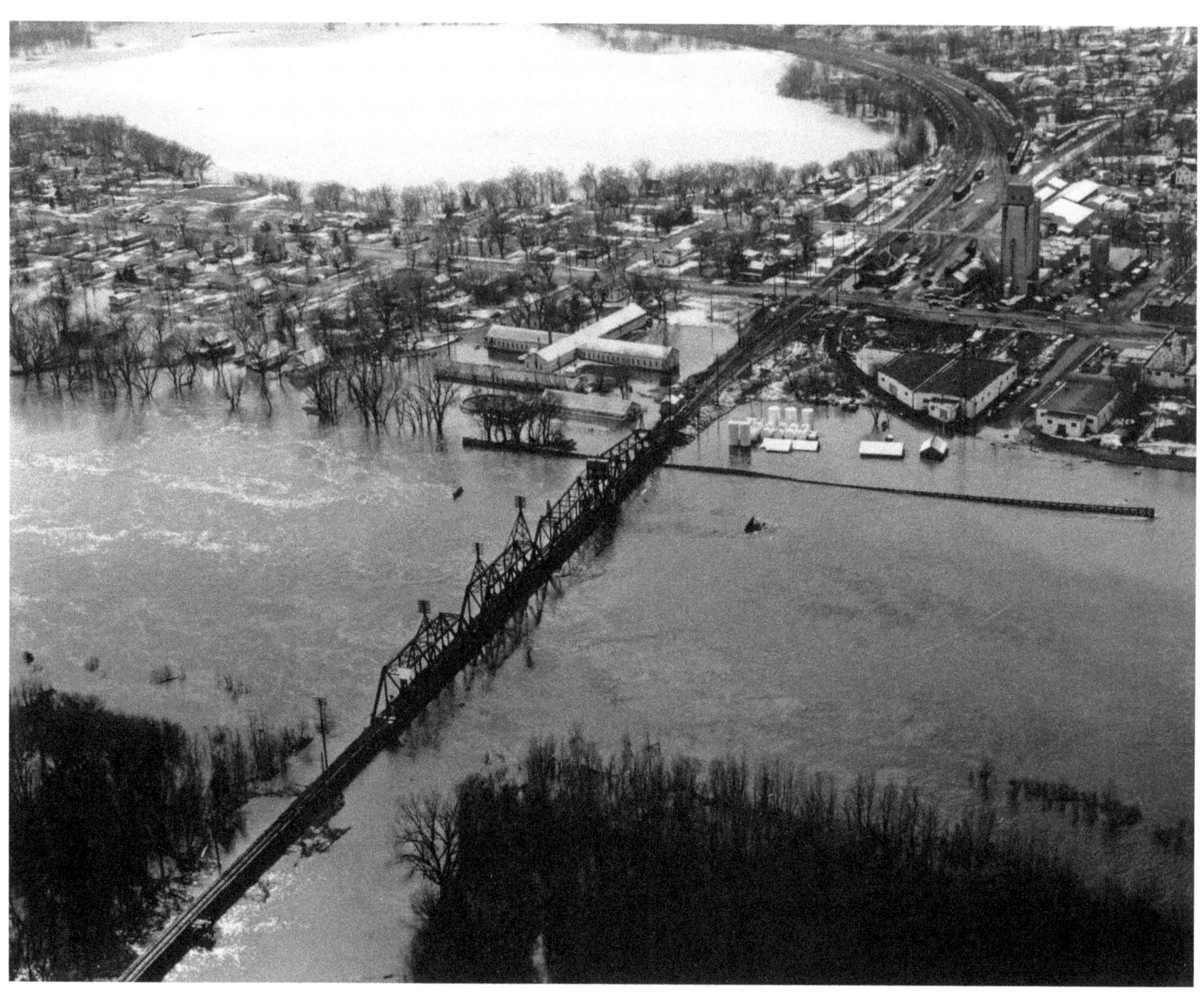

An aerial view of the severe flooding of the Minnesota River in the spring of 1965. Heavy snowfall and a prolonged deep cold delayed the thaw until April, when the melting snow caused record flooding.

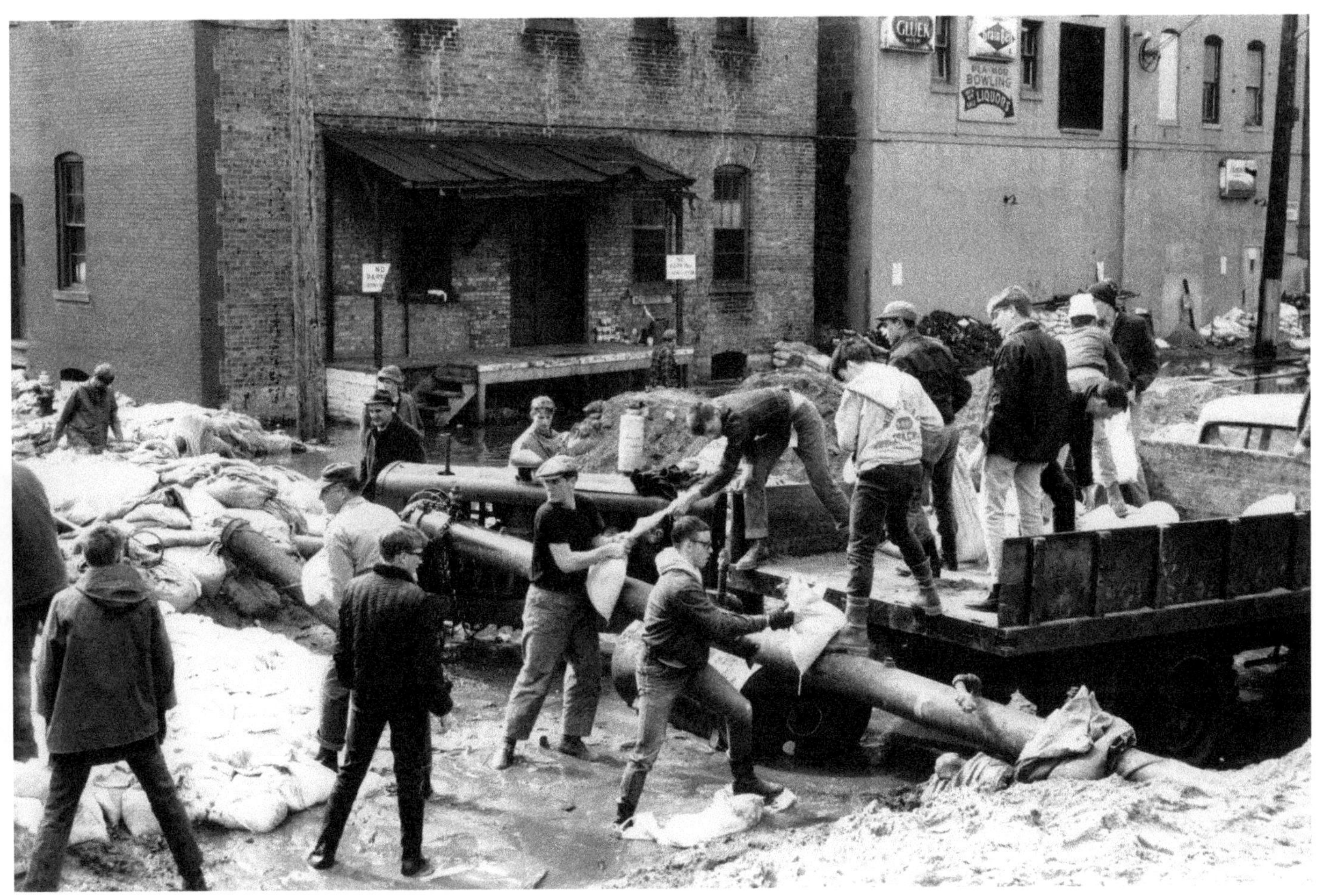


The flooding was so severe along Minnesota river cities in the spring of 1965 that legions of volunteers were needed for sandbagging. High school students in the Stillwater area were let out of classes to help sandbag around the St. Croix River, as were 50 convicts from the state prison at Stillwater.

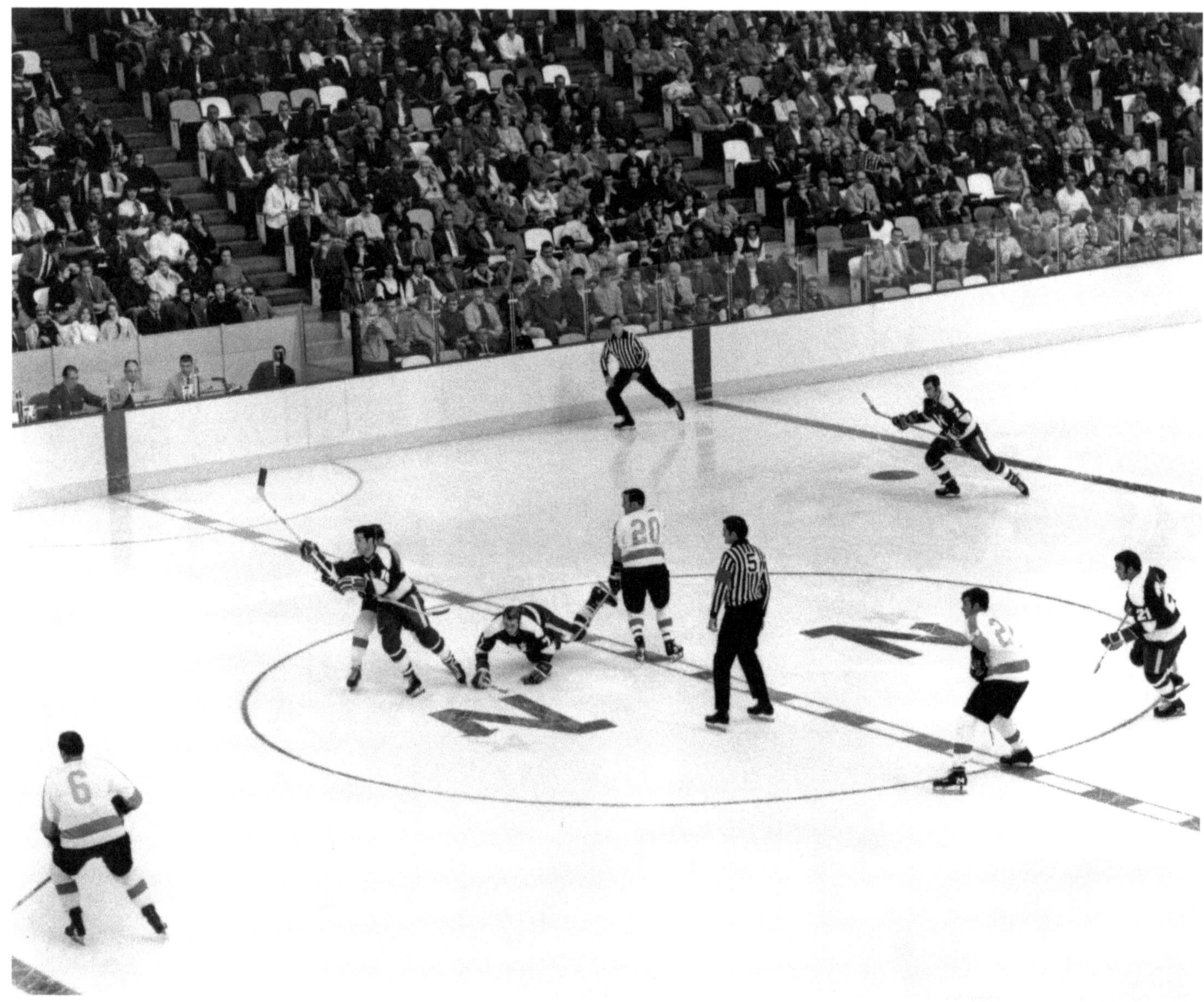

The Minnesota North Stars hockey team in 1969, their third season, at the Met Center in Bloomington. At the time, helmets were optional but rarely worn. A year prior, North Stars player Bill Masterton died due to a head injury during one of their games. Masterton was not wearing a helmet. His death gradually prompted a push toward mandatory helmet use in the National Hockey League.

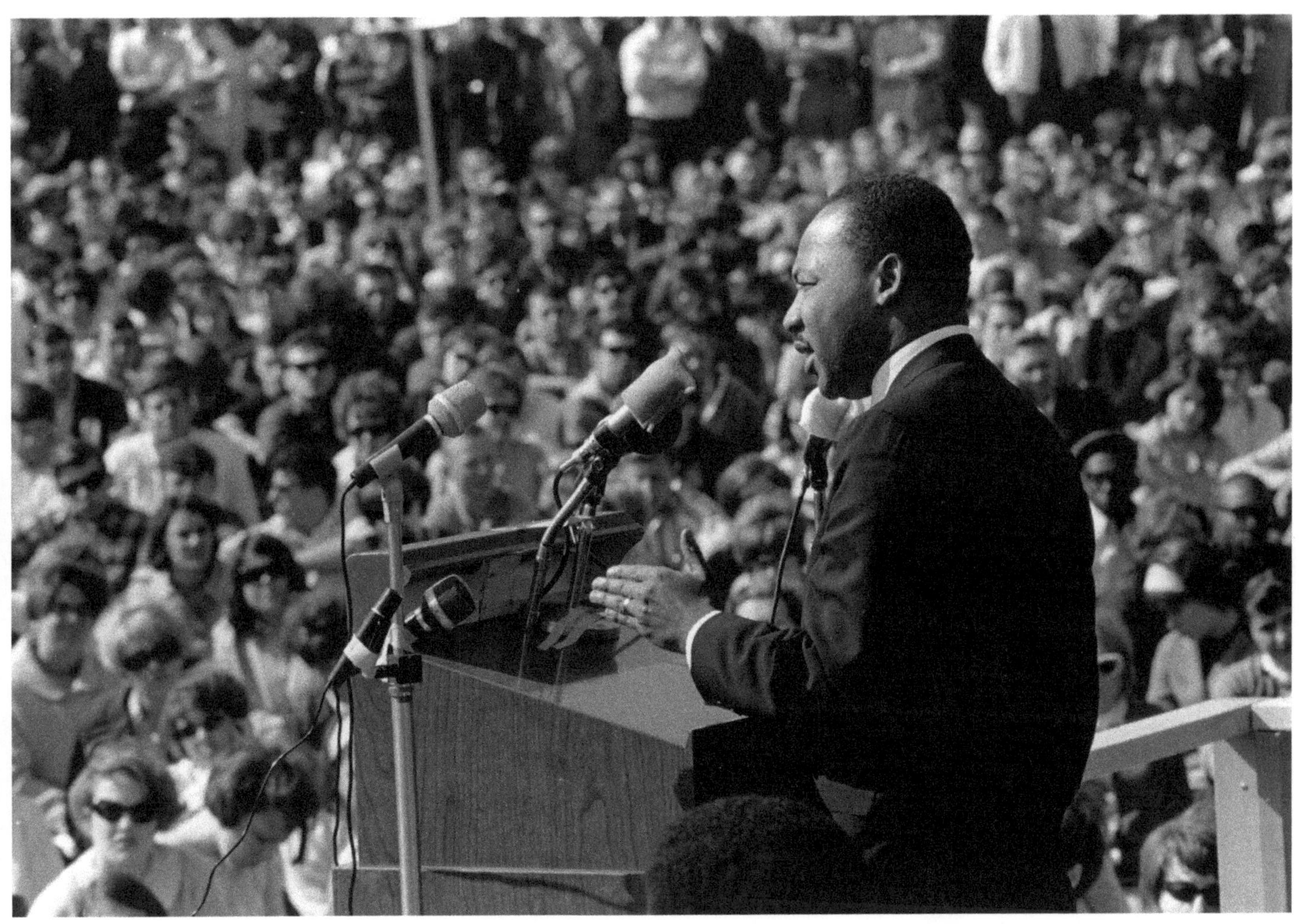

On April 27, 1967, Dr. Martin Luther King, Jr., spoke about racial inequality and ending the Vietnam War to a crowd of 4,000 at the University of Minnesota's St. Paul campus. Supporters were enthusiastic during King's nearly one-hour speech. Some students carried signs reading "King for President in 1968," even though King announced days before that he had no plans to run for president.

# Notes on the Photographs

These notes, listed by page number, attempt to include all aspects known of the photographs. Each of the photographs is identified by the page number, photograph's title or description, photographer and collection, archive, and call or box number when applicable. Although every attempt was made to collect all data, in some cases complete data may be unavailable due to the age and condition of some of the photographs and records.

**ii Duluth Facing Lake Superior**
Library of Congress
3c03216u-pan6a06963

**ii Minnehaha Falls**
Library of Congress
09967u-LC-DIG-ppmsca-09967

**x St. Paul and Superior Stagecoaches**
Minnesota Historical society
HE2.5 p30

**2 Bierbauer Mill**
Minnesota Historical Society
MB8.9 MK3.1 p11

**3 Settlers Seeking Refuge**
Adrian J. Ebell
Library of Congress
3a30396u-LC-USZ62-66542

**4 Incarcerated Dakotas**
Benjamin Franklin Upton
Minnesota Historical Society
E91.4S p53

**5 Ferryman**
Whitney's Gallery
Minnesota Historical Society
MH5.9 F1.3 r32

**6 Lumberjacks Sawing**
Whitney & Zimmerman
Minnesota Historical Society
HD5.22 r6

**7 Minnesota Avenue, St. Peter**
Minnesota Historical Society
MN2.9 SP2 r3

**8 Pigeon River Falls**
Adrian J. Ebell
Library of Congress
1s01740u-LC-DIG-stereo-1s01740

**9 Expedition Party**
Minnesota Historical Society
HE6.41N p12

**10 St. Paul's Episcopal Church**
William Henry Illingworth
Minnesota Historical Society
MS2.9 DU1 p23

**11 Logjam**
Benjamin Franklin Upton
Library of Congress
3b12287u-LC-USZ62-64698

**12 Ice Harvesting**
Whitney & Zimmerman
Minnesota Historical Society
HD7.7 r30

**13 "Chippewa Wedding"**
Whitney & Zimmerman
Library of Congress
3c07547u-LC-USZ62-107547

**14 Third Street, St. Paul**
William Henry Illingworth
Minnesota Historical Society
MR2.9 SP2.1 p436

**15 Ojibwe Winter Camp**
Minnesota Historical Society
E97.31 r16

**16 Minnesota House, St. Cloud**
Minnesota Historical Society
MS6.9 SC3.1 p1

**18 Minnesota House Barn**
Minnesota Historical Society
MS6.9 SC3.1 p4

**19 Hendricks House**
Caswell & Davy
Minnesota Historical Society
HF5.4 r49

**20 Saengerfest, Stillwater**
Minnesota Historical Society
MW4.9 ST9 p7

**21 Snowbound Train**
Elmer & Tenney
Minnesota Historical Society
HE6.43 r18

**22 Two Rowers**
Minnesota Historical Society
GV3.61B p28

**23 Velocipede**
Minnesota Historical Society
HE6.42 p11

**24 Minnesota Loan and Trust**
Minnesota Historical Society
HD6.73 p197

**25 Athenaeum**
Truman Ward Ingersoll
Minnesota Historical Society
MR2.9 SP5.3 h1

**26 Minnesota National Guard**
Minnesota Historical Society
U2.2 p38

**27 Laying Church Cornerstone**
Washington C. Fisher
Minnesota Historical Society
B1.11 p13

**28 St. Louis River Hunters' Camp**
Truman Ward Ingersoll
Library of Congress
3b44364-LC-USZ62-98278

**29 Dakota Indians in Pipestone**
Minnesota Historical Society
HD6.2 r58

**30 Boat Club Boxers**
Minnesota Historical Society
GV3.42 p24

**31 Atwater Croquet**
Minnesota Historical Society
GV3.19 p7

**32 Claim Shanty**
Minnesota Historical Society
HD3.4 r14

**33 Spiral Bridge, Hastings**
Minnesota Historical Society
Runk 1346

**34 Electric Automobile**
Minnesota Historical Society
HE3.1 p55

**35 Leech Lake Expedition**
Minnesota Historical Society
GV3.33 p38

**36 View from Dayton's Bluff**
Library of Congress
3b27005-LC-USZ62-80009

**37 Minnesota River in Mendota**
Edward Augustus Bromley
Minnesota Historical Society
MD2.1 p1

**38 Art Students**
Minnesota Historical Society
N1.2 p47

**39 Pillsbury Mill**
Norton & Peel
Minnesota Historical Society
MH5.9 MP3.1P p48

**40 Crowd at Depot, Red Wing**
Minnesota Historical Society
MG6.9 RW9 p4

**41 Minnesota River, New Ulm**
Library of Congress
3b36488u-LC-USZ62-90122

**42 Lumber Camp Scene**
C. A. Carlson
Minnesota Historical Society
Runk 3

**44 Stone Arch Bridge**
Library of Congress
4s18465u-LC-DIG-det-4a18465

**45 Hutchinson Aerial**
George R. Lawrence Co.
Library of Congress
6a20230u-pan 6a20230

**46 St. Cloud Aerial**
George R. Lawrence Co.
Library of Congress
3c25085-LC-USZ62-125085

**47 Wheat Harvest**
Sweet
Minnesota Historical Society
SA4.52 p37

**48 Portable Carousel**
Frances Benjamin Johnston
Library of Congress
3a46752u-LC-USZ62-46587

**49 Balloon Vendor**
Frances Benjamin Johnston
Library of Congress
3a46754u-LC-USZ62-46589

**50 Women Fairgoers**
Frances Benjamin Johnston
Library of Congress
3c22410u-LC-USZ62-122410

**51 Ore Engine**
Frances Benjamin Johnston
Library of Congress
3b45000u-LC-USZ62-98923

**52 Miners' Housing**
Frances Benjamin Johnston
Library of Congress
3b16639u-LC-USZ62-69197

**53 Digging Iron Ore**
Frances Benjamin Johnston
Library of Congress
3b16640u-LC-USZ62-69198

**54 Miner on the Mesabi Range**
Frances Benjamin Johnston
Library of Congress
3a47243u-LC-USZ62-47086

**55 Steamer Peerless**
Minnesota Historical Society
HE5.18 r105

**56 Seventh Street, St. Paul**
Library of Congress
3b05412u-LC-USZ62-57593

**57 Aerial Bridge**
Library of Congress
4a12863u-LC-DIG-det-4a12863

**58 Minnehaha Falls, 1906**
George R. Lawrence Co.
Library of Congress
6a19597u-pan 6a19597

**59 Bird's-Eye View of St. Paul**
Library of Congress
3c10667u-LC-USZ62-110667

**60 Taft in Ada**
Library of Congress
02187u-LC-DIG-ggbain-02187

**61 Taft in Northfield**
Library of Congress
3c01136u-LC-USZ62-101136

**62 Bryan Not Speaking**
Library of Congress
03085u-LC-DIG-ggbain-03085

**63 Downtown Goodhue**
Library of Congress
3b36519u-LC-USZ62-90153

**64 Watab Dam**
Library of Congress
17354u-LC-DIG-ppmsca-17354

**66 Albert Lea**
Frederick J. Bandholtz
Library of Congress
6a06767u-pan 6a06767

**68 Minneapolis Panorama**
Library of Congress
3c00417u-LC-USZ62-100417

**69 Red Jacket Bridge**
Library of Congress
3c21881u-pan 6a06678

**70 Paint Store, Shelly**
Fred Peerson
Library of Congress
3a42255u-LC-USZ62-41932

**71 Women's Suffrage Club**
Minnesota Historical Society
JZ.11 r3

**72 State Capitol**
Library of Congress
3b34859u-LC-USZ62-88433

**73 St. Paul Panorama**
Library of Congress
6a13551u-pan 6a13551

**74 Block-and-Tackle**
Library of Congress
3a47205u-LC-USZ62-47048

**75 Lake Calhoun**
Library of Congress
6a06831u-pan 6a06831

**76 Leech Lake Lumber Company**
Library of Congress
6a06714u-pan 6a06714

**77 Mississippi River, St. Paul**
Library of Congress
3c23510u-pan 6a06805

**78 Ayrshire Bull**
Library of Congress
3a46730-LC-USZ62-46563

**79 Fergus Falls Tornado Damage**
Walter T. Oxley
Library of Congress
6a06685u-pan 6a06685

**80 Bartenders**
Minnesota Historical Society
HF5.3 p11

**81 Munsingwear Employees**
Charles J. Hibbard
Minnesota Historical Society
I.125.20

**82 Cooling Off at Glen Lake**
Minnesota Historical Society
I.242.21

**83 Summertime Scene**
Minnesota Historical Society
GV3.62 p4

**84 Motorcycle Race**
Branch
Minnesota Historical Society
I.16.59

**85 Pillsbury Company Band**
Charles P. Gibson
Minnesota Historical Society
N5.21 p17

**86 Lumber Camp Cooks**
Minnesota Historical Society
HD5.1 p28

**88 Independence Day, Savage**
Minnesota Historical Society
GT4.5 p9

**89 Gymnastic Formation**
Myron Herbert Reynolds
Minnesota Historical Society
FM6.841 r16

**90 League of Women Voters**
Minnesota Historical Society
J7.12 r2

**91 Knute Nelson Funeral**
Minnesota Historical Society
GT3.7 r37

**92 Creameries Association**
Charles P. Gibson
Minnesota Historical Society
MH5.9 MP3.1L p29

**93 Coolidge Whistle-stop**
Minnesota Historical Society
J2 1924 r1

**94 Dayton's Department Store**
Minnesota Historical Society
MH5.9 MP3.1D p34

**95 Anglers**
Brown
Minnesota Historical Society
GV3.33 p10

**96 Women Playing Hockey**
*Minneapolis Journal*
Minnesota Historical Society
FM6.847 r4

**97 Harness Racing**
Minnesota Historical Society
FM6.541 p4

**98 Danish Festival**
H. Larson Studio
Minnesota Historical Society
GT5.3 p80

**99 Auto Race**
Minnesota Historical Society
FM6.542 p6

**100 Golden Gophers Football Crowd**
*Minneapolis Journal*
Minnesota Historical Society
FM6.845 r4

**102 Call of the Wild**
William F. Roleff
Minnesota Historical Society
GV3.61C p55

**103 Picketing the Minnesota**
J. H. Kammerdiener
Minnesota Historical Society
MH5.9 MP3.1M p157

**104 Minneapolis South High Football**
Minnesota Historical Society
GV3.13 p5

**105 State Fair Grandstand**
Minnesota Historical Society
FM6.54 p49

**106 Auto Ferry**
John Warner Grigg Dunn
Minnesota Historical Society
HE5.15 p7

**107 Columbus Statue**
Minnesota Historical Society
FM6.184 p10

**108 Job Seekers**
*Minneapolis Star Journal*
Minnesota Historical Society
HG4.1 p4

**109 Thrill Day Trains**
Minnesota Historical Society
FM6.543 p6

**110 Children's Day**
Kenneth Melvin Wright
Minnesota Historical Society
FM6.55Y p10

**111 Lindbergh Visit**
Minnesota National Guard
Minnesota Historical Society
por 7789 r39

**112 Future Musicians**
Kenneth M. Wright Studios
Minnesota Historical Society
FM6.55MU p9

**113 Kids' Checkers Tournament**
Minnesota Historical Society
GV5.11 r8

**114 Lock and Dam Number 4**
Library of Congress
8e01389u-LC-USW33-029106-C

**115 Hennepin Avenue Methodist Church**
Library of Congress
3b41900u-LC-USZ62-95764

**116 Camp Ripley Troops**
Minnesota Historical Society
U2.2 p35

**117 Death-Defying Act**
*Minneapolis Star Journal*
Minnesota Historical Society
FM6.543 p14

**118 Railroad Ties, Littlefork**
Russell Lee
Library of Congress
8b36596u-LC-USF34-030161-E

**119 Men in the Gateway District**
Russell Lee
Library of Congress
8a28733u-LC-USF33-011286-M3

**120 Columbia Hotel, Gateway District**
Russell Lee
Library of Congress
8a28732u-LC-USF33-011286-M2

**121 Mother and Daughter, Gemmell**
Russell Lee
Library of Congress
8a22125u-LC-USF3301-011299-M2

**122 Ojibwe Laborers**
Russell Lee
Library of Congress
8a21926u-LC-DIG-fsa-8a21926-011286-M3

**123 Blueberry Pickers**
Russell Lee
Library of Congress
8a21949u-LC-DIG-fsa-8a21949

**124 Ojibwe Blueberry Picker's Daughter**
Russell Lee
Library of Congress
8a21946u-LC-DIG-fsa-8a21946

**125 Red River Valley Migrant Worker**
Russell Lee
Library of Congress
8a22495u-LC-USF33-011389-M2

**126 Minnesota Armory**
Library of Congress
3c34597u-LC-USZ62-134597

**127 Potato Harvest**
Russell Lee
Minnesota Historical Society
SA4.54 p8

**128 Rail Yard**
John Vachon
Library of Congress
12291u-LC-USF33-T01-001506-M1

**130 Minneapolis-Moline Company**
John Vachon
Library of Congress
3c22731-LC-USF34-060226-D

**131 Roadside Vendor, Bemidji**
John Vachon
Library of Congress
8a04443-LC-DIG-fsa-8a04443

**132 New Ulm Business District**
Minnesota Historical Society
MB9.9 NU2 r10

**133 Tobogganing**
Minnesota Historical Society
GV3.77 p11

**134 Youth Football Halftime Show**
Minnesota Historical Society
GV3.13 p48

**135 Stephens Buick Fair Tent**
*Minneapolis Journal*
Minnesota Historical Society
FM6.55B r7

**136 Soldier Bugling**
*Minneapolis Star Journal Tribune*
Minnesota Historical Society
MH5.9 F1.7 p130

**137 Minnesota School of Business**
Norton & Peel
Minnesota Historical Society
Norton & Peel 137849

**138 Vulcan Krewe**
Minnesota Historical Society
MR2.9 SP9.1 1942 p2

**139 Meeker County Musicians**
John Vachon
Library of Congress
8c21002-LC-DIG-fsa-8c21002

**140 Quarter Launch, Port Cargill**
Minnesota Historical Society
HE5.14 m3

**141 Basswood Lake Portage**
Gordon Ray
Minnesota Historical Society
I.198.158

**142 Wartime Workers**
Norton & Peel
Minnesota Historical Society
Norton & Peel 143859

**143 Navy Recruiting**
*Minneapolis Journal*
Minnesota Historical Society
E448.21 r2

**144 Soldier on Leave**
Minnesota Historical Society
E448.251 r2

**145 Mother Reading Letter**
Minnesota Historical Society
E448.19 p19

**146 Major Richard Bong Brought Home for Burial**
Minnesota Historical Society
E448.27 p2

**147 V-J Day Celebration**
Minnesota Historical Society
E448.17 r15

**148 Agriculture Building Fire**
*Minneapolis Star Journal*
Minnesota Historical Society
FM6.55H p72

**149 Playing Horseshoes**
Minnesota Historical Society
GV3.52 p8

**150 Jitterbugging**
*St. Paul Dispatch and Pioneer Press*
Minnesota Historical Society
GV1.3 m3

**152 Minnesota Playground**
Minnesota Department of Conservation
Minnesota Historical Society
GV8.2 p10

**153 Sister Kenny Movie Premiere**
Philip C. Dittes
Minnesota Historical Society
MH5.9 MP3.10 p35

**154 Governor's Office Christmas Tree**
*St. Paul Dispatch and Pioneer Press*
Minnesota Historical Society
GT4.81 p83

**155 Little Train Ride**
Minnesota Historical Society
FM6.52 p18

**156 Republican Headquarters**
George Miles Ryan Studio
Minnesota Historical Society
J2 1948 p6

**157 Pure Oil Company Transportation**
Norton & Peel
Minnesota Historical Society
Norton & Peel 184626

**158 Wayzata Float**
Minnesota Historical Society
MH5.9 WY9 p1

**159 Colonel Bitler and Sun Valley**
Minnesota Historical Society
GV3.214 p7

**160 Couple in Front of Tepee at Itasca State Park**
Minnesota Historical Society
FM6.413 p4

**161 Boxing Match**
Minnesota Historical Society
GV3.42 p18

**162 Como Conservatory**
Riehle Studio
Minnesota Historical Society
MR2.9 SP4.1Cc p27

**163 Mayo Clinic**
*Minneapolis Star Journal Tribune*
Minnesota Historical Society
MO5.9 RC2 p7

**164 3M Building Explosion**
*Minneapolis Star Journal Tribune*
Minnesota Historical Society
MR2.9 SP3.1M p259

**165 3M Employees Treated**
*Minneapolis Star Journal Tribune*
Minnesota Historical Society
MR2.9 SP3.1M p259

**166 Payne Avenue Harvest Festival**
*St. Paul Dispatch & Pioneer Press*
Minnesota Historical Society
MR2.9 SP2.2 p238

**167 Planes in Ely**
Minnesota Historical Society
HE1.24 r19

**168 Bomb Shelter**
Minnesota Historical Society
E450 p15

**169 Ike Dirigible**
*St. Paul Dispatch & Pioneer Press*
Minnesota Historical Society
J2 1952 p17

**170 Duluth Superior Harbor**
Louis Perry Gallagher
Minnesota Historical Society
MS2.9 DU1 p8

**171 Red Lake Students**
Hakkerup Studio
Minnesota Historical Society
L3.2 p150

**172 Northern Minnesota Forest**
Norton & Peel
Minnesota Historical Society
Norton & Peel 216940

**173 Hub Shopping Center, Richfield**
Norton & Peel
Minnesota Historical Society
Mh5.9 RF3.1 p1

**174 Aquatennial Parade Spectators**
Minnesota Historical Society
MH5.9 MP9.1 1954 p28

**175 Ice Fishing**
Minnesota Statehood Centennial Commission
Minnesota Historical Society
GV3.34 p3

**176 Paul Bunyan Playground**
Kenneth Melvin Wright
Minnesota Historical Society
MB4.9 BJ6 p4

**177 Smokey Bear**
Norton & Peel
Minnesota Historical Society
Norton & Peel 227524

**178 Minneapolis Lakers**
Minnesota Statehood Centennial Commission
Minnesota Historical Society
GV3.12P p1

**179 Skate Sailing**
Minnesota Statehood Centennial Commission
Minnesota Historical Society
GV3.72 p10

**180 Swimming Hole**
Minnesota Statehood Centennial Commission
Minnesota Historical Society
GV3.62 p9

**181 Two-Millionth Ford**
*Minneapolis Star Journal Tribune*
Minnesota Historical Society
HE3.7 p22

**182 Model Posing**
Gordon Ray
Minnesota Historical Society
I.198.112

**183 Double Toboggan Slide**
Minnesota Historical Society
MR2.9 SP9.1 1957 p1

**184 Lutheran World Federation Assembly**
Minnesota Historical Society
B1.29 p10

**185 Maypole Dance**
Minnesota Historical Society
GT4.9 p23

**186 Delmar Hagen and His Oxcart**
Minnesota Historical Society
HE2.1 p5

**187 Hula Hoopers**
*Minneapolis Star Tribune*
Minnesota Historical Society
GV5.9 p17

**188 Hallie Q. Brown Camp Swimming Lessons**
Minnesota Historical Society
GV3.62 p61

**189 Children on the Capitol Staircase**
Minnesota Historical Society
FM6.15C p45

**190 Teacher Recognition Day at the State Fair**
Hasco Photographic Studio
Minnesota Historical Society
FM6.57 p31

**191 Horseback Square Dancing**
Hasco Photographic Studio
Minnesota Historical Society
GV1.3 r11

**192 Pillsbury Television Shoot**
Gordon Ray
Minnesota Historical Society
I.198.10

**193 Cuban Missile Crisis Protest**
*St. Paul Dispatch & Pioneer Press*
Minnesota Historical Society
E450 p4

**194 Vikings-Lions Game**
John Croft
Minnesota Historical Society
GV3.13P p14

**195 Capitol Christmas Tree**
Minnesota Historical Society
FM6.13 p93

**196 Minnesota River Flood**
Minnesota Historical Society
QC2.2d p115

**197 High School Students Sandbagging**
Minnesota Historical Society
QC2.2d r82

**198 North Stars Hockey**
Minnesota Historical Society
GV3.73P p8

**199 Martin Luther King, Jr., Speech**
*St. Paul Pioneer Press*
Minnesota Historical Society
E455 p4

# HISTORIC PHOTOS OF MINNESOTA

Minnesota's past is defined by its remarkable natural resources, and shaped by its native peoples and early settlers. From the fur trade and the establishment of Fort Snelling, to harnessing the power of the Mississippi River as a means to fuel emergent logging and milling industries, Minnesota's history is that of a land like no other.

Pioneering Minnesotans embraced everything that the sprawling prairies, rich farmlands, and more than 10,000 lakes offered. Boomtowns and small towns sprang up and were connected to the thriving metropolises of Minneapolis and St. Paul through a great labyrinth of railways.

From the time photographers first started pointing their cameras in the direction of Minnesota's land and people, crystallized moments from the state's history were captured, and stories preserved.

The archival images collected in *Historic Photos of Minnesota* offer unique insights into the state's not-so-distant past. Spanning more than 100 years, this book documents everyday lives and significant events in Minnesota's extraordinary history.

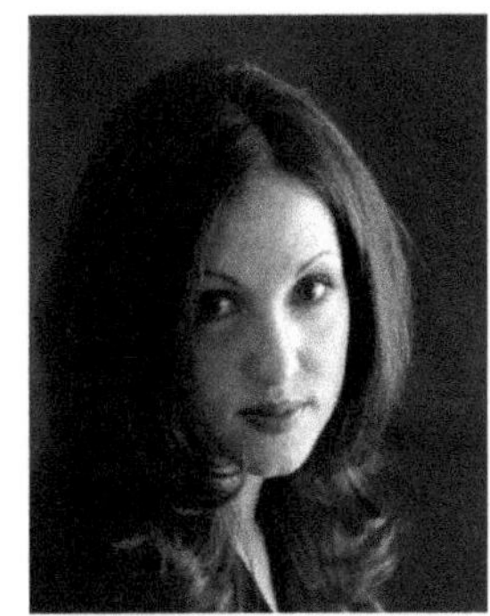

Susan Marks is a writer and documentary filmmaker. She holds a bachelor's degree in history, as well as a master's degree in liberal studies—with a focus on American studies, history, and film—from the University of Minnesota.

Susan authored the book *Finding Betty Crocker: The Secret Life of America's First Lady of Food,* and produced a documentary film about this famous Minnesota icon.

Susan lives in Minneapolis in a home once owned by famed Minnesota photographer Edward Bromley, whose photographs are among those appearing in this book.

WWW.TURNERPUBLISHING.COM